ARCHITECTURAL
COMPOSITION

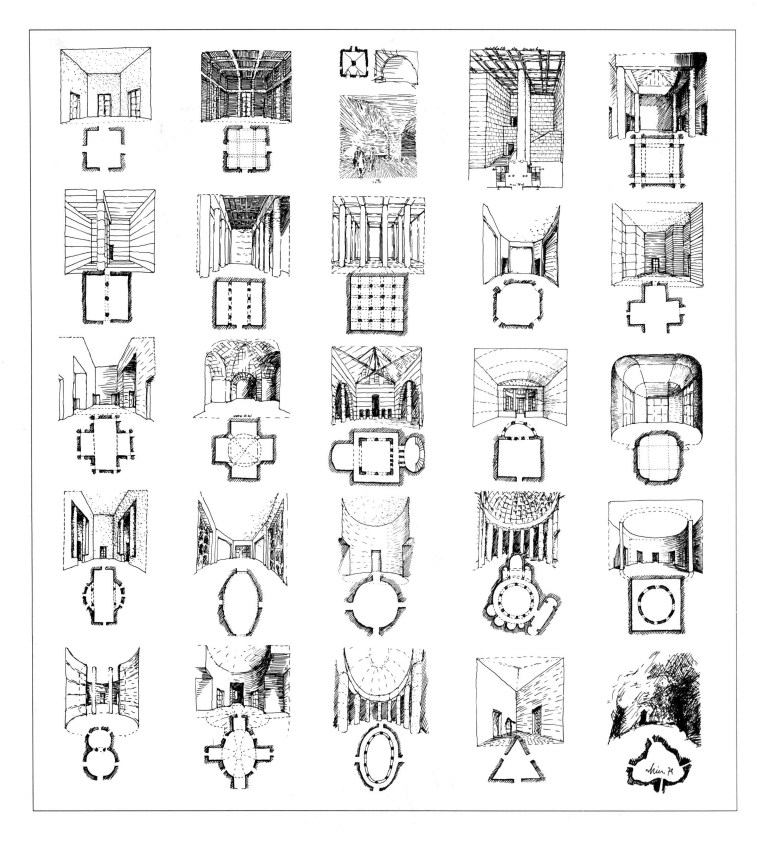

ROB KRIER

ARCHITECTURAL
COMPOSITION

NEW YORK

I would like to thank my publisher Dr. Andreas Papadakis who had the vision to commission this work over a decade ago, and for bringing it to completion together with his staff at Academy Editions. My work on this book has been supported by funds from the Department for the Development of Scientific Research in the Republic of Austria, and was carried out at the Institute of Building Form at the Technical University of Vienna. Collaborators: Margaret Cufer, Johann Kräftner, Robert Newald, Ute Schauer, Dietmar Steiner and Renate Stirk. Translated from the German by Romana Schneider and Gabrielle Vorreiter.

*For students of architecture,
patrons, politicians and speculators*

First published in the United States of America in 1988 by
RIZZOLI INTERNATIONAL PUBLICATIONS, INC.
597 Fifth Avenue, New York, 10017

Published in Great Britain in 1988 by
Academy Editions, 7 Holland Street, London W8

Library of Congress Cataloging-in-Publication Data

Krier, Rob.
  Architectural composition.

  Bibliography: p.
  Includes index.
  1. Architecture—Composition, proportion, etc.
I. Title.
NA2760.K68   1988   729   88–42691
ISBN 0–8478–0965–X

Printed and bound in Hong Kong

CONTENTS

FOREWORD

*'It is my aim
to rehabilitate
an architecture
that has become
dishonoured
and disgraced.'*

MOTIVATION

This book deals with the problems of architectural design and is aimed at students of architecture in the early part of their training. I am trying to bring out the connections between function, construction and the resultant architectonic form, and highlight architectonic interrelationships. I do not claim to promulgate an exhaustive design philosophy – my thinking and professional experience are still continually developing. My principal aim is to formulate and establish a set of ground rules that guide architectural composition. The rules are distilled into simple didactic formulae, easy for students to understand and employ.

Even though the architectural and art historical education of the average intellectual is extraordinarily superficial, he invariably ends up – as politician, financier or contractor – influencing architecture to a greater or lesser degree. I hope, therefore, that my 'design instructions' will benefit not only the expert, but also the 'layman', who has not enjoyed an architectural education. Much of this instruction should indeed be taught in our schools as general knowledge or as as part of a cultural history course.

The third chapter illustrates the spatial and structural elements in architecture with the help of carefully selected images. They constitute the summation of preliminary exercises, drawn by my first-year students at the Technical University in Vienna, before they took their first steps in designing.

The fifth chapter traces and analyses the building arts of the twentieth century and their developments. It takes the form of a critical discourse, examining the increasing banality and homogeneity of contemporary work.

All design considerations are restricted to living spaces, since they concern everyone. In our own homes we all, to some degree, suffer the daily confrontation with 'architecture'. It is, therefore, no wonder that our style of living – an expression of our way of life – mirrors an entire cultural epoch. It cannot be overlooked that our regional, cultural landscape – urban as well as rural – has fallen prey to oppressive industrialisation. Millions of faceless, ugly family houses – cluttered with nasty mass-produced furniture – spoil our countryside. Craftsmanship, together with its rich creative repertoire simply has been left behind. Planning the most economic and cost effective production methods is now confined to the drawing board – there in no longer scope for a cabinet-maker, for instance, to exercise his inventive mind. I do not maintain that the only way out of this dilemma is the return to medieval construction methods; however, as long as our building industry is controlled by ignorant speculators, I cannot imagine how the quality of mass-produced housing is to be improved.

Industrialists, like Michael Thonet, who invest their taste and organisational skills in the promotion of outstanding design prod-

ucts, are few and far between. When large firms, like 'Eternit', run competitions for a 'better living in the future', or the innovative use of their product, these are no more than gestures intended to cover up their true intentions, the brutal reality of which remain all too obvious. Their strategies are those of a politician running for re-election. However, the flowery aroma does not suppress the foul smell of a garbage heap. The good examples I have selected to illustrate my arguments are becoming increasingly rare in our present-day built environment. To search out a building of architectural distinction today, one has to embark on an exhaustive study tour. Where are our architectural students supposed to find cultural landmarks, so important for their architectural education?

One cannot blame the layman when, as a client, he makes the wrong decisions. Examples of good building are thin on the ground. The life-style of the rich has always been trend-setting for all the other income groups. This influence can only be rejected, since the difference between the rich man's and the poor man's taste is only one of scale – larger plot, larger house and larger pool. Their decorative 'kitsch artefacts' are quite interchangeable.

I do not wish to dwell on the sorry state of our present building industry, but I know this is not the last time that the anguish of our lost building tradition will drive me deep into despair. This emotion generated

in me the strength to pursue the fight against the prevailing stupidity in the building sector and has inspired me to write this book.

Just as in my book *Urban Space*, I shall frequently quote Le Corbusier. His theoretical and practical influence on twentieth-century architecture is extensive, and the artistic quality of his work sublime. Le Corbusier did not, in any of his innumerable essays, explain his way of designing. Therefore, the evolution of his design and thought process has never been given full didactic expression. All Le Corbusier ever mentioned were functional, structural and socio-economic factors, at the same time using nebulous poetic statements, such as: '. . . architecture is the play of forms under the light . . .' Or he speaks about an interior as 'espace indicible', inexpressible space! I would be the last person not to regard these poetic aspects as extremely important, but as a teacher, it is my responsibility to draw my students' attention to what I consider significant in the form-giving process of architec-

ture. This, I believe, can be done through a sequence of simple and easy steps.

THE CONFUSION IN
TODAY'S ART OF BUILDING

It comes as no surprise that in the light of today's architectural confusion the student is no longer able to draw a plain and simple window, for example; rather, he unwittingly apes what he has seen in the work of Le Corbusier, Aalto, Mies van der Rohe, etc. The results are fragmented walls drawn on asymmetrical plans with openings that playfully direct the light into sentimental, romantic motifs. The overwhelming concern is to produce a graphic *tour de force*. I am giving this example because I myself, for many years, have been fooled by similar half-baked theories.

The purpose of this book, among others, is to clean up the ideological nonsense in our profession. Where the rational use of our intellect has become diluted, dream-like visions begin to emerge and one gropes for architectural truths like and disciples of

Rudolf Steiner. Or one elevates *secondary themes* to *primary themes* in a bid to renew the profession (contextual building, democratic building, occupant participation, health-conscious building, energy-efficient building, light-weight construction, humane building, industrialised building . . .). All are desperate and one-sided attempts in the search for a lost theoretical framework.

IT CAN ONLY BE THE SUM TOTAL OF THE DEFINITIONS OF THE ELEMENTS, AS WELL AS THE COMPOSITIONAL RULES THAT DETERMINE THEIR JUXTAPOSITIONS!

I am not presumptuous enough to assume that I am here tinkering with a 'bible', rather I am trying to re-establish a set of basic principles that have gone astray.

FOR ME THEORY IS THE UNDERSTANDING OF THE USE AND MEANING OF OBJECTS, THEIR IDIOSYNCRACIES, CHARACTERISTICS AND EFFECTS.

CHAPTER I

FUNCTION CONSTRUCTION AND ARCHITECTURAL FORM

ARCHITECTURAL GUIDELINES

The following guidelines have been valid ever since man began to plan buildings rationally and aspired to architecture as an aesthetic product – in other words, to create buildings that are more than just an answer to programmatic problems.

FUNCTION, CONSTRUCTION AND FORM

are factors of equal significance and jointly determine architecture. No single factor should dominate.

FUNCTION AND CONSTRUCTION

are 'useful' elements whose rules always need to be acknowledged as a matter of course. However, a building can only be raised to the status of architecture through the additional fulfilment of aesthetic requirements.

THE FULFILMENT OF AESTHETIC REQUIREMENTS
DEPENDS ON THE FOLLOWING FACTORS:

–Proportion–Structure–Material and colour, and their artistic interpretation.

AESTHETICS

The sense of beauty in architecture is rooted in man's desire to bestow everyday objects with poetic content that will convey the spirit of his epoch to future generations. (' . . . it is useful, because it is beautiful . . . ' *A. de Saint-Exupéry*)

GEOMETRY

is the basis for all forms of architectural expression. As organised geometry, architecture draws its strength from opposing rather than adopting the laws of nature. Geometry is the creation of man.

SCALE

in architecture is not solely determined by technical, structural and economic factors; the dimensions of the human body as well as man's perceptions, behavioural patterns and emotions must also be taken into consideration.

ARCHITECTURE IN THE CITY

All new planning should submit to the overall order of the city. Its form should respond to existing spatial patterns.

THE URBAN SPACE

as a concept has been ignored in twentieth-century town planning. Our new cities are a conglomeration of free-standing buildings. Five thousand years of city planning history has taught us that the complex matrixes of streets and squares are successful communication networks and means of identification and orientation. Traditional concepts of urban space are still valid today.

HISTORY

The proper evaluation of our historical inheritance crystallizes our understanding of the past and teaches us how to plan for the future.

THE ARCHITECT'S RESPONSIBILITIES

The architect alone is responsible for what leaves his drawing-board and carries his signature. No politician or developer will bear the architect's cultural guilt for a botched environment. Our universities are responsible for preparing the next generation of architects for this almost insuperable ethical and moral duty.

No one of these factors must be neglected or over-emphasised during the design process. A one-sided solution would result in a 'deformed' architecture. However, it can be the architect's intention – depending on the problem and specific situation – to deliberately over-emphasise a certain form to create a special effect. Recent architectural history bears witness to a multitude of tendencies that are a result of far too narrow a vision: e.g. Functionalism, Constructivism, Formalism, New Brutalism etc.

I work from the principle that the harmony of form, function and construction leads to the right solution. Since the function and construction of a building are always visible, the built form is obviously inseparable from them. For this I will first consider function, and then construction, in relation to form. It is characterised by mutual dependencies and influences.

Using typologies, I shall illustrate the wealth of formal possibilities that – whilst meeting functional and constructional requirements – can be composed into architectural form. The true form of a building is the sum of its perceivable elements. I shall deal with them in a separate chapter in greater detail. In addition, colours, surface textures, materials, light and the quality of technical details play an enormously important role.

FUNCTION, CONSTRUCTION AND ARCHITECTURAL FORM

FUNCTION AND FORM

Architecture has to provide us with physical shelter from our environment, create a framework for our activities and, above all, express symbolic and ethical values.

The extent to which function influences architectural form becomes clear when we remind ourselves of the different uses of a building, and how certain activities can shape its form. The problem lies in the co-ordination of form and function. If this co-ordination cannot be mastered, the results are hollow forms and unsatisfactory living conditions.

Function is the fundamental starting point for all architectural expression. There is no need to labour the point that it is the architect's responsibility to fulfil all functional requirements of his buildings intelligently and to organise circulation as rationally as possible. The classic pitfalls are inadequate organisation and unsatisfactory planning.

Such examples are infinite; doors that jam and jar, ill-positioned toilet roll holders that bruise elbows, tiny washbasins that splash trousers etc. It is the architect's job to spare his client this kind of aggravation.

To plan a house with a logical and rational sequence of functions must be the architect's primary concern; yet it is only the starting point. Inhabiting a house must give enjoyment, pleasure and delight. No one would contest this simple statement, and yet it sparks off a fundamental ideological dispute amongst experts which is incomprehensible to the layman. To ascertain an individual's personal living preferences is indeed a formidable problem. Every human being has to answer this question according to his or her inherent spiritual and intellectual behavioural patterns. The experienced architect knows, however, that an individually tailored design solution has only 'one life'. When ownership changes, the

new occupant is left with two choices; either he resigns himself to his predecessor's living habits, or he sets about demolishing the walls of his new home, as far as this is structurally possible, to create his own living environment.

At this point we can, with a clear conscience, formulate a theory that has long been valid in architecture: a free plan and harmonious dimensions allow greater flexibility in the uses of a room. The social hardships of the interwar period gave rise to miserable tenement blocks. Only the best architects of the time successfully resolved the problem of reducing room dimensions without diminishing human dignity. Despite severe economic restraints, Le Corbusier created a living-cell for a family with several children that enjoyed the luxury of a double-height living room in his Unité d'habitation. It was an achievement that upgraded social housing enormously.

Too narrow a corridor

Too small an apartment

Le Corbusier: double-height living space

To the layman, architecture is what defines and sometimes fatally restricts his living space. He regards it as a commodity and spontaneously demands that it be 'enjoyable to use'. To combine this basic requirement with 'functional dexterity' is to choreograph the art of living, regarded as a matter of course by the rich. It is easy for the wealthy to enrich their daily lives with culture. Whether this is done in good taste is a different matter. The poor have more of a problem.

It has not always been this way! Today we admire the anonymous buildings of so-called primitive peoples. Their houses and living utensils exhibit unsurpassable taste, despite their primitive means. One reason for this high quality lies in a long and unbroken tradition, ensuring the continuous improvement and refinement of the product, and another is the hand-made quality of each item. People understood the processes by which objects were made. They lived in small communities and knew what went on in the workshops of their immediate neighbourhood.

Today we are no longer familiar with the methods by which our everyday objects are being produced. Not many people who settle into a new home know, or ever even meet, the architect. The designers of our furniture, lamps, cups and saucers remain equally anonymous. Only art lovers, *cognoscenti* and snobs bid for Mackintosh or Hoffmann chairs, Behrens cutlery, Bauhaus china and objects of a similar kind. Most of the everyday objects on display in department stores today are an insult to our aesthetic sensibilities, fulfilling only the interests of primitive sales strategies. No one can predict whether these tasteless artefacts will still be marketable in years to come. The consumer is not, after all, that insensitive and stupid.

———— ✳ ————

Modern interior, neutral, tasteful. House Tugendhat, Brno, Czechoslovakia, architect: Mies van der Rohe

Lounge interior, in the worst possible taste, as displayed by all department stores nowadays

Good old chair

Good modern chair (Otto Wagner)

Bad old chair

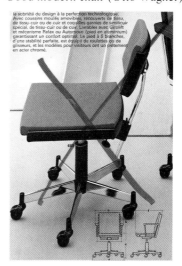

Bad modern chair

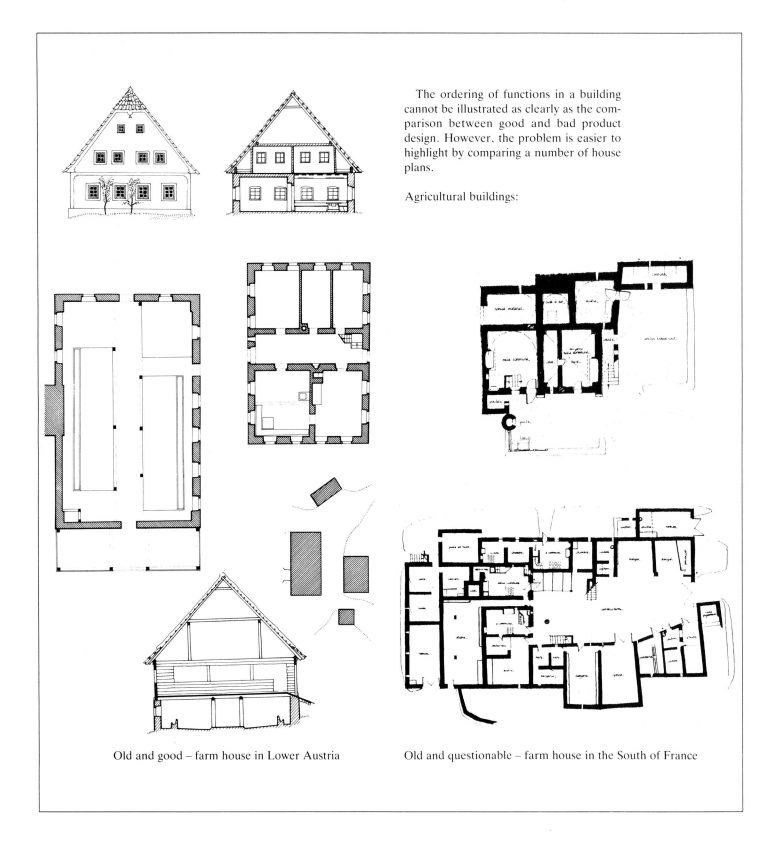

The ordering of functions in a building cannot be illustrated as clearly as the comparison between good and bad product design. However, the problem is easier to highlight by comparing a number of house plans.

Agricultural buildings:

Old and good – farm house in Lower Austria

Old and questionable – farm house in the South of France

Expensive buildings:

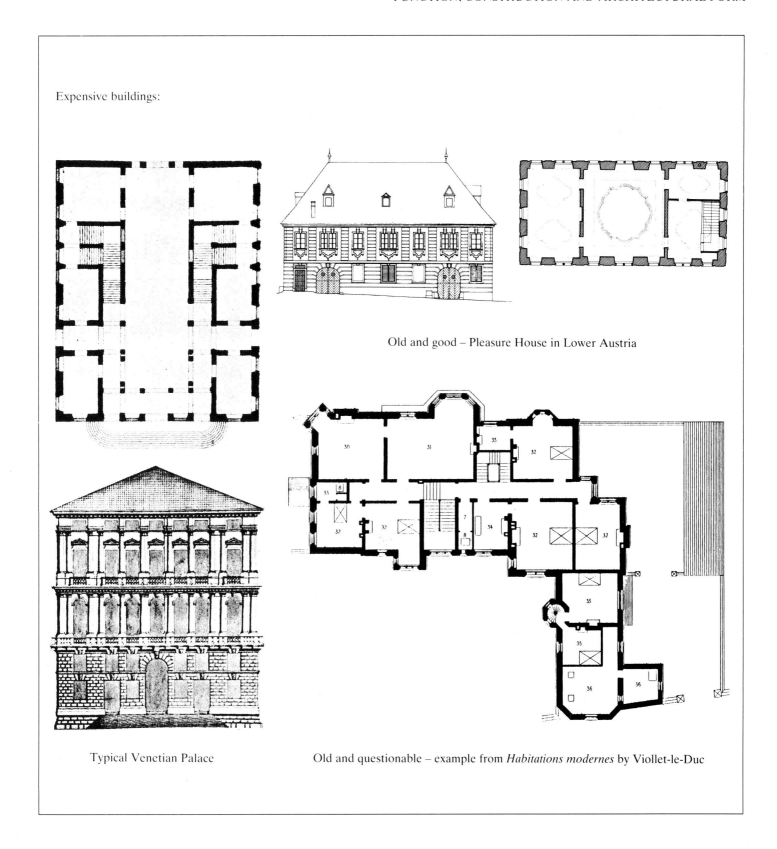

Old and good – Pleasure House in Lower Austria

Typical Venetian Palace

Old and questionable – example from *Habitations modernes* by Viollet-le-Duc

Inexpensive Modern buildings

Good example – worker's terraced house, architect: Tessenow

Bad example

Expensive Modern buildings:

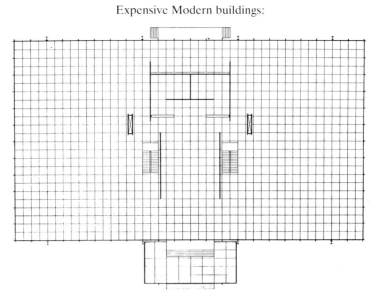

Good example – MIT, Chicago, architect: Mies van der Rohe

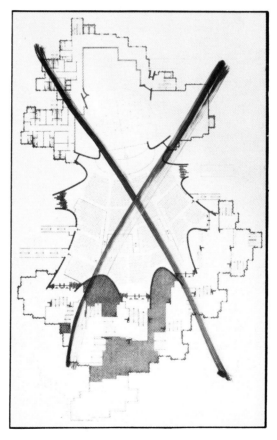

Bad example

Study of the Basic Types

The permutations of type for a domestic plan are very limited.

The three basic geometrical forms which can be developed into a plan are: square, triangle and circle

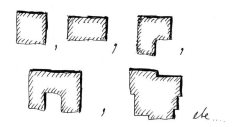

Each one of these basic forms can undergo manifold transformations, as illustrated here by the square:

Plan with autonomous cell-like rooms

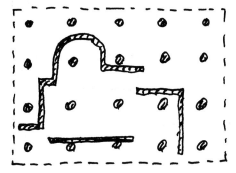

Plan with rooms flowing into each other

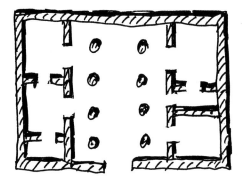

Plan showing the result of the superimposition of the two previous examples

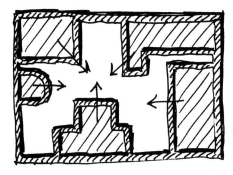

The organisation of the plan is either directed towards the centre

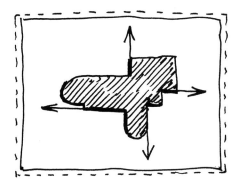

or from an inner core towards the outside

The same theme can be carried through the different basic geometries in regular and irregular form.

It is immediately obvious from these permutations that the design process can never be mathematically rationalised. The concept of organisation goes hand in hand with the idea of a spatial sequence. As stated above, architectural organisation cannot be stan-dardised. It does not follow that a perfect functional solution necessarily results in good architecture. To encompass our way of life, the entire aesthetic repertoire has to be pulled together and a balance created between 'tight' and 'relaxed' ordering (regular and irregular geometries).

The Organisation of Functional Sequences

The specific function of a house may suggest various constructional forms that channel working routines and modes of behaviour. *Orientation*, that is *'to find one's way around'*, plays a dominant role in this.

The most important organising and enclosing principles are demonstrated in the following sketches:

1. central/axial
2. linear
3. central and linear overlap
4. fork-like representation
5. network
6. superimposition on different levels
7. labyrinth

Systems of enclosure:

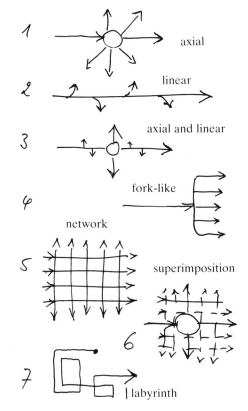

Historical examples illustrating some of the systems of enclosure. In the majority of cases we discover several layers of different systems superimposed.

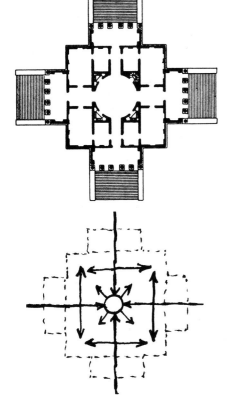

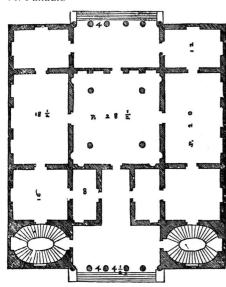

Villa Americo ('La Rotonda'), architect: A. Palladio

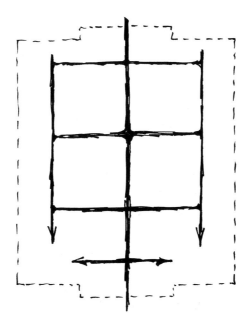

Design for a Palazzo for Gio. Battista Garzadore, Vincenza, (not realised), A. Palladio, *Quattro Libri dell'Architettura*, Book II

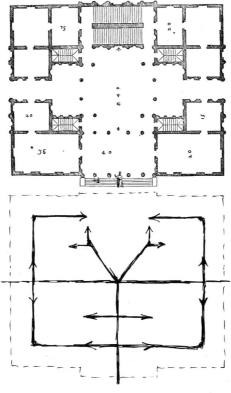

Design for a Palazzo for Gio. Battista dalla Torre, (not realised), A. Palladio, *Quattro Libri dell'Architettura*, Book II

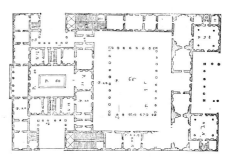

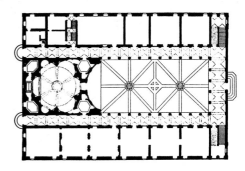

Villa with Tuscan atria, A. Palladio, *Quattro Libri dell'Architettura*, Book II

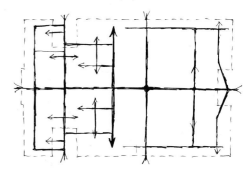

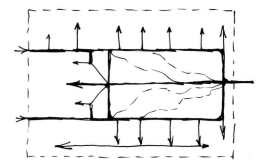

Palazzo della Sapienza, architect: Borromini

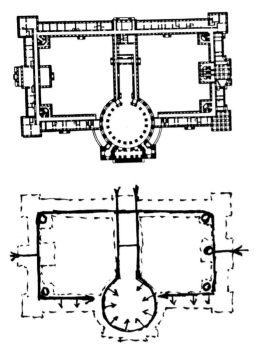

St. Blasien monastery, Baden

The circulatory route of a house begins at the main entrance, the garden gate or the portico. Here is the main threshold, between the public and private realm. The threshold acts as both demarcation line and connective tissue.

The portico is not accidental; it gives us a spatial and symbolic foretaste of the interior of the building. At the risk of being misunderstood, I pronounce the entrance the most erotically sensitive part of a house. Architecture, as one of the visual arts, has a symbolic dimension that should not be hushed up.

The porticos illustrated are unmistakable testimonies of their semiotic quality. Different cultural epochs have found their own expressions. The illustrations of porticos speak for themselves.

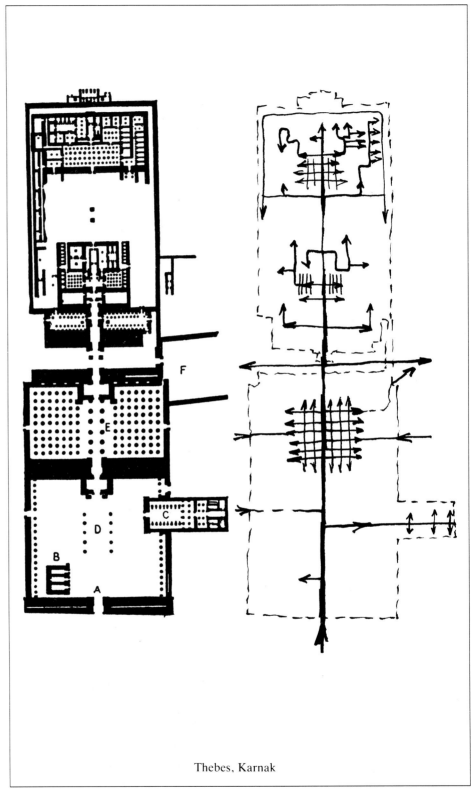

Thebes, Karnak

——— ❋ ———

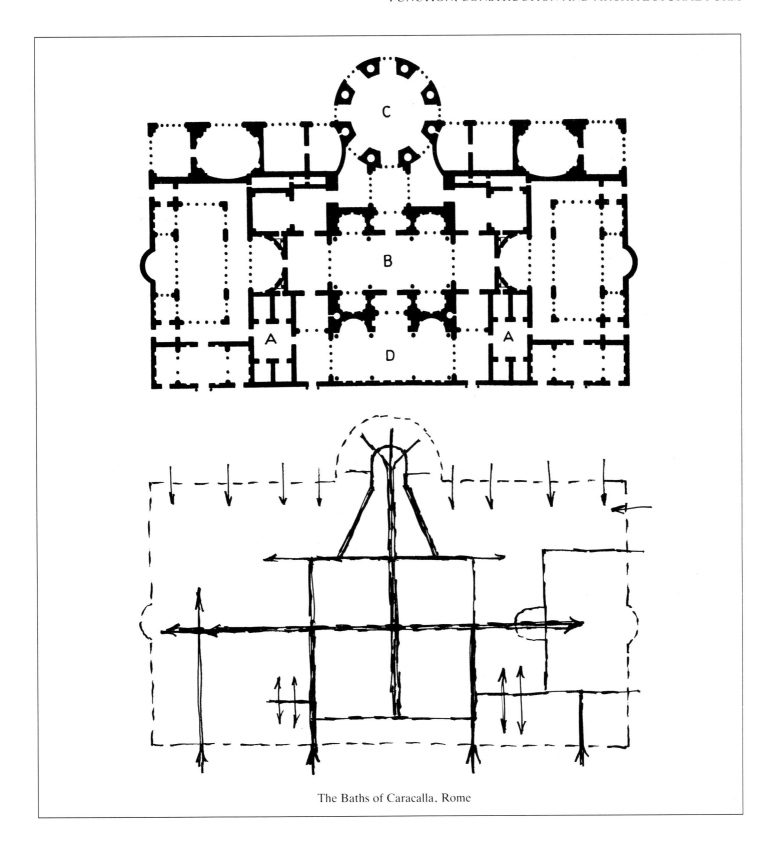

The Baths of Caracalla, Rome

Saqqâra, Djoser burial grounds, perimeter wall, c. 2600 BC

Banteay Srei, Gopura, Ishvarapura temple, gate tower

Jannpur Uttar Pradesh, Jämi Masjid, c. 1470-78

Uxmal, Governor's Palace, gate with Maja arch

St. Trophine in Arles

Notre Dame Cathedral, Rouen, 1281-1300

Fiesole, near Florence

Peterborough Cathedral, c. 1200

Eroticism is a constituent part of architectural choreography. Anyone who disputes this, has not yet enjoyed life to the full. Eroticism is a source of inspiration in all arts.

We have already talked about the main entrance to a house. One does not, of course, fall straight through the front door into the living room. A sober rationalist would call for a draught or entrance lobby to be inserted. The draught lobby is the epitome of a functional space; one does not tarry in it since its sole purpose is to exclude draught, to enable one to wipe one's shoes, deposit one's overcoat and gain access to the toilet.

If the client has enough money, the architect should always design some kind of entrance porch, however basic. The porch serves as a protection from bad weather and as a desirable prelude to the spatial experience of the interior. After the obligatory entrance lobby, the architect should plan a hall that clearly lays out the building's general system of organisation. You may laugh and think that none of this is possible in social housing, and I must admit you have a point. Poor people with little money are granted even less enjoyment of life. Yet, for the architect, the problem is only an intellectual one. Le Corbusier, in his Unité d'habitation, managed to harmonise hall, kitchen and living room into a wonderful economic and spatial unity.

Out of respect for mankind, it is an architect's moral duty to sacrifice some of his income rather than the quality of his design. The idea of the architectural foretaste to a spatial experience – expressed as a series of transitions – also exists in more complex relationships. In Bergamo, for instance, the transition is from market place, to churchyard, monastery, the Caesars' fora etc.

It is important to remember that private houses always engage in a particular relationship with public life, and are often miniature versions of the public, communal living realm.

The art of creating architectural foreplay – a sense of anticipation – begins not with the building itself, but long before; the garden gate, the path leading up to the house and the entrance itself demand careful thought and skilful manipulation.

What served as the hall in a nineteenth-

The sequence from garden gate to entrance door
can be illustrated graphically as follows:

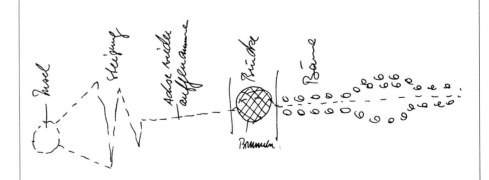

Approach, gate or porch, straight path . . . labyrinth,
depending on topography etc.

Straight path, overlayed by labyrinth, leading around an island,
branching off/upsetting the orientation . . .

Island, incline, axis continued, bridge/fountain, trees . . .

This is an example of classic garden landscape design.

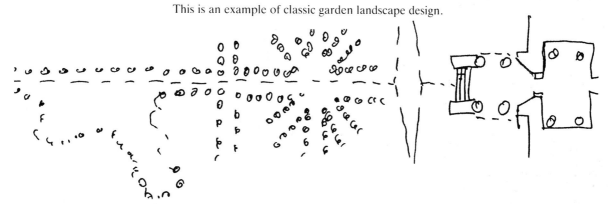

For a one-family house on a small site, only a fraction of the whole repertoire could ever be applied

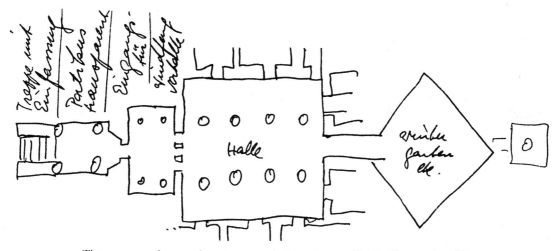

The sequence from main entrance to hall can be graphically illustrated as follows:

stairs with balustrades – transparent porticos – entrance door – draught lobby/ante-room – hall – winter garden etc.

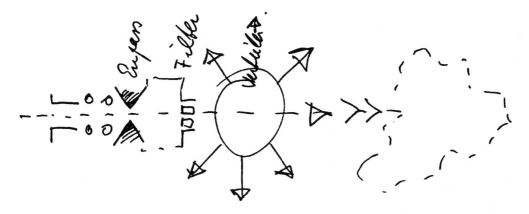

Narrow approach – filter – distributor

century civic building was the atrium in a Roman patrician's house – the space where the master of the house welcomed his guests. Rooms of different use and significance would branch off from it, controlled by a ceremonial system of order. All this sounds pretty genial. However, for architecture to become interesting, a certain effort, beyond the merely functional, needs to be made. Needless to say, the quality of the end product does not depend on the energy expended on it alone. I only mention this to safeguard myself from being labelled an elitist and reactionary by students and younger colleagues. Personal experience with students has taught me how quickly this classic historicist analysis can be condemned.

We have already discovered how difficult it is to describe the functions of a house without being constantly distracted by mere technicalities. How to design drawers and endless other banalities that make up the functional skeleton of a house – these considerations are important, but in the final analysis are of only secondary significance. This at least is my opinion and forms the basis of my philosophy.

To this day, I have not found a flat or house where I felt uncompromisingly comfortable, despite the fact that they all had a flushing toilet, hot running water, sufficiently lit rooms etc. The energy one has to expend in search of the perfect dwelling, in the right surroundings, is enormous. Until now, I have preferred to invest this time and energy in my work. However, I know full well that even I cannot endure this state of affairs much longer. The aesthetic component must, at some point, be solved satisfactorily, so that the few hours of relaxation in one's own home may at least be enjoyable.

——— ✳ ———

House in Berlin, architect: Tessenow

CONSTRUCTION AND FORM

Neither construction nor function can be isolated from the totality of architecture and expected to exist in their own right. Construction is closely related to function. A clearly defined concept of spatial organisation demands an appropriate structural solution. The more harmonious this unity, the closer one comes to the architectonic end product. There are three principal types of construction: massive construction, skeletal construction, and mixed construction. All three have been known to man for centuries.

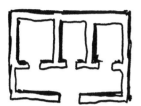

Solid wall construction

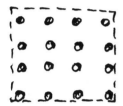

Skeletal construction

Mixed construction

The type of construction used depended on climatic conditions and the availability of materials in a particular region. Today, however, we seldom find an interdependence of climate, landscape and natural building materials. Types of construction for specific programmatic requirements are simply picked at random. Even consciously selected materials are seldom sympathetic to local traditions. Sadly, the choice between steel, concrete or timber is, more often than not, a financual one. Socio-political and economic market forces are having a devas-

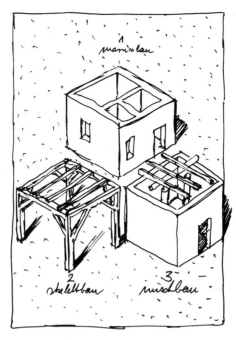

Massive, skeletal and mixed construction

tating effect on architecture. Internationally, systems of construction are becoming increasingly interchangeable. We are experiencing a *movement within world architecture which is in danger of producing total uniformity, smothering the relationship between ways of life and forms of construction.*

New production methods and new materials are unleashing a reservoir of previously unimaginable possibilities for the architect. In the twenties this was seen as one of the great opportunities for a new architecture; no one could have predicted the straggling course new technology has in fact taken. Prefabrication knows no limits in its perversion of structural forms.

In order to preserve the logical unity between function and construction one would choose either solid wall construction for a living environment with largely autonomous rooms, and skeletal structure for an open-plan spatial concept.

Solid wall construction, whether industrially prefabricated or constructed on site, by its very nature is not as spatially flexible as skeletal construction with its freer plan and inherent adaptability to changing living requirements.

On the other hand the characterisation of

these qualities can just as easily be reversed: the generously conceived massive structure is usually incredibly adaptable. Town houses built up to the turn of the century bear witness to this. The tailor-made programmatic solution of a skeletal building may prohibit changes of function, even if room partitions are only semi-permanent.

Any alteration to a temporarily conceived solution will demand substantial financial input that could have been saved by more generous spatial planning to begin with. Also, perfectly understandable human inertia has to be overcome before one gets round to converting a functionally redundant spatial entity. In addition, human beings adapt very quickly to given environmental conditions, even if they do not satisfy primary needs.

Let us investigate further the other qualities of the two primary construction types.

Massive or Solid Wall Construction

This type consists of a system of solid self-supportive wall elements made up of building blocks or of a monolithic nature.

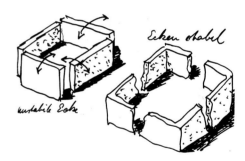

Four walls joined at the corners result in a stiff formation

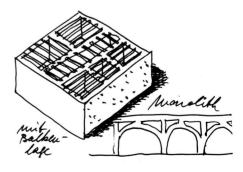

Ceiling construction: timber joists, vaults or pre-cast concrete panels

Openings in masonry walls are either bridged with large building blocks, timber or concrete lintels, or by arch formations

Concrete as a building material poses no limitation to the type and form of openings. The inherent and very real danger of this apparent freedom of expression is an aberration, since the use of concrete demands a very formal and structured discipline.

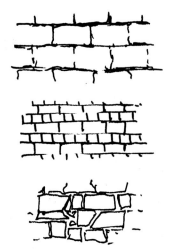

Solid wall construction, in particular, demands harmonious and well-proportioned window openings.

The deceptively simple architectural problem of punching a hole in a solid wall presents us with a wide range of elementary decisions and solutions. Walls are not simply punched through to admit light into the interior space. Through their arrangement and juxtaposition, openings form the most vital compositional elements in the architectural articulation of the facade.

The disposition of the openings can significantly affect the overall stability of the wall. If the number of openings is increased beyond a certain point, the laws for skeletal construction become applicable.

The Layering of Masonry Walls

Wall surfaces exhibit particular joint patterns characteristic of the building material used and can be aesthetically very appealing. The chapter on the elements of architecture deals with this in greater detail.

The type of joint pattern often reveals whether the wall is solid and load-bearing or merely cladded. It is, however, not always easy to make the distinction. In previous centuries, even the best architects imitated materials and wall structures with a variety of surface treatments. And, when even this proved too expensive, they just painted on the required joint pattern. This technique was commonly used in rural areas to imitate in a naïve and simplistic manner the prevalent urban culture of the time.

The quality of the material, its surface structure and line patterns can only be appreciated at close range. Such intricate examination reveals pores, veins, folds and minute hairs, just like the human skin: the object becomes visually and sensually interesting. The aroma of the materials, the structures and sub-structures of the patina are like veils of time, torn by wind and weather, and, together with the cleaning marks left by diligent charwomen, they enrich the building and make it more 'familiar'. In this microcosmos of detail, the colossus of technology fades into insignificance. The floorboards creak, the walls show cracks, the plaster work crumbles, walls are moist, a door is jammed or a window handle has fallen off. These are the trade marks by which I recognise my own house. The structure of the masonry is as close to my skin as the weave of my vest.

Supportive Wall Techniques

A wall's length to depth ratio is crucial to its structural stability. The simplest measure to safeguard against collapse is to ensure a sensible relationship between wall thickness and height. This method is not particularly ingenious. A far more interesting solution is to achieve structural stability with a sparing use of building materials.

The type of solution to this problem has fundamentally shaped architecture throughout history. Some of the stabilising techniques of masonry walls are as follows:

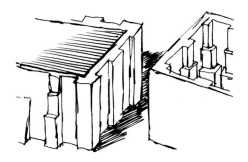

1. The pilaster-like strengthening of walls on the inner or outer face.

The flying buttresses of Gothic cathedrals are beautiful visual manifestations of the laws of statics.

The vaulting span of these open hall-like interiors could not possibly be achieved by filigree shafts in the interiors alone, unless used with elaborate iron bracings that would have impaired the spatial impact. Inspired by the noble thought to leave the sacred space as pure and light as possible and barring all show of strength, this ingenious method of transferring loads was developed. Its elegance was not to be secondary to the grace of the interior space. And, indeed, in classic Gothic cathedrals this has been achieved with unbelievable perfection.

I would like to describe only a small detail from this system: the seemingly ornamental turrets crowning the flying buttresses fulfil an eminently structural function. The arches transmit a sheer force onto the vertical piers, causing them to buckle and snap; the weight of the pinnacles, however, catches and retains this outward force and transmits it downwards through the piers into the ground.

2. Tapering of the walls from the ground upwards. In the example illustrated here, the measure expresses the different floor heights

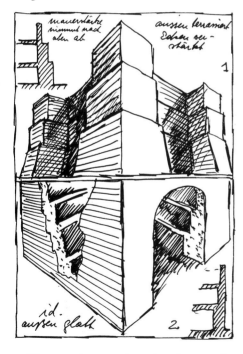

The tapering can also take place on the inside, leaving the exterior wall level

3. Widening of the plinth (base)
4. Reinforcement of the corners

5. Reinforcement of the building core by towers
6. Wave-like articulation of the wall
7. Cell-like or double membrane wall construction

All these structural tricks can find free expression on the exterior of the building; on the inside, however, they have to be compatible with comfort.

Skeletal Construction

With this form of construction the load-bearing posts and beams are physically independent of the exterior wall envelope.

The entire framework is self-supportive and independent of its infills. The static requirements of the skeletal framework influence its form considerably. The posts and beams cannot be joined as easily and simply as the first drawing might suggest. They have to withstand external forces without the complete framework collapsing.

The following methods are used to strengthen the frame:

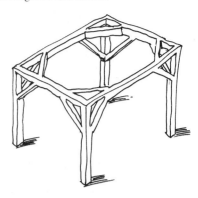

1. The four corners are stiffened

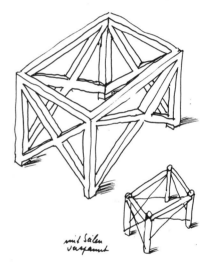

2. Lateral bracing stabilizes the structure

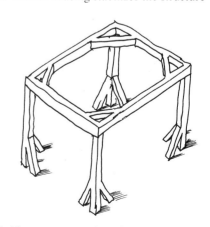

3. The posts are anchored to the foundations and the supported beams complete a frame

The type of material, whether timber, steel or concrete does, of course, significantly influence the method of stabilisation and the resultant form.

Method of tying post to beam, in timber construction

Post-Beam, steel connection (Savings Bank, Vienna, Otto Wagner)

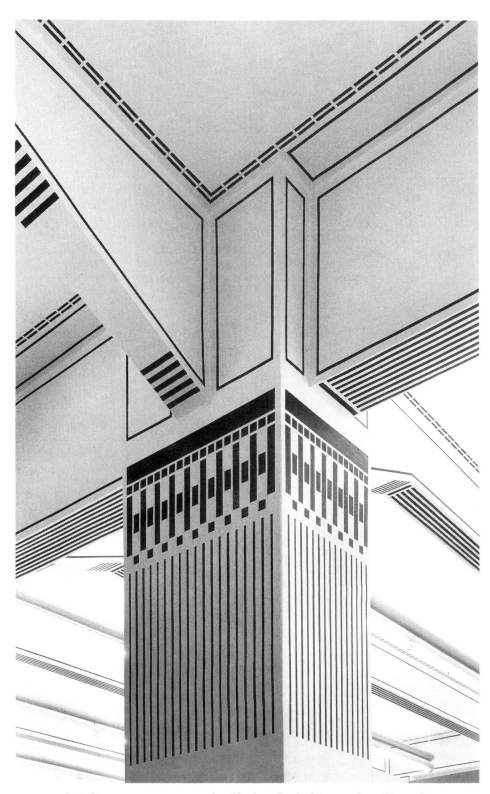

Post-Beam, concrete connection (Savings Bank, Vienna, Otto Wagner)

Stone skeleton (Roman Briscane, near Tebassai, Algeria)

Post-Beam, stone connection, brick, etc
(Hadrian's Villa, Tivoli)

Post-Beam, steel and timber connection

Post-Beam, brick and timber connection

Plans showing positioning of posts:

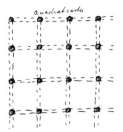

Square grid system

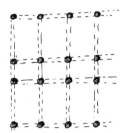

Rectangular grid system

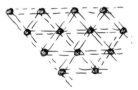

Triangular and sextagonal grid system

Irregular system

As the grid system becomes more complex, its functional and spatial limitations increase proportionally. The irregular, or wilful positioning of posts makes the supporting skeletal framework highly complicated since all the span dimensions are different.

Stabilising Cores in Skeletal Construction

In skeletal construction, the methods of stiffening and stabilising a building become increasingly involved as the number of floors increases. Most commonly, stair towers and lift-shafts are driven through the central core of the building to stiffen and stabilise and prevent it from being blown over.

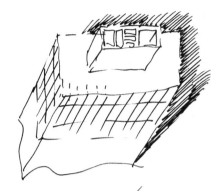

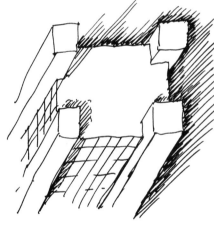

Flexibility of the Plan

In discussing function I have already mentioned that skeletal construction lends itself particularly well to a free and open plan.

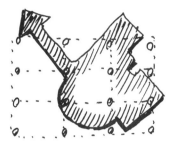

In the illustrated example the primary construction is perceived as a pure roof structure with the pavilion-like base slotted in. This conception is very material-intensive and therefore not normally economically viable. It formalises the idea of separate roof and dwelling from each other, and can be stylised to create great architecture

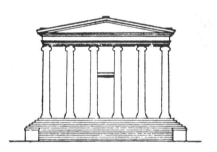

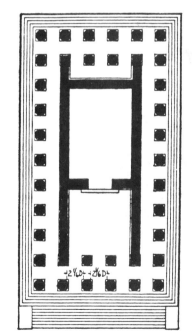

For example: the classical temple

Le Corbusier, for instance, borrowed architectural form from antiquity and reinterpreted it into a new architectural language. This architectural theme is particularly suitable in adapting to changing functional requirements. To ensure an ultimate flexibility of use, the idea must be given careful consideration from the earliest stages of the design process onwards.

In many cases, flexibility and transparency were quite simply seen as essential in the realisation of a contemporary architecture. The building's exterior frame was expressed as subtly as possible, making the distinction between interior and exterior space increasingly blurred and ill defined.

It is understandable today that the architects of the twenties, armed with a new technology and theory, aspired to create a completely new, extended and visionary aesthetic repertoire. The best of them succeeded. However, they then came to realise the limitations of these technological and creative advances. Their pupils and followers soon reduced those technological possibilities to unbearable platitudes.

Cladding the Skeletal Structure

From storey to storey lightweight cladding is fastened on to the structural framework of the building. It has to be appropriately dimensioned to withstand wind loads. The type of cladding and its proportion of glazing can be a personal choice. In the early twenties this technical innovation sparked

Le Corbusier, Villa Poissy

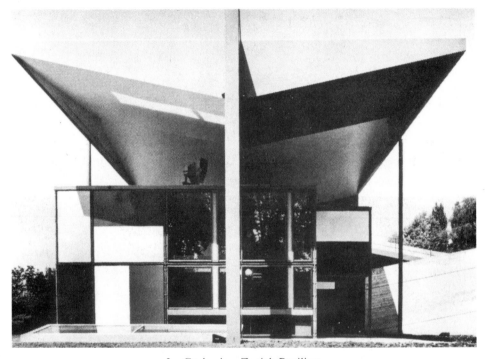

Le Corbusier, Zurich Pavilion

Mies van der Rohe, Barcelona Pavilion

———— ✳ ————

34

Unité d'habitation, Marseilles, Le Corbusier

Centre for the Visual Arts, Cambridge, Massachusetts, Le Corbusier.

off a true glass and light euphoria that found expression in numerable manifestos on glass architecture.

Today we see this problem far more clearly because we have subsequently come to understand the problems of glass-cladding in certain climates. Moreover, it seems absurd to glaze entire facades for the sake of an architectural ideology and then devise an elaborate system of sun shades to control the sunlight, or to provide permanent sun guards in the form of terraces or loggias.

Unfortunate experiences with the Maison du Salut and an office building in Moscow led Le Corbusier to use fixed 'brise soleils' (sunbreaks) in his later buildings. The plastic properties of this 'secondary' facade enriched Le Corbusier's architectural repertoire considerably. These are two examples of brise soleils and loggias in Le Corbusier's work.

In giving spatial expression to an interior, the type, form and size of the windows has enormous significance. The schematic 'screen' facade had a very negative and fragmentary effect. The doubtful argument to extend living space into nature, to let it spill over without transition, has destroyed *de facto* all essential spatial definition and alienated its geometry unnecessarily. In the chapter on architectural space, I shall take up the problem of fragmentation once again.

——— ✳ ———

**Mixed Techniques of Solid Wall
and Skeletal Frame Construction**

Skeletal construction is by no means an invention of modern building technology. Likewise, such modern architectural terms as 'adaptability', 'flexibility', and 'smooth transition between interior and exterior', are not twentieth-century inventions. Skeletal and solid wall construction are the earliest building techniques known to mankind.

Both techniques were employed to achieve the same goal: to create an enclosed habitat. The skeletal or structural framework was padded out with infill materials of various kinds. Roof structures, open to the air, were used to store food and feeding materials or for meetings and cult rituals. In the case of the latter, the building was especially elaborate. The Greek temple can be traced back to this early type. One does not have to go back to the temple's primeval origins to see that the ideal house type was, quite simply, developed into the monumental building type and enriched with sacral and symbolic significance. The enclosed cell had a transparent weather shield in the form of a colonnaded veranda or loggia wrapped around its perimeter walls.

Examples from Viollet-le-Duc's *Histoire de l'habitation*:

Stretched membrane construction

Skeletal construction

Skeletal framework interwoven

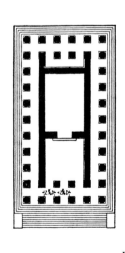
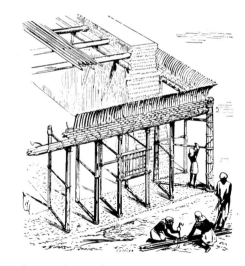
Example: temple . . . hut

Solid wall and skeletal construction mixed

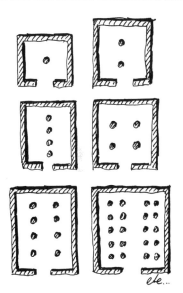

The roof structure is supported from the inside

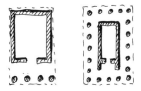

The house under one roof, or house with overhanging canopy

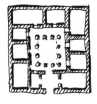

House with atrium; the interior courtyard opens to the sky and harbours its own colonnade; none of the rooms has unrestricted views, or opens out into nature. The courtyard house is, in a sense, the reverse of the verandah house and is of course much more suited to the dense urban context than the detached house.

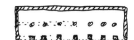

Colonnaded hall

Arcaded street

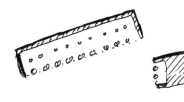

Agora

Forum, cloister style

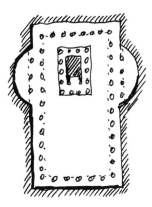

Forum with temple

Looking at it another way, one could say that a small living-cell was placed under an essentially free-standing roof construction. By this method the clay walls of primitive houses were protected from rain. At the same time, the overhanging roof provided the desired sun shade.

The house in this archaic form unmistakably articulated the interior space as a unit enclosed on all sides, and the ante-room as the intermediate space under the open roof with its solid wall at the back and posts, piers or columns looking out.

To compose a house with only open and flowing rooms is questionable. An open-plan room only gains its strength when contrasted with a closed room. The longing for a change in light intensity alone must lead us to this conclusion. Here, a purely architectural problem was thrust aside by seductive technological innovations.

Mixed forms of massive and skeletal construction are illustrated here.

Historically domestic and public architecture have always influenced each other. House and temple, courtyard house and forum not only have direct morphological connections but also feed from each other. History teaches us that a building type only survives the test of time if its functional and aesthetic qualities are in equilibrium. Columns in front of a house, or within an interior courtyard, are not only climatic filters but also splendid elements of architectural expression. Le Corbusier's efforts to carve out the building mass into cell-like units by means of loggias and to prop it up on stilts had similar architectonic motives.

———— ✳ ————

The charm of mixed construction lies to a large extent in its structural and spatial complexity. Let us start by comparing two interior spaces: the nave of an Early Romanesque and a Gothic cathedral.

In Romanesque architecture, the side arcades are simply carved out of the solid walls, without any special articulation, as in the clerestorey; this nave wall is still clearly reminiscent of a normal house facade.

During the Late Romanesque period the composition and technology of this rather filigree wall composition was being developed step by step.

On the lower level the wall has been completely dissolved, and the column with capital and base has been articulated as an autonomous building element. The triforium or blind storey is closed to the outside but opens into the sacral space, while the plastically articulated gallery serves no direct function. The clerestorey, just above the triforium, serves as the actual light infuser of the interior space.

Early Romanesque

Gothic

———— ✳ ————

The third example of a Gothic space, the Jacobin Church in Toulouse, illustrates that increased simplification of the building type heightens transparency and overview but some of the tension is lost in the process. With mixed construction the number of different materials used plays an important role. For example:
–   Solid wall construction on the outside and timber or steel construction inside.
–   Massive core with inset timber, steel or concrete structure.

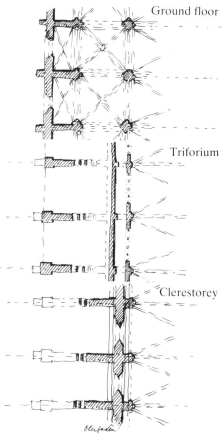

Ground floor

Triforium

Clerestorey

Wall articulation of a Gothic cathedral

Jacobin Church, Toulouse

Bibliothèque Nationale, Paris, architect: Labrouste, 1862

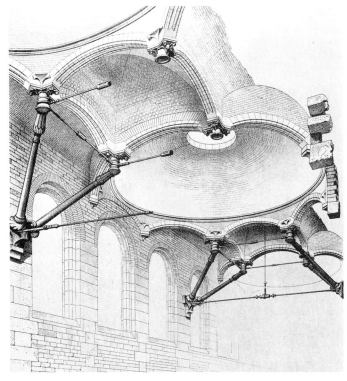

Hall construction, architect: Viollet-le-Duc, 1865

Corn Exchange, Leeds, architect: C. Brodrick, 1861

CHAPTER II

ON
ARCHITECTONIC
FORM

ON ARCHITECTONIC FORM

So far we have examined the significance of function and construction in architectural composition. Should we have considered a third factor? Is there more to the definition of architecture than function and construction? Are there aesthetic requirements that determine architecture independent of function and construction? According to our original mandate, a building is only perceived as architecture if the two basic factors are enriched with an aesthetic sensibility. Describing the two basic factors, we have not exclusively talked about the purely factual and technical attributes of functional co-ordination and systems of construction, but have always hastened to emphasise the resultant formal properties. Does this therefore render the chapter on architectonic form redundant? No . . . for a number of reasons!

1. There are architectural rooms and objects that have abstract, symbolic and cultural significance as monuments. They can be designed independently of function and construction, purely according to aesthetic principles.

2. In building, the art of beautifying the 'useful' calls for more than a few simple tricks. When we earlier talked about 'architectural composition', we had a very complex package of rules in mind – the aesthetic operators of architecture. They are, as we shall presently see, no less complicated than the rules of composition in music.

3. For the diligent architect, the poetic dimension Le Corbusier so often referred to is, in the end, no gift from heaven. He has to understand the rational methods by which he can reach those dimensions. There are no fixed rules or absolute laws that define the creation of architectural form and guarantee to meet every aesthetic condition, thus doing justice to our poetic pretensions. The architect, like every artist, has to sense precisely when, during the act of creation, rational thought processes are played out and when the intuitive process takes over.

If you think I am making a mockery of this irrational component you are quite wrong. I am wholly serious about it and not only because my own experience has taught me that day-dreaming can suddenly and without apparent reason lead to a solution that would never have arisen from a purely rational and mathematical path.

Poetic intuition is not transferable and cannot be taught. One may merely suspect its significance.

It takes an unbelievably long time to find within you the artistic orientation that corresponds to your temperament and gives unmistakable expression to your abilities and inclinations. I personally had to tread a path plastered with uncertainties before having the merest hunch of an artistic position. My education at the Technical University in Munich is to blame for many of my detours, since it failed to implant in me a theoretical backbone. Perhaps it was lucky, since without this back-breaking effort I might still today be under the spell of an inflated self-confidence.

The architectural design process can be outlined as follows:

1. General considerations about the ordering of functions, based on the requirements of the particular design programme. Choice of construction type and suitable materials.

2. Next, one has to decide which geometric pattern the architectural layout is to follow. In most cases one only reaches a decision after numerous experiments in various directions have been made and it becomes clear which geometry is most suited to meet a particular programme and its limitations.

3. Only now does the purely arithmetic puzzle begin to take form. The geometric shapes drawn on the paper are joined-up sections that need to be felt in their two-dimensionality before being projected upwards and co-ordinated.

First we define the interior of a house before going on to wrap a skin around the articulated plan and formulate it into a building. Only now does one begin to make aesthetic corrections; working from the inside towards the outside, or the outside inwards.

It is, of course, also possible to project a certain function and construction into a preconceived building concept. Neither function nor construction must be compromised in this reverse process, i.e. in every case the process must be fully reversible.

In the case of urban designs, after having clarified all functional interrelationships, one has to decide which urban formation seems most appropriate – whether street or square – how these spatial entities are to be shaped, the co-ordination of architectural types, and how the whole system is to be knitted into the existing urban fabric.

In architecture, the interior space and the urban space are very closely related.

As soon as an architectonic system takes on physical form, point, line and plane patterns take effect on the inner and outer surfaces of the system. What do we mean by that?

– Walls, floors and ceilings are planes.

– Window cross-bars and mortar joints are line structures.

– Lamps, installation fittings, holes, etc.

make up point patterns, as do many other architectural elements. All these elements have their own material-related characteristics and thus their own 'colour'.

4. Space, solid, plane, line and point obey the rules of spatial composition. They can be artistically distorted or manipulated. Without wishing to elaborate at this point why this or that distortion technique is employed, I should first like to introduce you to the rules and then, with the aid of examples, uncover the causality of the processes. An element can be:

    a. bent
    b. divided
    c. segmented
    d. added to
    e. superimposed, intertwined
    f. perspectively distorted
    g. deformed

By 'deformed' I mean in this context 'a deformation beyond recognition'.

5. All these processes of spatial composition can – in the geometric sense – lead to regular, irregular or hybrid forms.

6. Proportioning. I would like to talk about this rule of spatial composition in the design process quite independently, since it influences and controls all architectural elements.

7. Scale or geometric ratio is the last and most dominant factor in the architectural design process. Once fixed, the geometric ratio acts like an umbrella, with every part of the building depending upon it.

———— ✳ ————

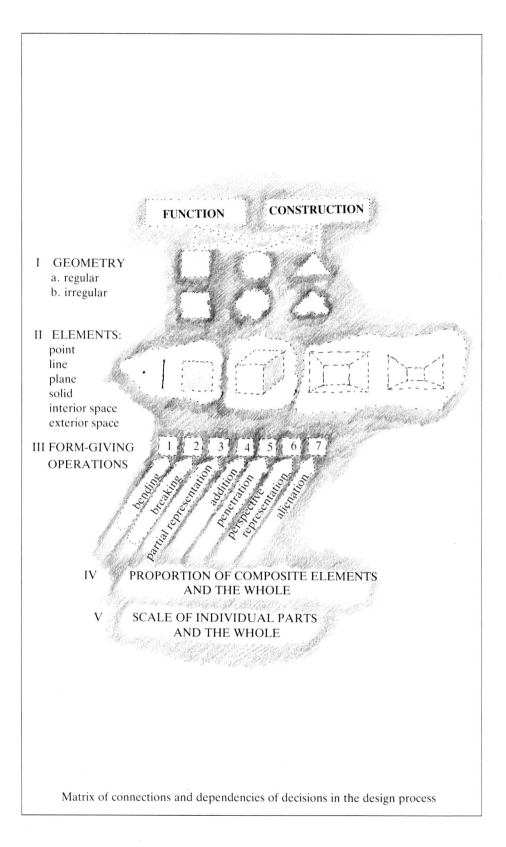

Matrix of connections and dependencies of decisions in the design process

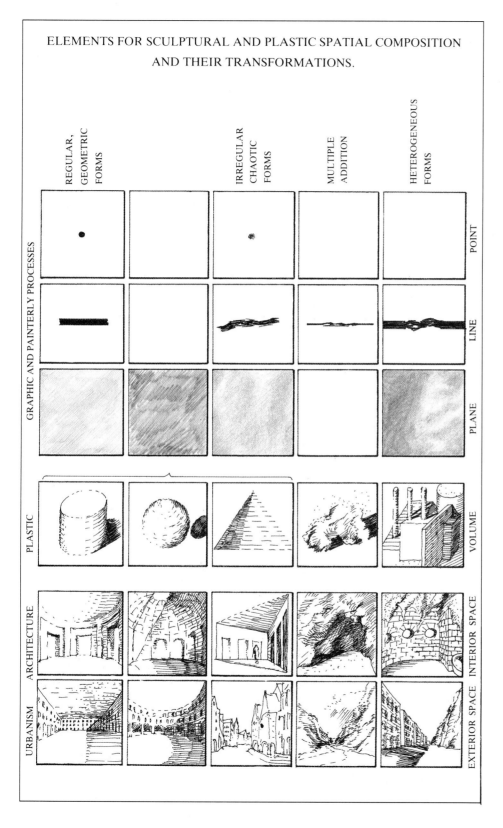

ELEMENTS FOR SCULPTURAL AND PLASTIC SPATIAL COMPOSITION AND THEIR TRANSFORMATIONS.

BASIC FORMS OF THE ELEMENTS

The basic forms of these elements are: regular or geometric, irregular or chaotic, or a mixture of both.

For the dot, line and plane, this simply means the manipulation of light and colour values. For the solid it is the primary forms; cylinder, sphere, cone, cube, pyramid or a random rock that might symbolise the irregular body, and finally, the heterogeneous solid made up of different figurations.

The interior space of all these bodies may be directly related to their exterior form. If we remove the upper limits of these spaces and differentiate the scale, we can speak of urban space, natural space, landscape or of their dialogue.

———— ✳ ————

1. Kink, Bend, Fold

The first possible transformation of these elements is kinking and bending. By this method lines can be deformed at will, either geometrically regular or irregular. Handwriting patterns demonstrate all the different permutations of this method. A neatly folded piece of paper, a soft cloth regularly pleated, a rippled water surface, a seat cover or a puckered trouser hem: these are all manifestations of bending (in the widest sense of the word) a plane. A soft or crooked stick, a twisted branch and a flexed knee are all examples of bent bodies. An elongated space, a corridor for example, can have one or several regular or irregular bends. The Olympic swimming stadium by Behnisch and Frei Otto in Munich has almost all its planes folded or deflected. (This morphological observation does not bespeak quality.) Contorted corridors also result in rooms with twisted walls and vice versa. In urban planning, meandering roads twisting and turning are part of this theme.

———— ✳ ————

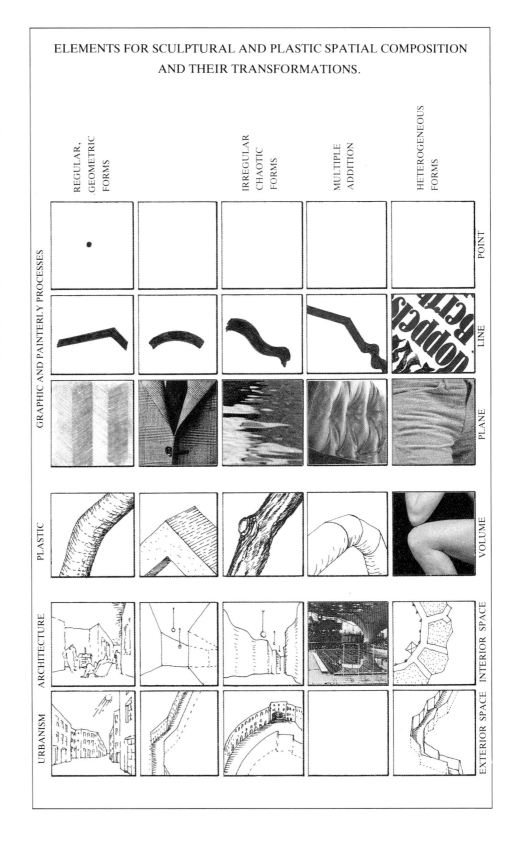

ELEMENTS FOR SCULPTURAL AND PLASTIC SPATIAL COMPOSITION AND THEIR TRANSFORMATIONS.

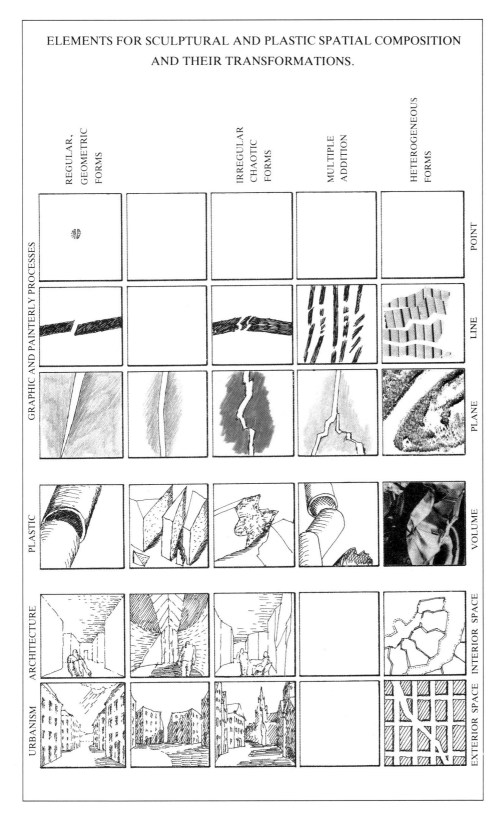

ELEMENTS FOR SCULPTURAL AND PLASTIC SPATIAL COMPOSITION AND THEIR TRANSFORMATIONS.

2. Break, Cut

The second transformation consists of dividing, breaking, separating and cutting up. On a microscale, a dot or point can, of course, be sub-divided, and lines, surfaces and forms broken up into sharp or jagged pieces. A crashed car is a dramatic example of all kinds of mangled surfaces and elements. A building can be split in two by a squabble over property, the power of the traffic planners, or a war – as well as by functional and constructional interests. Walls and ceilings can be divided to give an interior space a fragmentary character and, on the outside, an irregularly curved, completely glazed cladding can create the illusion that the building is somehow broken.

An interrupted street or square pattern, or the irregular grid-pattern that runs through Broadway in New York, are examples of interrupted or divided urban space.

———— ✳ ————

3. Segment

This transformation is related to the preceding one. It emphasizes the fragment that results from the breakage of a complete part. The fragment and its broken edge are suggestive of the original form. Parts of lines, planes and solids, with ragged and smooth cleavage lines, are all illustrated here. Segments can sometimes express more than the whole. Looking just at a mouth, for instance, can often reveal more about a person than the entire face.

If we dissect a building by cutting away one of its exterior walls and replacing it with a plane of glass, all we are left with is a fragment of the original. The interior rooms bereft of a wall are now fragmented. The layman might consider this a perfect improvisation. However, if we look more closely, we realise that we are being confronted by the prototype of the so-called 'modern building type', in which interior space as well as the building corpus remain fragmented.

This comment may be interpreted critically. The one-sided and biased emphasis of a design process always has a weak theoretical foundation. Glass buildings will soon be distinct for energy reasons, rather than because of form-giving insights. An empty, burnt out house is illustrated here as a symbol of spatial fragmentation.

In modern city planning, the enclosed urban core of the pre-industrial city has been lost through fragmentation. The interior and exterior space of the twentieth century has fallen victim to the same plight.

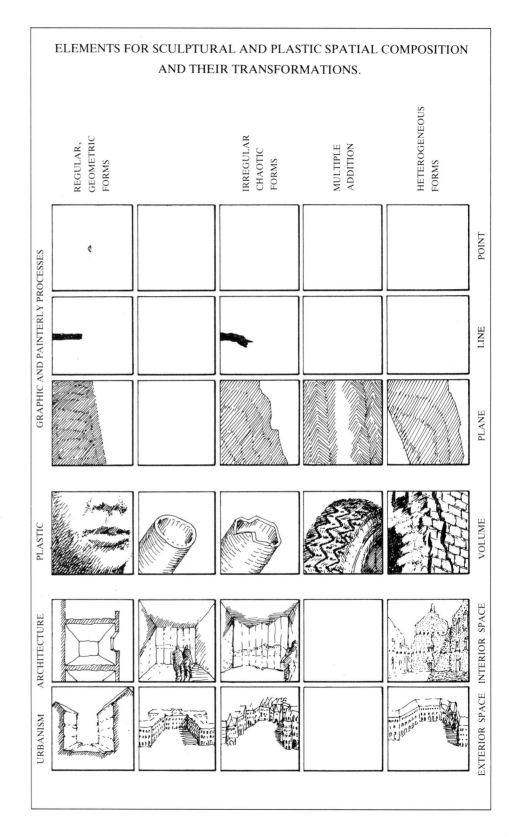

ELEMENTS FOR SCULPTURAL AND PLASTIC SPATIAL COMPOSITION AND THEIR TRANSFORMATIONS.

———— ✳ ————

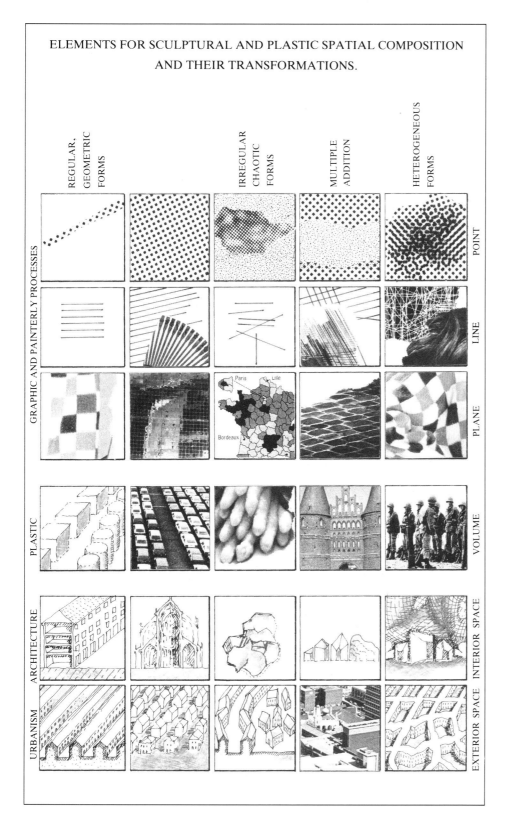

ELEMENTS FOR SCULPTURAL AND PLASTIC SPATIAL COMPOSITION AND THEIR TRANSFORMATIONS.

REGULAR, GEOMETRIC FORMS — IRREGULAR CHAOTIC FORMS — MULTIPLE ADDITION — HETEROGENEOUS FORMS

GRAPHIC AND PAINTERLY PROCESSES

PLASTIC

ARCHITECTURE

URBANISM

POINT — LINE — PLANE — VOLUME — INTERIOR SPACE — EXTERIOR SPACE

4. Addition–Friction–Accumulation–Stacking

Every scanning pattern, in graphics as well as painting, is the addition of dots, lines and planes.

A row of boxes, oil drums or houses, a flow of cars, a bunch of asparagus, a pair of towers and a battalion of soldiers are randomly selected examples of addition and repetition of geometric and non-geometric solids. Today, mass production has given this form-giving process a tenuous value.

The piling of rooms on top of one another, the addition of room floor plans of equal or different scale (in this case the floor plan of a Gothic church), the addition of regular and irregular spatial units or their superimposition (a soft membrane harbours strong geometric forms): all these represent only a fraction of the possibilities in the realm of interior spaces.

The composing of spaces in relation to one another enhances the theme of addition and bestows it with an aesthetic background. The tension lies in the variation of the joining elements. The stringing together of identical parts soon becomes very boring. The first two illustrations in the 'town planning' sequence highlight this point: a typical terrace house community in the twenties and a rigid suburban colony of villas. The spaces between the buildings are identical and therefore interchangeable; private and public spaces can hardly be differentiated. Courtyards should not be added on in such a way that you only ever find one house between two halves. Schematic building patterns of this kind are reminiscent of the massed housing blocks of the nineteenth century, leading to the formation of ghettos in the cities.

———— ✳ ————

49

5. Penetration–Superimposition–Interlacing–Meshing

Nature offers the best examples to illustrate the various transformation sequences. Looked at from a distance, the foliage of a tree can be perceived as a diversified and interesting superimposition of dot matrixes. The details of a knitted cardigan, a bicycle spoke, a braid of hair or a shopping net all illustrate the superimposition and inter-weaving of lines. The network of twigs and branches of a barren tree should also be added to this list.

The overlaying of different colour trans-parencies can produce fascinating colour effects, and a highly interwoven material can lead to equally interesting results. The painter Albers delighted in the overlaying of differently coloured squares.

A rod pushed through a fixed fence post, a building element that grows out of or into a rock are all examples that serve to illus-trate the principle of penetration. The pic-ture of the glass house in the grounds of Castle Schonbrunn in Vienna is a beautiful example of penetration through trans-parency of the outer skin.

The cross-over between transept and nave on the plan of a Gothic cathedral symbolizes one of the most perfect articula-tions of this theme. Piranesi conceived fan-tastic spatial penetrations in his 'Carceri' drawings.

In urban planning the pertinent examples of transformation would be a crossroads or a square intersected by numerous side roads.

6. Emphasis on Foreground and Background in Perspective Representation

The clarification of foreground and back-ground or the feeling of depth are the con-cerns of these transformations.

Dot and line patterns can be drawn to suggest a feeling of perspective: either by emphasising the foreground through bold lines that thin out gradually as they advance further into the picture plane, or by project-ing all the lines towards one vanishing point as in a one-point perspective. Planes are treated similarly. Landscape paintings only evoke a feeling of depth if the different picture planes are determined mathe-matically.

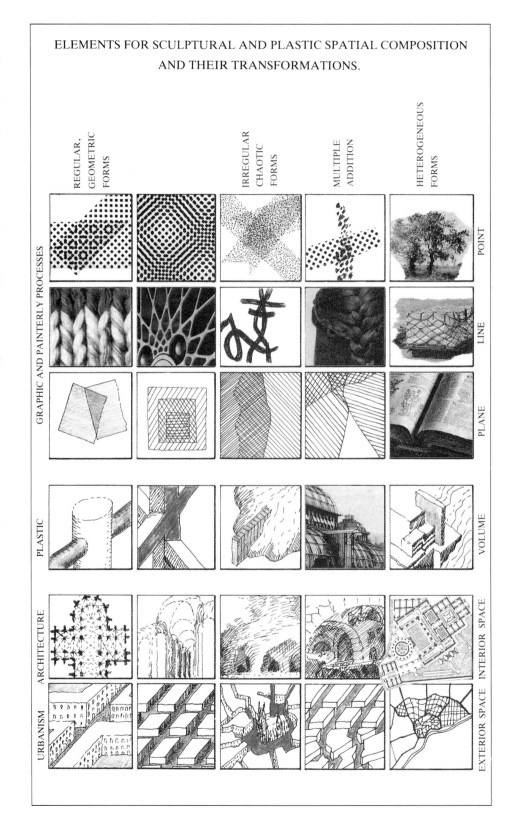

ELEMENTS FOR SCULPTURAL AND PLASTIC SPATIAL COMPOSITION AND THEIR TRANSFORMATIONS.

ELEMENTS FOR SCULPTURAL AND PLASTIC SPATIAL COMPOSITION
AND THEIR TRANSFORMATIONS.

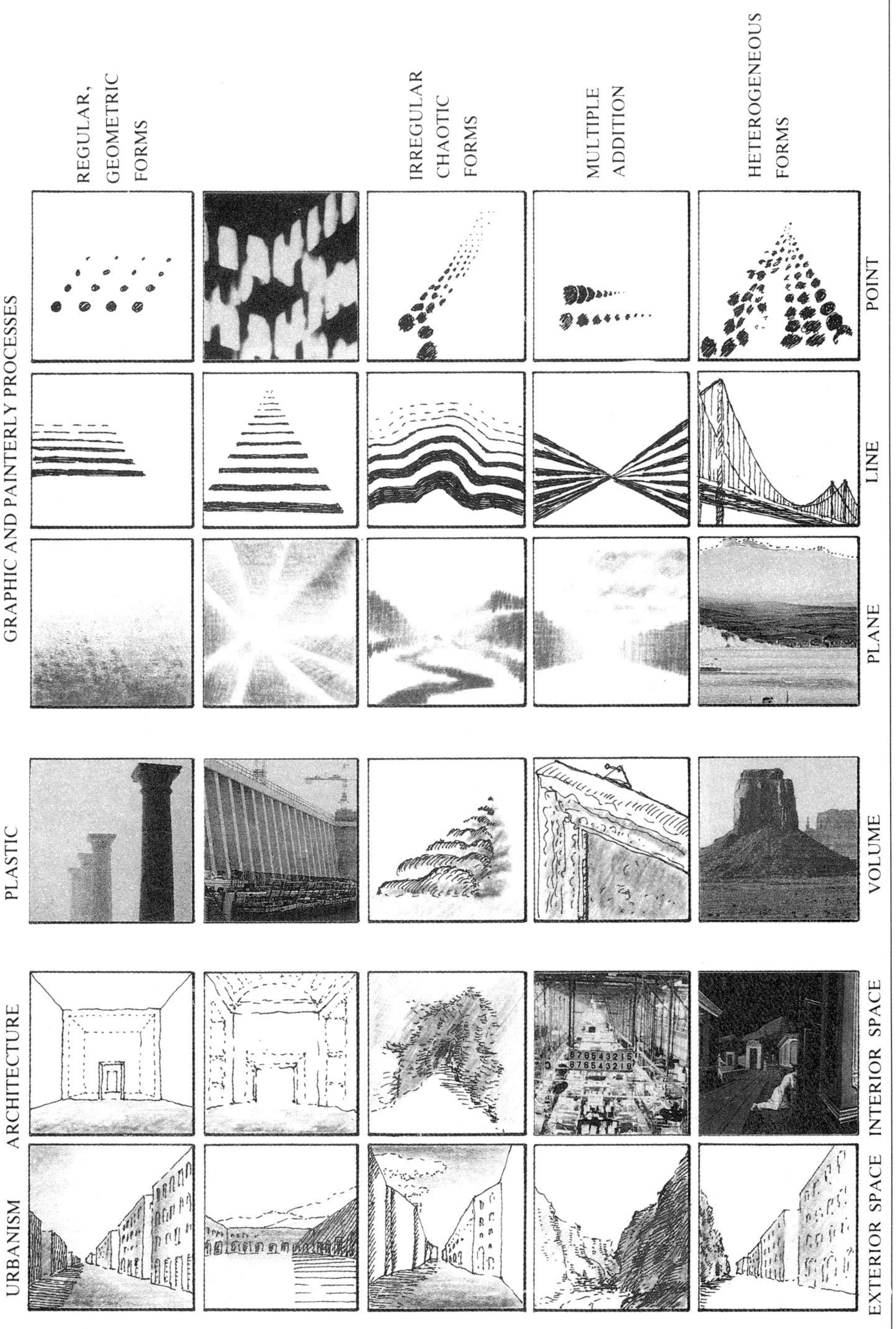

REGULAR, GEOMETRIC FORMS

IRREGULAR CHAOTIC FORMS

MULTIPLE ADDITION

HETEROGENEOUS FORMS

GRAPHIC AND PAINTERLY PROCESSES

PLASTIC

ARCHITECTURE

URBANISM

POINT

LINE

PLANE

VOLUME

INTERIOR SPACE

EXTERIOR SPACE

The stringing together of building elements in a strong linear order intensifies the feeling of depth in an urban composition as well as in the landscape. The traditional picture frame is often employed to condense a piece of architecture and space.

The most ordinary interior space can acquire a feeling of depth through purely constructive or decorative means. In this the location of light sources plays a crucial role.

Through their mastery of perspective drawing, baroque artists transformed flat church ceilings into visual illusions of soaring vaults.

In the inner city, a feeling of depth can be evoked through straight running streets and wide open spaces. However, only places of particular significance should be designed with this effect (e.g. Champs Elysées, Place de la Concorde).

In Bellini's design of St. Peter's in Rome, the arcades on either side of the square become wider as they approach the dome. This visual trick intensifies the feeling of depth and deceives the observer into perceiving the enclosing walls as parallel.

The rue de Tournon in front of the Palais de Luxembourg in Paris opens out in a similar manner towards the palace facade.

In Palladio's Teatro Olimpico in Vicenca, the street scenes taper towards the building, bestowing on it a feeling of depth that borders on the fantastic.

Nature too, offers perfect examples; a river bed cut deep into the rocks mysteriously ebbs away along its meandering path.

The contrast between built city and nature can, through clear demarcation of both parts, promote a feeling of space.

———— ✳ ————

7. The Alienation of Elements

Alienation is the manipulation of an element through distortion of scale or inversion of its original meaning. Ledoux's spherical house or the accessible Eva by Niki de St. Phalle belong to this morphological category.

A dot or a line enlarged under a microscope, a plane (such as a carpet) rolled up into a body, a piece of aluminium shaped into a receptacle, a statue turned into a high-rise building, or Adolf Loos' Doric column imagined as a skyscraper, a fossilized skeleton, a deformed baby and many other examples are all inversions and deformations of the original elements.

Many fashionable tendencies in architecture have claimed to revolutionize the building industry with their innovations. But the short life of these movements is testimony to their feeble theoretical stance.

The skyscrapers of some cosmopolitan cities have surpassed all human dimensions with over-scaled entrances, and are examples of alienation. In stark contrast, the awe-inspiring portals of cathedrals do have symbolic significance and a direct ritual function. At Piccadilly Circus in London, for instance, one hardly suspects houses behind the plethora of billboards and advertising signs. The dramatic alienation of the urban structure inevitably leads to its destruction. Ruined cities, like Pompeii or Leptis Magna also belong to this category.

8. Unequally Emphasised Transformations and Elements

This is a critical category. Looking at the elements and their different transformations it has become apparent that a one-sided manipulation, which only focuses on one point of view, always has a weak influence and remains of limited significance. 'Monostructures' are of limited complexity.

I am convinced that in any discipline a true masterpiece only passes the test of time if based on a multi-layered design concept. Such a rich concept can never be unravelled at first glance. Its true content is only uncovered after prolonged study, with some questions always remaining unanswered.

The work of many modern artists is only skin deep; after the first 'aha effect', little remains. The paintings of Paul Klee, however, are infinitely rich and fascinating

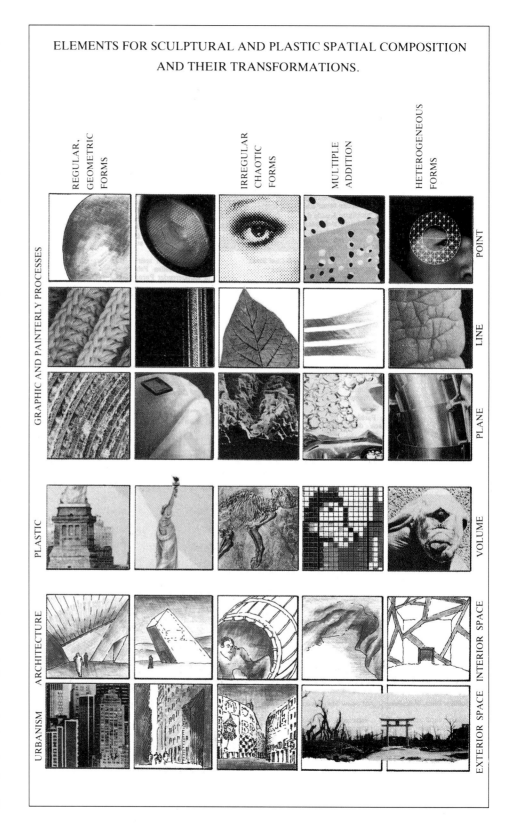

ELEMENTS FOR SCULPTURAL AND PLASTIC SPATIAL COMPOSITION AND THEIR TRANSFORMATIONS.

ELEMENTS FOR SCULPTURAL AND PLASTIC SPATIAL COMPOSITION AND THEIR TRANSFORMATIONS.

in their poetic quality despite their deceivingly simple pictorial expressions. Even with all the abstraction Klee's paintings have not lost the figurative element. Mondrian, however, never went beyond his mystic numbers. The 'Monochromes', like Mark Rothko, deny themselves the message, subscribing instead to the meaningless.

In architecture, inside as well as outside, the same problems are also relevant. A sparse, well-proportioned space can hold a wonderful fascination. Romanesque or Gothic cathedrals undoubtedly have more to offer. Expressionistic spaces suffer from the one-sidedness of their formulation, as well as the over-emphasis of their structural extravaganzas. In city planning, 'structures à redents' by Le Corbusier or the hexagonal structures by Candilis, Josic and Woods for Toulouse le Mirail, are spatially accentuated, yet their similar and serialised repetition negates the effect. No clear hierarchy between public and private spaces is set up. The proposals made by Friedman and the Japanese Metabolists were far more extravagant but, after a few years, were no longer being discussed.

The most important result of this examination is the synchronized appreciation of all design-related medias – from graphics to urban planning – and the clarification of their interconnections. Only by dissecting and disentangling the creative and design processes will compositional interrelationships become apparent.

———— ✳ ————

9. Superimposition and Interplay of Dot – Line – Plane – Volume – Interior Space – Exterior Space

I should like to elucidate the complex superimposition and interpenetration of all these elements and their different transformations by means of six examples, all taken from the realm of nature.

No one can question their quality.

In my creative work nature is a deep source of inspiration. All cultural epochs have drawn on nature and no doubt will continue to do so in the future. The growth patterns of nature have a great deal in common with the rules of artistic composition.

In the visual arts, in architecture and in city planning in the twentieth century, the one-sided and isolated emphasis on the element is, in contrast to earlier cultural epochs, especially widespread: for example, De Stijl with dot, line and plane patterns, Fontana with canvas cut-outs and Yves Klein with monochrome paintings. In architecture since the turn of the century, two seemingly disparate schools have evolved; one working with regular, the other with irregular forms. Each trend has produced astonishing results – the Chicago School on the one hand, and Gaudi, Steiner and the 'Morning Light' group on the other.

If we leaf through history we always find the classical examples to be in the middle ground between the two extremes.

I have often asked myself how anyone can resist the forms of nature, composed, as they are, of only the most essential elements – the starlit sky as prototypical dot pattern; the tree as line structure; the sea and sky as planar patterns; a piece of rock or the mountain as prototype solid; the forest and cave as natural interiors; the canyon; the clearing and, finally, the landscape in all its imaginable variations: the most basic of exterior spaces. There is no art form that

man has not already seen in nature.

Here are a few characteristics of nature's form-giving quality which even the modern artist should learn from:
–The fascination of the spatial effect; the tangible dimension of the earth below, the ethereal dimension above.
–The whole spectrum of light nuances and their delightful interplay.
–The movement of individual elements.
–The static state of others
–The permanence of the drama, the transmutation and regeneration through its own resources.
–The multitude and harmonious balance of its structure.
–The unqualified power and dimension of being – ideas we can hardly comprehend intellectually. You may hold it against me that it is easy to impress with such ideas. The painter, sculptor and architect do not have such an *oeuvre* at their disposal. Their main weapon in their creative duel with nature is the intellectual and spiritual dimension.

The possible manipulations of the elements – dot, line, plane, solid and space – tabulated here are by no means exhaustive. Whatever new materials and tools will extend and enrich the creative repertoire, the basic elements remain the starting point for any artistic expression, whether in two or three dimensions.

New technical advances have broken into the static structure of traditional techniques of representation.
MOVEMENT through the machine.
MUTATION of the pictorial elements through chemical interaction.
EXCHANGEABILITY through building block compositions and mobile objects.
KINETIC PICTURES through film technique, etc . . .

To consider the basic design elements

objectively expels some of the pathos traditionally associated with the creative process. It is also an attempt to establish some system of order in the emotions of people who find our environment worthy of contemplation and wish to communicate their insights and experiences to others. The tools, however, must always remain subordinate to the intention, which can neither be learned, nor, in its intangibility, objectively manipulated. In the end it is intention and motivation, the creative motors, that determine the rational or irrational choice between the available elements and their possible modulations.

Should someone seek a guide book or a catalogue listing the laws of design, I can only advise him to collect and register everything he can possibly lay his hands on.

The ultimate and finest teaching material is our surroundings with all its mobile and immobile things; at will we can grasp, lift, toss, love or hate them.

The transformation processes I have listed here are only a collection of rules and guidelines, they do not guarantee good design. However, we must know and understand them so that our design decisions may never be haphazard.

This is as far as the general overview goes. It was necessary to establish the position of architecture among the visual arts. Architecture has not been called 'the mother of all the arts' for nothing. It is the epitome of all the creative processes, a kind of 'umbrella discipline'. Should it fail to fulfil this role the building is reduced to a utilitarian object devoid of cultural significance.

To avoid superficiality we must take a more detailed look at architectural form. We shall follow the sequence of our already established framework and with the help of examples try to reconstruct individual design processes.

* * *

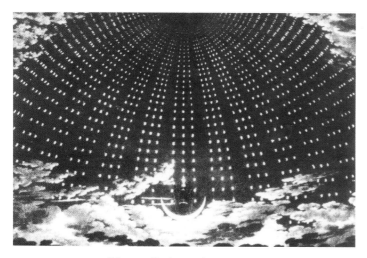

The starlit sky as dot pattern

The forest as archetypal line structure

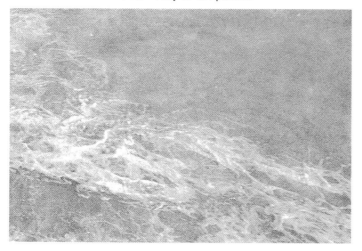

The sea, the sky as plane patterns

Mountains as prototypes of solids

The canyon/gorge as natural exterior space

The cave as natural interior space

RETRACING THE ARCHITECTURAL DESIGN PROCESS
Primary building types

The following six groups of figures are to be read from left to right. Each vertical group represents one type of construction: solid wall construction, skeletal construction, mixed construction. The three primary geometric forms – square, triangle, circle – are always grouped horizontally. In each case the regular and irregular formal manifestation is illustrated.

The dotted plans only roughly suggest the geometric operation and are merely conceptual. The modulation of the interior spaces and building corpus in the third dimension had to be neglected.

And now the primary building types themselves:

a. Solid wall/massive construction:

All spaces, though different in dimension, share a comparably intimate and intro-verted character. Their order follows a hierarchy. The only wall openings are doors and windows. The wall surfaces are by far the most dominant elements. The windows are of traditional upright format and admit well-apportioned light.

b. Skeletal construction:

Typically these are infinitely adaptable large rooms, allowing evenly distributed natural light to permeate through large glazed exterior walls and creating a neutral spatial impression with little compositional articulation. The abundant use of glass and metal endows the building with an abstrac-tion that is characteristic of its type and function.

c. Composite or mixed construction:

This type, in all its conceivable figurations, offers the richest and most exciting spatial and formal repertoire. The hierarchy of the interior spaces can convey a special ceremonial quality, with major and minor rooms of clearly differentiated tectonic character. This building type is particularly suited for public functions and sacral spaces. It can, of course, also find application in private houses with ever-changing functional requirements, where the skeletal framework within the interior has not been designed according to aesthetic considerations, but principally to affect a free-standing plan.

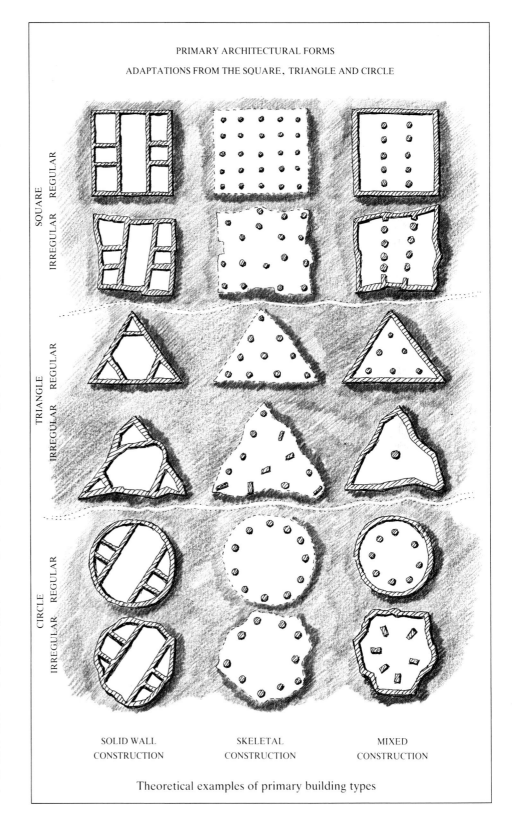

PRIMARY ARCHITECTURAL FORMS

ADAPTATIONS FROM THE SQUARE, TRIANGLE AND CIRCLE

SQUARE — REGULAR / IRREGULAR

TRIANGLE — REGULAR / IRREGULAR

CIRCLE — REGULAR / IRREGULAR

SOLID WALL CONSTRUCTION

SKELETAL CONSTRUCTION

MIXED CONSTRUCTION

Theoretical examples of primary building types

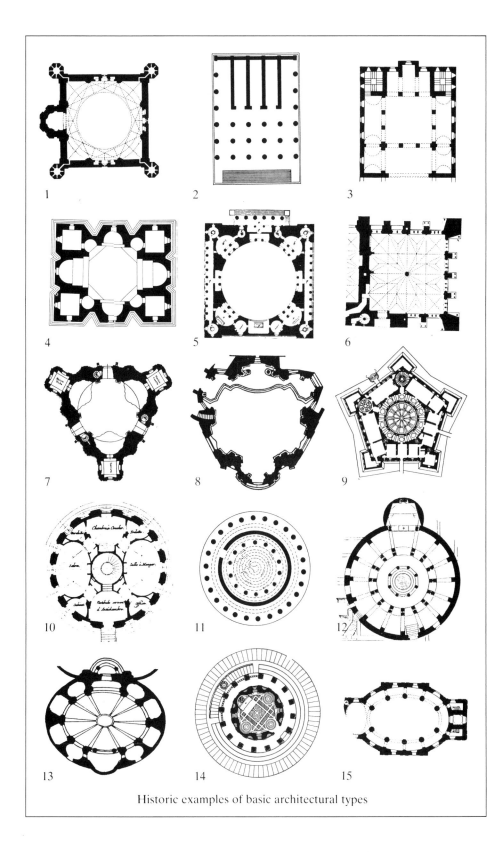

Historic examples of basic architectural types

Considerations concerning the spatial division, apportioning of rooms and positioning of structural supports are to meet functional and structural as well as spatio-aesthetic requirements. This is true for all three types of construction.

Explanatory notes to historic examples of basic architectural types, 1-15:

1. Bischapur (India), burial site of Mahmud Aoil Schah, 1626-56
2. Falerii, Etruscan Temple
3. Corvey, Westwerk, 873-85 AD
4. Wagharschapat, Hripsime Church, 618 AD
5. Initial design for the Roman Catholic Church in Karlsruhe (West Germany), F. Weinbrenner, 1808
6. Marienburg, Grand Master's Palace, monastic order, fourteenth to fifteenth century
7. Paura near Lambach, Holy Trinity Church, J.M. Prunner, 1715-17
8. Munster (Westphalia), Clemens Church, Schlaun, 1744-53
9. Caprarola, Palazzo Farnese, G. Vignola, 1559
10. House in the shape of a column for M. de Monville
11. Epidauros, Tholos, Polyklet the Younger, third century BC
12. Nocera, S. Maria Maggiore, fourth century
13. Rome, S. Andrea al Quirinale, L. Bernini, 1678
14. Rome, Tempietto di S. Pietro in Montorio, D. Bramante, after 1500
15. Steinhausen, Pilgrimage Church, D. Zimmermann, 1728-33

———— ✳ ————

1. Operation: kinking, bending

Some of these figures look rather arbitrary. I must admit, drawing these six plates, the compulsion to play the musical scale to its last note was often greater than the belief in the absolute sense of some figures. Examples of this kind are found in organic village structures.

We often find bent square, rectangular or triangular houses on street corners and crossroads. Contoured circular figures are more likely to be solitary objects.

A kink in the geometry of a plan can be used as a special spatial feature, or to provide space for a spare room – if the regular geometry of the other rooms needs to be retained.

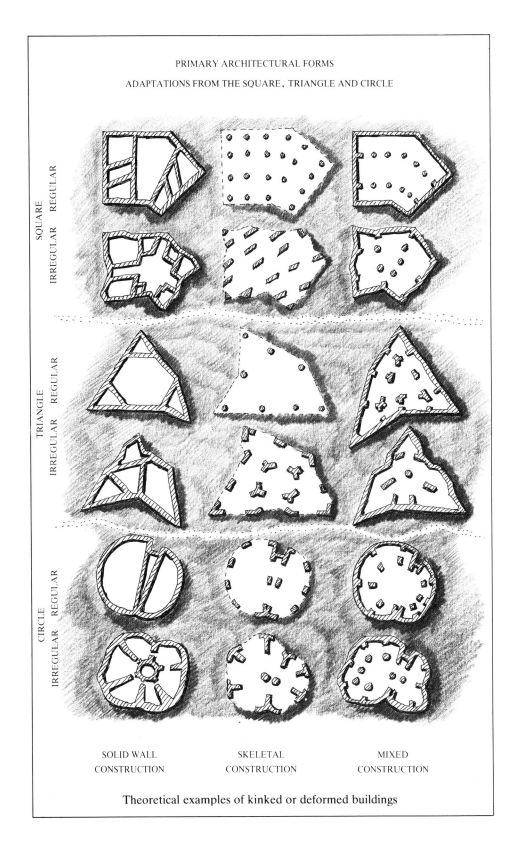

PRIMARY ARCHITECTURAL FORMS

ADAPTATIONS FROM THE SQUARE, TRIANGLE AND CIRCLE

SQUARE REGULAR

SQUARE IRREGULAR

TRIANGLE REGULAR

TRIANGLE IRREGULAR

CIRCLE REGULAR

CIRCLE IRREGULAR

SOLID WALL CONSTRUCTION

SKELETAL CONSTRUCTION

MIXED CONSTRUCTION

Theoretical examples of kinked or deformed buildings

— ✳ —

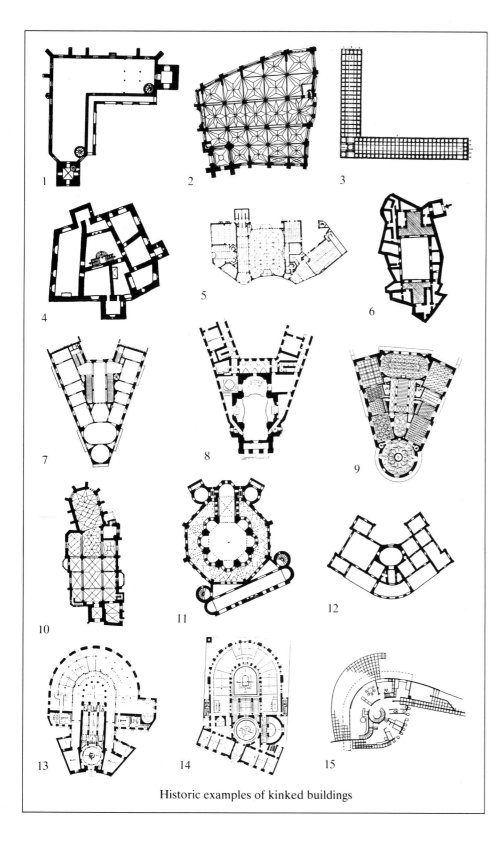

Historic examples of kinked buildings

Explanatory notes to historic examples of kinked buildings, 1-15:

1. Freudenstadt Church, c.1600
2. Melun, Saint-Aspais
3. Tahull, Santa Maria, 1123
4. Fenis, fortification
5. Brussels, Maison du Peuple, V. Horta, 1896-99
6. Cairo, private houses, seventh century
7. F. Weinbrenner, sketch design for a private house in Baden-Baden, 1826
8. Salzburg, Ursula Church, J.B. Fischer von Erlach, 1699-1705
9. F. Weinbrenner, sketch design for a private house in Karlsruhe, nineteenth century
10. Spitz, Community Church, after fifteenth century
11. Ravenna, San Vitale, completed 547 AD
12. Baghena, Villa Palagonia, eighteenth century
13. Otto Wagner, Post Office Savings Bank, Vienna, competition design, 1880
14. Vienna, Landbank, Otto Wagner, 1883-84
15. Zell-am-See, Heyrovsky Residence, L. Welzenbacher, 1932

2. Operation: Dividing and Breaking

Take, for instance, a path that leads across a plot. The owner is forced to segment his building on one or more levels to ensure the public path remains unobstructed. This condition can generate a design of unusual spatial quality. In Vienna, the passage from the Hofburg to the Michaeler Platz serves as a beautiful example. The passage opens up into a magnificent domed space within the building. Should it be necessary the entire building could be split open and the upper storeys reconnected via bridges.

If functional requirements do not demand connections between the separate building units, the relative hierarchy of the individual building masses can be carefully composed. To emphasise and clarify the design concept further, the 'cut' walls facing inwards could be articulated with light and transparent materials, in contrast to massive perimeter walls facing outwards.

———— ✳ ————

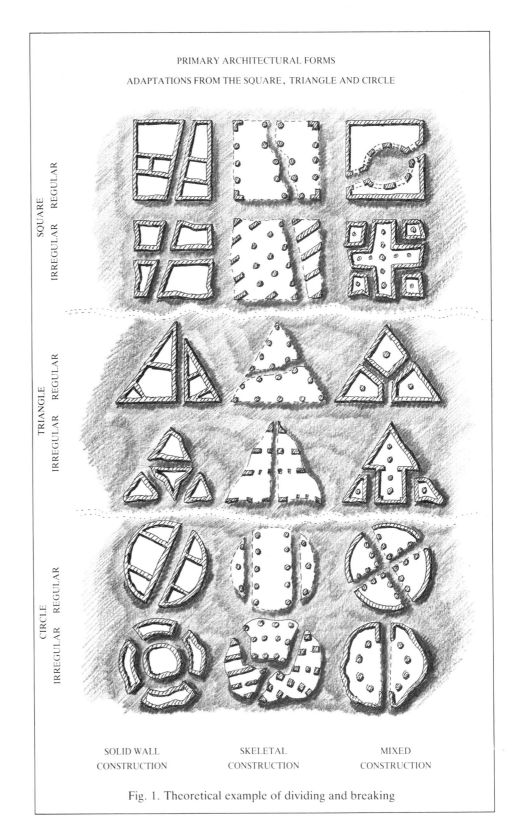

PRIMARY ARCHITECTURAL FORMS

ADAPTATIONS FROM THE SQUARE, TRIANGLE AND CIRCLE

SQUARE REGULAR

SQUARE IRREGULAR

TRIANGLE REGULAR

TRIANGLE IRREGULAR

CIRCLE REGULAR

CIRCLE IRREGULAR

SOLID WALL CONSTRUCTION

SKELETAL CONSTRUCTION

MIXED CONSTRUCTION

Fig. 1. Theoretical example of dividing and breaking

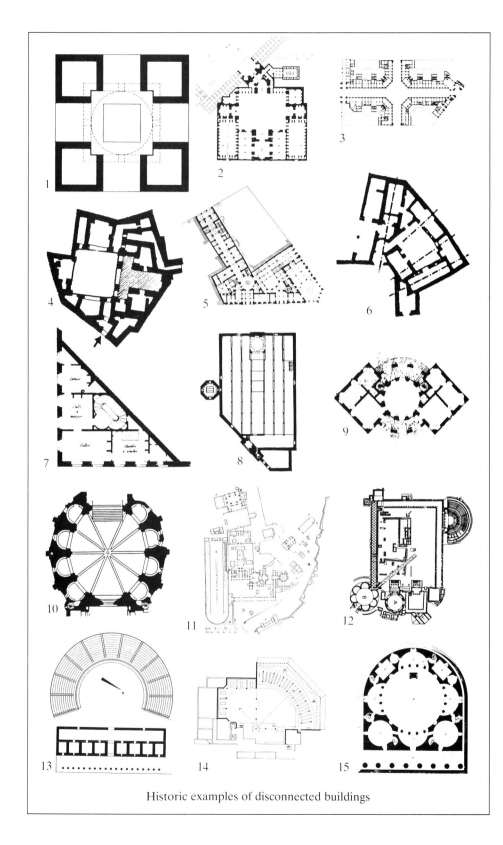

Historic examples of disconnected buildings

Explanatory notes to historic examples of disconnected buildings, 1-15:

1. Neisar, Tschahar Tak, fire altar 229 AD
2. Isfahan, Emperor's Mosque, 1612-30
3. Galleria Vittorio Emanuelle, takes up several fields
4. House in the Old City, Cairo, seventeenth century
5. Vienna, previously Austro-Hungarian Bank, H. Ferstel, 1856-60
6. Dar Dallaji, Sidi Bousaid, ground floor
7. From Durand's *Leçons d'architecture*
8. Eshrefoghlu, Turkey, Mosque to Beysehir
9. Old Hanseatic pleasure houses, Rossau, J.B. Fischer von Erlach
10. St. Gereon, Cologne, 1219-27
11. Constantinople, plan of the Palace Quarter
12. Square, Galleria Emanuelle
13. Ephesus, plan of the original Hellenic theatre
14. History Faculty Library, Cambridge University, Stirling and Gowan, 1964-68
15. Preliminary conceptual design for the Roman Catholic Church in Karlsruhe, F. Weinbrenner, first quarter of the nineteenth century

———— ✳ ————

3. Segmentation, Fragmentation

It sounds absurd to represent a building unit as an isolated fraction of an overall concept. It is the result of topographical, juristic or other more overriding reasons. Essentially, the patched-up building fragment lives off all its tragic and romantic associations.

James Wines and SITE are playing quite seriously on this musical scale. Like the surprises in a baroque pleasure garden, I can imagine those curiosities to be quite fun, but not as warehouses on an American freeway. Through their wit and irony they may break the monotony of this tedious stretch of tarmac, but I think it's best not to talk of architecture here.

I consider the fragment legitimate only if it is the result of serious and real limitations that do not permit an alternative solution.

However polished the aesthetic solutions (as in Hollein's administrative building for his Museum in Mönchengladbach), I cannot subscribe to them. For me, a purely artistically inspired fragmentation is a fraud.

Why then do I even bother to mention this operation? Well, it happens to be one of the drawers in my morphological box and needs airing from time to time. I am myself confronted with this situation in the case of a building project. Political and other reasons, which I do not want to go into here, allowed me to realise only a quarter of my proposed scheme for the Schinkel Platz in Berlin. The entire scheme could have been built without much difficulty. Opponents of this urban concept, however, devised all kinds of tricks to strangle the plan. I fought like mad to rescue the idea of the square. One square wall is now being built and, if fate is unkind, it will stand as a fragment. I have consciously taken this risk because I refuse to believe that intrigues of this kind can run full circle. The Schinkel Platz project was originally planned for the Internationale Bauausstellung in Berlin 1984, but since it has been excluded from all the IBA publications it has become clear how jeopardised the project is.

In many instances city plans have been stitched together like fragments of a puzzle and, God knows, have not always been guided by common sense and rationality.

——— * ———

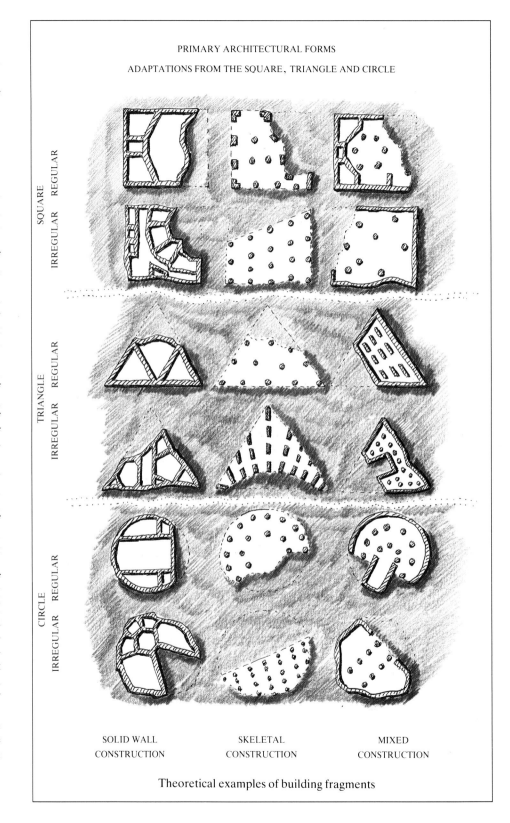

PRIMARY ARCHITECTURAL FORMS

ADAPTATIONS FROM THE SQUARE, TRIANGLE AND CIRCLE

SQUARE REGULAR

SQUARE IRREGULAR

TRIANGLE REGULAR

TRIANGLE IRREGULAR

CIRCLE REGULAR

CIRCLE IRREGULAR

SOLID WALL CONSTRUCTION

SKELETAL CONSTRUCTION

MIXED CONSTRUCTION

Theoretical examples of building fragments

ON ARCHITECTONIC FORM

PRIMARY ARCHITECTURAL FORMS

ADAPTATIONS FROM THE SQUARE, TRIANGLE AND CIRCLE

SOLID WALL
CONSTRUCTION

SKELETAL
CONSTRUCTION

MIXED
CONSTRUCTION

Theoretical examples illustrating the addition of buildings or building parts

4. Addition, Stringing Together, Accumulation, Stacking, Layering . . .

This somewhat simple arithmetic operation is most common in architecture. Every village or town configuration is made up of the continuous or disparate addition of built units. Individual building complexes, however, may consist of identical, similar or geometrically different building elements, culminating in a serial or harmonically differentiated order.

The theme of addition in its innumerable facets continues into the many details of the individual building units: the layering of bricks, the repetition of columns, doors, windows, loggias, balconies, railings, steps etc . . .

Schematic succession soon runs the danger of monotony. Rhythmic accentuations must break the sequence. Every function offers a potential motive to break what might otherwise be a monotonous sequence.

It is my contention that even the most limited monofunctions of a building give rise to adequate variation and rhythm. All too often we see modern curtain walls where staircases, toilets, storage rooms, offices and living rooms all carry the same signature. I consider this to be a cardinal sin and the key mistake in architectural composition.

I would particularly like to emphasise that the rhythmic accentuations, depending on the make-up of the building unit, can be regularly or irregularly, symmetrically or asymmetrically distributed. The former has made its presence felt across all cultural epochs. Modern architecture since the twenties has favoured asymmetrical accentuation. One of the main reasons for this turn-around was the decampment of the then prevalent, academically over-bred 'architectural pomposity'. Symmetrical composition seems to have been trampled to death. As appropriate examples I should like to mention the monument for Vittorio Emanuele in Rome or the Law Courts in Brussels. Symmetry was superficially condemned like the pitched roof and upright window. These were cardinal sins against the Modern Movement.

———— ✳ ————

It soon became apparent that asymmetry was far more difficult to handle than symmetry. In both cases, the main problem is to balance the chosen vocabulary. The consciously selected principle of disorder and disturbed balance leaves a fading feeling of helplessness, unless it is mastered ingeniously. Le Corbusier had command of the problem with his sure instinct for good proportions. Mies van der Rohe, on the other hand, swiftly moved on to concentrate on the classical symmetrical order. The defamation of symmetry is by no means over. Pre- and post-war propaganda architecture of the European dictatorships, including East Germany, have contributed to the problem. But the principal orders in symmetry cannot be called into question by minor derailments.

Personally, I have never had any spiritual problems with symmetry. The construction of the human body and our facial lines, based on the same principle, surely cannot be despised? Unfortunately, it is infinitely difficult to compete with the perfect proportions of nature's marvels and translate them into buildings. Nevertheless, some fine examples have been realized in the course of history. They should be carefully studied, providing one has the instinctive ability to determine their quality.

These things have long been known and a great deal is being written about them. You need not bother to waste your time on objects of mediocre quality. I always advise my students to limit three-quarters of their scheme to regular or symmetrical composition and assign no more than a quarter to chaos and disorder.

The entrance door to a house, for example, cannot always be located in the centre of a facade. This functionally dependent asymmetry can, however, easily be balanced by a calm window composition on the upper floors. (See, for example, my designs for the Dickes residence and the first Spandau House.)

In architecture, as in music, the quality of repetitive elements lies in their rhythmic cadence and interesting variation.

———— ✳ ————

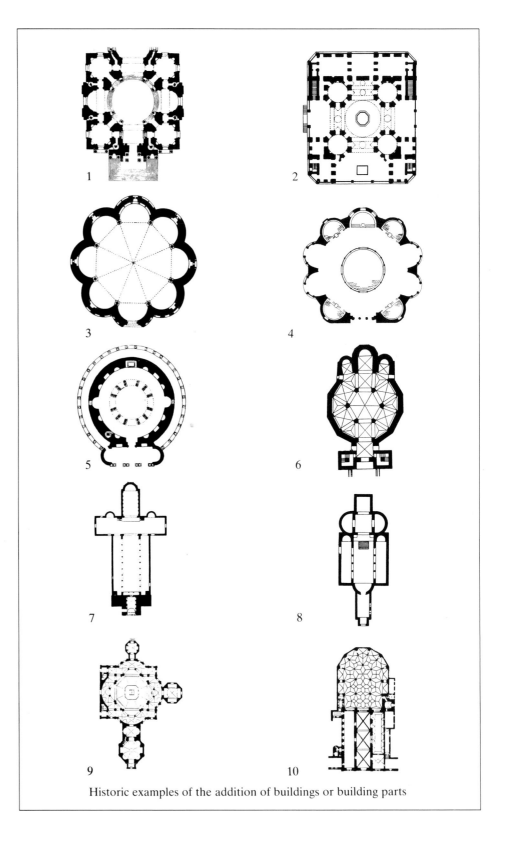

Historic examples of the addition of buildings or building parts

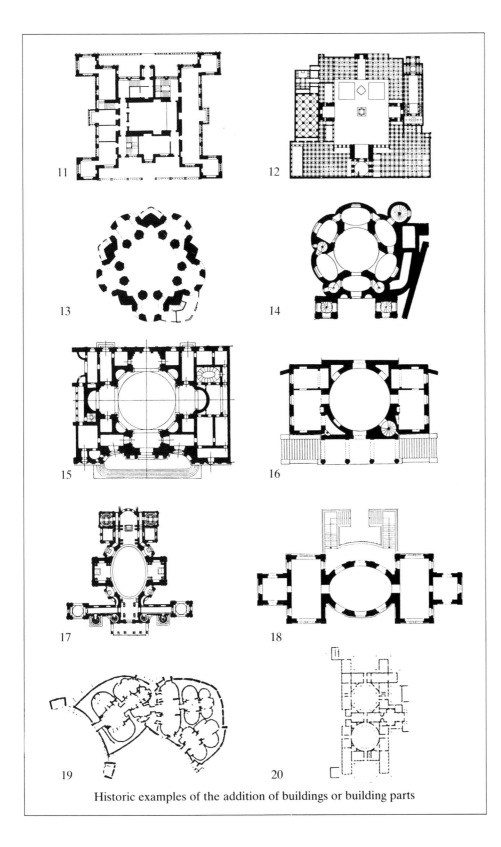

Historic examples of the addition of buildings or building parts

Explanatory notes to historic examples of addition of buildings or building parts, 1-20:

1. Paris, Invalidendom, J.H. Mansart 1675-1706

2. Isfahan, Hescht Bihischt, Garden Pavilion

3. Entraigues, S. Michael, twelfth century

4. Rome, round temple of Minerva Medica, third century

5. Rome, S. Constanza, 340-55 AD

6. Wimpfen/Tal, Ritterstift Church, 979-98 AD

7. Hersfeld Monastic Church, after 831AD

8. Reichenau-Oberzell, St. George, c. 900 AD

9. Milan, San Lorenzo, before 395AD

10. Salzburg, Franziskanerkirche, long house 1221, choir, H. Stethammer 1408-32

11. Wollaton Hall Notts., R. Smythson, 1580-88

12. Isfahan, Masdschid-i-Dschuma, Friday Mosque, ninth to fourteenth century

13. Saar, St. Johann Nepomuk on the green hill, J.S. Aichel, 1719-22

14. Frain, Castle Church

15. Rome, S. Agnese, Rainaldi and Borromini, 1625-50

16. Karlsruhe, 'pleasure house' in the garden of the Count Palais, Weinbrenner, 1801-03

17. Vienna Karlskirche, J.B. Fischer von Erlach, 1716-25

18. J.B. Fischer von Erlach, 'pleasure house' in Neuwaldegg

19. Tarnien/Malta, Megalith – Temple, 1200 -1900 BC

20. B. Peruzzi, design for a monastery, sixteenth century

———— ✳ ————

5. Penetration, Superimposition, Interweaving . . .

This design operation is the most interesting in architecture. The interpenetration of two building units brings about a conflict on the inside and outside that has led to the most fantastic results in building history. The crossing in a Gothic cathedral, where transept and nave overlap, is one of the most beautiful examples of this theme. The rhythmic interpenetration of different geometric spaces in Roman thermal baths also illustrates this operation exceptionally well.

Mixed construction facilitates the most perfect articulation of this design procedure. Massive walls and transparent collonades are the clearest and most exciting manifestation of penetration and superimposition. The chapter on construction describes the structure of a Gothic cathedral which relates to this theme. Here, the vertical as well as the horizontal penetration of spaces has been accomplished perfectly.

The Weissenberg Sternschloss near Prague is as an architectural rarity incorporating two superimposed equilateral triangles. The interior spaces developing from this juxtaposition are most interesting (see illustrations of superimposed triangles, massive construction).

The free-standing roof spanning one or more building units certainly belongs to this theme; a favourite theme of Le Corbusier, he used it in his Zurich Pavilion and at the Palace of Justice in Chandigarh. The wide-spanning roof construction of Frei Otto and Buckminster Fuller form a secondary climatic envelope around a large number of buildings and these also belong to this category.

The interlocked cylinders of Melnikov's private house perfectly illustrate the interpenetration of two circular plans. By shifting the floors and inserting a staircase, Melnikov has very skilfully solved the problem of the 'collision zone'. The cylinder facing the street has been cut open in a fragmented fashion to make room for a large window opening.

Important buildings throughout history richly illustrate this theme.

———— ✳ ————

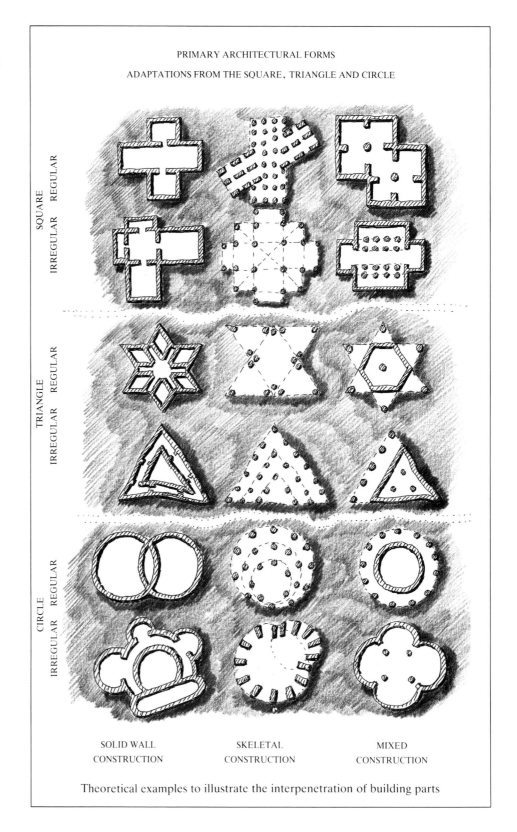

PRIMARY ARCHITECTURAL FORMS

ADAPTATIONS FROM THE SQUARE, TRIANGLE AND CIRCLE

SOLID WALL CONSTRUCTION · SKELETAL CONSTRUCTION · MIXED CONSTRUCTION

Theoretical examples to illustrate the interpenetration of building parts

Historic examples of the interpenetration of building parts

During the penetration of two or more building units the definition of the individual parts, in terms of their hierarchy and scale, plays an important role.

Primary and secondary parts must be easily distiguishable. The tension in the entire composition is thus heightened. German hall-like churches such as the Frauenkirche in Munich or the Dom in Noerdlingen are, without doubt, magnificent constructions but in their dramatic staging of interior space and building structure are not comparable with the cathedrals of Chartres or Reims.

The accompanying historical examples are intended to illustrate the morphological studies. Each example should actually be explained in some detail, but alone would fill an entire book. In the chapter on the architectural elements I have discussed Palladio's art in composing spaces in relation to one another. This type of spatial analysis will be helpful in gaining a better understanding of these plans.

Quite deliberately, I won't get involved in semiotic interpretations I know nothing about. For me a building is a tectonic structure with a sober, grammatical background that I am trying to explain. I shall leave out all literary overtones which, admittedly, may well be of significance. They are, however, alien to my own more mediterranean architectural interpretation.

Explanatory notes to historic examples of the interpenetration of building elements, 1-20.

1. Spalatio, Diocletian's Palace, 295-305 AD
2. Kalat Siman, Monastery Church, early fifth century
3. Wells Cathedral, c.1300
4. Lincoln Cathedral, thirteenth century
5. Salisbury Cathedral, 1220-60
6. Rome, Circular Temple by the Tiber
7. Aachen, Pfalzkapelle, 798 AD
8. Vienna, old Hanseatic 'pleasure house' in Rossau, J.B. Fischer von Erlach, c.1690
9. Baalbek, Circular Temple
10. Vicenza, Basilica, A. Palladio, after 1546

11. Constantinople, Sergius and Bacchus Church, 527AD
12. Nowgorod, Sophian Cathedral, 1045-52
13. Rome, St. Peter's, design by Peruzzi, 1505
14. Agra, Taj Mahal, 1630-48
15. Bonn, Castle Poppelsdorf, De Cotte, after 1715
16. Hanau, Flemish and Walloon church, 1600-08
17. Turin, S. Lorenzo, G. Guarini, 1634-80
18. Kappel/Waldsassen, Holy Trinity Church, G. Dientzenhofer, 1685-89
19. Wahlstatt, Monastery Church, K.I. Dientzenhofer, 1727-31
20. Prague, St. Nikolaus/Kleinseite, Chr. and K.I. Dientzenhofer, 1673-1751

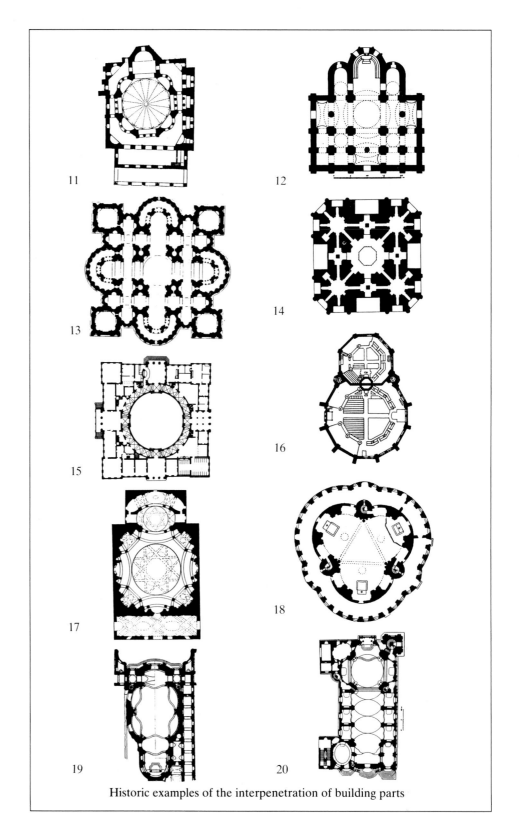

Historic examples of the interpenetration of building parts

———— ✳ ————

Carved into the landscape, raised from its coincidental mass, made to serve a useful purpose and to protect, formed to lend meaning to existence, often maltreated, broken, destroyed beyond hope of regeneration . . . Time will give a spiritual quality to all stone.

A connecting link across a valley or bearer of supply lines . . . this technique has brought magnificent structural achievements. But with a few exceptions, the theme has never been treated by classical architecture with the same devotion as other monumental buildings. The field offers inexhaustible possibilities for powerful gesture. It is a pity that architects have left it almost entirely to engineers.

In a miraculous filigree nature has left us a magnificent encyclopedia of possibilities which could be exploited in building. For thousands of years the basic forms of architecture have been given significant interpretation in stone. The modelling of the shaft, the base and the capital with their complex visual and structural requirements has matured to perfection over the course of time.

The most obvious, perhaps even the most archaic, building technique is to lay stone on stone and thus to form an homogeneous constructed mass. A long wall must either be thick enough to stand alone or it needs to be supported by a system of pillars, ribs and terracing, outer covering or network.

The spaces inside the building, nests we decorate for our daily comfort, the objects which fill our lives with warmth and nostalgia—this is our second skin and we allow no-one, to force it on us. The architect creates the shell, which is dead until its inhabitants fill it with life. But he still has the obligation to give his houses as full a form as possible, so that they become a well-modulated sounding-board for everyday life.

The enclosing and protecting wall, the differentation of rooms inside, windows as sources of light, doors as entrances and exits, the roof to keep out the rain and cold . . . all this, thematically, technically or in the architectural aesthetic need no longer be questioned today. Following the destruction of a deep-rooted tradition in the twenties, we must start again, learning to build from the fundamentals.

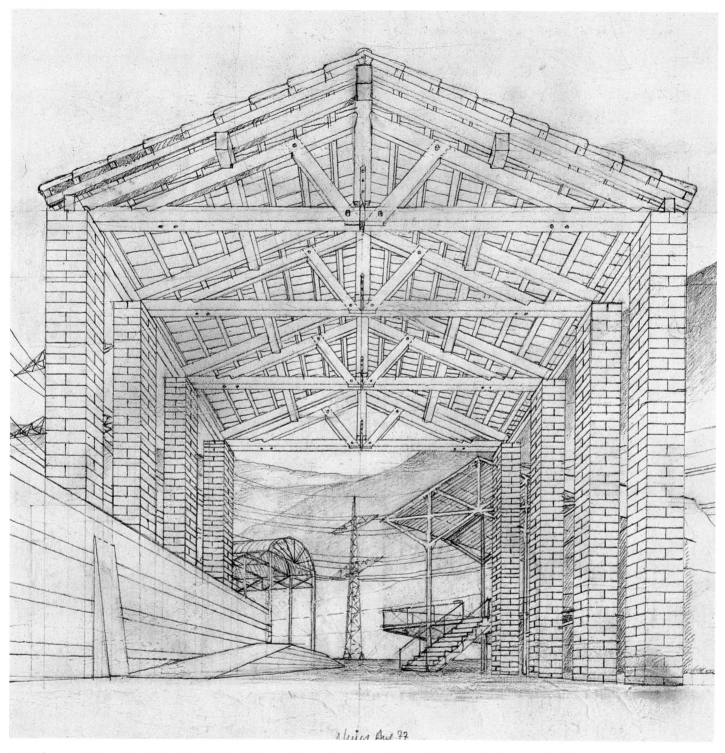

A roof supported by pillars is the simplest kind of protection against the weather, and for centuries has served as barn, storehouse, market . . .
In Antiquity, the protective roof with the 'cella' beneath became the symbol of the ideal house and the prototype of the temple. This architectural theme has lost none of its importance today, enabling dramatic interplay between essential architectural elements.

The geometry of the single house derives its force from the contrast with living nature. The greater the density and number of houses, the greater the displacement of nature and the environment and thus the more important the artificial spaces, become. Streets and squares are the vehicles of public life, while quiet cells in the form of courtyards are places of refuge, intimacy and retreat.

CHAPTER III

THE
ELEMENTS
OF
ARCHITECTURE

Typology of Interior Spaces

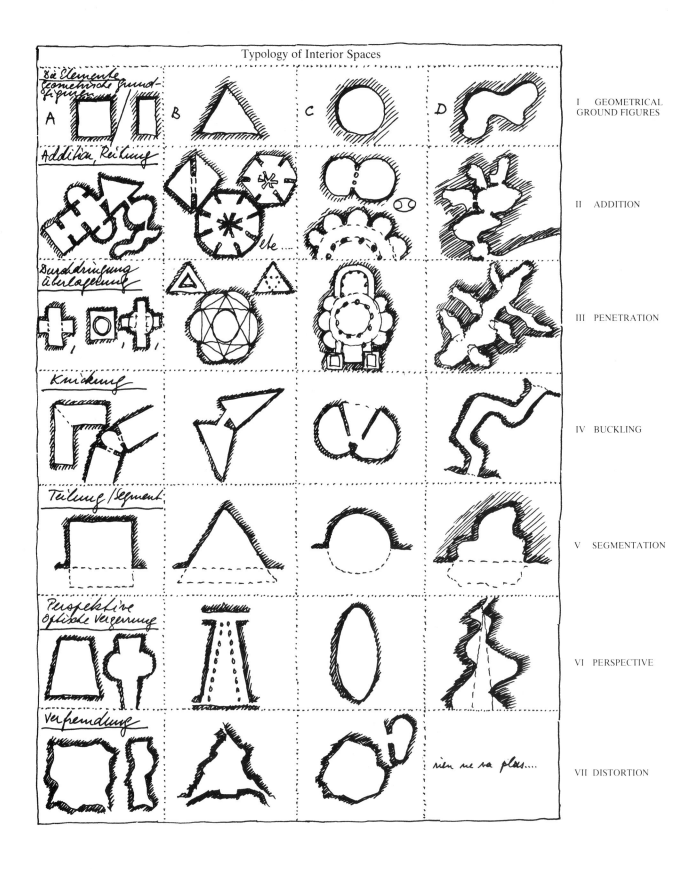

I GEOMETRICAL GROUND FIGURES

II ADDITION

III PENETRATION

IV BUCKLING

V SEGMENTATION

VI PERSPECTIVE

VII DISTORTION

70

THE ELEMENTS OF ARCHITECTURE

EXPLANATIONS RELATING TO THE TYPOLOGY OF INTERIOR SPACES

The diagram shows in the horizontal the geometrical ground-plan forms: square, triangle, circle and the amorphous figure; and in the vertical the possibilities of transformation of these basic elements by way of addition, penetration, buckling, breaking, accentuation of the perspective, or effect of depth and distortion. These operations are put together side by side without any valuation. The examples presented here, however, are only a fraction of the variants created so far by human ingenuity.

At this point I would like to suggest that, from the history of building, one should picture the great variety of forms for oneself and refresh it again and again by way of drawing exercises.

Addition

Addition is the most elementary principle of order. With the most simple way of addition, the elements are only closely joined and form an accumulation or a group. Their relation to each other ensues from the proximity, a so-called topological relation (Norberg-Schulz) resulting in an irregular, amorphous shape. In contrast to that, geometrical relation means a relation which is created by a geometrical principle of order, e.g. by axiality or parallelity. The basilica serves as an example in which several similar elements of space are arranged in parallel. In the perspective of depth, a series of impressions of closed spaces of nave and side-aisles emerges, whereas in the transverse direction, because of the transparency of the order of columns, the entire space can be perceived. By augmenting the heights of side-aisles towards the nave, the latter is especially accentuated and the orientation towards the altar is emphasised. We have here the different heights of spaces as a means of design to express the hierarchy of spatial elements.

Penetration

1. Two or several spaces of different geometrical form overlap and merge into a new shape. In this process one space, or even both, will be deformed, i.e. their formal separation would be senseless, because it would yield fragments.

2. Two spaces being overlapped retain their independence, remain recognisable, and together create a new spatial quality. The crossing of the cathedral is a classical example: the longitudinal aisle and the transept penetrate each other and form a common space which is emphasised by a dome or a tower.

3. When two spaces overlap in a way that one includes the other, this gives rise to space within space. If the interior space is bordered by rows of columns and segregated from the enclosing space, the entire space remains to be experienced simultaneously. Classical examples of this kind of spatial penetration are to be found in Egyptian Baldachin Temples. The closer the two spaces move together, i.e. if they become nearly equal in size, one gets the impression of *one* space with a double enclosure. Louis Kahn, for example, sets circular spaces into square bounds for light penetration. Through different openings in the walls, the light is filtered when required, and indirectly led into the interior.

Further possibilities of transforming basic geometrical forms are the processes of buckling, bending, breaking, separation and fragmentation. This happens mostly if several elements of different geometrical shape should be joined together, and if one has to adjust to the other. Let us imagine an octagonal space which is surrounded by a corridor. Because of the given geometry of the octagon, it has to be buckled several times, in a sense to submit itself to the geometrical form. However, it can achieve an independent spatial quality if the buckling points, by expansion, are made into joints. Or another example, which very often can be found in housing construction in the nineteenth century, in Weinbrenner's work for instance: in a given ground-plan form, which very often resulted from the shape of the site – perhaps a triangle as the residual site between two streets – the main spaces were inserted as independent forms – as circle, square or oval. Between them and the exterior skin, spaces of deformed shape remained, which sometimes had the awkward effect of being merely remnants, because they orginated from something which was of more importance. So they offered the possibility of accommodating technical facilities. But often they are independent localities of the 'in between' and have enough spatial charm to accommodate staircases, for instance.

The 'perspective distortion', i.e. the artificial manipulation of the effect of depth, can be created by simple geometrical tricks, as Scamozzi did with his stage sets in the Teatro Olimpico in Vicenza; and Bernini in both his design for St. Peter's Square, and his famous staircase in the Vatican, the Scala Regia.

The 'distortion' of a geometrical form can in most cases be attributed to fateful, historical events.

The examples of interior spaces listed here do not in any way represent a complete typology. The drawings illustrated have emerged from exercises with my students carried out in the first year of their course. I am of the opinion that the decisions which form the design of a space, or a building, can only be completely understood if they have been apprehended through drawing them. It may be noted that my students draw exclusively in Vienna, so that they learn to recognize the city in which they study with all its qualities and the characteristic features of its local architectural tradition. That modern architecture thereby gets the shorter end of consideration is not surprising. The good examples in modern architecture are anyway too rare.

Interior Spaces

As the starting point of architectural composition, the smallest spatial unity, the interior room, should firstly be studied. Normally an interior space has for its bounds walls, piers, ceiling and floor, being the traditional elements. Windows and doors serve as connections with the exterior. By these, the technical elements of a space are determined. It becomes comprehensible and describable by the definition of its size, proportion (relationships between length, height and width) and shape. These components refer directly to the function of the room because they allow for the residence of people, the accommodation of furniture and the execution of certain activities.

Shapes and atmospheres of spaces can be described. At first we recognize the geometry of a room, e.g. cube, cylinder or different forms mixed together. We can also specify the exact sizes and identify the proportions by relating length, width and height. Although we still describe rooms according to their basic geometrical forms, clear and simple spaces nowadays have an almost elitist character. The so-called liberation of spaces by modern architecture has given rise to the unfortunate term 'flowing space'. Spaces were separated into areas, only able to function, but without contributing to better functioning. The repression of clear geometry has not resulted in a truly free and poetic solution of room forms, but in deformed structures which no longer allow a

meaningful relationship between wall and opening. The nature of a room is very much determined by its enclosure, which demarcates it from the exterior and turns it into an interior space. Let us consider the geometry: a sphere has a maximum enclosure. In geometrical terms, it cannot be connected to another form. In accordance with that, the circular room is not directional and rests in itself. Symmetry emphasises independence. In a rectangular space, the enclosure is created by the uninterrupted relationship between the four walls, especially the integrity of the corners. Rounded corners emphasise the enclosing character of the walls. By different treatment of the surfaces in terms of colour and texture, by arrangement of openings and incidences of light, the enclosure of a space can either be emphasised or broken.

More difficult is the description of the quality of a space. Very often when we describe their character, we talk about small, spacious, low, high, oppressive, friendly, comfortable, cold or warm rooms. Very often for these appraisals of a space, not only its geometry but also its attributes are crucial. In this sense every interior space offers a complete 'cultural image', given by proportion, light penetration, structure, furniture and accessories.

Already the accentuation of the surfaces confining the room adds to its character: dividing vertical and horizontal elements, floor texture, ornaments and mouldings on ceiling and walls, extensions, bays, colours and materials etc. The basic forms are equally changed by piers standing free in the room. New spaces 'within the space' are created. According to their purpose, they articulate and structure; they form transparent walls dividing the space, and because we move in the room, new perspectives, vistas and space relationships emerge again and again.

With the knowledge of these effects, the architect can give to a room the character which suits its function and significance. He can create a sacred space which makes people worship, a lecture-hall helping people to concentrate on listening, or an office room which, because of its functionalism, places work in the foreground.

Finally, owing to tradition, symbolic

meanings can be attributed to certain forms. Archeologists and ethnologists have intensively concerned themselves with the significance of certain forms of space. Psychologists too, like C.G. Jung, made important contributions to the exploration of archetypes. Hanns Sieder, through extensive research in his book *Urformen der abendländischen Baukunst* (Archaic Forms in Western Architecture), comes to the following thesis: 'Considering . . . existing forms, excluding each other in the circular or rectangular house, it is conceivable from what is known about the different stages in change of house construction in Italy and Greece, that we can trace back precisely the genesis of a rectangular house born out of a circular house via oval and apse-shaped preliminary forms. Decisions of that kind in favour of the circular or the rectangular house are rooted in the entire existence of the human being; they are not at all left to the free will. *Cultures not yet formed or no longer sound, make formless buildings.*' Sieder also maintains that certain geometrical forms of spaces gave expression to a corresponding physical and spiritual attitude: 'A non-directional circular space allows for relaxation and concentration. An oval-shaped space encloses two points of encounter. The form of the apse has risen from the feuerschism ('firescreen') to the symbolic place of spiritual promulgation. A broad space becomes a place of preparation, a longitudinal space a route leading to somewhere. Both spatial directions meet in the square–the crossing–the place of ritually structured concentration.'

Of course the mythically influenced attitude concerning the effect of spaces does not apply to such a degree to contemporary architecture, e.g. housing construction. But it is crucial to bear in mind that certain rooms furnished in a certain way can actually and significantly stimulate and influence the spirit and emotions of the inhabitants. This is also warning to those who think that the size and form of a room are determined only by the space requirements of standard furniture, rather than other spatial qualities. Only if we succeed in understanding the relationship between form, proportion, effect and usefulness can we achieve a meaningful and well-balanced composition.

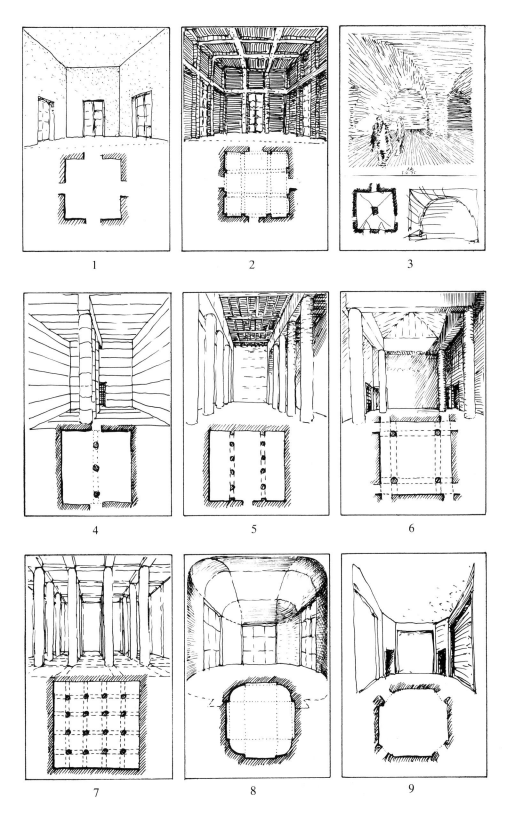

Square Interior Spaces

The square remains clearly recognisable at best by means of an all-round symmetrical arrangement of openings. A well-balanced spatial effect without direction is shown in illustration 1, in which the openings are placed on the room axes. Going beyond this, the space can be structured by way of a subtle, square grid of pilasters, door lintels and beams. As the geometry of the space is specially supported, the square achieves an even more powerful expression (illustration 2). Also in illustration 3, we have a square ground-plan, but a space with a completely different centre of gravity because of the pier and cross-vault. Here, the tectonics of the vault are more important than the ground-plan. In illustrations 4 to 7, examples of structures are shown which – often for technical or functional reasons – give to the space entirely different relations and directions. They alter the scale, and are confusing when it comes to describing the proportions. When divided by means of a row of piers (illustration 4), two equally relevant rectangular spaces are created. By the division of the square into three parts in one direction (illustration 5), the emphasis is laid on the 'main space' in the middle. This intensification can be reversed if the middle part which one enters is narrower than the two border areas. In this case the space in the middle gains the character of a route, and so the areas on each side become more significant. Illustration 6 shows an enclosed space with a skeletal canopy construction inside. A space within a space emerges. By that, the shape of the entire space is intensified; the canopy defines an almost sacred area and the edges become a silent zone; a threshold area which, although existing inside the space, does not fully belong to it.

The fully skeletal interior space (illustration 7) is of course only conceivable at a larger scale. Illustrations 8 and 9 show the centralisation of the square by way of rounded or bevelled edges. These 'manipulations of the edges', however, need to be minor in proportion to the sides, in order to avoid indistinct spaces. Otherwise this superimposition may easily provoke associations with a circular or octagonal space.

Distorted, Basically Square, Geometries

Such spaces only possess the notion of 'centrality' found in the original basic geometrical form. Because of bays and frontal threshold areas, the following examples (illustrations 1 to 3) have an intermediate position between 'pure spaces' and a series of spaces. Windows and doors in the bays form particular architectonic spaces with strong individuality. They almost force the middle of the space to remain void because the user's attention is focused on the bays.

Rhythmic Series of Spaces

(illustrations 4 and 5)

Stations of a route with a small entrance area which functions as a 'border-crossing'. The anteroom has a clear orientation: a rectangle which accompanies the route and prepares us for the main space. This main space has the form of a square, but only at its final window front does the route end. The route is mainly recognizable by its series of spaces in perspective. Such an effect is prohibited in illustration 4 where four columns form an additional spatial filter, which psychologically 'stops' the route.

Rectangular Interior Spaces

The simple, rectangular space with an open pitched roof (illustration 6) is an archetypal form for the house. It is to be found as sepulchre, as well as barn or garden house. This form of space is a good example of the significance of used materials. From the rush-hut to the solid stone shrine, the meaning and character of the space can thereby be subjected to a complete transformation. The surface texture determines the whole range of what is precious to what is merely make-shift. This is something that applies in general to every space, but here this fact is particularly evident.

In rectangular spaces (illustrations 7 and 9), the location of the openings is particularly significant. If they are positioned in the short sides (illustrations 7), the room gains an airy atmosphere with a clear alignment along its longitudinal axis. By inserting rows of piers, this tendency is more manifest. The dark side-zones can be assigned to secondary purposes and activities. A longitudinal barrel (illustration 9) emphasises even more the closed cross-direction.

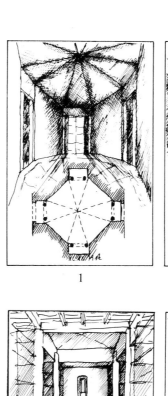

1

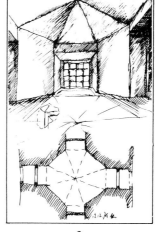

2

3

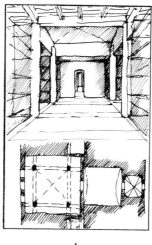

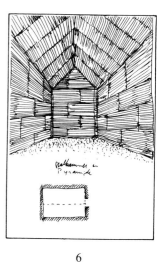

4

5

6

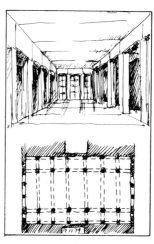

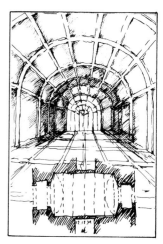

7

8

9

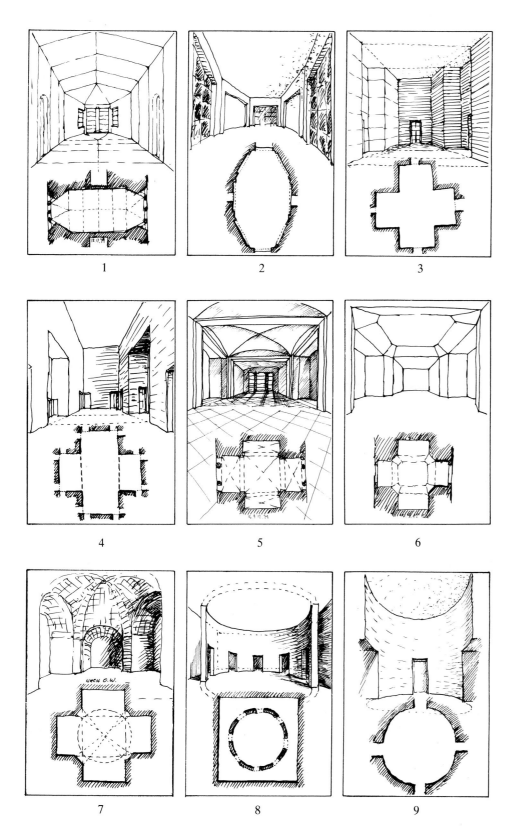

1

2

3

4

5

6

7

8

9

Octagonal Interior Spaces

The variants of octagonal spaces presented here (illustrations 1 and 2) have, according to contemporary understanding, quite an exotic character. However, they do reveal some advantages. When stretched, octagonal spaces develop a clearly defined middle zone and two narrowing edge areas. The room thus if necessary gains an intimate stability.

Cross-shaped Interior Spaces

The crucial problem with cross-shaped interior spaces (illustrations 3 to 7) is the valuation of the two directions. Illustration 3 shows the interpenetration of two rectangular spaces of the same kind. If one focuses only on the inner part, the equivalence of the spatial areas is without any doubt still existent. But this space also has openings – doors or windows – which because of different valuations, immediately establish a hierarchy to the spatial areas. I would like in this context to cite Palladio's Villa Rotonda as an example, a building with a similar ground-plan where the effect of the different prospects is noticeable. A space having an intrinsic hierarchy of directions will be achieved, if for example the proportion of one part is changed. Illustration 4 shows the effect that can be gained by such an arrangement: one part of the space is elevated and thereby demotes the side parts to bays. A focus to the central space (illustrations 5 and 6) is reached by a cross-vault, or even more so by elevating the crossing area. This space, which is called 'crossing' in centralised plan churches, has a supreme symbolic and mythical significance.

Circular Spaces

Illustration 8 shows a round wall-shell within a square room, establishing a particular inner area. By the principle 'space within space' residual areas remain which have been developed to perfection, especially by the American architect Louis Kahn, resulting in interesting spatial effects. The circular space in illustration 9 belongs like square and cross to the 'archetypal forms' of architecture. The extreme spatial consequences require a well-considered discretion as to practical application. Psychological aspects have also to be taken into consideration; not every human being can cope permanently with such a powerful form.

The overlaying of two basic forms – the square and the circle – has been attempted in illustration 1. Compared to the altitude of the cube, the cylinder is lower and therefore four segments remain as bays. This is an example of the differentiation of heights in a room and the resulting effects. Nowadays, thinking in three dimensions is very often neglected when it comes to design. The circular space with the square canopy in the middle (illustration 2) intensifies the significance of the central space. At the same time the room gives the impression of openness. A heterogeneous space with many side-rooms and bays (illustration 3) determines its centre by way of an inserted circular space formed by piers and covered by a dome. This is a technique which can also be applied to later adaptations of existing spaces where one often achieves valid architectural results. Circular spaces, to develop their spatiality and functional usefulness, need a certain minimum dimension which should not be underestimated. Height and form of the ceiling are especially crucial. In illustration 4 a high circular space is cut through by a bridge which, because of its transparent structure, allows perception of the overall space. This example also hints at the fact that circular rooms, being non-directional, are often used in a boundary position as the mediation of spaces with multidirectional structure. Illustration 5 describes two cylinders which interlock. The transparent tangential zone offers a fascinating experience of space. A famous example in architectural history is the house of the Russian constructivist Constantin Melnikov. Illustrations 6 and 7 show circular spaces in each case being related to other rooms. The latter are designed as loggias or anterooms which surround the central space. These arrangements give the circular space an ambivalent role: it is a space of tranquility, void of furniture and other equipment, but also serves as a kind of distributor, being in the best position to connect different routes and meanings. Illustration 9 actually belongs to the theme: composition of spaces. In plan, square, octagon and semi-circle form a rhythmic sequence of spaces. It is important to note how clearly geometrical forms can be brought into correlation.

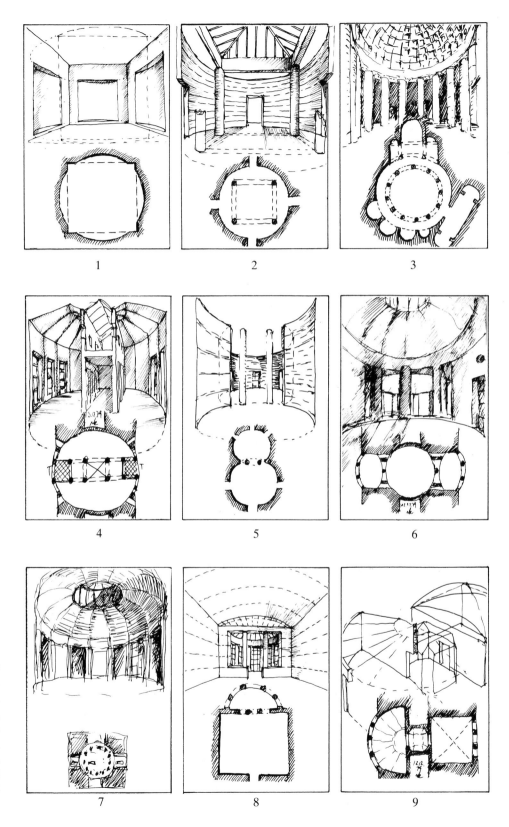

1

2

3

4

5

6

7

8

9

Addition and Penetration of Spaces in Practical Examples

The basic forms dealt with above can give rise to innumerable combinations of spaces; so it is out of the question that the employment of clear forms restricts creative imagination. Considering the mighty heritage of architectural history, the aberrations of modern architecture have proved one fact: spaces which can be described, which are conceivable in real terms, have the advantage of multifarious ways of utilization; still – and this fact cannot be pointed out often enough – a building exists in general longer than its initially assigned utilization. Illustration 1 shows a square, tent-shaped space, formed by an inner shell which separates it from a corridor. The route leads from a representational staircase–inserted in an ellipse–to an ante-space filter into the main room. In illustration 2 a directional rectangular space leads to a semi-circular one which has a relieving effect, promising a pleasant vista. Narrowness of the two spaces creates an important tension. In the space which is shown in illustration 3, it is the vaulting of the rectangular space which creates a relationship with the semi-circular forecourts. Illustrations 4 and 5 picture examples of simple series of spaces: through an entrance area one reaches a rectangular room which is terminated by a semi-circle which is its culmination. Illustrations 6 and 7 prove that it is also possible to give rectangular spaces a centre by way of widening and the superimposition of a central circular space. The last two examples, illustrations 8 and 9, deal with a rectangular space with curved ends. It gains different spatial effects by way of its inner configuration or widening.

Oval-shaped spaces (illustrations 1 to 3) are not a modification of circular spaces, but stand as an independent type which, since the Renaissance, has always been seen as a contrast to the circle. The circle represents a mono-centric view of life, the oval shape a duo-centric one. The circle was favoured by the conservative, neoclassical theorists (Alberti, Bramante) in the Renaissance, whereas the moderns (Peruzzi, Serlio) preferred the oval, which reached its prime in the Baroque.* Of course from a formal point of view, the oval allows for similar operations as does the circle.

However, similar to the rectangle, the oval is directional.

Triangular spaces (illustrations 4 to 6) are conceivable as special forms because of their pointed edges, which are difficult to fully utilize. For practical reasons, the triangle is often deformed; the edges are cut off or the three sides are rounded out. The Trinity churches of the baroque are known examples of this. For secular purposes, the triangle is suitable as mediation of three distinct directions of traffic routes, or if a trunk road splits into two less important ones.

Special shapes (illustrations 7 to 9) stretch from all possible polygons to the irregularly modelled space – the cave.

To end this chronology, it may be remarked that all spaces should have in common defining borders. A space should always allow itself to be defined, described and understood without one having to take refuge in its atmospherical values to begin with.

See Lotz, 'Die ovalen Kirchenräume des Cinquecento', in *Römisches Jahrbuch für Kunstgeschichte*, 7th volume, 1955.

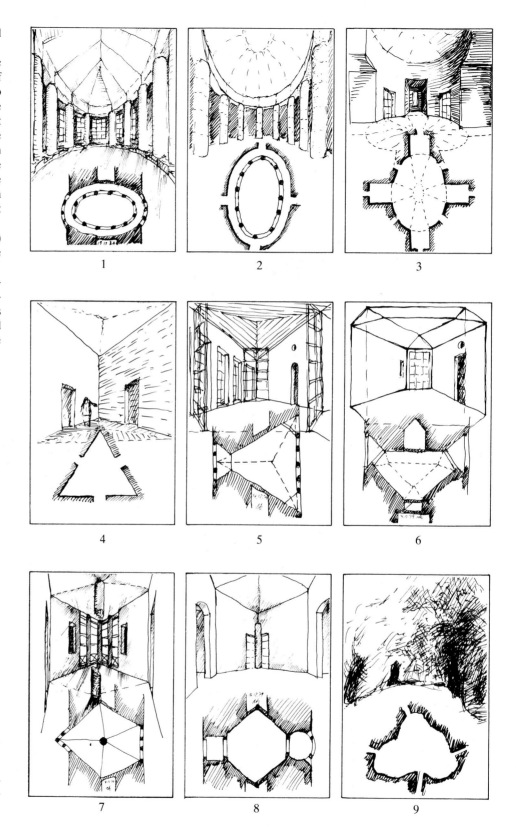

1

2

3

4

5

6

7

8

9

Hall of Columns, Vienna, by T. von Hansen, 1873-83

Court Library, Vienna, by J.B. Fischer von Erlach, 1721-35

Teatro Olimpico, Sabbioneta, by V. Scamozzi, 1588

'Knize' store, Vienna, by A. Loos, 1909-13

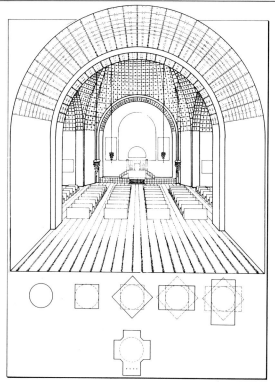

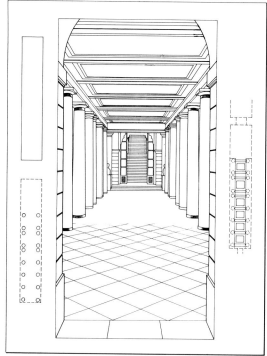

Student works on the theme of Interiors

INNENRAUM

Heilig Geist Kirche
von Josef Plečnik
Herbststraße 82
WIEN XVI

Grundrißentwicklung
aus dem Quadrat, das
von einem Rechteck im
mittleren Teil des Raums
überlagert wird.

Ein kleineres Rechteck
schneidet aus dem
überhöhten Mittelteil
seitliche Säulengänge
heraus, die an ihren

Enden von je 4 Säulen
getragen werden. An
den Eingangsbereich
werden die Stiegenauf-
gänge angegliedert.

MARTIN
PALMRICH

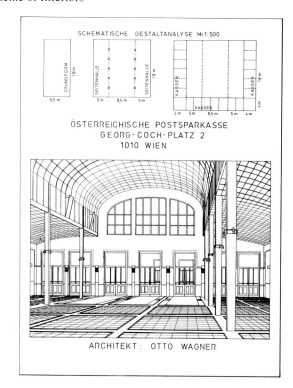

SCHEMATISCHE GESTALTANALYSE M=1:500

ÖSTERREICHISCHE POSTSPARKASSE
GEORG-COCH-PLATZ 2
1010 WIEN

ARCHITEKT: OTTO WAGNER

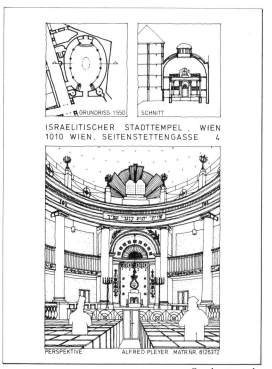

ISRAELITISCHER STADTTEMPEL, WIEN
1010 WIEN, SEITENSTETTENGASSE 4

PERSPEKTIVE   ALFRED PLEYER MATR.NR. 8126372

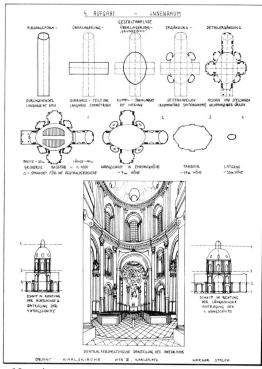

Student works on the theme of Interiors

JOHANN BERNHARD U. JOSEF EMANUEL FISCHER VON ERLACH 1721-1735
WIEN HOFBIBLIOTHEK PERSPEKT. U. GRUNDR. D. PRUNKSAALES AUSSCHN.

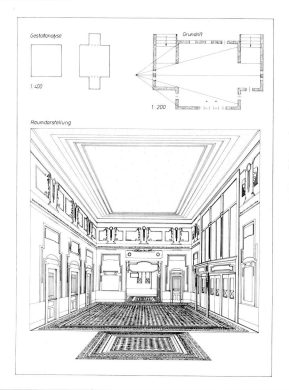

The Art of Composing Spaces

Guided by the work of Palladio, I would like to demonstrate how spaces should be brought into sequence in order to create spatial and aesthetic relationships. It is not sufficient to be well acquainted with the quality of a single space as such. One must also be able to join spaces in a way that together they make an interesting composition.

1. Teatro Olimpico, Vicenza, 1580

The auditorium deviates from the semi-circular Vitruvian type, common at that time, because of lack of space. It is a half amphitheatre in plan with rising tiers of seats. At the level of the top tier, the space is terminated by a colonnade consisting of blind and free-standing columns giving access to the stairs which are situated in the corners. This self-contained geometrical space appears as if inserted into an irregular larger one. The stage is linked with the audience by way of a rectilinear *scenae frons:* a richly structured facade with five openings through which seven 'streets' are visible in exaggerated perspective. This permanent setting, representing a city in Renaissance style, only allowed for the performance of classical plays.

2. Palazzo Porto, Vicenza, 1549

The central space of this complex is an inner courtyard which is situated between two identical palace blocks, one for the use of the master and his household, and the other for guests. The two living areas with identical facades are situated between two public streets. One enters the palace through a vestibule with four columns supporting a cross-vault. From there a narrow corridor leads to central cortile which on each side has five axes. The space between the two columns in the centre is bigger than that between the others: 6.3 : 6.3 : 8 : 6.3 : 6.3 (feet). The columns are two storeys high and support a gallery on the level of the upper floor which is also held by smaller pilasters opposite the columns. The only element that has no symmetrical counterpart is the main staircase which is situated at one side of the courtyard equally distant from the two entrances. Palladio's intention was to focus attention on the cortile, being the most beautiful part of the palace. The

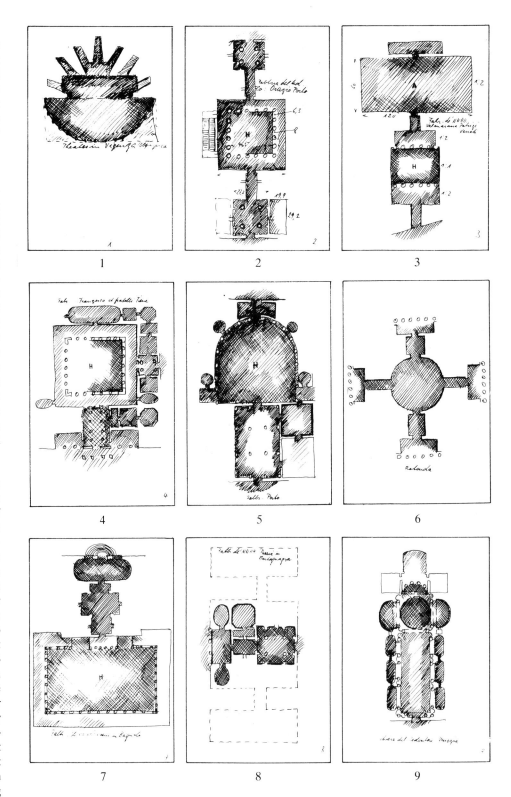

Diagrammatic interpretation of Palladio's ground-plans

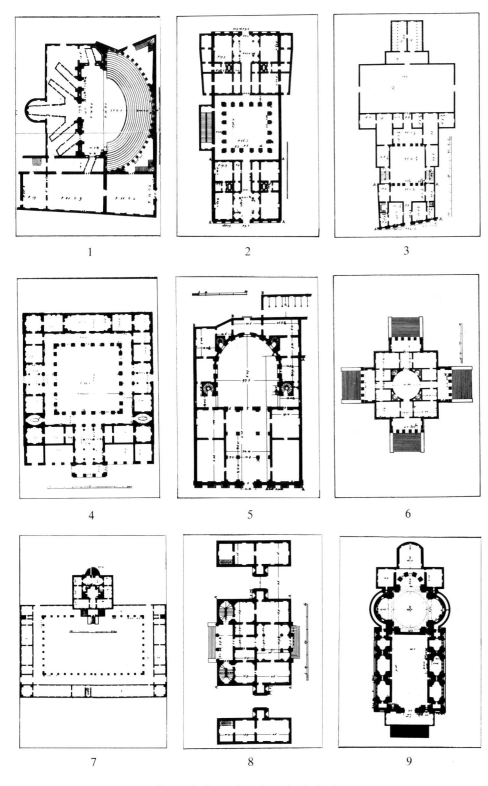

Ground-plans of projects by Palladio

staircase is rather modest in terms of spatiality. Palladio never created large-scale connecting spaces between the different floors. It was only in the baroque that the staircase became a theatrical event. In the Venetian type of palace it always remained a secondary element. Much more important was the rhythm of spaces to be experienced when walking through the rooms : the vicissitude of wide and narrow, square and rectangular spaces suggesting either to linger or to continue on one's way.

3. Palazzo Valmarana, Vicenza, 1565
The sequence of spaces in this palace corresponds in a marvellous way to a cadence of different light intensity. One enters the building through a dark narrow corridor which leads to a dim arcaded hall, the transparency of which gives access to the bright square inner courtyard. The space between the columns diminishes from the middle towards the sides: 2 : 4 : 4 : 7 : 4 : 4 : 2 (feet). Therefore the light penetration is more intense in the middle of the space where one actually walks. On the other side of the courtyard one enters again a dim hall which mediates between the exterior and interior, and which on both sides is narrowed by one vertical axis. Then a dark corridor, which is shorter than the first one, leads into a garden which has a proportion of 2 : 1.

4. Palazzo Thiene, Vicenza, 1542-6
The ground-plan of this palace is one of the most interesting in Palladio's early work. From a tripartite entrance hall, the portal of which is emphasised by a portico, one arrives in a square inner courtyard which is surrounded by an arcade. The corners seem to be denser because their high rectangular openings are only 4 feet wide whereas the normal openings are 8 feet wide. The same rhythm is applied to the organisation of the upper floor. Of interest is the variety of different spatial geometries which are arranged round the courtyard within the whole complex forming a consistent series of spaces. Square rooms alternate with oblong or transverse rectangular spaces. Corners are articulated by way of the octagonal room-width bays. The staircases are oval in plan.

5. Palazzo Porto, Piazza Castello, Vicenza, 1571

Only two window axes have been built from this design (bottom right). The facade's dominant feature is a gigantic order of columns. A spacious tripartite entrance hall was meant to lead to a courtyard constituted by a rectangle and a semi-circle. The concave back wall absorbs movement in the direction of the longitudinal axis. Spiral staircases are grouped around the courtyard for access to the building.

6. Villa Rotonda, Vicenza, 1566-7

The Villa Rotonda is the most consistent example of a symmetrical plan. The idea for such a composition was certainly also due to the topographical character of the site, a gently sloping hill. Palladio's intention, to constitute a relationship between the landscape and the building, is manifested by way of the broad external stairs on all four sides of the villa. As they rise towards the house, they form a built continuation of the natural hill. The entrances on all four sides are emphasised by porticoes for the enjoyment of the views all round. Inside, the two main axes run through narrow halls, slightly wider on the entry axis, and meet in a round central space which is two-storeys high and covered by a dome. In contrast to the plans which I have described before, it is not the axis of depth that is the main principle in this case, but the harmonious arrangement of rectangular rooms with a circular main space in the centre.

7. Villa Pisani, Bagnolo di Lonigo, 1542

The main entrance is situated on a longitudinal side of the spacious rectangular courtyard which is mostly surrounded by an arcade. The columns of the arcade are interrupted in the entrance area giving way to a triple flight of stairs and a portico. The vestibule leads directly into the cross-shaped vaulted main space. The passage to the garden is through a transverse rectangular loggia which has two semi-circular terminations on the short sides.

———— ✳ ————

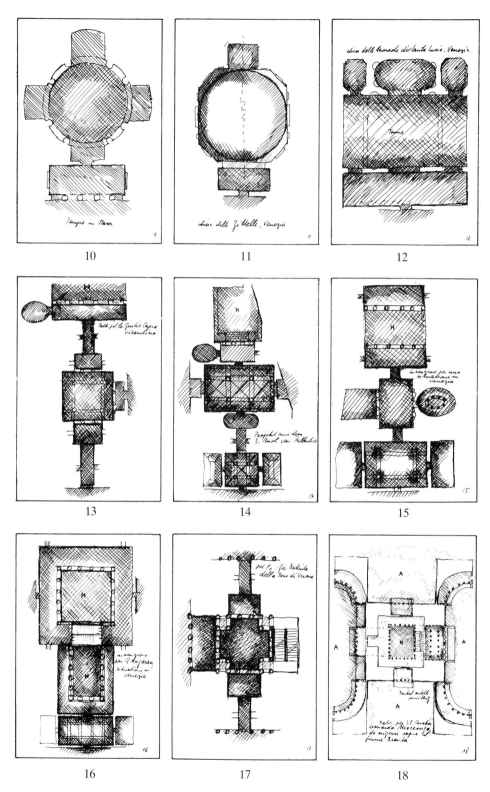

10   11   12

13   14   15

16   17   18

Diagrammatic interpretation of Palladio's ground-plans (continued)

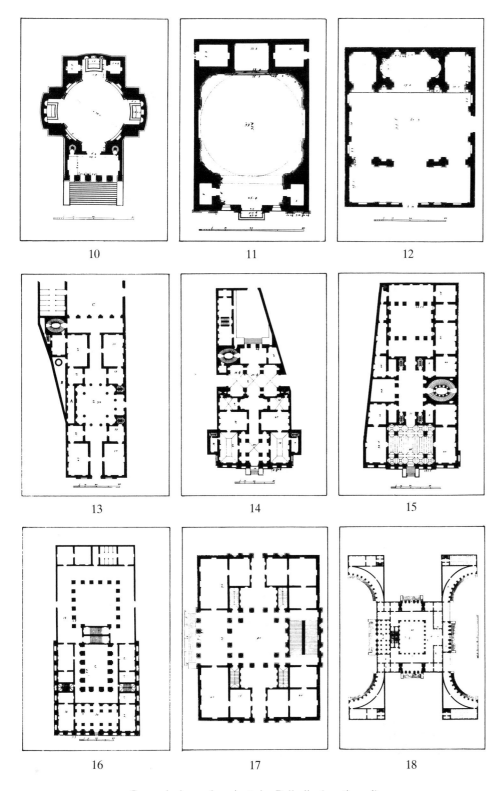

10　　　　　　　11　　　　　　　12

13　　　　　　　14　　　　　　　15

16　　　　　　　17　　　　　　　18

Ground-plans of projects by Palladio (continued)

8. Villa Pisani, Montagnana (Padua), 1552

From the street and an outside staircase, one arrives directly in the square main room which, by way of four free-standing columns supporting a transverse barrel vault, is divided into three zones. A corridor gives access to the loggia where the position of the columns corresponds to that of the main space. From here one has access either to the upper part of the building by way of two oval staircases on each short side of the loggia, or one continues on axis into the garden by way of an outside staircase.

9. Chiesa del Redentore, Venice, 1576

The ground-plan consists of three spatial areas which correspond to different functions. The church is entered and a long rectangular nave provides the spatial frame for the processional route of the faithful. The direction of movement is emphasised by the longitudinal barrel vault and the double columns of both sides of the nave, which in each case constitute a niche. The nave terminates at the most important part of the church, the self-contained chancel which is covered by a dome and is accessible from all sides. The space is enlarged on three sides by way of apses. The back of the middle apse is a wall of columns through which the choir can be viewed.

10. Tempietto Barbaro, Maser, 1580

A rectangular portico gives access to a circular domed space. To this space chancels are attached which are situated on the prolongation of the main axes. They have rounded back walls and thereby correspond to the form of the main space. The entire composition is orientated towards the centre, as with the Villa Rotonda.

11. Chiesa delle Zitella, Venice, 1579

A rectangle, which is enclosed from the outside, includes a basically square main space in its central area covered by a dome. The edges of this room are bevelled in order to mediate square and circle. A rectangular anteroom supporting a barrel-shaped vault is extended in front of the main space. In contrast to the Tempietto Barbaro (10), the entrance axis is orientated towards a single chancel which is attached to the opposite side of the main space.

12. Chiesa di S. Lucia, Venice, 1564

Here also, we have an enclosed, nearly square plan, which has no projections or additions. From an anteroom one arrives in a rectangular main space which is covered by a transverse barrel vault. The chancel is situated in the prolongation of the longitudinal axis with semi-circular niches added to it; it is flanked to the left and the right by minor square chapels with compound columns in the corners. The emphasised transverse direction of the main space creates a calming counter-balance to the movement axis of entrance to altar.

13. Palazzo Capra, Vicenza, 1563-4

Similar to the Palazzo Porto (2), a rhythmical, symmetrical sequence of spaces develops along the axis of depth. A narrow corridor leads to a widened anteroom and finally to a quiet square inner courtyard surrounded by an arcade supported by four free-standing columns. Traversing the courtyard, the rooms gradually narrow again, leading into a loggia followed by a second and larger courtyard.

14. Project for a Palace in Venice, 1553

This project discloses a very eventful sequence of spaces along a longitudinal axis. The square entrance hall is structured by way of four free-standing columns carrying a cross-vault above. This room is followed by two basically rectangular spaces at right angles to each other with similar dimensions which, when taken together, form a T-shape. The transverse room has semi-circular apses added to its short sides. From there one reaches the rectangular main room which picks up the motive of the four columns from the entrance hall. This space is enlarged to the left and right by a second axis. A small loggia creates the transition to the courtyard and, on the left, gives access to the oval staircase into the house.

15. Project for a Palace in Venice

When compared with the former example this project shows a similar organisation; however, the situation is different. The transverse rectangular entrance hall is bigger and again is constituted by four free-standing columns. A short narrow corridor leads to a smaller oblong hall which to the left receives light from the adjacent courtyard, and to the right gives access to the main staircase. A second short corridor leads through an arcaded hall into the courtyard which, on its opposite side, is confined by a second arcaded hall.

16. Palazzo Angarano, Vicenza, 1564

The ground-plan is constituted by a sequence of three spatial units, where one prepares for the next. All areas have in common the motive of the position of columns but differently applied. The entrance hall is structured by way of two rows of columns in transverse direction and corresponding half columns recessed into the walls. The adjacent first courtyard, with an arcade, has the same width as the entrance hall, but is much deeper. The columns surround the courtyard only on three sides and, as arcades, support a gallery. The open fourth side of the entrance axis gives access to the main staircase so that the narrow passages on both sides of the staircase into the second arcaded courtyard appear as prolongations of arcades of the first courtyard. The larger courtyard is again surrounded by an arcade with the exception of the staircase area. By spacing of the rows of columns, the width of the two other spaces is taken up again.

17. Palazzo Torre, Verona, 1561

This building is free-standing and has an enclosed rectangular ground-plan. The two main intersecting axes determine the organisation of different spaces. The shorter entrance axis leads first of all into a rectangular space, then into the square main hall, and from there again into a rectangular space which accommodates the main staircase. The three rooms have the same width and are transparent because of the columns. The longer axis runs through the two side entrances which, by way of narrow corridors and small anterooms, leads again into the central hall. The principle here is the gradual widening of spaces towards the centre.

18. Villa Mocenico, 1564

The whole composition is orientated towards the central hall as is the case with the Villa Rotonda. The difference here is that a definite main axis exists. On two sides exterior spaces are created by way of quarter-circle arcades which prepare for the interior. Here we also have located the main entrances, whose porticoes consist of eight columns, whereas the side-entrances on the other sides only consist of six columns. One of the main entrances is especially emphasised by way of an entrance hall with free-standing columns and the adjacent main staircase.

*   *   *

Roof truss of a hall for drying clothes, Burano, Veneto

Roof truss of the San Francesco church, Ravenna

Glyptothek, Munich, by L. von Klenze, 1816

Domed Hall, Palais Rasumofsky, Vienna, by L. Montoyer, 1806-07

Ceilings and Floors

These examples should only serve as a small indication of what we have lost in terms of treatment of the most important surfaces of an interior space – the floor and the ceiling. The surface of a room which we use each day, on which we walk all the time, cannot be dealt with only in terms of usefulness or ease of maintenance. The same applies to the ceiling, the termination of a space above our heads. A space's significance and use, independent from its size, can be adapted and structured by way of an intentional and painstaking treatment of these surfaces. Centralised spaces can be emphasised, lines of movements can be represented. No carpet covering the entire floor can have the effect which is so clearly achieved by separate beautiful rugs on a hard surface: the creation of small islands within a space, of informal borders which underline the employment and structure of the room; and which also, when looked at, give rise to a little happiness and relief. With one example, I would also like to explain the economic aspect of a sound treatment of surfaces. At the moment timber ceilings are very popular. But many people prefer to use cheap veneered panels, or even foam rubber beams with an embossed wood pattern. After some years such junk becomes dusty, scratched and mean-looking, and has to be replaced by a new ceiling. Compared with this, we still find in old houses unpainted ceilings made of natural timber. Every few years they are cleaned with soap and brush and thereby develop over time a silky lustre, a patina, which makes the material, in the course of time, more and more beautiful.

These three examples demonstrate the principle of floor and ceiling corresponding to each other. They show how the two surfaces are brought into relationship by way of formal and constructional compositions. The first example (illustration 1) is the banking hall of Otto Wagner's Post Office Savings Bank in Vienna. The glass bricks of the floor correspond to the glass roof in its tendency towards dematerialisation. The piers emerge from the floor partitions and penetrate the roof into infinity. Also in the next example (illustration 2) the compartments of the vault correspond to those of the floor. The transverse arches of the ceil-

Student works on the theme of Ceilings and Floors

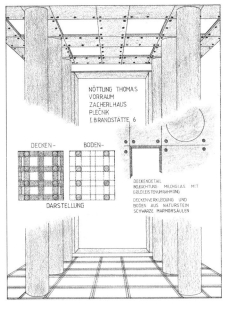

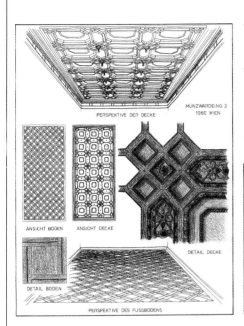

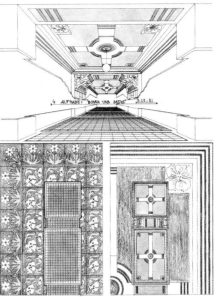

ing are represented in the floor, the tiles of which repeat the diagonal principle. A classical, geometrical order is applied in illustration 3. Josef Plećnik created an almost sacral space when designing the entrance hall for the 'Zacherlhaus' in Vienna (illustration 4). From a shiny floor made of natural stone, black marble columns rise and break through an exquisitely detailed bright ceiling. The close positions of the marble columns, and their significance as part of the composition of the space as a whole, make it necessary to leave them without base and capital. What is most crucial is the envelope of the whole space.

Student works on the theme of Ceilings and Floors

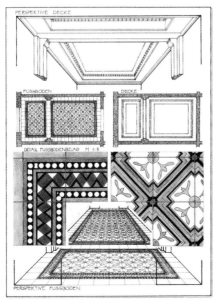

———— ✳ ————

Floor, Domed Hall, Palais Rasumofsky, by L. Montoyer, 1806-07

Court Library, Vienna, by J.B. Fischer von Erlach, 1721-25

Terracotta pavement, town hall area, Vienna, c. 1900

Church am Steinhof, Vienna, by O. Wagner, 1905-07

Timber roof structure, eighteenth century

Klosterneuberg Monastery, by J. Kornhäusel, 1836-42

Dome Room, Palais Rasumofsky, by L. Montoyer, 1806-07

Church am Steinhof, Vienna, by O. Wagner, 1905-07

Columns and Piers

Centuries of architectural culture have created an inexhaustible variety of forms of columns and piers. In Greek architecture epochs were named after their orders. Time and again the proportioning and decoration of a column or pier served as an indication and characterisation of a certain architectural style. The students' drawings which accompany this chapter should serve to remind us of this. It remained for our times to give up the continuous refinement of this archaic form. A column has a relationship with the ground and has to carry a load; this alone should have been sufficient enough to bestow higher considerations on these two properties. Concrete or brick piers are problematic due to the vulnerability of their edges, which up to a certain height require special protection. The reason for the employment of banal concrete, steel or timber

Student works on the theme of Columns and Piers

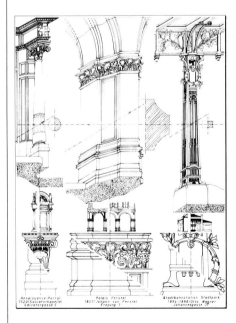

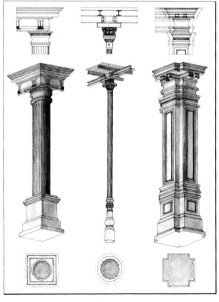

———— ✳ ————

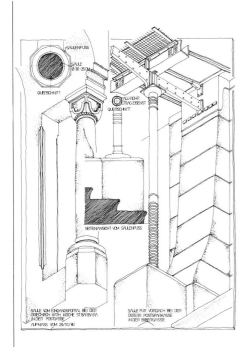

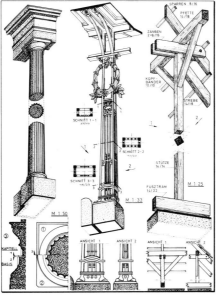

Student works on the theme of Columns and Piers

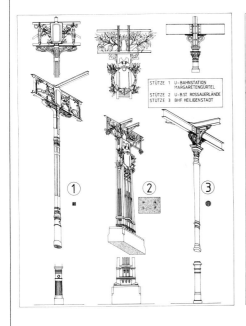

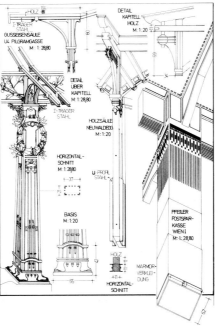

piers nowadays is very simple and clear: it is due to high wages which have far exceeded the price of materials. Experiments with concrete piers by Morandi or Nervi, for example, are no longer possible because the making of them has become too expensive. Exposed steel piers had to disappear from the classic repertoire of architecture due to rigorous fire regulations; and the quality of timber which is generally available today is so poor that it hardly allows for artisan treatment. Does all this mean the end of the column and pier as an element in architectural creation? Of course, the high wages for fabrication are justified. But it would be important to make society appreciate the significance of architectural design and architectural themes, and to thereby gain public support which would make it meaningful again to learn from the ancients how to use columns as a structural device.

———— ✳ ————

Arcade of a building from the Middle Ages, Bologna

Base of a pier in the Golden Hall of the castle Hohensalzburg, c. 1500

Base of a pier, Basilica San Vitale, Ravenna, 545

Four Piers of a stairwell, Vienna, early nineteenth century

Portal of the Heiliggeistkirche, Vienna, by J. Plećnik, 1910-11

Villa Sarregno, Santa Sofia di Pedemonte, by Palladio, 1569

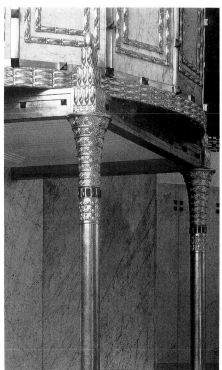

Further examples of Columns and Piers

Doors

If one considers the conception of an interior space, every opening, whether door or window, means the violation of the wall. These violations, however, give the room its direction and its appropriate meaning. Doors play a decisive role in this context because they prepare the visitor for the spatial event to come. The significance of the door should therefore be considered from different standpoints.

A crucial pre-condition for our reflection is to recognize the door as being an important symbol. This banal statement makes sense if one examines the many versions of door formats available at present. We are used to a door having the form of an upright rectangle. Here the most popular sizes lie in the proportions 1 : 2 to 1 : 3 (illustration 1). Beyond this, the meaning of a door can vary according to its purpose. A low door for instance, which gives access to the parlour of an old farm house, clearly communicates that the private area is to be penetrated into. Doors of the same kind can be emphasised individually by way of additional openings on the sides or above (illustration 2). This kind of articulation also facilitates orientation. It is not always the scale of the human body which determines the size of a door. Especially in monumental buildings, the dimensions of the openings derive from the proportions of the receptive space. Quite often for everyday purposes, a door within a door was conceived, which could be used easily by people just wanting to go through. But when major events occurred, the entire over-dimensioned door was opened. Descendants of these palace doors are still to be found in bourgeois houses of the nineteenth century. The normal folding-door of a Viennese bourgeois house had a width of 1.25 metres and a height of 2.50 metres. But normally only one half was opened (about 60 cm width) – seemingly nowadays a hardly bearable standard. (I am always amused to see some 200 students who came to my lectures at the Technical University in Vienna going in and out through such a narrow slit without anyone having the idea to open the second wing of the door; a good example of the relativity of function.)

1   2   3

4   5   6

7   8   9

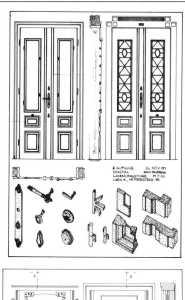

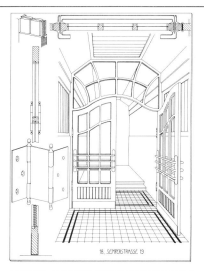

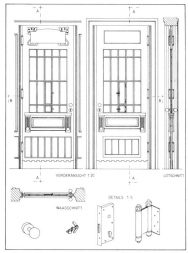

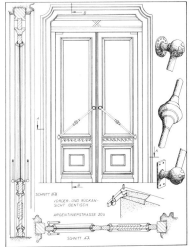

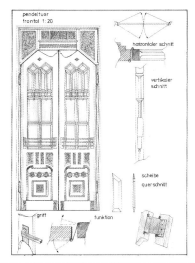

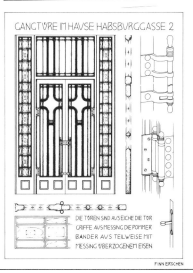

More determined by function is the position of a door. But even under complicated functional constraints, it is possible in most cases to find an appropriate position which is in geometrical harmony with the room. Illustrations 3 to 6 show attempts to create a precise relation between wall and opening. Of prime importance are the proportions of door height and door lintel to the residual surfaces at the sides of the door opening. As a rule it might be appropriate to apply the system of proportion which determines the ground-plan and the elevation of a building also to the secondary elements such as windows and doors. If it is not possible to coordinate door and wall in this way, there are other devices to nevertheless achieve a harmonious space. Relatively simple is the creation of niches in a wall or the concentration of a group of doors and windows. A more difficult method, but one which helps to enrich the spatial atmosphere, is to insert bays which by way of piers are separated from the actual room and would cushion irregular positions of doors. This 'filter' in front of the opening would create a proper door space which is sympathetic to the functional structure of the actual room (illustration 6). The combination of door and window elements (illustration 7) is very appropriate, especially in the case of balconies, terraces and loggias. It is essential, however, that a distinction in terms of proportion and size between door and window is retained.

Before I end this section, I would like to mention some technical and constructional factors relating to doors. The violation of the wall caused by a door can best be overcome by fair-faced brickwork. The arrangement of lintel and door leaf is determined by the logic of the brickwork structure, and the frame is secured in the masonry accordingly. If the walls are plastered, the door frame in most cases simply surrounds the opening.

Student works on the theme of Doors

And because of the incessant cracks between timber, plaster and wallpaper, the inhabitant realises very soon that these different materials are difficult to join properly. With old doors, these weak areas were resolved by way of richly profiled frames and the employment of beautiful timber. In addition to that, the decorators used mouldings to achieve a proper transition from door frame to wall. (A fantastic example is Otto Wagner's design for the management rooms in the Post Office Savings Bank in Vienna. The doors are treated as logical elements of the composition of the wall surfaces; the wall panels are therefore of the same timber as the door and window frames.) Our contemporary standard door sets offer few possibilities in terms of design. Today we can only concentrate on the quality of proportions, the material and colour. The steel frame is merely the representation of a frame around the plain door leaf. I think there is no longer any sign of the old type of door. Seemingly our building industry is only interested in crushing natural products such as timber into fibres only to later glue the stuff together again and to roll it into big sheets. The technique of making panels out of boards had led to astonishing results which became real works of art.

Door between stairwell and entrance hall, Amerling House, Bäckerstrasse, Vienna

Greenhouse in the Burggarten, by F. Ohmann, c. 1900

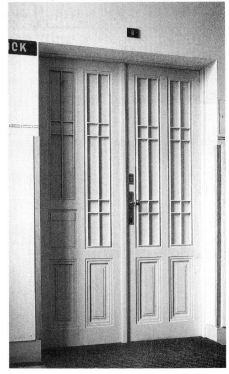

Entrance door and vestibule door, house in the Döblergasse, Vienna, by O. Wagner, 1912

———— ✳ ————

Former railway station in the Karlsplatz, Vienna, by O. Wagner, 1898-99

Portal in the fishmarket in Laibach, Yugoslavia, by J. Plećnik, 1939-40

Control Room door, Kaiserbad Dam, Vienna, by O. Wagner, 1906-07

Door to mausoleum, San Vito di Altievole, the Veneto, by Carlo Scarpa, c.1970

Door Handles

I'll permit myself one small observation on this apparently insignificant theme, for strange as it may seem, the door handle is the architectural detail that we have most daily contact with. It's not a detail we're likely to overlook, either. Think of how uncertain we feel in front of an unfamiliar door: does it open inwards or outwards, do we push or pull it? The door handle is an extremely difficult architectural 'sign', because each new variant will not be automatically understood by the user. There's still no universal rule for opening doors: instead there is a technical gadget, a bank of light which forces part of the facade – usually a glass part – to yield before the person approaching it. This is a really cunning machine, for if you dare to hesitate between the open doors, they'll close and catch you like a rat in a trap, making you the object of your fellow-citizens' scorn. Thus an apparent gesture of courtesy brings with it a small loss of freedom of choice.

The tactile quality of a proper door handle is another thing entirely. One should be able to take it in one's hand and the door should open comfortably. A whole thesis could be written on what kind of door handle is best for what kind of door. Here, however, there is only enough room to reiterate the importance of this unprepossessing detail, which can be simply stated by the fact that no architect wants to irritate the users of his building as they enter it.

Biedermeier door handle, Vienna

Door handle on the portal of Laibach Library, by J. Plećnik, 1930-32

Door handle in Holyhof, Vienna, by Arch Perco, 1928

Door handle in the Government Printing Office, Vienna, by J. Hoffmann, 1900s

———— ✳ ————

Door handle on the aluminium-clad door to the
house at No 3 Döblergasse, by O. Wagner, 1912

Windows

The theme of this section is the window and its relationship to interior space. Its effect on the outside, the facade, is dealt with in the section dealing with the composition of the facade.

With respect to the relationship between window and interior space, first of all the window's function as the source of light is of great importance. To be more specific, we should talk about the effect penetrating light has on the interior space. To the same extent that a room is created by its wall surfaces, it is enlivened by light. One may think of a sunbeam striking upon a white wall or producing reflections somewhere in the room. The play of light and shade creating bright and dark zones in a room, motivates our awareness of the space – whereby not only the source of the light, the window, remains in our consciousness, but also the illuminated surfaces of the room: the texture of the walls, a sparkling floor, furniture or other objects which are given prominence by the light. Therefore the design of an interior space and the choice of materials and colours, should always take into account the effect of penetrating light.

One aspect that is quite often underestimated is the quality of light and its dependence on the time of the day, season, weather, cardinal points and intensity. All this results in certain though changing light atmospheres which we experience as harsh, soft, subdued, dazzling, sparkling, obscure, misty etc. It is also important to find out what quantity of light is appropriate for a space. Too little light can only be complemented by artificial illumination; too much or too direct light should be filtered with the help of devices such as shutters, blinds, lintels, transparent curtains and plants. Also forms of double skin wall construction which allow indirect (i.e. its intensity weakened) light to penetrate are a good and appropriate solution.

I do not allow my students to design horizontal ribbon windows, because I want them from the first moment on to tackle the problems of the window and its significance for the room. In the end, light coming from a ribbon window only has a very monotonous and banal effect on space. Therefore for housing developments, the appropriateness of ribbon windows is rather limited. I am of the opinion that single sources of light offer an opportunity for the space to be lit in a much more exciting way while they also allow the creation of areas in shade which are very pleasant in time of direct sunlight penetration. Equally doubtful in terms of benefit is the fully glazed wall or curtain wall. The excessive amount of light is exhausting for the eyes, and oddly enough, after having torn up the wall, one has to counteract the implications of excessive light by way of special sun protection equipment. The room itself is completely open only on one side, its geometry is destroyed, and the tension between inside and outside is diluted. But, if for functional or design reasons one wall of a room has to be left open, it is much better to apply an architecturally effective method, such as a row of piers or well-ordered bars, which would not destroy, but enrich, the interior space. As we are not in favour of the ribbon window, we have to come to terms with the position of the window. In general, we can establish that if a room is penetrated by light only from one side, which in the extreme case could be direct sunlight, an uncomfortable dazzle will easily result. But if the main source of light is balanced by a smaller window on another side – the opposite one would be best – or from above, then the room will be better lit. Even reflective masonry surrounding big windows can soften the contrast between the bright outside and the dark inside.

Not only is the way in which light affects the interior space significant when talking about the position of a window, but the view presented is also important. The window frames a certain part of our environment and makes it into a kind of picture, but one which is changing constantly, very much in contrast to the motionless painting on the wall which can be an artistic substitution for what might be seen through a window. The awareness of the outside world is intensified by a cross window, or generally by windows with structuring bars, and becomes weaker the bigger the window opening is. Thus windows or glass walls which are too big, which open up the interior space totally, make the room uncomfortable; the feeling of safety and security is lost. If nevertheless a generous transition from the inside to the outside is desired, one should not think of achieving this in an abrupt way, but gradually, by way of loggias or transparent and lightweight projections (verandas for instance). If we consider all the points which are significant when dealing with the window – such as light penetration and its effect on the interior, light quality, position of the window, view from the window – then it becomes obvious that, strictly speaking, the window deserves as much care as does the actual room.

Basic Forms and Bars

The square, the triangle and the circle are the basic geometrical forms for the window. The latter two, however, have to be regarded as special forms. Traditionally they were used for spaces of eminent or solemn significance. It is therefore recommendable to treat circular and triangular windows with great care, and to use them sparingly so that their meaning is not trivialised. Otherwise they would degenerate to negligible graphic attributes too quickly (illustration 1). The classic window has a rectangular upright format. For thousands of years of architecture, this kind of light source has proved to be the most economic both in terms of construction and in optimal terms of function. Related to constructional considerations, the simple argument against broad windows is that they violate the wall considerably. In terms of function, the upright window has evolved to meet most simply and efficiently the requirements for sufficient light, air and view.

The square window, although representing a precise form, is a very abstract and, in addition, a very banal format. It can be appropriate if in the composition of a facade it is used as a harmonizing element together with other forms.

In anonymous rural and urban architecture, square window formats are almost exclusively used for secondary utility spaces. Very rarely are they applied to domestic buildings. Several times when I thought I had discovered a square window, it turned out in fact to be slightly rectangular. The exact square has also the disadvantage of appearing distorted when viewed from a certain angle, face to face it takes on a

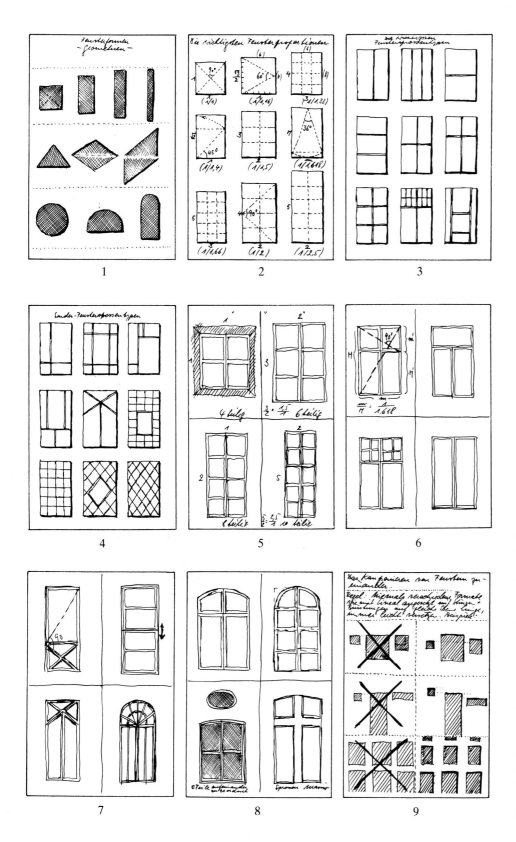

1

2

3

4

5

6

7

8

9

horizontal format. The most common window proportions result from the division of the circle into three parts (1 : 1.16); the division of the circle into four parts (1 : 1.4); the Golden Section; and the proportion 1 : 2.5 (illustration 2).

I should mention that all my recommendations concerning different aspects of design, although they may sound irrefutable, always allow for first-rate exceptions. I refer only to Le Corbusier's 'ribbon window' or Aldo Rossi's 'square window'. Window divisions are firstly related to the kind of opening one is dealing with. They have to comply with basic function, such as opening, ventilation and cleaning. In addition to these, window bars can be employed for the aesthetic structuring of the window plane (illustrations 3 to 8). This latter design responsibility has been very much neglected in recent years. It was thought to be enough to satisfy the passion for an unhindered view by way of panorama glazing, which was made possible by the products of the glazing industry. Very often as a result, the intimacy of a space was destroyed; tasteless 'curtain culture' was the user's response. Because of all these reasons one should go back again to sensible divisions for the window and reconcile its design with that of the facade.

The simple divisions, depending on the kind of opening, are horizontal or vertical, and the superimposition of these two. The common 'window-cross' has been quite successful. It is economic in terms of timber consumption and handy in terms of ventilation and cleaning. One of the top casements can open separately by way of a lever mechanism. The lower side hung casements also allow for the unavoidable curtains to be moved aside when the window is to be opened. If people have fear of heights, they can lean on the closed casement and look out through the other opened one (illustration 6).

The examples in illustration 4, which show different arrangements of bars, are rather decorative. These windows are special in terms of their structure, their figuration, the tension between larger and smaller divisions; they have an independent architectural significance. The window surface itself becomes an important element of design. It would be precarious to replace these kinds of windows by synthetic or panoramic glazing. They would destroy the texture of the facade.

A successful bar pattern in architectural history is the multiple division of the window in fairly exact square compartments (illustration 5). For this type, the different thickness of bars is a characteristic which results from the constructional functions of frame and thinner elements.

Vertical sash-windows, common in Great Britain, allow for the greatest graduation of ventilation. Both halves of the window can be moved upwards and downwards and they can remain in any position – air can enter either from the top or the bottom. Special forms of windows dealt with here are seen as derivations of the rectangular window (illustrations 7 and 8).

As regards the combination of different window formats, I would like to suggest a simple 'peasant's maxim' (illustration 9):
1. Different window formats should never line up with either their lintels or their sills. Otherwise this would be a typical result of T-shape thinking. Cut the formats out of dark cardboard and move them around on the facade drawing; you will learn quickly how to avoid banal solutions. The tension of the formats one to another is geometrically measureable.
2. One should be careful with the addition of identical formats both in the horizontal and the vertical direction. If one tries to alternate the sizes storey by storey, it will become evident how lively the relationship between opening and masonry can become (illustration 9).

Window Figures
Window figures are created when different formats are brought into aesthetic inter-dependence. They can even be set in an architectural frame to become a particular element of the facade. I have sketched some examples to explain what I mean: Palladio (illustrations 1, 2 top 3), Schinkel (illustrations 2 bottom, 4, 5 top and middle, 6, 7), Gaudí (illustration 8) and Le Corbusier (illustration 9).

Window figures are always divided into different elements. Openings with different functions and meanings are combined to form an 'image'. The result is an exciting conduct of light into the interior and an

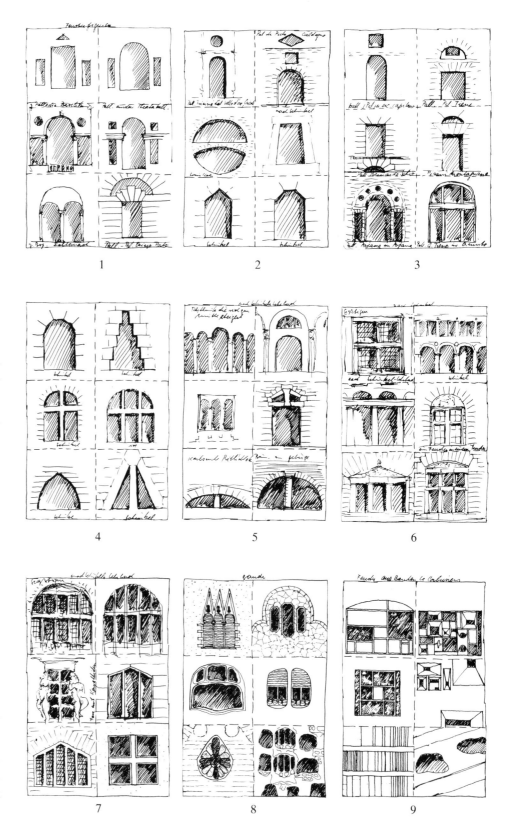

1

2

3

4

5

6

7

8

9

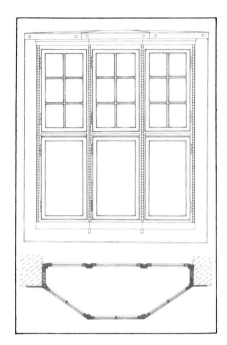

No. 70, Sternwartestrasse, Vienna, By F. Federspiel

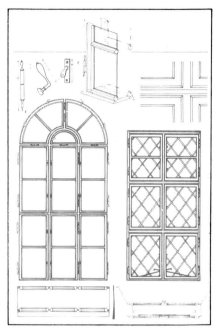

No. 12, Akademiestrasse, Vienna, by C. Vostrovky, and 'Schloss Schönbrunn', Vienna, by G. Aicher

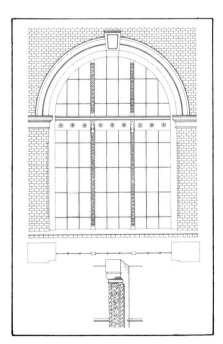

Markethall in Landstrasse, Vienna, by J. Dürrhammer

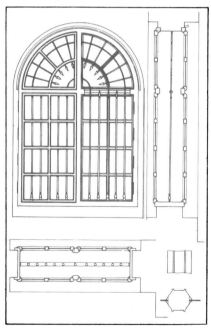

Building at Minoritenplatz, Vienna, by E. Aicher

architectural articulation on the outside. Window figures are also especially addressed to exterior space. Here the relationship to the overall facade is crucial.

The Window as Room Divider

The examples in this plate have been measured up by students from old Viennese buildings. They show the refined treatment, the richness in detail and the significance which was applied to the window. The bay window in illustration 1 is designed as a special room. A window is not merely 'a hole in the wall', it defines a real space with an area in front of the window, a breast-wall zone and an exterior space. This is best described by the experience we have when approaching a window: we are no longer inside and not yet outside. Behind us lies the protecting room and in front of us the exterior world. The window has to be easy to reach to be used. It should also tell us something about the significance and situation of the rooms behind. Illustrations 1, 2 and 4 also show windows where the space between exterior and interior windows can be used. By this, an optimal response to different climatic needs is ensured, because several casements are available to be opened or left closed. This works much better than even the most sophisticated modern ventilation systems (if they work at all!). These hints advocate that the window should be understood as a spatial element and not as transparent wall.

———— ✳ ————

A special theme is introduced by the arched window (illustrations 2, 3 and 4). Although dividing the arch is an extremely risky task in aesthetic terms, this was often undertaken to emphasise certain windows over others. In the nineteenth century the arched window was also used in engineer-designed buildings. But the bars in the arch already usher in the domination of the machine (illustration 3).

Heinrich Tessenow had strong opinions about filling in parts which came into conflict with the overall form; especially when – as with the arched window – a rectilinear division meets with an arch so that unsightly residual areas remain. As much as an arched window can be very attractive, these difficulties should not be brushed aside. Alberti has probably expressed the most severe restriction concerning this problem: 'In these Sorts of Apertures various designs have been commended; but the best Architects have never made Use of any but Squares and straight Lines.' *

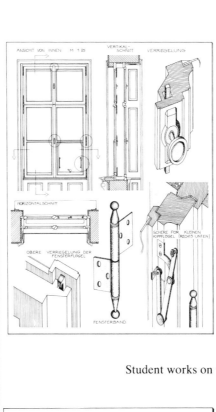
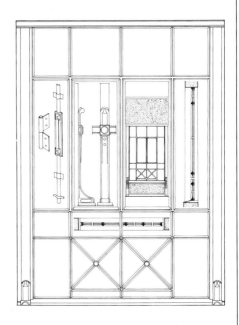

Student works on the theme of Windows

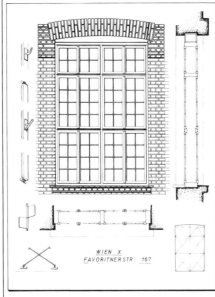
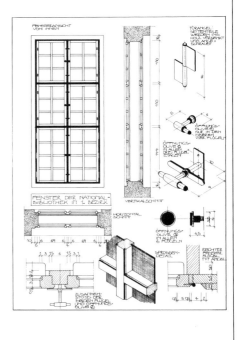

*Leon Battista Alberti, *Ten Books on Architecture*, English translation published by Alec Tiranti, London 1965, Chapter XII.

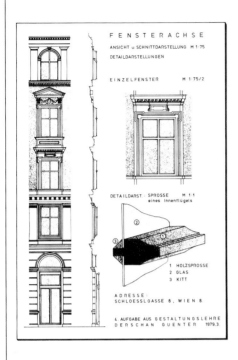

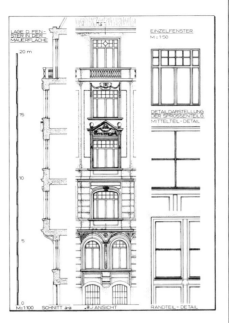

Student works on the theme of Windows

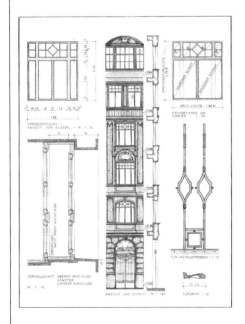

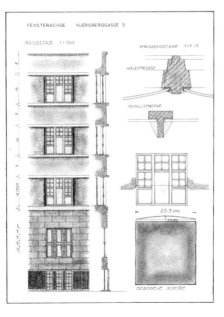

Facade and Window Axis

Further reference to a contemporary grievance is given by these facade segments. The windows let us imagine the wonderfully high rooms behind. It is really questionable whether the lowered ceiling heights in council housing represent such striking progress. Of course they are cheaper than the old ones. Bathrooms and toilets are expensive; but would anybody think of ignoring them in council housing because of cost factors? I just want to hint at the priorities which should govern us when making buildings. Unfortunately one priority, the quality of the space, has been most easily renounced. And what has also been lost in this context is the high, representative window. Therefore, again an admonition from Alberti about the treatment of windows: '. . . from whatever side we take in the Light, we ought to make such an Opening for it, as may always give us a free Sight of the Sky, and the Top of that Opening ought never to be too low, because we are to see the Light with our Eyes, and not with our Heels; besides the Inconvenience, that if one Man gets between another and the Window, the Light is intercepted, and all the rest of the Room is darken'd, which never happens when the Light comes from above.'

———— ✳ ————

Without intending to anticipate the section on facades, I would like to show here parts of facades which relate to the vertical gradation of windows. The examples demonstrate that in former times the valuation and meaning of particular storeys was also applied to the design of their windows. The arrangement in these buildings represented social conditions, because different storeys were inhabited by members of different social classes. Nevertheless today we are attracted by this differentiation not only for nostalgic reasons. It allows for spontaneous orientation, the recognition of particular storeys and a precise architectural designation. To achieve this, it is not absolutely necessary to use different window formats for special storeys. Different materials on the facade can also support a similar effect.

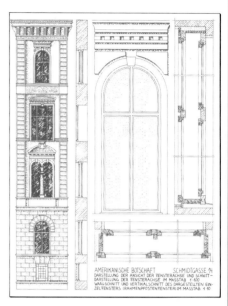

Student works on the theme of Windows

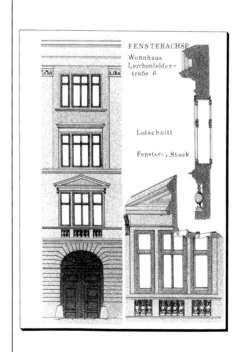

Upper Belvedere, Vienna, by J. L. von Hildebrandt, 1721-22

Palm House in the Burggarten, Vienna, by F. Ohmann, c. 1900

Stadtbahn station at the Gürtel, Vienna, by O. Wagner, 1896-97

House Knip, Vienna, by J. Hoffmann, 1923-24

'Pawlatsche' (pergola), Graz, nineteenth century

Children's Refuge, Vienna, by J. Plećnik, 1907-08

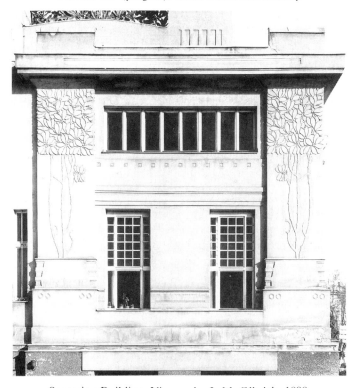

Secession Building, Vienna, by J. M. Olbrich, 1898

Building on Michaelerplatz, Vienna, by A. Loos, 1910

House on the Schottenring, Vienna, by O. Wagner, 1877

House in Schulergasse, Vienna, nineteenth century

Industrial Museum, Vienna, late nineteenth century

Former stage-set depot, Vienna, by G. Semper, 1873

Zacherlhaus, Vienna, by J. Plećnik, 1903-05

Former Stadtbahn station, Karlsplatz, Vienna, by O. Wagner, 1898-99

Stock Exchange, Vienna, by T. von Hansen, 1874-77

Leopold wing of the Hofburg, Vienna, by P. Luchese, 1660-6

Staircases

The staircase is the vertical element of access in a building, which enables one to ascend and descend from one storey to the next. The primitive forerunner of the staircase is the ladder. It is the shortest connection between two places, but it is also steep and hard to use. In most cases it is not firmly installed in order to be used flexibly, and therefore lacks any proper spatial or architectonic quality. The other extreme, the ramp, allows for an almost imperceptible transition from storey to storey. The differences in height are very easily overcome. But the space which is required for a ramp is considerably larger than for a staircase because of the gentle rise of the former.

The function of a staircase determines its form and at the same time shapes the enclosing space. We perceive either a straight flight or two opposite diagonal flights which cut through the space, or a winding movement which turns upwards. The way a staircase runs; whether it requires a – typically vertical – well; where it fits into the ground-plan; its construction and material are all aspects which contribute to its form.

A short glance at history shows the changing emphasis which was given to the staircase. The Romanesque spiral staircase, for instance, had no light and having the shape of a tube filled a special recess in the masonry or was pressed into a circular tower. It fulfilled the purpose of transporting people upstairs and downstairs like a vertical corridor. During the Gothic period, the outer skin of the staircase was articulated by arcades, columns and tracery. Light could therefore penetrate and it could be looked through. In the sixteenth century we have stair towers which were extended vertically beyond the buildings they belonged to, having a 'crow's-nest' on top. Here the motive of the staircase is linked with a social function. In baroque palaces the well of the staircase becomes a representative Hall. The staircase itself is gorgeous in detail, oversized and runs up in several flights. It is full of light and sometimes ends under a mighty cupola. The actual purpose of the staircase is dominated by the notion of representation. The typical staircases in residential buildings in Vienna reached their prime in the nineteenth century: curved stairs of natural stone, free projection over one side, minimal thickness of material, generous gaps between flights, artistically designed bannisters and profiled handrails. The well was in most cases illuminated by a roof-light and quite often, besides water taps, contained sculpture or stone benches. In Otto Wagner's residential buildings these details have been executed as real masterpieces.

In the years after the war, space was cut down for economic reasons and the large-scale staircase has been sacrificed without hesitation. This is why we have merely functional staircases in our modern buildings. They appear as an addition of disjointed sections with tiny landings and minimal flights. The generous gap between flights, which allowed the view from storey to storey, has almost completley gone.

The staircase, which formerly was an important area of human communication, has to be given back its appropriate significance in a building. Solutions for stairs on a more appropriate scale are still possible. It is not difficult to create them as spaces which we find pleasant, which receive enough light and allow views to the outside, and which are enlivened by a sunbeam penetrating through a roof-light. The widths do not need to be enormous: 1.10 metres to 1.20 metres is enough, if landings intervene which allow for conversation or resting on a bench.

The most important requirement of a staircase is that the degree of rise is as gentle as possible, in order to reduce to a minimum the effort necessary for climbing. To determine a convenient angle of rise, first of all the stride of a human being must be taken into consideration, which on average has a length of 63 cm. It is assumed that the movement in vertical direction requires a double effort in comparison with the horizontal one. This means in arithmetical terms, one tread and twice the riser should make 63cm. The most comfortable staircase according to Viennese tradition has risers which are 14cm high and treads of 35cm width. Unfortunately most staircases are steeper with risers of 18 to 19cm because a reduction in floor space can be achieved. If the height of steps is less than 14cm, the bottom line of convenience is reached because difference in altitude is only very slowly mastered.

The staircase and its surrounding space are an essential part of the architectonic composition of a building. Its function of giving access to different storeys can only be achieved in a meaningful way if this quality is immediately obvious; in other words, if it is clear that the staircase serves as a device of orientation in a building. Today one makes do with technical and graphical guiding systems instead of organising routes and stairs in a way that by their position, by way of their relations to the entrance and their particular form, the plan of the building can be understood and visitors can easily orientate themselves. If a building has to accommodate several staircases, the hierarchy of significance and frequency in terms of use can be manifested in design, while unmistakable areas are created. Form directly fulfils function. Here the whole richness of typological variations is at our disposal.

Staircase

Similar to the ladder put against a wall, the straight stair is the simplest solution. Illustration 1 shows an example which is fitted into a frame of piers and beams. If a straight staircase is situated in a bigger space, access to the different storeys can be given by way of a gallery (illustration 2). This type works very well in public buildings. The respective stair to the next storey is easy to find, and the gallery allows all rooms on one level to be entered without difficulty. More economical in terms of space, and therefore better suited for housing developments, is the square well with straight flights of stairs of the same size as the landings (illustration 3). One common solution is the development of two straight flights with an intermediate landing (illustration 4). If the landing is bordered by an exterior wall it is possible to arrange for the well to get natural light. Three flights of stairs (illustrations 5 to 7) have to be seen primarily as being related to representation. They almost directly ask for 'dignified striding'. The example in illustration 5 is suitable for repetition over several storeys. A broad staircase starts with one flight until the intermediate landing is reached, at which point it turns into two flights which are narrower than the first one. However, the example in illustration 6, where two flights rise in different directions from the intermediate landing, has its best effect if applied only once in a building. In illustration 7 two flights of stairs from opposite directions meet to become one stair. This form is recommended especially for passage-ways with two entrances, as they can be approached equally from both directions. The type in illustration 8, which is a flight of two stairs with preliminary steps leading to it, demands integration into a high space which allows the whole staircase to be looked at from elsewhere. A very costly solution is shown in illustration 9, where stairs change their direction on every level to give access alternately to opposite sides.

——— ✳ ———

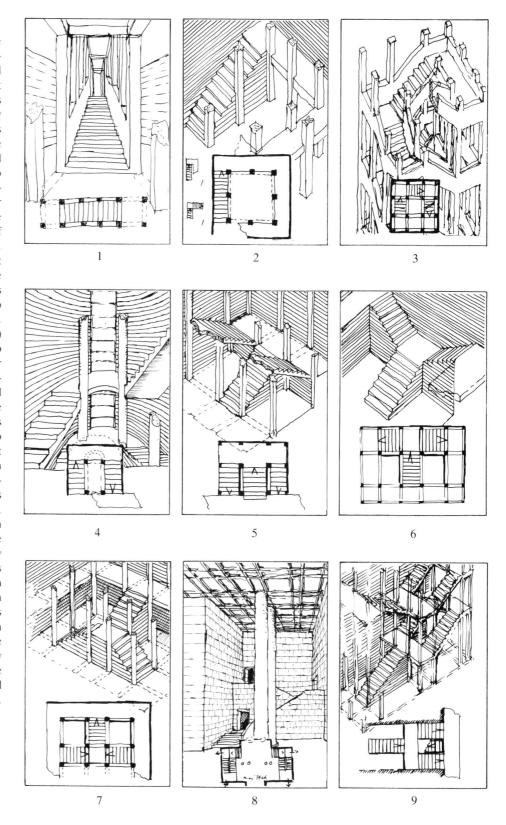

1

2

3

4

5

6

7

8

9

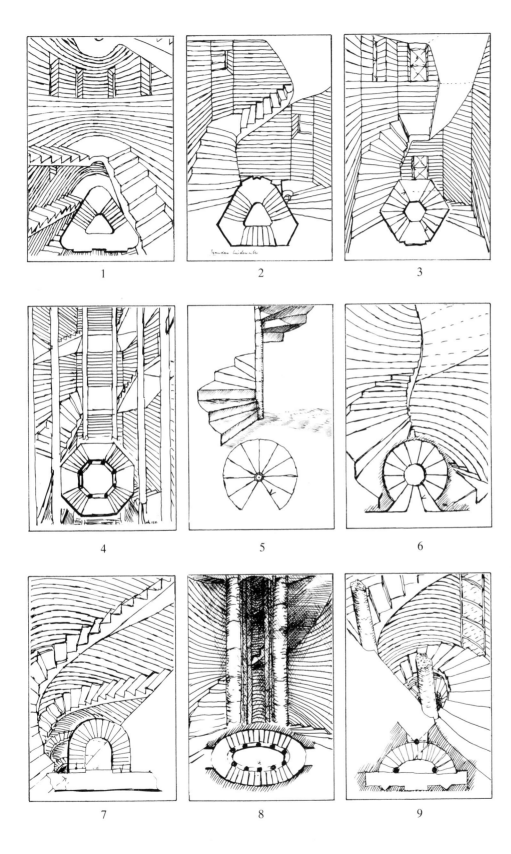

1

2

3

4

5

6

7

8

9

This can be suitable for special solutions.

The geometrical modification of the straight staircase leads to spiral stairs. In difficult spatial situations, for instance corners, a two-flight staircase on a triangular ground-plan can be applied (illustration 1). A variation of this form is a stair rising in three flights on a triangular ground-plan (illustration 2), but here only a small landing remains. Two flights of stairs on a polygonal ground-plan – for example a hexagon (illustration 3) – provide the well with a high spatial quality. Illustration 4 is more related to the exploitation of a geometrical form where the sides of an octagon are constituted alternately by flights and landings.

Illustrations 5 to 9 show examples of spiral staircases. The very narrow newel staircases (illustrations 5 and 6) are difficult for elderly people and unsuitable for bigger objects to be transported. This is not the case with winding staircases on half-circular (illustration 7) or oval ground-plans (illustrations 8 and 9). Here it is also possible to find one's own walking rhythm by either climbing on the inner or the outer side. What should be avoided is the alternation of circular and straight steps, because this makes it very difficult to find one's natural walking rhythm.

———— ✳ ————

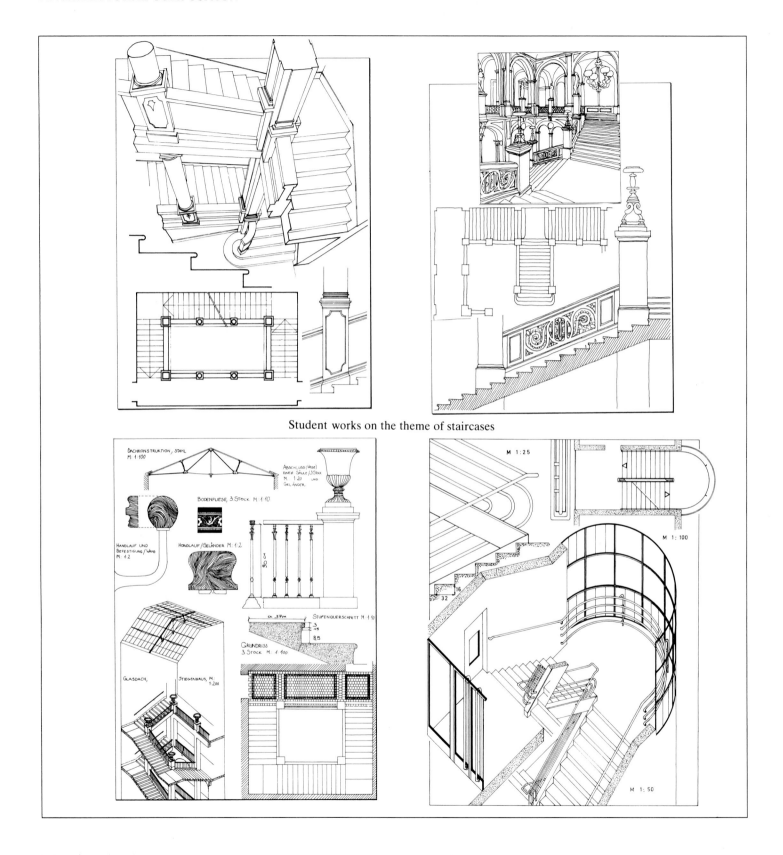

Student works on the theme of staircases

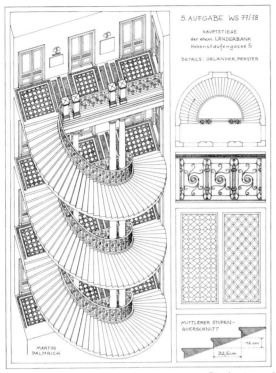

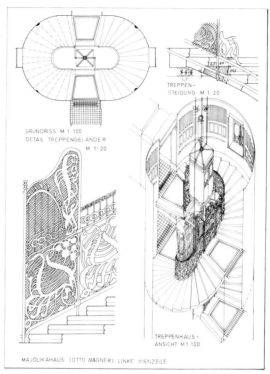

Student works on the theme of staircases

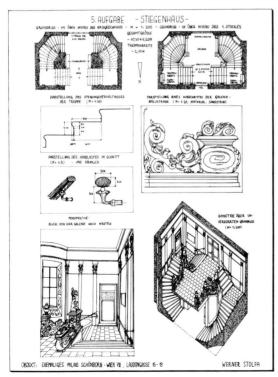

Staircase, Biedermeier period, Vienna, c. 1830

Staircase, Biedermeier period, Margarethenstrasse, Vienna, c. 1830

Spiral staircase and staff staircase, Post Office Savings Bank, Vienna, by O. Wagner, 1910-12

Staircase, Seilerstätte, Vienna, first half of nineteenth century

Entrance hall, Landstrasse, Vienna, by J. Brychta, 1862

Staircase, monastery near Vienna, by J. Kornhäusel, 1834-42

Former Bank, Hohenstaufengasse, Vienna, by O. Wagner, 1883-84

Staff staircase, Post Office Savings Bank, Vienna, by O. Wagner

'Majolikahaus', Rechte Wienzeile, Vienna, by O. Wagner, 1898

Building at Michaelerplatz, Vienna, by A. Loos, 1910

Neu Hofburg in the Heldenplatz, Vienna, planned by G. Semper from 1869, completed by L. Baumann

Facades

The facade is still the most essential architectural element capable of communicating the function and significance of a building. I say 'still', having in mind its theoretical destruction proclaimed in the twentieth century where the ideology of the free-standing object, visible from all sides, became predominant. The perfection of the building body had priority over the creation of a specific 'show-side' facing the street. It is only in recent years, after the rediscovery of the importance of the public realm and the value of urban life, that the facade regained a new valuation.

The facade never only fulfills the 'natural requirements' determined by the organisation of the rooms behind. It speaks of the cultural situation at the time when the building was built; it reveals criteria of order and ordering, and gives an account of the possibilities and ingenuity of ornamentation and decoration. A facade also tells us about the inhabitants of a building, gives them a collective identity as a community, and ultimately is the representation of the latter in public.

The root of the word 'facade' stems from the Latin 'facies' which is synonymous with the words 'face' and 'appearance'. Therefore, if we talk about the 'face' of a building, the facade, we mean above all the front facing the street. In contrast to that, the back is assigned to semi-public or private exterior spaces. Both these phenomena of front and back relate – roughly speaking – on the one hand to public responsibility and on the other hand to the private self-representation of the inhabitants. Compared with the more representative character of the street facade, the back of a building is more open and communicates with courtyard, garden and landscape.

The often-used framed facade made of light material and glazing is too standard in type and too abstract in character for housing developments. It does not allow for aesthetic differentiation and is too vulnerable and transparent. Such a 'skin facade' has nothing to do with the appropriate facade for a residential building, which should be more closed and concealing towards the street, in order to protect the private sphere of the inhabitants. All these requirements are still best met by the solid facade whose massive, protecting exterior wall is perforated by openings to let air and light penetrate into the interior of the building. Also, in terms of energy consumption the solid facade is without doubt much more appropriate, because its exterior wall has a higher thermal storage capacity. In Austria, the energy problems caused by glass facades have already been taken into account. In public buildings a smaller proportion of windows in a facade surface is allowed as compared with previous years. This proportion between opening and plane has at least stopped the unhindered development of curtain walls, and has helped the solid facade to gain new topicality.

The composition of a facade, taking into account the functional requirements (windows, door openings, sun protection, roof area) is essentially to do with the creation of a harmonious entity by means of good proportions, vertical and horizontal structuring, materials, colour and decorative elements. Since Vitruvius architects have been trying to develop metrical relations which would give an ideal order and structure to the facade – and also to floor plans and rooms. This was thought to be the way of achieving absolute beauty. Especially in the Renaissance, such attempts were referred to systems of numbers and rules of proportions. Plato's philosophy was taken as a basis, as were the thoughts of Neo-Platonism. Saint Augustine approved – and so Renaissance artists were thoroughly convinced that the whole universe was a mathematical and harmonious creation. By such thinking, rules were established which Wittkower describes as follows: '. . . If the laws of harmonic numbers pervade everything from the celestial spheres to the most humble life on earth, then our very souls must conform to this harmony . . .'*

But the aim of reaching a harmonious beauty cannot be achieved only in this way. One needs only to consider that the oblique view given from the bottom of a building, together with the constantly changing contrasts and effects of depth caused by light and shade, prevent us from perceiving such truly calculated proportions exactly. Nevertheless it seems very important to me to examine window proportions with the help of the Golden Section, and equally to study the proportions of opening and parapet, base and total height etc. This exercise will lead after a while to a 'natural' sense of pleasant, harmonious proportions, e.g. a well-balanced composition. It is the rhythm in architecture which, similar to music, arouses emotions in us. Therefore it is possible to transfer conceptions of musical theory directly to architectural composition. The polarities of tension-relaxation, event-interval, accord-contrast; the principle of repetition; the process of the theme being carried through in variations; all create the

Let us, for example, reflect on window openings which repeat themselves again and again, which in succession with the wall elements, create the contrasts of open-closed, dark-light, smooth and rough surfaces. At the same time because of periodical repetition they produce a quiet order and vary the same theme from storey to storey by way of – for instance – rhythmical diminution towards the top (appropriate because the light quality increases).

An important aspect of structuring the facade is to make a distinction between the horizontal and the vertical elements, each of which can, in themselves, create an adequate general effect. Normally the proportions of the elements should correspond to those of the whole. Accordingly in low broad buildings, windows, bays, etc., broad proportions would predominate, whereas in high buildings slender elements give a sense of the large being found in the small and the small being found in the large, as it is similarly experienced in nature.

Following the ordering principles of a facade, the constructional conditions can be made visible, e.g. by channelling the bearing forces into piers. This articulation of verticality would emphasise a particular effect of the facade. However, this is not to put construction too much into the foreground or to show every nail or joint, but to reveal the nature of construction and craftsmanship.

Besides construction there are many other things necessary in terms of function or simply narrative elements which add to the animation of the facade: window surroundings and lintels to articulate the independence of the windows, rain-pipes, shutters, roof projections which give shade, mate-

rials that emphasise the masses (rustication) or loosen them (reflecting marble), window boxes and Virginia creeper give the building a summer or winter appearance.

The horizontal layering of the facade results from the different areas of function. In principle, a facade should never be designed without horizontal differentiation. A clear differentiation is especially appropriate between the ground floor, the ordinary storeys and the attic. The facade as 'built border' acts in a similar way to the portal: in German the word for wall is 'Wand' which has to do with 'wenden' (to turn) or with 'Wandlung' (change); the wall is therefore the place where the exterior turns into the interior and vice versa. This transitional zone has the function of exchange, becoming more lively if the surface has a certain plasticity and if movement is evident. By way of wall projections, ledges and pilasters the plane of the surface develops three-dimensionality, becoming a relief, whereby

light and shadow, foreground and background, become perceptible.

The facade as a whole is composed of single elements, the latter being entities themselves with an expressive capability of their own. The composition of a facade, however, consists of structuring on the one hand and ordering on the other. The elements base, window, roof etc., which by their nature are different things, will also therefore be different in their forms, colours and materials. All these parts should remain recognisable individually, although the common language binding them to the whole has also to be found. However, not every means of connecting or matching is sensible: for instance to locate the upper edges of windows and doors in one line would contradict the different meanings they have. If the heights are staggered, the common factor could relate to similar proportions or shading gradations of a basic colour.

If we do not approach the design of a

facade as an autonomous work of art, but in context with adjacent historical facades, it is necessary to employ different elements which separate the new from the old as well as ones which join and connect both. Thus the choice of elements should first of all be related to the language of the historical facades. Parts of them, or particular aspects, will be taken across, a purporting continuity being achieved by such a thematic approach. But genuine continuity is only conceivable once the independent quality of the new facade, and its new conditions and demands are upheld. The relationship between old and new is in any case a dialogue, a conversation between the past and the present.

*Rudolf Wittkower, *Architectural Principles in the Age of Humanism*, Academy Editions, London 1988, p.38.

This plate shows fundamental possibilities for the design of a facade. First of all, with small sketches, I would like to again hint at the decisive role geometrical proportions play for the harmonious appearance of the facade (illustration 1). Considerations of this kind are, of course, not to be separated from the whole building body. If, because of a disadvantageous site or restrictive building regulations, an unsatisfactory solution of the facade will transpire, this can be at least partially prevented by careful composition, i.e. a deliberate zoning of the facade (illustration 2). Yet when applying this kind of deliberate zoning, harmonious geometrical proportions have to be paid attention to (illustration 3). By the distribution of windows in the facade, a particular effect can be emphasised or suspended (illustration 4). Here the possibilities range from a regular distribution of equal windows to an irregular and figurative arrangement. Windows can be combined in small groups to form particular figures, or they can divide the facade by being almost separate elements (illustrations 5 and 6).

While windows are the most important means of composition, the facade itself can be treated as a sculptural part of the building. Specific parts of the building can be exposed (illustration 7), whereby the foreground and the background of the facade are determined (illustration 8). The superimposition of different building parts is yet another subject of composition, which will be dealt with again in the section on the three-dimensional composition of a building (illustration 9).

——— ✳ ———

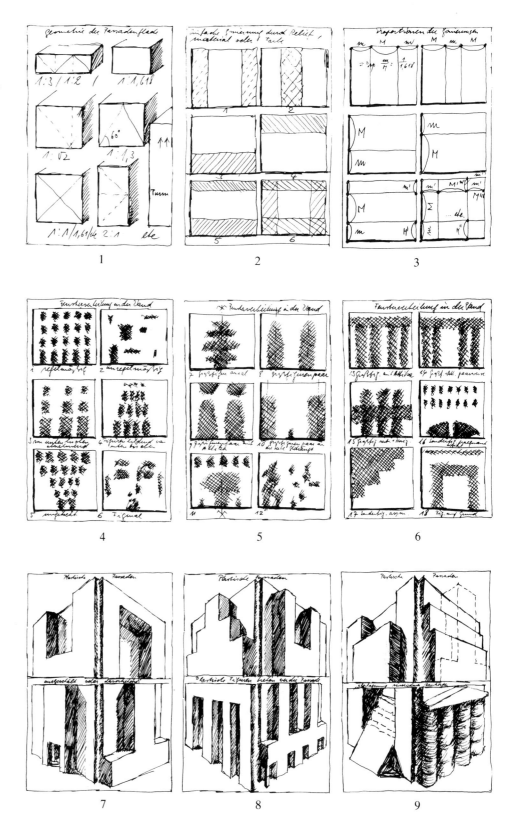

1

2

3

4

5

6

7

8

9

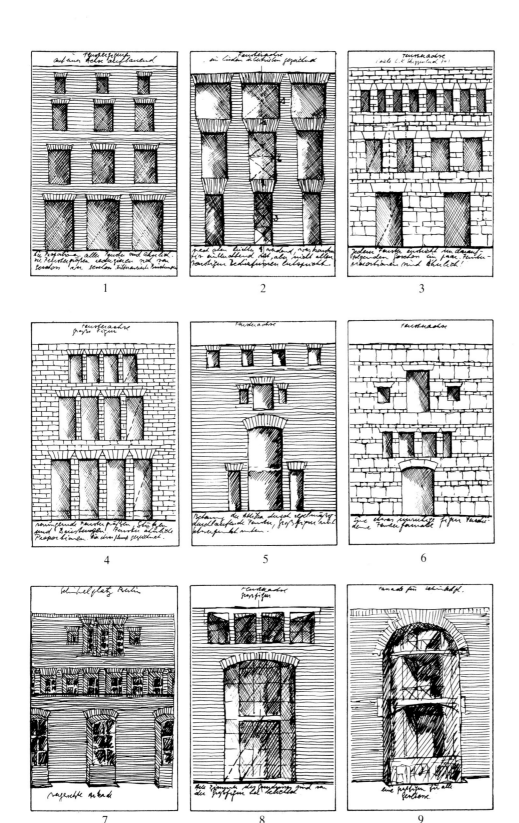

By means of the parts of elevations, shown here, the theme of facade figures running through vertically can be explained with examples.

Illustration 1: The distribution of windows is based on their axes. Similar window proportions are reduced in size according to storey. This motive underlines the perspective of the facade; it makes the building appear higher, and symbolises the need for more light penetration into the lower storeys of buildings in narrow streets.

Illustration 2: Here the windows increase in size which makes the facade appear lighter and symbolises its constructive logic.

Illustration 3: An almost 'mathematical' order is achieved by doubling the number of windows in each storey and, at the same time, by reducing their formats. Thus a very active facade provides nevertheless the same amount of opening space in each storey.

Illustration 4: Similar in appearance to the example shown in illustration 1, this figure, however, is not determined by the axes of the windows but by the grouping of windows together.

Illustration 5: A figure in an almost literal sense develops from this arrangement of windows, which is based on the coordination of different formats on one vertical axis. Here the emphasis lies on the entrance and the articulation of the attic by way of a regular series of equally sized windows.

Illustration 6: This uneasy figure has a rather casual effect composed of different window formats. It is important at this point to again call attention to the spatial effects of interior rooms which can lead to such figuration on the facade.

Illustration 7: A projected base with regular openings (instead of pilasters), allows for the zone above to employ a new, independent, organisation of windows. This is a popular motive in 'big city' architecture, where the ground floor has a separate meaning.

Illustration 8: One vertical element accumulates all necessary openings of the adjacent rooms.

Illustration 9: The same figure as the only opening element in the facade; a gigantic figure which runs through all storeys. The scale of the building must be able to cope with such a monumental opening.

These examples no longer show only parts of the facade. Slender high buildings are demonstrated in their total composition and serve for each theme.

Illustration 1: A regular window composition based on axes. From bottom to top increasing sizes of windows culminate in a large-scale top floor.

Illustration 2: Clear separation into three zones: the ground floor with large-scale openings; a middle area with windows regularly distributed; and a light skeletal storey.

Illustration 3: Here the sizes of the windows are dimensioned in a way that the wall surfaces are largely reduced to 'piers' and 'beams'. However, because the window sizes vary in each storey, one cannot call this type a skeleton facade.

Illustration 4: The old theme of the 'piano nobile', the main floor of a house, is emphasised here by a closed attic zone.

Illustration 5: The exterior flights of stairs give the ground floor a public character. The large studio windows of the top floor indicate a clear difference in valuation compared with the small windows of the intermediate storey.

Illustration 6: A large-scale hall of columns, almost like a 'stoa', constitutes a powerful order which can also conceal the irregular and lively interior of the building.

Illustration 7: Elegant, slender window slits are bound together by a constructional arch, and form a figure with the circular windows of the attic storey. Thus a serial motive becomes an image.

Illustration 8: The zoning of this facade resembles the 'building block' principle, with its different surfaces and window partitions. It gives the impression of relatively independent storeys being piled up.

Illustration 9: Here we have an irregular facade structured according to the interior organisation of spaces. One should not underestimate the difficulty of distributing windows this freely, because it requires adherence to quite precise proportions relating the openings to one another. Excellent taste can lead to a harmonious yet free design, but a 'secret' principle of order is also the foundation of these kinds of composition.

——— ✳ ———

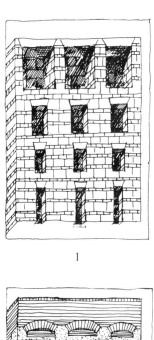

1

2

3

4

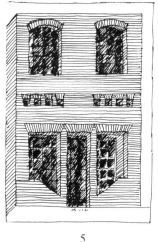

5

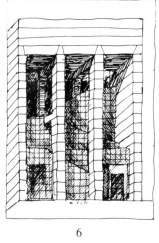

6

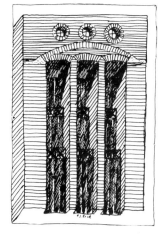

7

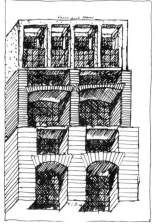

8

9

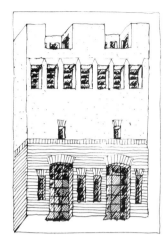

1

2

3

4

5

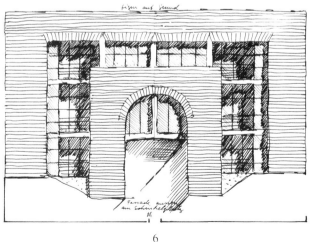

6

Complete compositions are also shown in this plate. They cannot be applied arbitrarily, but can reinforce the whole 'tendency' of a building.

Illustration 1: The base is clearly distinguished from the rest of the building by having a different surface. Because of the terraces being cut out from the attic storey, the building has a battlement-like termination.

Illustration 2: This facade figure unfolds from the bottom to the top like a tree-top or a goblet. One may also find that the significance of the individual storeys diminishes towards the top.

Illustration 3: Here a plastic figure, a portico, projects from the building whereby the entrance is clearly emphasised.

Illustration 4: In contrast to illustration 2, the facade figure tapers off towards the top. Oddly enough, although the order is reversed, we do not perceive a change in meaning. Probably it is the hierarchical structure of the facade as such which suggests a hierarchy of significance.

Illustration 5: A projected arcade is subdivided by a loggia on first floor level. A socially useful interspace is created, which almost gives the idea of theatrical staging.

Illustration 6: The gate motive in front of a largely glazed facade clearly demonstrates the problematic nature of the figure-ground relationship. The layering of the facade ranges from the opening of the gate, to the light background, until finally the surrounding frame of the building is reached.

———— ❈ ————

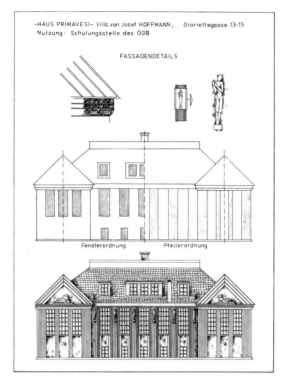

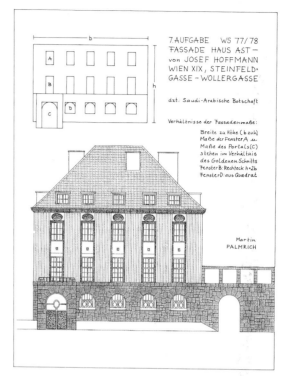

Student works on the theme of Facades

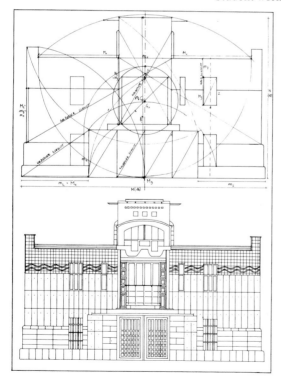

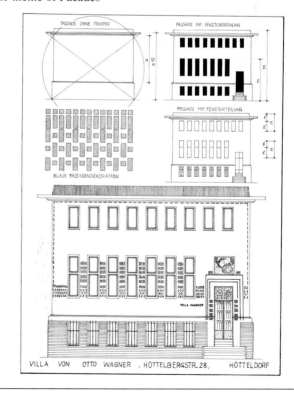

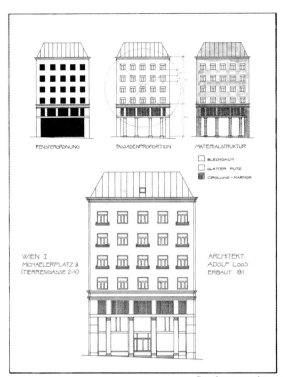

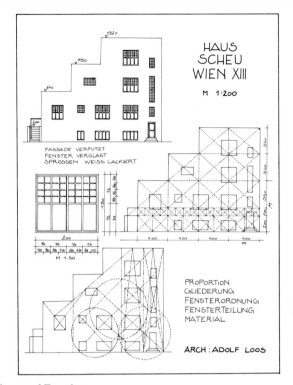

Student works on the theme of Facades

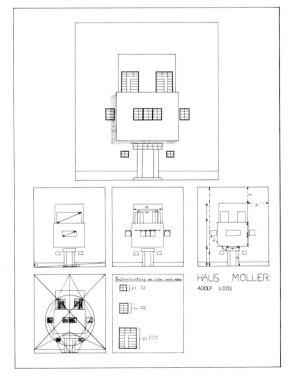

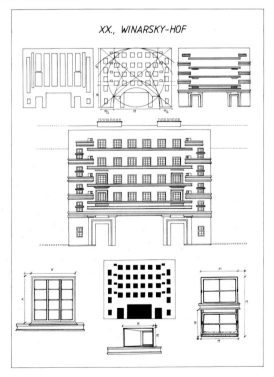

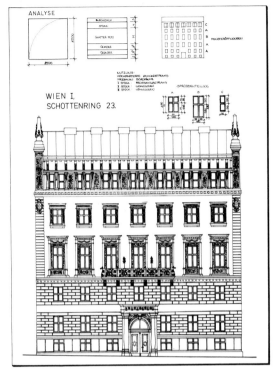

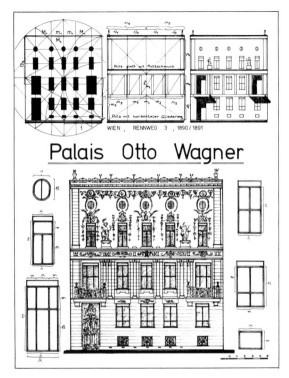

Student works on the theme of Facades

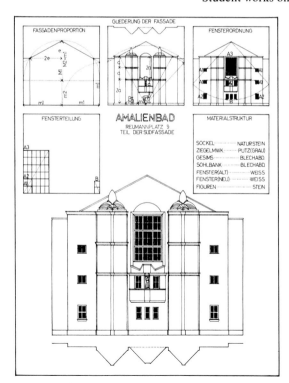

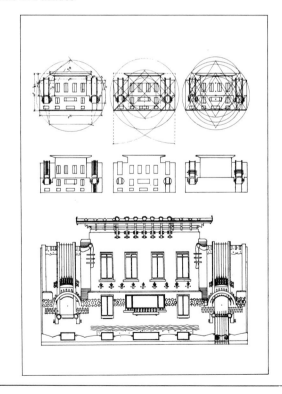

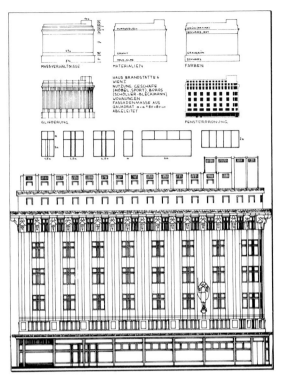

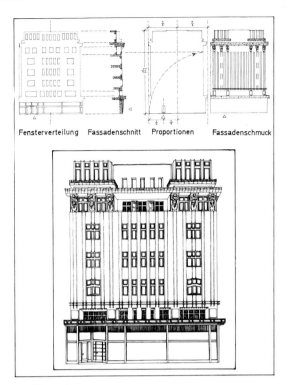

Student works on the theme of Facades

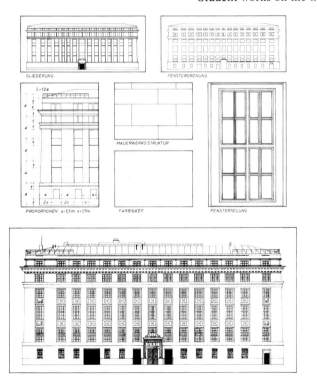

On the Layering of Masonry

By bonding individual stones together they become a steady wall. Large, heavy natural stones can be laid without mortar (dry stone walls). When the stones are smaller they must have smooth supporting surfaces and be bound with mortar and possibly also braced.

Technical perfection and aesthetic appeal go hand in hand – the more precision that goes into the laying of the stones, the greater the rewards in terms of formal quality. The following are examples – some of them historical – of different types of the mason's craft.

CYCLOPEAN MASONRY: Irregular, large blocks of stone are piled on top of each other, often without horizontal layering. Gaps and holes are plugged with lime or small stones. Examples: the Mycenaean era.

POLYGONAL MASONRY: This is a technical and aesthetic advance over Cyclopean masonry, in which polygonal blocks are arranged according to size and form. Example: old Italian cities.

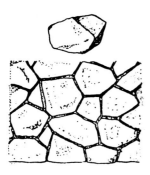

RUBBLE MASONRY: Rubble, the by-product of demolition, can be used for cellar or garden walls.

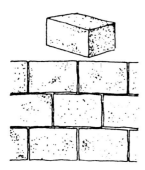

ASHLAR MASONRY: Consists of quarried stones with regular, parallel surfaces and mostly exact edges. The Egyptians used this type in their stone buildings. In addition, there are a number of special types with uneven visible faces.

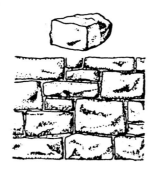

RUSTICATED MASONRY: Stones with rough-cut faces, a technique found in the ancient world, but particularly popular during the Early Renaissance.

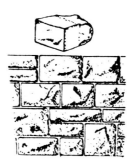

DIAMOND MASONRY: Here the visible faces of the stones are cut in the shape of a pyramid. Examples: Italian Renaissance.

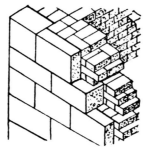

MIXED MASONRY: By this one understands a wall of brick or concrete block with a rubble or ashlar veneer. This technique has been used since the Middle Ages.

BRICKWORK: The brick is the foremost standard building component. Because it can be mass-produced, it can ensure the highest level of regularity. Examples: Mesopotamian high cultures, Roman brick building, Gothic.

BONDS: Bonds occur between alternating courses of stretchers and headers (block bond, cross bond) or in the rhythmic alternation of stretchers and headers in each course (Gothic, Flemish, Mark-Brandenburg). In figurative or decorative bonds the bricks have only a filling function (Roman mesh bond, textile patterns and plant motifs in Mesopotamian high cultures). In these cases, polychromy can be applied as an additional formal tool. Examples: Roman Tower, Cologne; Country wall, Constantinople; Arsenal, Vienna.

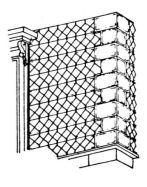

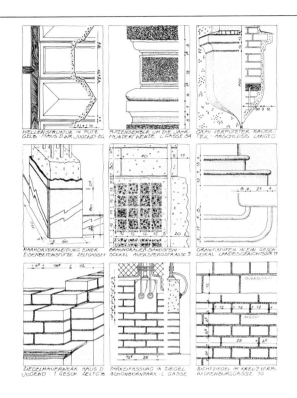

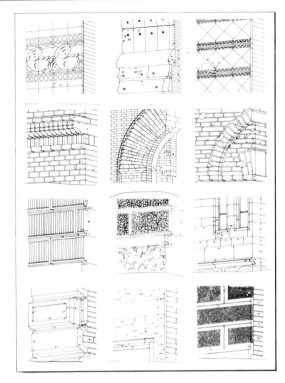

Student exercises on the theme of Masonry Structures

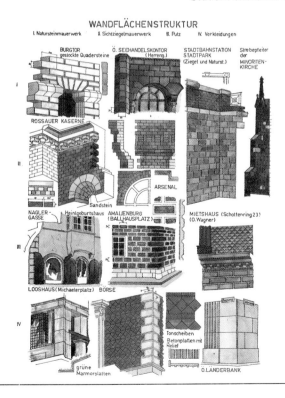

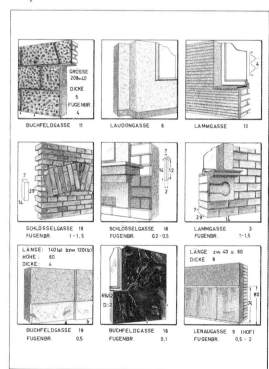

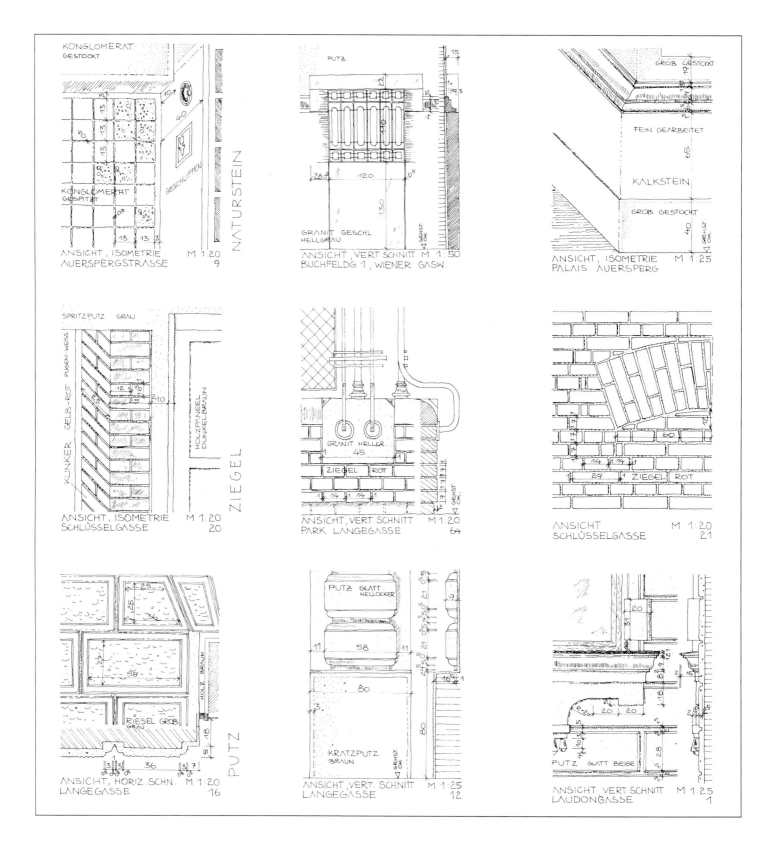

KONGLOMERAT GESTOCKT

KONGLOMERAT GESPITZT

GESCHLIFFEN

NATURSTEIN

ANSICHT, ISOMETRIE   M 1:20
AUERSPERGSTRASSE   9

PUTZ

GRANIT GESCHL
HELLGRAU

ANSICHT, VERT. SCHNITT M 1:50
BUCHFELDG. 1, WIENER GASW.

GROB GESTOCKT

FEIN GEARBEITET

KALKSTEIN

GROB GESTOCKT

ANSICHT, ISOMETRIE   M 1:25
PALAIS AUERSPERG

SPRITZPUTZ GRAU

KLINKER GELB-ROT FUGEN WEISS

HOLZPANEEL
DUNKELBRAUN

ZIEGEL

ANSICHT, ISOMETRIE   M 1:20
SCHLÜSSELGASSE   20

GRANIT HELLGR.
45

ZIEGEL ROT

ANSICHT, VERT. SCHNITT M 1:20
PARK LANGEGASSE   64

ZIEGEL ROT

ANSICHT   M 1:20
SCHLÜSSELGASSE   21

HOLZ BRAUN

RIESEL GROB
GRAU

PUTZ

ANSICHT, HORIZ. SCHN. M 1:20
LANGEGASSE   16

PUTZ GLATT
HELLOCKER

KRATZPUTZ
BRAUN

ANSICHT, VERT. SCHNITT M 1:25
LANGEGASSE   12

PUTZ GLATT BEIGE

ANSICHT, VERT. SCHNITT M 1:25
LAUDONGASSE   1

Wood as a wall veneer

Wood as a floor covering

Wood and glass panel construction

Monolithic stone construction

Rough-cut rusticated masonry

Sandstone and brick

Geometrically profiled rusticated masonry

Marble steps, exterior

Marble steps, interior

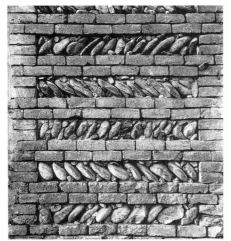

Brick with *Wacken*

Bricks of various sizes

Brick and sandstone

Plaster pillars, wood balconies, roof tiles

Bolster masonry

Granite, concrete and plaster

Rough and smooth plaster

Steel structure

Masonry with marble and ceramic veneer

Entrances and Portals

On the way from the street into a building one passes through different gradations of what can be called 'the public'. Immediately, the position of the entrance and the architectonic significance it is given demonstrate the role and function of the building. Thus the main entrance of a large public building would not be a tiny hole located somewhere where nobody would find it. Equally it would be inappropriate for a modest house to be approached by a representational drive or large-scale flights of stairs.

The portal marks the transition from the public exterior to the private interior. It is an element of self-representation for the inhabitants. The route from the portal to the vertical means of access forms an individual space or series of spaces; this fact is much too seldom taken into account.

Portals and entrances have nowadays been mostly degraded to residual spaces. They merely suffice the requirements of building regulations. Uppermost in perversity is the combination of the entrance for vehicles – into a courtyard or underground car park – with the entrance into the build-

ing. For the pedestrian, only a narrow path along the wall is left. Thus, by passing the rubbish containers, one hurries to the safe apartment door, swearing at the dirty and devastated entrance; and what else can be expected from such a built reality?

Other bad examples are the so-called entrance halls of the modern centres of power; the office towers and insurance palaces. We find an open ground floor, flattened by the load of the ascending storeys, and awkwardly structured by wall partitions, greenery, mural pictures and orientation boards. Without all this crap, the entrance hall would be just an area without meaning. One should ask a visitor leaving one of these places whether or not he could remember the space. He would not even understand the question. For this reason the following examples of student works have been chosen which clearly demonstrate the spatial qualities of entrance areas.

A notable example is the solution for the entrance to the former 'Länderbank' by Otto Wagner. The round vestibule, which is non-directional, acts as a distributor. Three different areas (banking hall, entrance and

main staircase) are thus held together. A richly decorated Art Nouveau portal is illustrated next. As the actual door into the building is recessed, an ante-space is created which is made into a porch.

The Palais des Beaux Arts shows an interesting sequence of spaces. A round vestibule prepares the visitor for the following architectural event. A small flight of stairs narrows the space, which then opens into an irregular hexagon. After this landing, which is separated from the actual stairwell by wall projections, the route terminates in a staircase which ascends in three flights. There were times when even the entrance areas to blocks of council flats received the necessary design attention. This is clearly visible in the example of a Viennese 'Gemeindehaus' from the years between the wars. The portal is emphasised by a frame of bricks. A spacious porch opens into a proper vestibule with inviting bottom steps of a staircase and two doors; one giving access to the house, the other leading into the courtyard. Here a simple entrance has been turned into an enjoyable meeting place.

Vestibule of a house with Doric columns, Vienna, 1830

Entrance to a house in Resselgasse, Vienna, by J. Kornhäusel, early eighteenth century

Veranda and staircase, house in Resselgasse, Vienna, by J. Kornhäusel, eighteenth century

Entrance hall of bourgeois residential building, Vienna, c. 1900

Entrance hall to a townhouse in Vienna, c. 1900

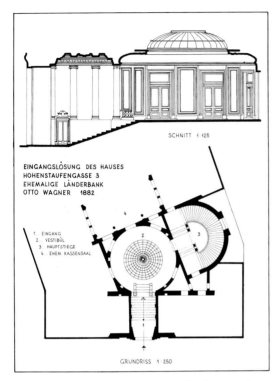

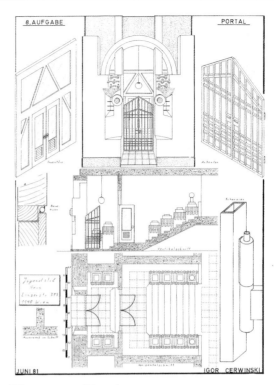

Student works on the theme of Entrances and Portals

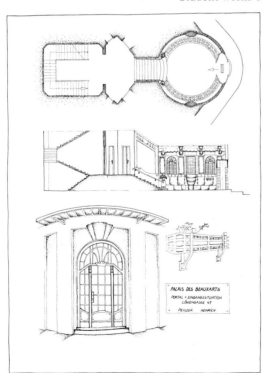

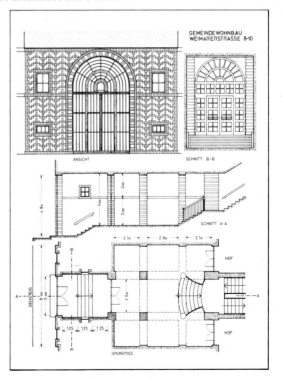

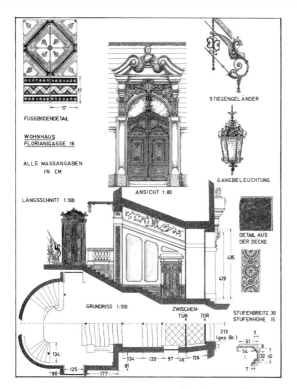

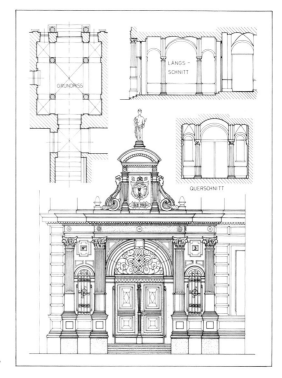

Student works on the theme of Entrances and Portals

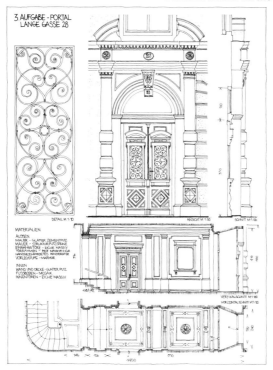

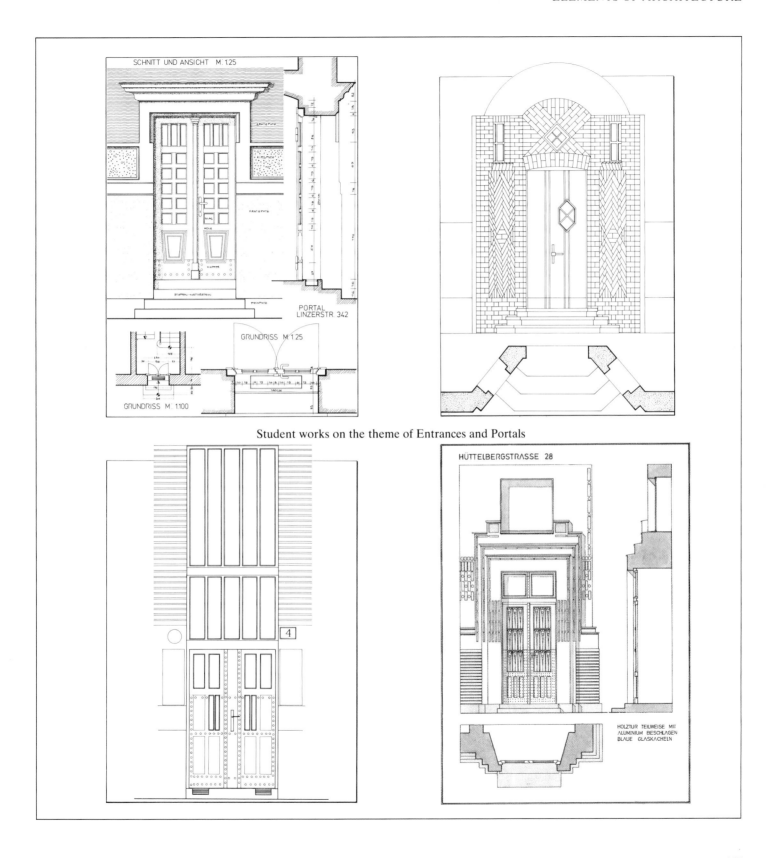

Student works on the theme of Entrances and Portals

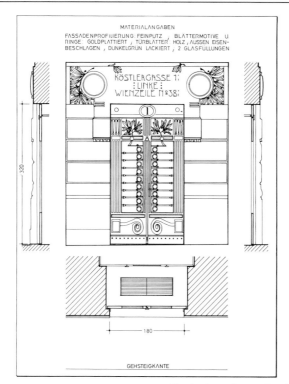

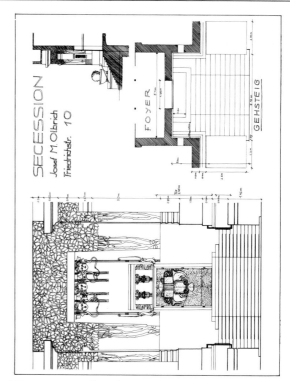

Student works on the theme of Entrances and Portals

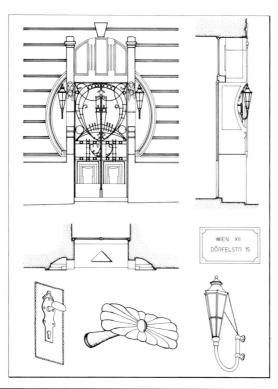

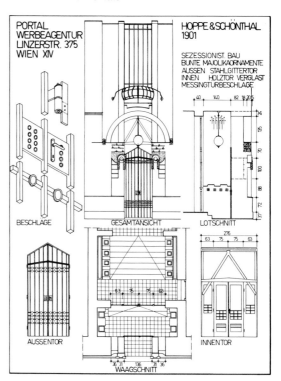

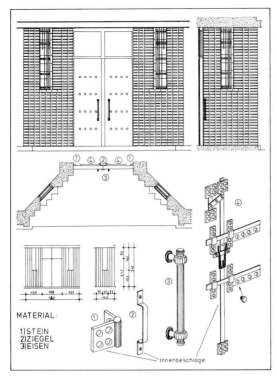

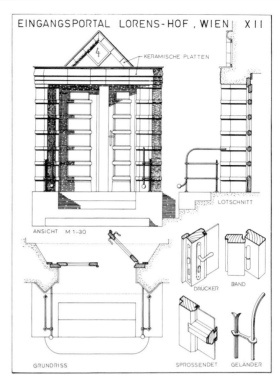

Student works on the theme of Entrances and Portals

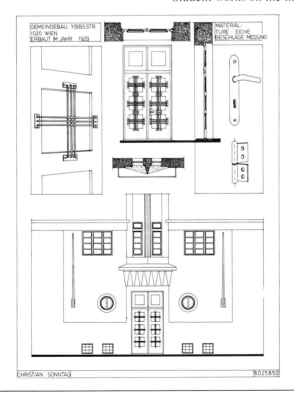

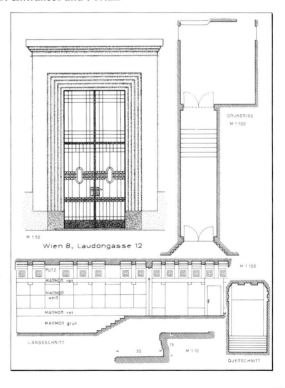

Villa Pisani, Montagnana, by A. Palladio, 1552

Palais Pallavicini, Vienna, by F. von Hohenberg, 1783-84

Secession Building, Vienna, by J. M. Olbrich, 1898

Mausoleum, San Vito de Altievole, by Carlo Scarpa, c. 1970

Villa della Torre in Fumane, the Veneto

Rosenburg Castle in Lower Austria, late sixteenth century

Old Währing Cemetery in Vienna by Korompay, 1827

Portal to a factory in Krumnussbaum, Lower Austria

Arcades

Who owns the arcades? Are they related to the street or the building? Or do they even belong to the pavement, creating its proper space? The arcade is determined by this ambivalence of application, but it is also an intermediate space which can be used and interpreted in many different ways. It can fulfil semi-public functions by being projected in front of a building whereby the user is neither outside nor inside the building. But the space of the arcade is also capable of assuming an independent public role. It can almost grow into the building behind, and thereby become an arcaded building. Finally there are examples where, in the course of time, arcades have been filled in or walled up in order to gain additional space. (When old buildings are in the process of being restored, hidden arcades are often found behind plaster and brick walls.)

The arcade is a collective urban element. For its construction, it is necessary not only to gain the agreement of the neighbours in the particular street affected, but also to gain the permission, and even the instruction, of the building authorities. Once the arcade is built it becomes an individual urban element which is largely understood to be independent from the building behind. The reason why there are so few arcades built today is probably due to a lack of common sense when it comes to the determination of common urban elements. However, the usefulness and enrichment of the arcade for urban life has been proved for centuries.

———— ✳ ————

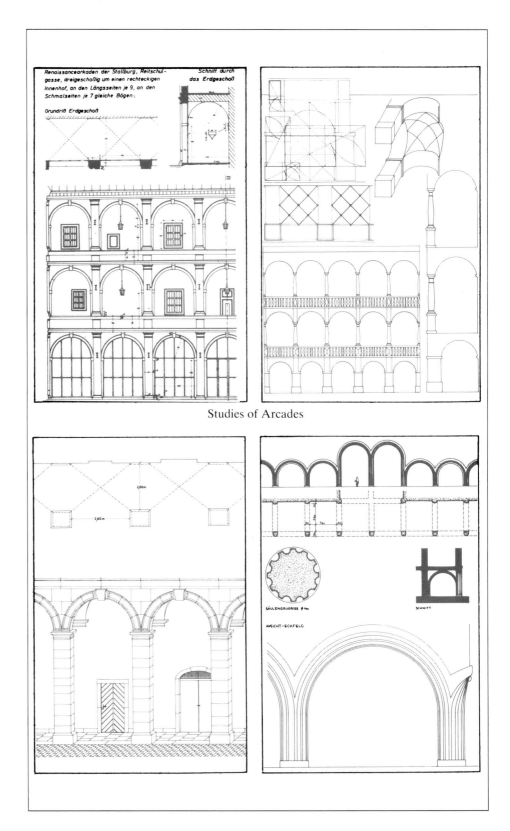

Studies of Arcades

Studies of Ground Floors

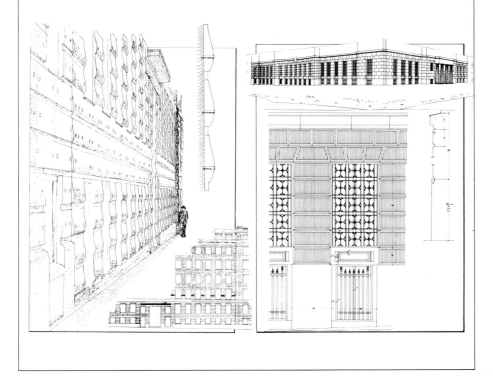

Ground Floors

The base for a building, its ground floor zone, is without doubt the most important urban element of a facade. As it constitutes the transition to the ground, or the pavement, it is exposed to considerable strain, and therefore the material used for this zone is usually more durable than that used for the rest of the building.

The ground floor has a particular importance in urban life. Because this area is most directly perceived by people, it often serves for the accommodation of shops and other commercial enterprises. Given the nature of business, such a ground floor zone is also subjected to frequent change, especially in terms of its fittings. It is to be recommended therefore that the ground floor be given a robust, neutral structure which can cope with 'parasitical architecture' such as shop fittings. The examples here show different kinds of bases. They range from neutral backgrounds for large openings to buildings with a rejecting, even closed, character, whose ground floors do not, for some reason, have a public function.

— ✳ —

Palazzo dei Diamanti, Ferrara, sixteenth century

Bologna Town Hall

House in Lastenstrasse, Vienna, by R. Oerley, 1907

Base of a campanile in Comacchio, by Emilia Romagna

Bay-windows, Balconies and Loggias

Similar to arcades, bay-windows, balconies and loggias are to be seen as independent spatial units. They are in any case genuine enlargements of the apartment, providing a sense of stepping out of the building – out of the facade – although still being in the private realm. In addition to that, these elements allow for a better view of urban life; they open up 'new prospects' in the true sense of the word.

To a greater extent than the balcony, bay-windows and loggias also represent an enrichment of the interior space which lies behind, because they divide it into spaces of different value.

Another important argument in favour of bay-windows and loggias stresses their climatic function. They form a buffer zone to the exterior, which is of great advantage in terms of the energy consumption of the apartment. Experiments with winter gardens and projected conservatories have revealed interesting results which, although known long ago, were largely ignored in the recent period of energy wastage. After the last war, when only a few households were equipped with refrigerators, these parts of a building were often used for the storage of food during the winter. Even the intermediate space between double glazed windows also served for this purpose.

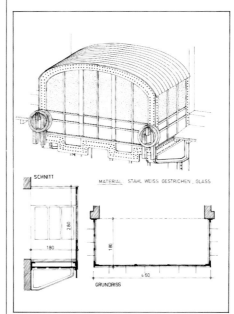

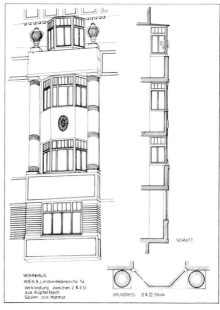

Student works on the theme of Bay-Windows, Balconies, Loggias

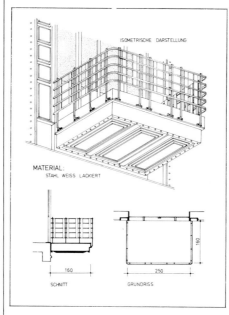

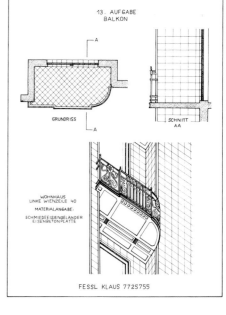

———— ✳ ————

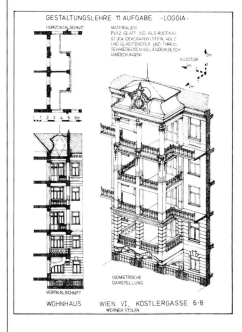

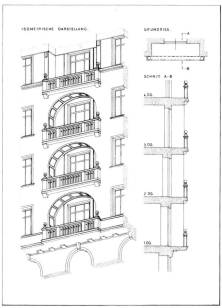

Student works on the theme of Bay-Windows, Balconies, Loggias

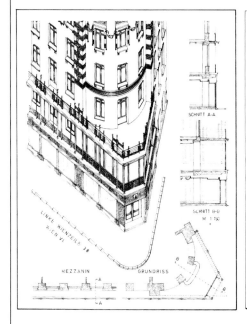

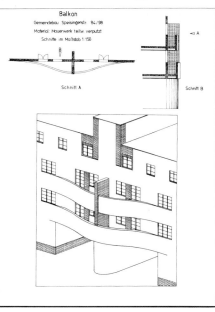

Two variants of bays are shown in illustrations 1 and 2. The bay-window in Otto Wagner's 'Schützenhaus' in Vienna (illustration 1) is conceived as a little building on its own; a pulpit above the river. Another building in Vienna reveals a bay element which vertically reaches over the entire facade creating the motive of a small building which is projected from a large one (illustration 2). The two balconies shown in illustrations 3 and 4 are remarkable in terms of their painstaking, constructional treatment of the soffit.

Bay-windows, balconies and loggias are also very suitable for the functional structure of the facade. However, it goes without saying that these elements should not be distributed on the surface at random. I would recommend a concentration over several storeys.

The loggias shown in illustrations 1 and 2 are examples of representational building projections. The loggia in illustration 1 measures nearly three square metres and thereby almost resembles the size of a proper room. This clearly invites possible use as a room. In contrast to that, the arches dominating the loggias in illustration 2 constitute a representational frame, and more likely only invite the inhabitants to have a brief glance at the street. Here, the interior space is probably much more important, with the loggia serving as an additional filter of the exterior. Especially at the times when the French windows are open would it suggest an optical enlargement of the room behind.

The degree to which these kinds of elements are also appropriate for the articulation of an important part of the building is shown in illustrations 3 and 4. The contour of a street corner is taken up again by the first two storeys of a corner building (illustration 3). But, as the angled rooms do not seem to be very suitable for apartments, the corner is interrupted by a cylinder which provides space for a terrace and, in addition, monumentalises the corner of the building, especially when viewed from a distance. The big 'hole' in the facade of the 'Gemeindehaus' (illustration 4) achieves a positive meaning by way of curved balconies, which have the effect of modulating the building mass.

———— ✳ ————

Biedermeier house, Josephsstadt district, Vienna

House in Maximiliansstrasse, Munich

Kaiserbad Dam, Vienna, by O. Wagner, 1906-07

House in Penzingerstrasse, Vienna, early twentieth century

Pavilion, Charlottenburg Castle, Berlin, by K. F. Schinkel, 1824-25

Glazed loggia in Pötzleinsdorferstrasse, Vienna, c. 1900

House at No. 15 Steingasse, Vienna

Public housing in Vienna, by Chartelmüller, 1928

Railings

While this theme appears at this point in the book, it is relevant to many other spatial problems, as shown by these examples drawn from the most diverse parts and spaces of buildings.

One could start by saying that a railing is necessary wherever there is some danger to using a space. It is also a physical barrier that can be set up where the use of the space must be restricted if social conventions are to be upheld. On top of these problems of danger and ordering comes the rather harmless requirement of defining space.

This makes a minimum of three requirements which can determine the form of a railing. The ordering role of a railing – although there 'fence' might be a more appropriate term – is illustrated by the fact that the police vetoed a proposal to remove the railings in the Volksgarten park, which lied between the Ringstrasse and the most important government buildings in Vienna,

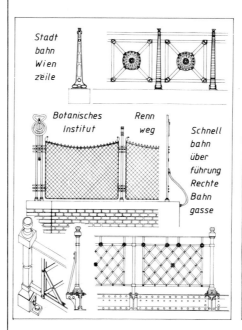

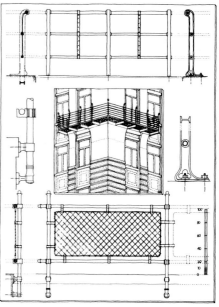

Studies of Railings

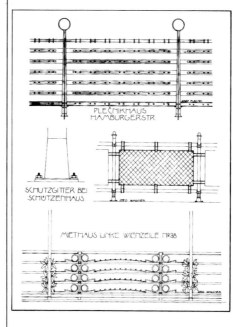

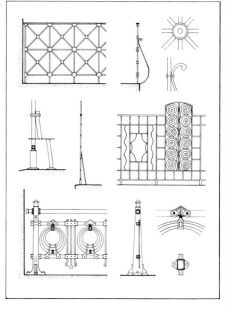

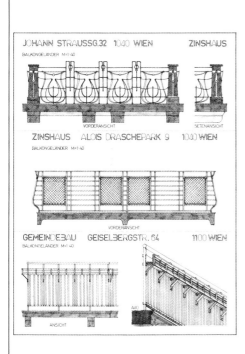

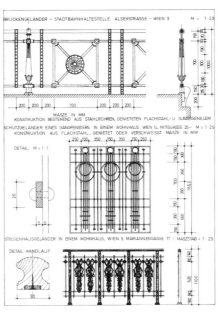

Studies of Railings

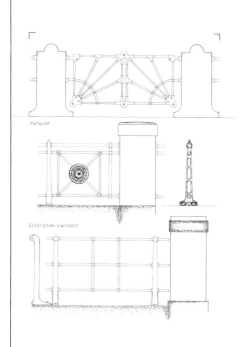

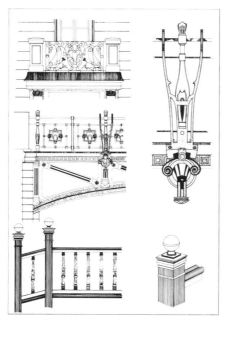

on the grounds that unruly demonstrations might get too close to the centre of power. However these social problems should not concern us anymore here: in any case, it is no longer the architect's responsibility to build fences to preserve State order. (The use of architecture as an ordering factor is muchmore subtle now.)

Let us therefore stick with the simple railing that fences off a space to protect the user. We must decide whether this runsalong a path, and so requires a continuous hand rail, or whether it just marks a boundary, and does not have to provide support. These factors can also determine the design. The finest and most appropriate material for railings is still iron, with wire mesh, a flexible combination of stability and transparency. All other materials are limited in comparison. The examples illustrated here show the many options available for binding and connecting railings: it is up to the architect to use these to the full.

———— ✳ ————

Castle Bridge in East Berlin, by K. F. Schinkel, 1819-24

Schlosspark Bridge, Laxenburg, near Vienna, nineteenth century

Castle Rudolf, Vienna, by Th. von Hansen, 1872

Post Office Savings Bank, Vienna, by O. Wagner, 1904-06

Garden fence in Mauer-Öhling, Lower Austria

Augarten Bridge in Vienna, by H. Gessner, 1929-31

Staircase, Klosterneuburg Monastery, by J. Kornhäusel, 1836-42

Detail of a Venetian bridge

Railing, Parliament Building, Vienna, by Th. von Hansen, 1873-87

Railing on the Kaiserbad Dam, Vienna, by O. Wagner, 1906-07

Stair railing, Loos House, Michaelerplatz, Vienna, 1910

House at No. 3 Döblergasse, Vienna, by O. Wagner, 1912

Railing in the Vestibule of the house at No. 3 Döblergasse, by O. Wagner, 1912

Roof and Attic Storey

Nowadays one apparently only comes across two types of roofs: the flat roof, and the normal pitched roof. We should look at the variety of possibilities and meanings that this important part of the building has, bearing in mind that it is a building's termination towards the sky. The meanings which language attaches to roofs are very instructive. For instance, the term 'roof landscape': it rises from the buildings like a skin and, overtopped by higher silhouettes or public buildings, this artificial thing becomes a second plane between sky and earth. In general, the roof involves an ambiguous, undefined space which nowadays is mostly sacrificed to a radical exploitation of the building volume. But we should not completely forget this reservoir of secrets and memories. Here the objects of the past, the history of the inhabitants, and therefore that of the building itself are preserved.

For all this there is a simple explanation. The attic is a free place, a residual space, a storeroom, a play area for children. It is often full of corners, mostly dark and dusty, the opposite of the exterior world. The roof is the crown of the building, the evidence of its meaning showing the pride and dignity of the building itself.

The crown is carried by the building body. Visually it is the termination of the facade, often with an attic storey inserted, by which device the roof is withdrawn from people's eyes. Therefore the top floor zone, the attic storey, is much more important for the design and composition of the facade than the actual roof.

The facade is protected from the weather by a cornice, or by any other projecting moulding. On top of these could be a small balustrade – as if there was a terrace behind – to hide the mysterious roof. At important points the attic storey is broken through by domes and towers which simply have the purpose of 'crowns'.

The necessity of the attic storey being treated in a special way, in terms of form and function, results from the simple fact that a building has a top and a bottom. The bottom is the base which has to communicate its particular relationship with the earth. At the top everybody should know that the building ends there.

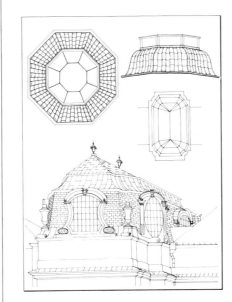

Student works on the theme of Roofs and Attics

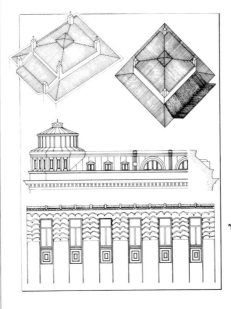
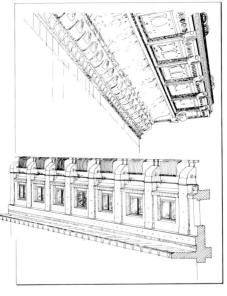

Basilica in Vicenza, by A. Palladio, 1546-49

Cathedral in Ferrara, after 1135

Bourgeois residential building at Dannebergplatz, Vienna

Castello Sforzesco in Milan

'Ankerhaus' in Graben, Vienna, by O. Wagner, 1895

Palm House in the 'Burggarten', Vienna, F. Ohmann, c. 1900

Ground-Plan and Building Form

A long-standing error in contemporary architecture is the belief that there is a logical connection between the function and the form of a building; or even that the latter is a result of the former. But as this irrevocable equation of a direct analogy of function and space, or form, is non-existent, an attempt was made to create an auxiliary theory which ended in a diffused, vague definition and vindication of architecture. Seemingly the infinite possibilities which lie in the relationship of function and form were not understood in a positive way. No ground-plan or building can be traced back directly to a function. Always in architecture, certain 'types of spaces' will be applied. They are ultimately relatively independent from the initially required function which existed at the beginning of the planning process.

Therefore let us assume that the design of a building develops from the interdependence of the requirements of the users – the functions – and the types of spaces which are provided by architecture. Requirements alone do not make a building. If so, all doors would be opened to 'hypertrophic ferocity' and the disruption of buildings.

The majority of functions and ground-plans are easily capable of being related to simple types if the rules and procedures of function are understood. Within itself, every type provides enough freedom of design. Experience shows that with the clarity and simplicity of the ground-plan, and the form of a building, the possibilities of different uses increase.

Quite frequently, the argument is put forward that confinement to precise building types would restrict the individuality of architectural design. But it is exactly this excessive individuality which leads to the nowadays much lamented wildness in architecture and its lack of conception.

In contrast, the examples which follow show the possibilities of individual differentiation of buildings with similar ground-plans. An additional aid in the design of a building is the analysis of the topographical and typological situation of the surroundings, and the tradition of the respective area. In principle, one should always presume that every site has its own social and historical meaning. To discover, and to in-

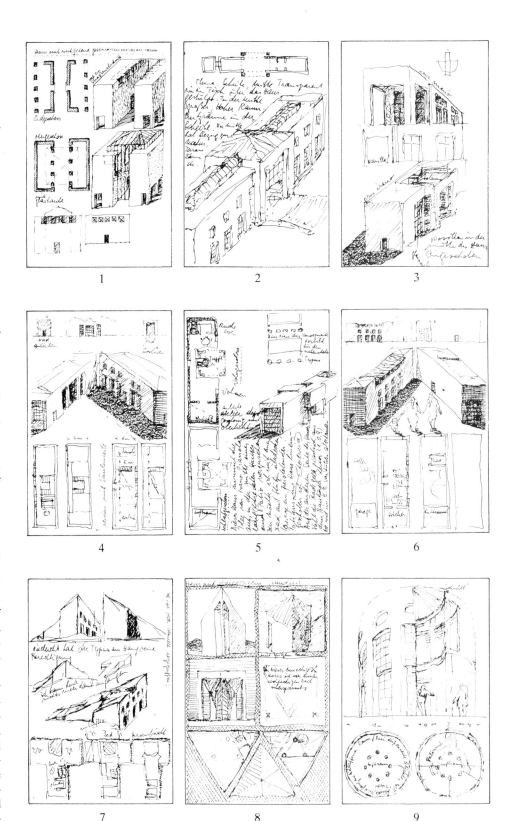

1   2   3

4   5   6

7   8   9

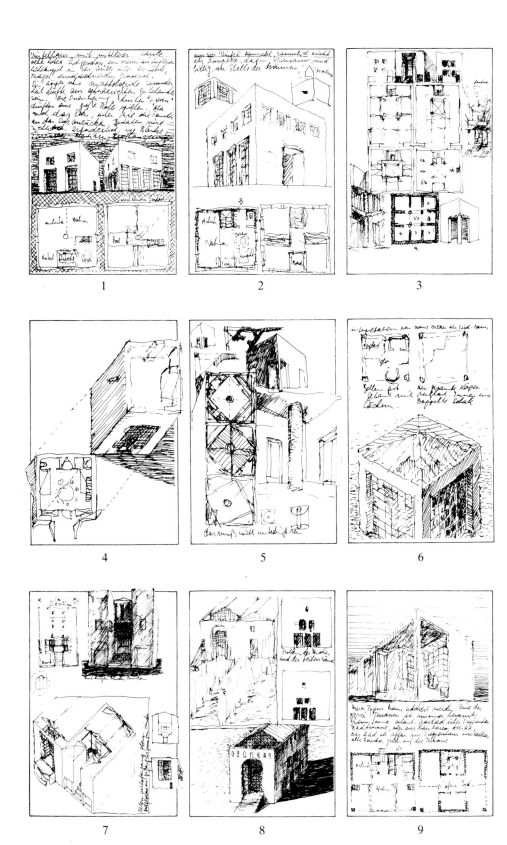

1

2

3

4

5

6

7

8

9

vestigate, its implications is a pre-condition for the cultural understanding of an architectural design. Every place has its specific conditions and its history. People have given meaning to even the most desolate prairie, the seemingly untouched desert, and the most inaccessible mountain areas. Legends and myths do exist, and certain places evoke associations for many people. No place is a virgin piece of land.

The choice of the building type and the building form is dependent on these general specific conditions, which mean more than mastering the requirements of a building's future inhabitants and its architectural possibilities. Without taking into account the complex situation of a particular site, a building is merely a trivial throw-away product; and without the involvement of the cultural heritage, every solution must remain individualistic and arbitrary.

The art of architecture, the decision on the building type and the design of the building itself, begin with the deliberate superimposition of the conditions of the place with the requirements of the inhabitants. If he takes these pre-conditions seriously, every honest architect will therefore quickly consider a simple, understandable and appropriate building type.

Development and Composition
Every ground-plan should be conceived and developed in relation to space. Here, often from the client's side, the first obstacles to understanding occur, because he is normally inexperienced in spatial imagination. But there is a useful rule of thumb which might help in this situation: at the beginning of a building process, the architect should never confuse or overwhelm the client. Simple geometrical basic forms also provide sufficient possibilities for spatial surprise. This kind of discipline excludes much unnecessary estrangement, because it involves concrete experience and understanding.

Then the work on the form of the building can be started. Once its rough contours are visible, the requirements of refining become the next step. Openings are brought into a rhythm, and are combined to form a motive; exterior spaces, such as terraces, balconies or loggias are added, not as missing pieces, but as a kind of second layer to the building.

The most important problem when designing a building is probably the determination of the line which has to be drawn between interior and exterior space. At this point, the whole range of possibilities of how to create an appropriate transition from the private sphere to the public realm comes into question. A change in conception occurs whereby these two different spaces have to be taken into consideration. In contrast to a much cherished ideology of architects advocating the unlimited transition of interior and exterior, the user in general knows very well where to draw the line between these spaces.

Square Buildings

For the study of simple geometrics related to the conception of residential buildings, I would like first of all to talk about the square. The following three plates will deal with this basic form and will show how it allows for the manipulation of the space within. The most decisive question which arises when designing square rooms is probably what to do with the centre; whether to fill it in or to keep it void. The square Roman house had its fireplace exactly in the centre, whereas the entrance was of minor importance, and therefore situated in a corner of the building.

As a geometrical object, the cube most clearly communicates the notion of enclosure and also the symbol of stability. The cube therefore, among the Platonic solids, symbolises the earth.

The sub-divisions and fragmentations shown in the following plates should first of all be understood independently of function and use. They simply state principal formal possibilities which give rise to definable rules of how to solve the conflict of enclosure and division, and, by way of interior structure, how spatial effects are changed.

To commence the sequence we can consider the all-round enclosure, which is orientated towards the centre, where the similarity of division is emphasised by a pier (illustrations 1 and 2). Spatial focus is mainly determined by the position of the staircase. This is the case in the building shown in illustration 3 despite the living areas running through. Illustration 4 demonstrates the superimposition of a circulation axis with a

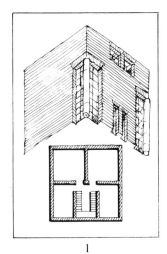

1

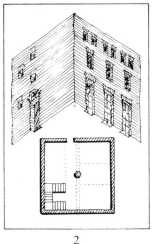

2

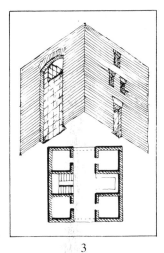

3

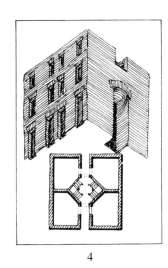

4

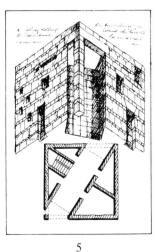

5

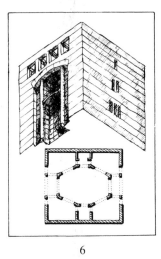

6

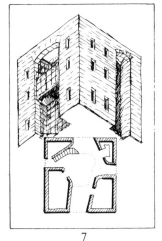

7

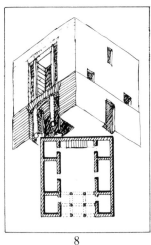

8

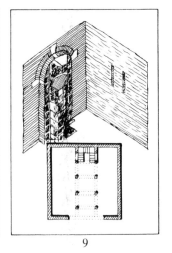

9

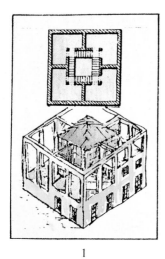

1

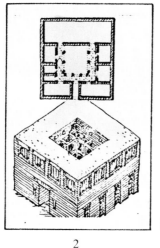

2

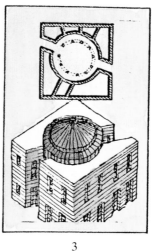

3

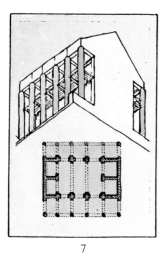

4

5

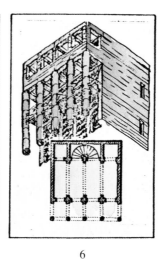

6

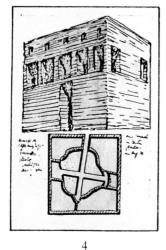

7

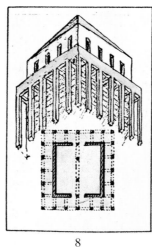

8

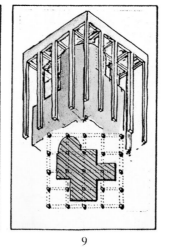

9

central staircase, by which device the centre of the building is clearly determined. Illustration 5 concerns a directional division, by which the building is sub-divided into two, or several, zones representing different spatial valuations. A common practice is to sub-divide the building into a main zone and two subsidiary zones (illustration 6), whereby the main space can have its own geometry to emphasise its particular position. The interior fragmentation of a solid appears in illustration 7. The square remains by way of its bordering lines, but in terms of its interior, it allows for complete freedom of spatial arrangement. Thus the square is left recognisable only when viewed from the outside.

Illustrations 8 and 9 show examples of one-directional space. One side of the square is accentuated by a large opening and thus constitutes the main side, the facade, of the building.

The centralised vertical arrangement within a cube is divided into quarter segments, each of which starts at a different height (illustration 1). The shape of the square is repeated in the gap between the stairs in the central well. This method is also applied in principle in the next example (illustration 2), where the centre is constituted by an atrium.

As with all other simple geometrical forms, the square can also be superimposed on other forms. Illustration 3 shows a cube being cut through yet having a central hall. The contrast between solid and amorphous basic forms, that is between hard and soft, results in exciting spaces (illustration 4).

Different forms within a composition appear to be punched out (illustration 5), whereby the residual spaces – with walls of different thickness – disregard the overall shape of the enclosure.

The gradual disintegration of the square is shown in illustrations 6 and 9. Only piers remain of the basic geometrical form, so a second spatial layer develops, which is useful for the mediation of interior and exterior.

The square in general, being a neutral and non-directional basic form, asks for dialectical contrasts, like a frame which surrounds changing images. So the inner spaces themselves can be created as geometrical forms, or they can follow the lines of movement within a building.

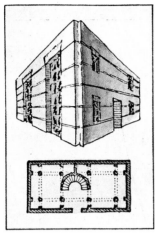

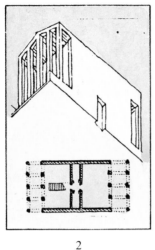

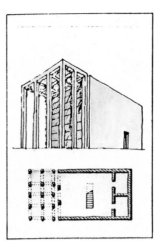

1   2   3

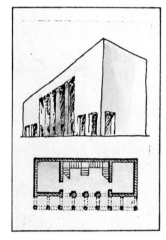

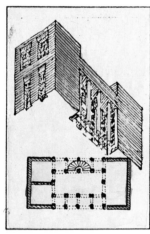

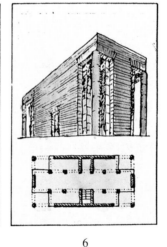

4   5   6

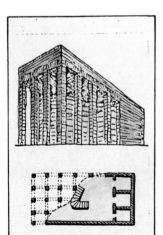

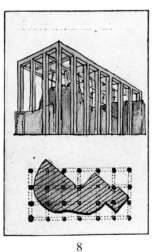

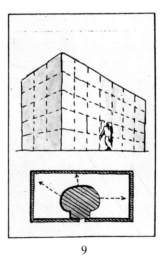

7   8   9

The examples of this plate show super-impositions of solid and skeletal building parts. Columns are never only constructional elements, as they always create an independent spatial layer or an additional ordering factor to the structure of a space. Therefore the rhythm of piers has to be well-considered.

In illustration 1 we have an interior structure which is constituted by piers and pilasters. This sub-division almost directly provokes a certain valuation and use of the spaces created; main and subsidiary spaces become obvious.

The examples in illustrations 2 and 4 show the fragmentation of rectangular solids by way of projected loggias. In illustration 5 the middle part of a building is loosened to become a central hall, the two remaining corner towers forming prominent terminations to the building.

A lively combination of solid and skeleton building parts ensues if they are superimposed (illustration 6). The result of this method is that two different rectangular structures seem to be integrated with one another.

In illustration 7 and 8 these two principles of defining a space simply co-exist. The first example (illustration 7) shows a solid part juxtaposed with a hall of piers, whereas in the second example (illustration 8) the constructional possibilities of solid and skeleton are deliberately opposed.

Finally, the rectangular solid can also be understood as a container which accommodates a free-form (illustration 9).

———— ✳ ————

Rectangular Buildings

Rectangular ground-plans are clearly directional; the extension of the rectangle therefore has certain effects on the division of the ground-plan. Also, the building has a clear direction of movement which influences the way it is used, unless this direction of movement is terminated by subdivisions and – above all – by the position of the staircase.

Another aspect of rectangular ground-plans affects the design of the building itself. The different valuation given to the facades on the long and the short sides can hardly be changed by means of composition. That means that here the possibilities of design are limited.

One possibility of the typological structuring of a rectangular building is to situate the staircase in parallel with a long side (illustrations 1 to 3). By so doing, a longitudinal zone is created which separates main subsidiary spaces from each other.

If the long sides have a centre, the building is automatically divided into two halves (illustrations 4 to 6). Thus a staircase in the centre makes possible the division of the whole into two spaces of equal value (illustration 4). These can be further sub-divided (illustration 5). With a central hall running through vertically (illustration 6), this kind of division is even more distinct.

———— * ————

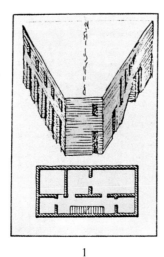

1

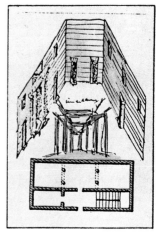

2

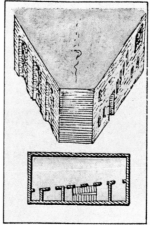

3

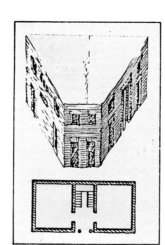

4

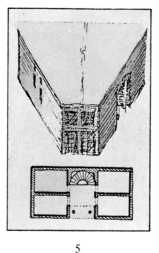

5

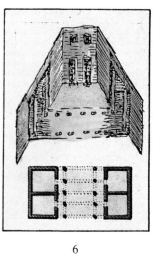

6

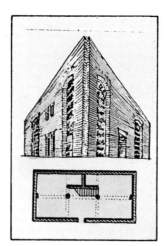

7

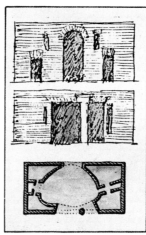

8

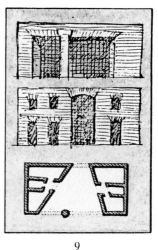

9

A special form of the square is constituted by the loosening of its sides and by the accentuation of its four corners. Massive corner towers define a transparent interior space (illustration 1), or are reduced to bay-like projections from a solid core (illustration 2). The co-existence of two different building forms is achieved by the surrounding cube being fragmented, whereby the solid form lying behind becomes visible (illustrations 3 and 4). A variation of this type is shown in illustration 5. A central cylinder serves as the main space and at the same time as a distributor, giving access to the corner towers each of which have different spatial geometries.

Le Corbusier also concerned himself with the square. Illustration 6 shows a studio building which reveals a poetic structure. The next example (illustration 7) suggests a central core from which very different spatial divisions are possible without destroying the overall form of the building.

The sketches in illustrations 8 and 9 are attempts at structuring a square facade. As already mentioned in the section on facades, the geometrical reality of a facade can, by way of visual manipulations, develop into one with a different effect.

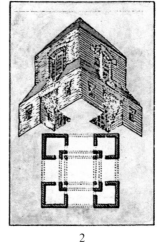

1

2

3

4

5

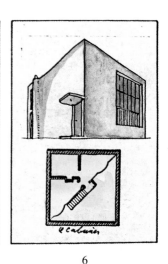

6

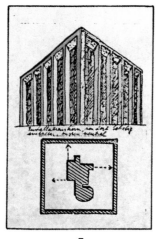

7

8

9

———— ✳ ————

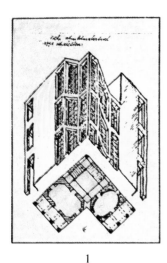

1

2

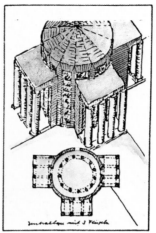

3

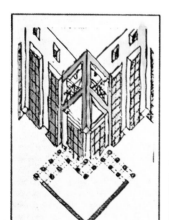

4

5

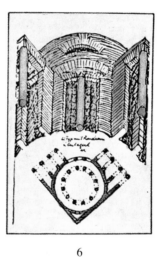

6

7

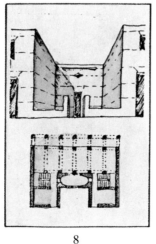

8

9

L-shaped Ground-Plans

L-shaped ground-plans are especially suitable for arrangements of buildings because of the protected free space which is created between them. The examples shown here are geometrical types developed from a square, a quarter of which has been left void. They differ from the functionalist L-type, where the living area is situated in the shorter wing and the bedrooms are joined together in the longer one. The disadvantage of L-shaped building types lies in the possibility of dark corners at the junction. It is advisable to use this space for subsidiary rooms or staircases.

Illustration 1 shows an example where the staircase is located in the joint, the space in the wings having loggias in front. The superimposition of L-form and the square gives rise to the exterior space being fixed (illustrations 2 and 3). In the next example the edge consists of massive walls (illustration 4), whereas the open sides are relieved by piers. Illustration 5 represents an assemblage of independent building elements. A transparent tower accommodating the staircase is flanked by two solid towers. The next example shows an L-form being superimposed with a cylinder, which becomes the dominating figure of the building. The two wings are built as verandas.

U-shaped Ground-Plans

These building forms still inevitably have a masterly character. The distinct symmetry with its defined centre is so dominant that a mitigation by way of fragmentation or similar techniques is difficult to achieve. Illustration 7 shows this classic type.

Its retracted courtyard is closed by a pergola. The opposite effect is gained if a pergola constitutes the long side of a building (illustration 8). By this, the transverse main space is clearly defined, the two wings being left to accommodate the subsidiary rooms. In illustration 9 the long side of the building is terminated by a buffer zone with subsidiary spaces. The centre is dominated by a staircase, and the side wings accommodate two main spaces.

A representative forecourt is shown in Fig. 1. The spatial organisation, with the semi-circular stair in the centre, clearly reveals the side with the two wings as the most

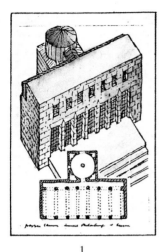

1

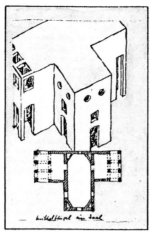

2

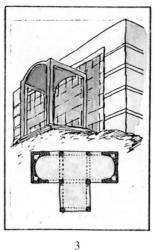

3

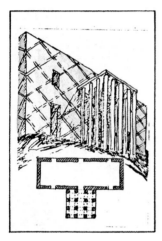

4

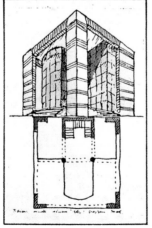

5

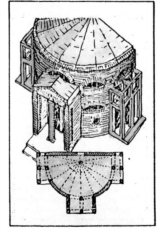

6

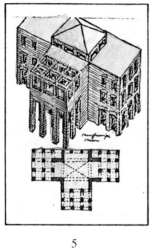

7

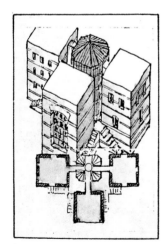

8

9

T-shaped Ground-Plans

Within the main space, a row of piers creates a filter in front of a tower which is a kind of annexe (illustration 1). A transverse main space is emphasised by the dissolution of the side wings (illustration 2). The massive corners of the longitudinal parts of a building (illustration 3), give the space in the middle its direction. This is broken by a light loggia projecting from the building. This type has been built as a four room maisonette apartment in my project for Ritterstrasse in Berlin. The direction of the main space of the building shown in illustration 4 is clearly visible.

The enclosed rectangle can have a projected pergola. In illustrations 5 and 6 we see the solid parts of two buildings being shrunk into a core. In both examples the T-shape is ony constituted by piers.

A building with an opposite development is shown in illustration 7. The core is entirely dissolved by a transparent staircase tower, and by isolation from the other three towers.

If the T-shape is superimposed with a circular or semi-circular cylinder (illustrations 8 and 9), which can also be designed as monumental main spaces, the projections recede to become merely emphasised entrances.

———— ✳ ————

T-shaped Ground-Plans

This type offers manifold possibilities of interpretation. It can be a centralised building with three extensions, a longitudinal building with an accentuated centre, or even the combination of four centralised buildings forming a T-shape.

One realises that it is the projecting part of the building which constitutes the real challenge for the design of this building type: is it a triumphant portico projecting from the facade; is it simply an extension on the back; or are the two side wings merely extensions of a centralised building? It is clear that the particular building parts have to be treated very carefully according to their valuation. Otherwise the intended meaning can easily turn into its opposite.

The projecting part of the building in illustration 1 seems to result from a need for additional space. The long side accommodates all subsidiary rooms and the entrance; and the staircase pushes the 'middle' part out towards the front. Illustration 2 consists of four individual solids, whereby the central dark one functions as the element of access to the building. It is also the central part in illustration 3 which gives access to the building. The side wings are distinguished from it by way of transparent joints. The building in illustration 4 is divided in transverse direction due to the arrangement of the subsidiary rooms. The central part is clearly the main space. This kind of division is also applied in illustrations 5 and 6. However, the main space here is even more articulate.

The simple method of superimposing the T-shape with a square potentially allows one to get rid of the dark zones constituted by the inner corners (illustration 7). The exterior piers of the loggias determine the form of the square; the walls the T-shape. If the exterior space is filled with pergolas (illustration 8), the whole complex is supplemented to become a rectangle on plan. This shows that through architectural treatment of residual spaces it is possible to gain complete building forms. In contrast to that, we see in illustration 9 one building part being almost separated, as the longitudinal principal part is especially emphasised. Because of the entrance by way of the tower-like building part, it receives a centre.

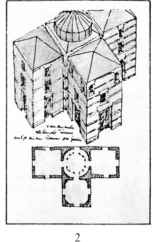

1

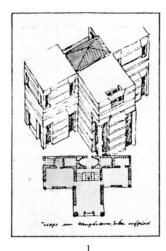

2

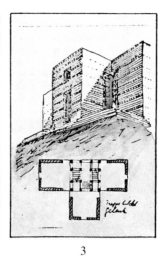

3

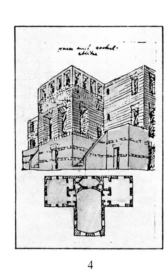

4

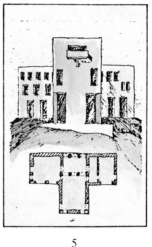

5

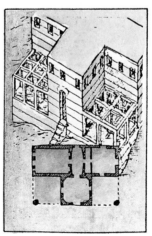

6

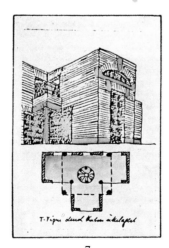

7

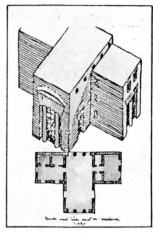

8

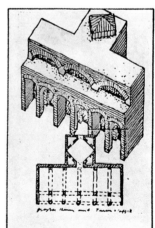

9

V

important one visually. In Fig. 2 the house type is viewed only as a shell for accommodating a variety of spatial geometries. The tendential resolution of the U-type is shown in the next example (Fig. 3), through the addition of a tower, which is inserted in the middle of the two wings, thus becoming the principal space.

Towers

The tower is a special form in that it does not tend to lend itself well to a rational division of space. Nonetheless, this form is still important because it is an appropriate means of plugging gaps in the fabric of a city. It is also an independent building type suitable for urban monuments. An octagonal tower has a central space ringed with supplementary spaces (Fig. 4). Triangular towers are difficult to handle. A regular division of space inevitably produces sharp-angled left-over areas (Fig.5). A better arrangement can be achieved with an inscribed hexagon (Fig. 6), in which just three smallish triangular areas are unusable. The problem of a round tower is solved in Fig. 7 with the division of the space into two semicircles, one massive, the other transparent. Fig. 8 shows what happens when this is overlaid with a rectangle – a rational, usable main space. The composition of regular and irregular spaces appears topographically determined (Fig. 9). Here the tower seems to be a continuation of the cliff, an effect which required the foregoing of a geometrically simple exterior form.

———— ✳ ————

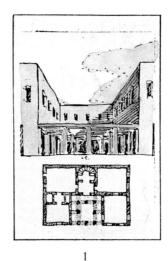
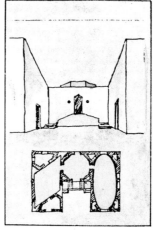
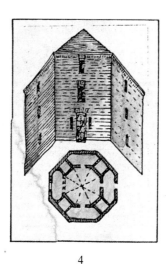

1

2

3

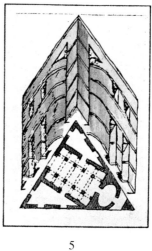
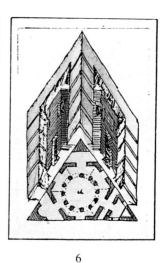

4

5

6

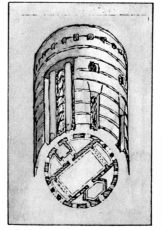
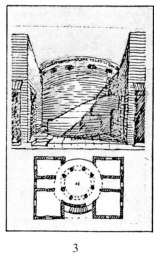

7

8

9

1

2

3

4

5

6

7

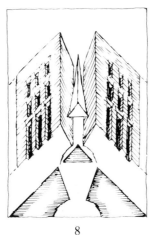

8

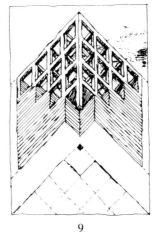

9

Building Corners

The corner of a building is one of the most important zones and is mainly concerned with the mediation of two facades. During the past decades this subject in architecture has been largely neglected. Nowadays, as a result of simply lining up buildings, the corner as a particular part of the building has not received the necessary acknowledgement and treatment.

In contrast to this, the following sketches should demonstrate some possibilities for special corner treatment. The first example shows (illustration 1) that the corner has also been dealt with in modern architecture. Guiseppe Terragni and the Russian Constructivist Golosov achieved similar results by emphasising the corner of a building by way of a glass cylinder. This solid carries the architrave of the top storey like a huge, dematerialised round column. The turning of the corner is especially emphasised by a projecting frame which marks the actual termination of the building (illustration 2). In illustration 3 the psychological shearing off of the corner is counteracted by way of an inserted pyramid, a sensitive but perhaps too powerful a protection of the corner. The rounded, retracted corner shown in illustration 4 is emphasised by a similarly shaped row of columns creating a filter and reducing the dark zone often associated with a deep corner. In illustration 5 the corner is formed as a building in its own right – a tower. The problem of connecting the tower with the street facades is solved by the employment of loggias. Illustrations 6 and 7 also present corner towers which in terms of their proportions are to be regarded as classical solutions.

———— ✳ ————

The curve, the circle and the turning of a corner are, in formal terms, logical means of protecting a corner. Parts and elements of the facade, without being broken, can thereby be 'wound round' from one facade to the next. The tower allows for a proper termination of the side facades and creates an additional accentuation.

The emptying of a corner or, in other words, a corner being opened up is shown in illustration 8. The small monument with its outward edges takes up the alignment of the two adjacent facades. The example presented in illustration 9 is a useful solution both in constructional and functional terms: the stepped form and the dissolution into pergolas allow for a positive response to the otherwise large dark zone of a corner. By opening the corner towards the top such problems are removed.

———— ✳ ————

1

2

3

4

5

6

7

8

9

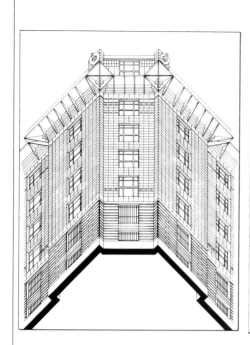

DRUCK- und VERLAGSHAUS   KIESEL - SALZBURG

Student works on the theme of Corner Buildings

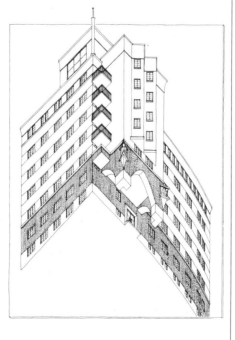

Illustration 1: A masterly achievement in terms of the most subtle and yet accentuated development of a corner is realised in Otto Wagner's Post Office Savings Bank in Vienna. The surfaces of the last vertical window axis of the side facades are drawn forward and stand out almost like a frame, terminated by the bevelled corners above. The setback also accommodates a vertical window axis and signals the development of a diagonal prospect from the building. Three elements, the two vertical parts of the 'frame' and the corner itself are held together by a projecting cornice, the consoles of which constitute the point of transition of the different parts. All this prepares finally for the corner to be crowned by a tower.

Illustration 2: A ground level pavilion in front of a building corner completes the alignment of the two facades which approach each other at an acute angle. The actual corner facade, which is slightly concave and terraced towards the top, recedes. The setbacks of the storeys end at top floor level which is emphasised by a window situated in the vertical axis, and is crowned by two statues. In addition, this corner is separated from the side facades by way of recessed corners.

Illustration 3: This building shows the transparency of mediation of the different building levels. The entrance area reaches symmetrically right round the corner and, by way of a wall band above, is connected with the side facades. The plaster joints at the end of the side facades mark their termination. The loggias finally allow the bevelled corner to widen towards the top whereby a plane is created. This is flanked by two flagstaffs, which help evince the corner as being a complete form.

Illustration 4: This example shows the penetration of a corner. One side penetrates the other and develops into an expressive gateway structure. The small balconies at the corner do not represent the prolongation of the facade, but the penetration of the corner.

------ ✳ ------

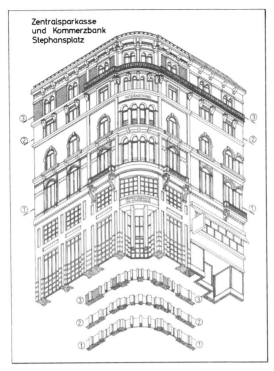

Student works on the theme of Corner Buildings

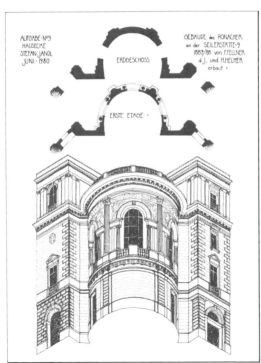

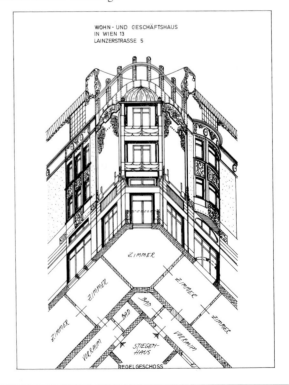

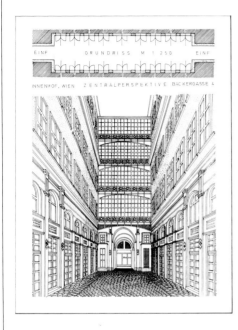

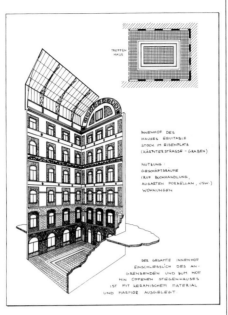

Student works on the theme of Interior Courtyards

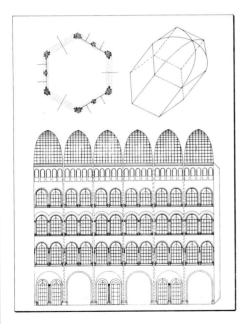

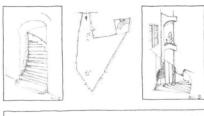

Interior Courtyards

Interior courtyards are not independent elements, but the outcome of a certain kind of building. We should not concern ourselves here with original historical and rural forms of this type, so the 'atrium' and other similar types of courtyard buildings will not be at issue. What will be dealt with in this context are examples of courtyards as they are found in cities. Courtyards are semipublic spaces which are for the use of the community concerned. They can also be part of an informal route network of passages and thoroughfares which give access to various parts of the city (illustrations 1 and 3). A large roofed courtyard, a hall so to speak, is especially useful in public buildings as a device of orientation. It also removes the tightness of an office complex and allows for additional ventilation and illumination (illustration 2). As a residential courtyard within an urban development (illustration 4), the courtyard is a common space used by the inhabitants of the adjacent buildings. Especially because of excessive traffic, the streets and therefore public life are often restricted in cities; the courtyard has thus gained a new significance. Today one should strive to locate apartments orientated towards a quiet courtyard rather than towards the street. This is a development which is only beginning but which will result in greater support for, and consideration of, existing and new interior courtyards. The required changes to traditional building types must, however, be made sense of.

———— ✳ ————

Interior courtyard between Wollzeile and Bäckerstrasse, Vienna

Vista between Lerchenfelderstrasse and Neubaugasse, Vienna, 1800s

Palais Epstein in Vienna by Th. von Hansen, 1870-75

Courtyard in the Justizpalast in Vienna, by A. Wielemanns, 1875-81

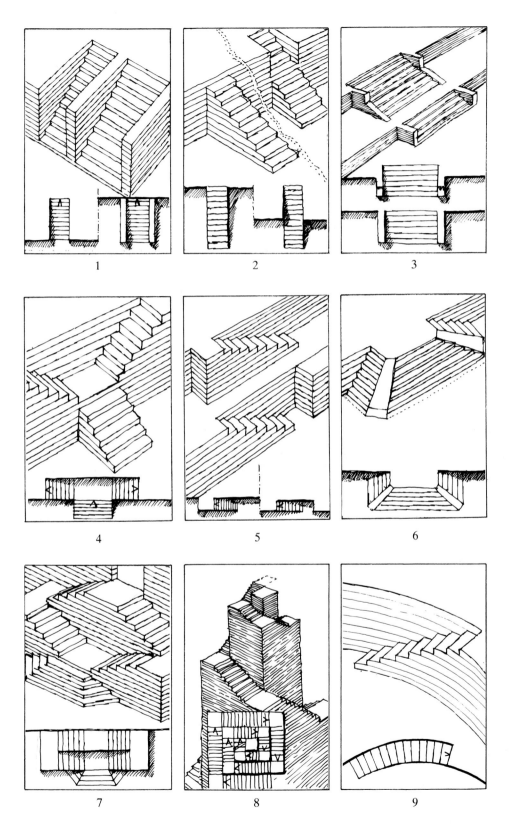

1

2

3

4

5

6

7

8

9

Outside Staircases

As the term already implies, outside staircases form part of the exterior space. They are human structures of landscape which also act as markers in natural and urban environments, and communicate their public use. We can think, for example, of a large baroque outside stair which, although related to an axis, also leads away from it and therefore engenders moments of contemplation. Another example would be a footpath in the countryside. If simply made steps emerge in hilly terrain then we know that this path is often used by people, and that it facilitates walking.

Beyond this, outside staircases also create their own space, become points of encounter, meeting places, or simply points from which beautiful views can be enjoyed. I think it is not necessary to enlarge upon the fact that these characteristics have largely been lost, and have been substituted by the simplistic idea of the 'shortest connection between two points'.

Illustration 1 shows a simple straight staircase cut into the upper level of a building. Already at the bottom level, one comes under the influence of the upper level because of the stair. One can then slowly ascend it. However, the degree to which a staircase is projected from its upward termination (illustrations 2 and 3) determines the different possible relationships between the two levels. If our sense of spatiality was still intact, we would realise the difference.

What we nowadays experience instead is somebody rushing up the stairs and getting confused because, as is shown in illustration 4, one staircase often turns at right angles into two.

Staircases which run parallel to one another (illustration 5) give every level an independent, yet equal significance. This arrangement resembles terraces. Illustration 6 shows an almost semi-circular staircase running up in three flights suggesting a slope. Stairs which separate and come together again have a special character because of the way they are used by the public (illustration 7). People meet and separate again; they can time their walking speed either to encounter others or to avoid them. One could almost call this an example of 'freedom of use'. Illustration 8 shows an interesting though special form. A stair rises like a spiral and at the same time it narrows. From the beginning, the user becomes aware that the stair is going to end at a certain point. The example presented in illustration 9 again shows a cut-in staircase which is now curved and runs parallel to the upper level.

Illustration 1 here represents the opposite effect of that gained in illustration 9 in the former plate. Here the curved form of the stair gives the impression that the upper level has a greater significance than in the previous example.

The semi-circular staircase shown in illustration 2 emerges from a particular level to lead up to the next one. Initially one moves away from it to come back to it again on another level. The next example considers a staircase which is again cut into the ground (illustration 3). Only after having moved on to the bottom step has one really left the area concerned. A bold variation of opposite staircases is shown in illustration 4. The division into main levels and intermediate landings is striking. The following staircase (illustration 5) also possesses an intermediate landing. From half way up one has already entered the sphere of the upper level. This effect of an 'exterior' and 'interior' to a staircase is even more explicit in the simple, yet in another way sophisticated, arrangement shown in illustration 6. One half of the stair is 'heaped up', the other half 'cut in'. Apart from the variety of possible lines of movement and connection, the circular intermediate landing clearly manifests a meaningful centre. Examples of representational front staircases are presented in illustration 7. Here the upper level clearly has the prominent meaning. A rare example for an exterior stair is a spiral staircase (illustration 8). As a 'functional winding' it is a forerunner – or maybe a result – of the Tower of Babel, of which the last example (illustration 9) is even more reminiscent.

———— ✳ ————

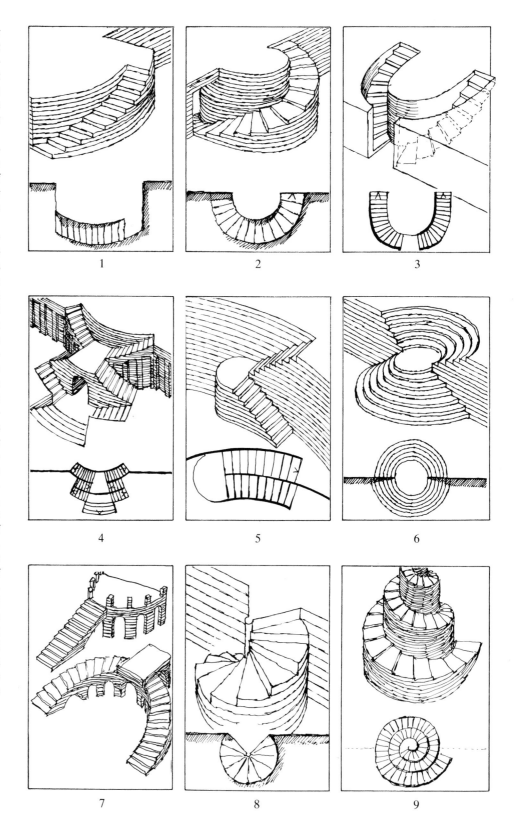

1

2

3

4

5

6

7

8

9

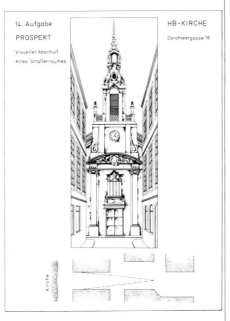

14. Aufgabe
PROSPEKT

Visueller Abschluß
eines Straßenraumes

HB-KIRCHE

Dorotheergasse 16

STANDPUNKT
SCHAUFLER-
GASSE

BLICKRICHTUNG
MICHAELER-
PLATZ

Student works on the theme of Prospect

VOLKS
GARTEN

METASTASIOG

MINORITEN
KIRCHE

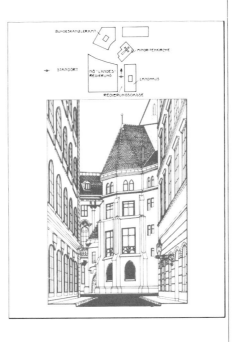

Prospect

With the issue of the prospect, although it is closely related to architecture, we leave the 'building' as an independent subject of design and set out to think about public space. It has already been hinted at that the obligation of every building is to be integrated into its specific urban tissue. A special problem in this context is presented by the 'prospect'.

Let us take the common case of a street or a square that is to be terminated by a building – our building. This termination is not to be treated as an accident; the facade of the building concerned has to react to this specific situation. While the street as such is a symbol of infinity, its termination communicates the fact that a destination has been reached. This destination, the facade of our building, must respond to this event, must catch the eye; only then will the building make sense and be integrated into the urban context. If we are committed to our responsibility for urban space, we have to respect its laws. That we have regard to the effect of prospects has nothing to do with a deliberate monumentalisation of buildings, but with rendering respect to the urban texture. A prospect at the end of a street makes the eye rest, gives it a target, and thereby symbolically shortens the way to the destination.

By taking into consideration the effect our facade has on adjacent street alignments, we communicate our concern for the rules of the place where we build. We should not make people think about our building in the sense that a space ship has landed in their town by accident. What we should care about is giving evidence that we are going to continue to build more for this specific place – our place.

Towers and Monuments

Building is always about the occupation of a place. Architecture is about setting marks. In the free countryside we come across a tower. It directs our way. Lighthouses, chimneys, steeples, city gates, defence towers etc. belong to the archetypal symbols of uprightness. Towers symbolise human achievement, the triumph over earthly matters. Without doubt every tower has a monumental character as it rises above the environment. I can see before my inner eye certain modern architects shaking a warning finger at me. Monumentality? If one dares to talk about this last taboo of the Modern, one is too easily accused of having a longing for a totalitarian state of affairs. What a stupid and short-sighted fallacy! A monument is of course first and foremost a sign of power. Only the mighty potentate could afford to rise above his subjects by way of architectural manifestations. But his monument will outlast him and will be celebrated by future generations as a cultural testimony. Without these 'signs of power' there would be no such thing as architecture; we would dwell in a desolate steppe.

Monuments always were, and still are, cult objects which have meaning and value for a community. Because of their symbolism, they express a common will or confession. Monuments do not need to be towers or high-rise buildings. A small wayside shrine suffices as a sign of human existence. Let us try to find out what the term 'monumentality' really means. It certainly implies a lasting piece of architecture; it also conveys the beauty of destruction.

On the 16th of May 1871, the Vendôme Column with the statue of Napoleon I was destroyed by fighters of the Paris Commune. What do we learn from such an example, to which many others could be added? We learn that the destruction of a monument is a symbol; a symbol for the will of a society. We, however, preserve and care for the monuments of the past. Sometimes it appears that the rescued statue of a past sovereign compensates for the destruction of entire historical urban quarters. While our society destroys valuable testimonies of the past, it clings to nice little monuments but is unable to create new ones. Historical worship of heroes is certainly not in accordance with our understanding of democracy. But is there nothing left we can believe in? Democracy does not stand in need of erecting monuments – it legitimises itself by testimonies of monarchic and autocratic power. From the monuments which have not been built, we can learn about the self-valuation of a society and what position architecture has in it. *A society which does not believe in its survival is incapable of the symbolic representation of its aim, and therefore incapable of building.*

1

2

3

4

5

6

7

8

9

CHAPTER IV

ON
PROPORTIONS

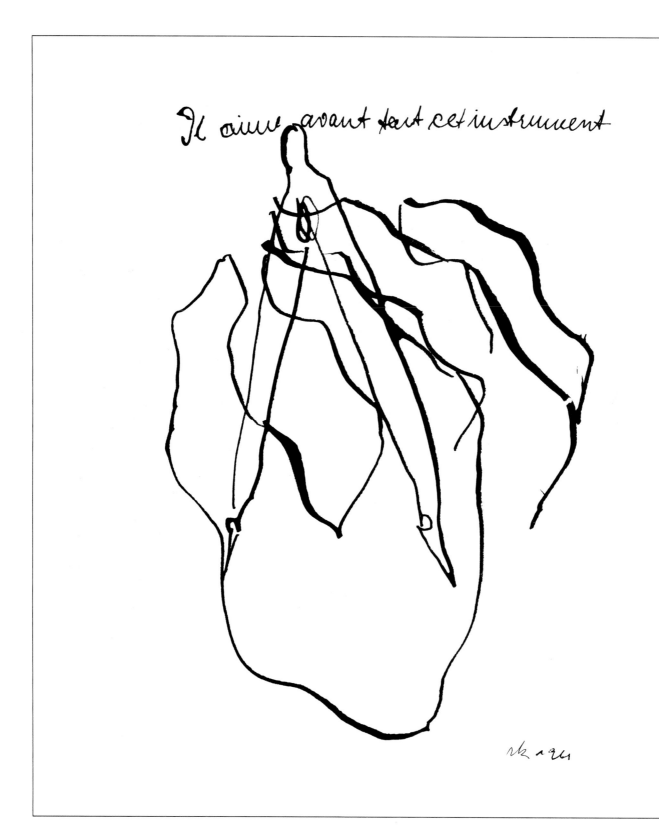

PROPORTIONS

This chapter on proportions is of particular significance in the field of architectural composition. Having selected the basic type and the elements for a building, a suitable scale has to be worked out that governs the dimensions of individual parts and their interrelationships. The main question facing us is to what extent the purely functional and structural requirements can be aesthetically manipulated by controlling proportions.

There are no rules to guide us in this. Only experience can help us appreciate the beauty of those things which countless philosophical observations and artistic exaltations have proclaimed to be aesthetically perfect. I shall recount some of my own observations on nature and on buildings whose quality of form has already been recognised. We are not dealing with scientific novelties but with subjective relationships whose interpretation springs from the problematic of the architectural profession.

Every artist has to formulate his own theory. Just as nature permanently seeks to destroy its order, so every creative impulse is generated by questioning and re-evaluation. In the course of exploring a problem, age-old experiences come into play which have to be rediscovered by each new generation.

MY EXPERIENCES WITH PROPORTIONS IN ARCHITECTURE

Early on in my study of architecture I stumbled upon Le Corbusier's 'Modulor', the fantastic little figure bible that offered the key to 'God's pleasure garden' (L.C.).

My history teacher, Krauss, a stickler for precise figures as his surveys in Paestum show, did nothing to encourage me in my study of sources. Those 'mystifications', as he called them, were alien to him. At the Technical University in Munich, they had quite forgotten about a dissertation Ernst Moessel had submitted to Professor Theodore Fischer in 1915, entitled 'Circular geometry: the law of proportion in antiquity and the middle ages'.

Moessel, like Krauss in his fifteen years of academic research, sought to substantiate his arithmetic examinations with scrupulous and pedantic exactitude. It is this esoteric mathematical preoccupation which renders his work, like that of many other researchers, inaccessible to the average architect.

On the other hand Le Corbusier, the intuitive mathematician, is much closer to our hearts. Following my natural inclination I shall try to make the study of proportion equally clear. I shall recall my own study in this field and how I utilised my discoveries.

The survey and measured drawing exercise I undertook of the Gothic cathedral at Auxerre, the northern gateway to Burgundy, constituted a decisive phase in my architectural development. I used the study of this valuable architectural model to gain significant insights into the complexities of architectural composition before embarking on my first independent design at university.

I was well aware that I could not grasp everything at once. However the year I spent with my friend Friedemann Wild, studying the cathedral and the then still intact medieval town centre, was without doubt the most beautiful and exciting experience of my entire architectural education.

Equipped with theodolite, plate camera, plumb line and tape measures, we set about attacking the monster's belly. The verger of the cathedral gave us free lodging in an adjacent abandoned timber-frame cottage. In return, we promised him copies of all the plans we drew up.

The parts of the building constructed between the thirteenth and sixteenth century exhibited the wildest irregularities, making our survey unbelievably involved and complicated. The memory of clambering about in the roof trusses and climbing the interior walls and facades still sends shivers down my spine.

*   *   *

The Pantograph

To chart the innumerable geometric figurations of the cathedral at Auxerre, we had to devise a multitude of tools and gadgets; one of them was a simple piece of string. Using it we could, through repeated probing, accurately determine the centres and radii of arched segments.

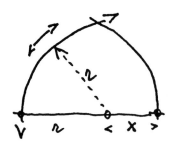

Once the radius had been found, I tied two knots in the string, then, measuring distance x, the figure was determined.

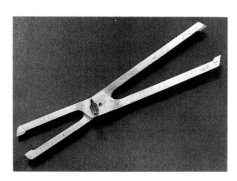

In order to investigate the similarity between different pointed arch configurations in windows with elaborate tracery work, we improvised a proportional compass by pinning two rods together.

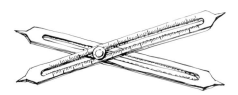

The length of the rod was equal to the base of the pointed arch configuration. The radius of the arch was marked with a nail. We were employing an instrument the Ro-

mans knew as a 'proportional divider'. Moessel had discovered it in a museum in Pompeii. The geodesists also knew it as an instrument of enlargement with variable adjustment.

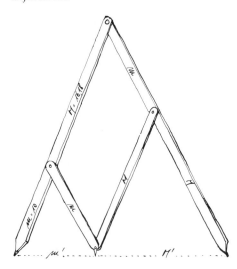

Stone masons know the proportional divider in this form.

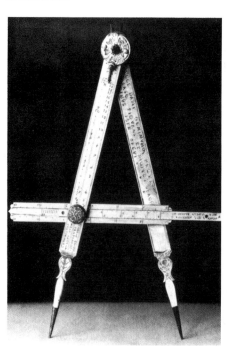

This instrument was used as a proportional divider by Christoph Schissler the Elder, of Augsburg, in 1580. The required proportion can be read off the horizontal slide rule.

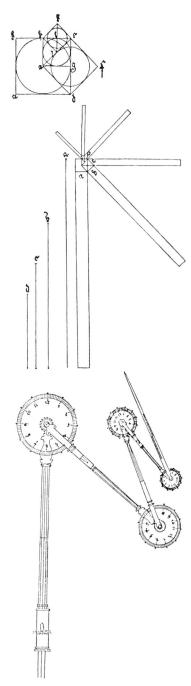

Proportioning instruments by Dürer (1525), taken from *Underweyssung der Messung* (Instructions in Geometry).

I am using my own surveying experience to explain in the simplest way how a proportional divider can be employed to divide a circle into three, four or five segments.

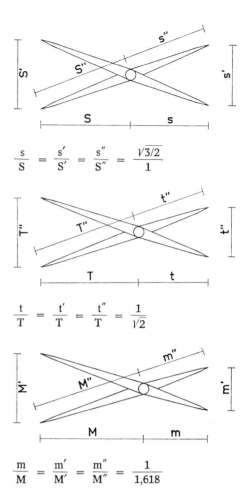

$$\frac{s}{S} = \frac{s'}{S'} = \frac{s''}{S''} = \frac{\sqrt{3/2}}{1}$$

$$\frac{t}{T} = \frac{t'}{T} = \frac{t''}{T} = \frac{1}{\sqrt{2}}$$

$$\frac{m}{M} = \frac{m'}{M'} = \frac{m''}{M''} = \frac{1}{1,618}$$

The relationships marked off by this divider result from dividing a circle into five or ten segments and are referred to as 'relationships of the Golden Section', used by Le Corbusier for his Modulor sequence. It is, however, only one of many proportional sequences to be found in architecture. Besides the Golden Section, the two most important relationships are the segmentation of a circle into three or six parts (1 : $\sqrt{3}$, 1 : $\sqrt{3/2}$), and into four or eight parts (1 : $\sqrt{2}$).

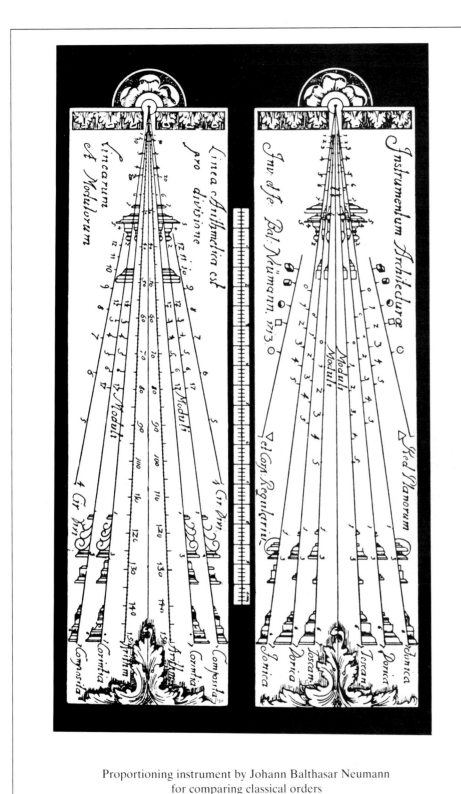

Proportioning instrument by Johann Balthasar Neumann
for comparing classical orders

These relationships are marked on the proportional divider with indentations. By changing the position of the pin joint, the proportion of the marked off distances is altered.

Perhaps, one day, the drawing supplies industry will take up my suggestion to market a divider of this kind. A home-made instrument of timber or brass is always more fun. One should knock up a number of these dividers, all different in size, so that they could even be used for drawing up large plans.

A selection of proportional dividers, constructed by my students

————— ✳ —————

180

Proportional Looking Glass

Proportional Looking Glass

I built this useful little instrument to observe proportions during my architectural excursions. It consists of two clear plates of plexiglass with their planes parallel to each other. Expandable rubber pads sit on each one of the four corners. The distance between the two perspex plates is variable, according to the focal length of the envisaged object. The distance between the two plates is measured and, with a slide rule or calculator, the relationship between the two distances can be ascertained. This instrument is obviously not very accurate but is just as useful as paces for exploring a building. Apart from that it encourages one to study buildings in a more direct fashion than through studying books.

Division of Circles into Three, Four and Five Segments

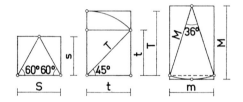

The three geometric figures illustrate how, with the aid of a set square and a compass, the above-mentioned proportions can be constructed.

To gain a deeper understanding of the dimensions that result from those three geometric operations, I invite the reader at this point to take a compass and scale and check the dimensions of these figures for himself.

This form of geometric manipulation can be very useful for certain design operations.

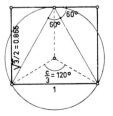

A General Overview of the
Segmentation of a Circle into Three Parts

In an equilateral triangle the base to height ratio is $1 : \sqrt{3}/2 = 1 : 0.86$ or height to base relationship is $\sqrt{3}/2 : 1 = 0.86 : 1 = 1 : 1.15$.

Originally, the static performance of a building structure, that is to say its load distribution, was determined by the method of triangulation. (See Dehio, *Untersuchungen über das gleichseitige Dreieck*, Strasbourg 1894).

I am fond of using rectangles into which equilateral triangles can be inscribed when determining the overriding building form. Examples of this in my own buildings are the Siemer residence, the Dickes residence, or the right arm of the engaged portico of the house on the Ritterstrasse in Berlin. I am not pretending that I share a deep relationship with triangulation for any other reason.

I shall return to this topic later with reference to the cathedral at Auxerre. The mystic interpretation has practically vanished from the artistic world of creativity. Its place has been taken by surrealistic, literary and socio-critical associations. In the case of the Viennese artist Walter Pichler, for instance, the mystic part is one of many interpretations; it is of equal importance and often expressed with a cruel honesty that lends his work a deep poetic significance.

In architecture, geometry plays the role of quantitatively controlling the harmony of a building that would otherwise remain nebulous and only vaguely defined. Intuition gives us the impulse and, like sleepwalkers, we are drawn in a direction that at some point has to be intellectually justified.

The reference to mystic and symbolic figures may be justified in the case of sacral buildings, but what has it to do with an ordinary house?

The temple epitomizes the seat of God, but is no more than a glorified version of an immortal's home. The temple is recognised by everyone as unique in its physical form, conspicuous in its monumentality and in its essence the ideal prototype house. The house on the other hand is thought unassuming, rational, functional, yet noble in its scale. And because man and God are dependent on each other for their existence, the desire of the former to be just like the latter is understandable. Thus, man's house will always aspire to be a noble imitation of the archetypal temple.

Segmentation of a Circle into Four Parts

The square, the simplest geometric figure, is deceptive in its purity.

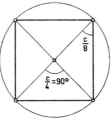

$$\text{ctg } c/8 = 1.00$$

By rotating the diagonals about the centre of the circle, we produce a rectangle with a base to height relationship of
$1 : \sqrt{2} = 1 : 1.141$.
These are the same proportions as a Din A4 format.
On its side the base to height relationship is:
$1.41 : 1 = 1 : 0.7$.
In the house for Mr. and Mrs. Dickes, I managed to inscribe the entire superstructure, including the roof, into a square; in the

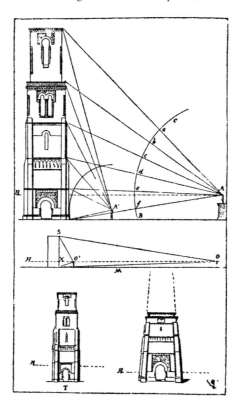

Siemer house only the south facade; and in the first of the Spandau houses the central tower elevation.

Square dimensions in buildings can, unfortunately, never be perceived as exactly square due to a certain degree of optical distortion. The square always seems to be shortened in height or depth. Therefore this dimension should always be stretched slightly. The windows in the house on the Ritterstrasse in Berlin only appear to be square because their width to height ratio is $1 : 1.5$. The height becomes the base line of an equilateral triangle.

All proportions constructed on plan are in reality never perceived the same by the eye. The perspective distortion, and the fact that the building normally rises far above the horizontal eye level, alters these dimensions considerably. The farther the distance from the building, the truer our perceived dimensions.

Segmentation of a Circle
into Five and Ten Parts

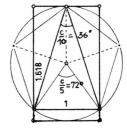

Fig. 1.
$2 \times \text{SIN } c/20 = 0.618$
Height to base $= 1 : 1.618 = 0.618 : 1$
Angle $c/10 = 36°$ is inscribed in a triangle whose base to side relationship is ruled by the Golden Section $1 : 1.618$

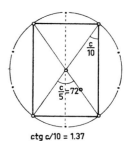

$$\text{ctg } c/10 = 1.37$$

Fig. 2.
A rectangle inscribed in a ten-sided polygon. The relationship of the sides is
$1 : \text{ctg } 36° = 1 : 1.37$

Further rectangles that result from the regular segmentation of the circle:

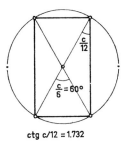

ctg c/12 = 1.732

Fig. 3.
Division by six.
Base : Height = B : H = 1 : ctg 30° = 1 : 1.732

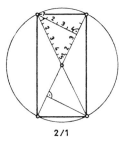

2 / 1

Fig. 4.
After Pythagoras.

Divide the radius by five, erect a vertical on the intersection between the second and third division. Connect the point where the vertical meets the circumference with the centre of the circle. You can then inscribe a triangle in the circle whose sides share a relationship of 3 : 4 : 5. The two points where the radius touches the circumference form the base about which a rectangle is constructed with a base to height relationship of B : H = 1 : 2.

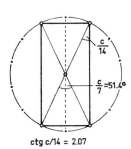

ctg c/14 = 2.07

Fig. 5.
Segmenting the circle by seven.
B : H = 1 : ctg. 25.7° = 1 : 2.07

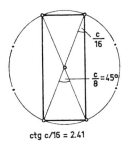

ctg c/16 = 2.41

Fig. 6.
Segmenting the circle by eight.
B : H = 1 : ctg 22.5° = 1 : 2.41

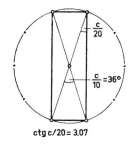

ctg c/20 = 3.07

Fig. 7.
Segmenting by ten.
B : H = 1 : ctg 18° = 1 : 3.07

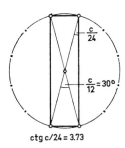

ctg c/24 = 3.73

Fig. 8.
Segmenting by twelve.
B : H = 1 : ctg 15° = 1 : 3.73

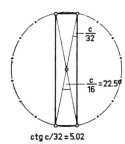

ctg c/32 = 5.02

Fig. 9.
Segmenting by sixteen.
B : H = 1 : ctg 11.25° = 1 : 5.02

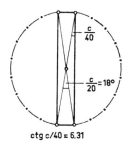

ctg c/40 = 6.31

Fig. 10.
Segmenting by twenty.
B : H = 1 : ctg 9° = 1 : 6.31

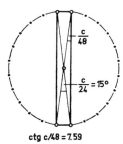

ctg c/48 = 7.59

Fig. 11.
Segmenting by twenty-four.
B : H = 1 : ctg 7.5° = 1 : 7.59

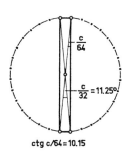

ctg c/64 = 10.15

Fig. 12.
Segmenting by thirty-two.
B : H = 1 : ctg 5.62° = 1 : 10.15

Now, let us repeat this figure game on larger forms that illustrate the division into three, four, five, six, eight and ten parts respectively, and bring the figures into a far clearer and more meaningful relationship.

**Segmentation of a Circle
into Three, Six and Twelve Parts**

We divide the circle into six parts. In each case the equilateral triangle is superimposed twice on the figure. There is no need to make it stand out. As already discovered, the base to height relationship is
$1 : \sqrt{3}/2 = 1 : 0.866$.

The resulting figure sequence is as follows:
. . .0.649 : 0.749 : 0.866 : 1 : 1.154 : 1.33 : 1.539 : 1.777 : 2.05 : 2.36 : 2.73 . . .

The rectangle, constructed from opposite points of the star, has a side ratio of
$1 : \sqrt{3} = 1 : 1.732$.

This gives rise to the following sequence:
. . .0.333 : 0.577 : 1 : 1.732 : 2.999 : 5.19 : 8.989. . .

The three equilateral triangles have their sides divided up into three equidistant parts by virtue of their superimposition.
Base line: $1 : 3 = 1/3$

This gives rise to the figure sequence
. . .0.11 : 0.33 : 1 : 3 : 9 : 27 : 81 : 243 . . .
and $2 : 3 = 0.66$
$3 : 2 = 1.50$
$0.43 : 0.66 : 1 : 1.5 : 2.25 : 3.375 : 5.062 : 7.593.$

Two equilateral triangles superimposed on the diameter of the circle divide it up into four equal parts
$2\sqrt{3}/3 : 4 = \sqrt{3}/6 = 0.288$

We are already familiar with the resulting relationship
$1 : \sqrt{3}/2 = 2\sqrt{3}/3 : 1 = 1/3 : \sqrt{3}/6 = 1 : 0.866$

One side of the hexagon rests on the base line. This can be joined up with the side directly opposite to create a rectangle. The mathematical relationship between its long and short side is
$1 : \sqrt{3} = \sqrt{3}/3 : 1 = 1 : 1.732$
$\sqrt{3}/2 : \sqrt{3}/3 = 0.866 : 0.577 = 1.5 : 1 = 3 : 2$

The resulting number sequence is
. . .0.29 : 0.44 : 0.66 : 1 : 1.5 : 2.25 : 3.37 : 5.06 . . .

The relationship between base line 1 and the circle diameter is $1 : 2$.

———— ✳ ————

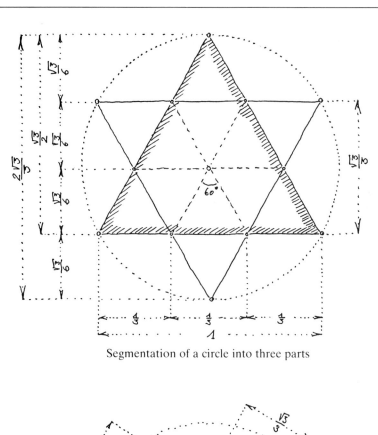

Segmentation of a circle into three parts

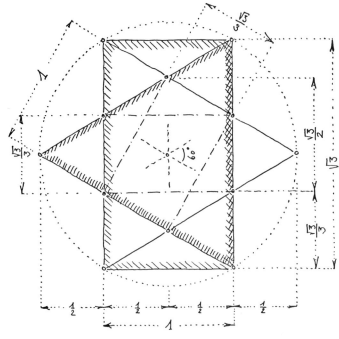

Segmentation of a circle into six parts

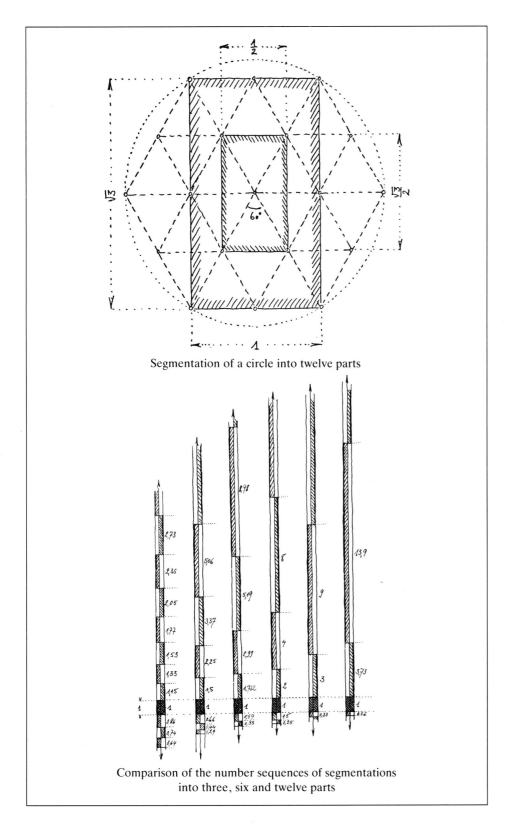

Segmentation of a circle into twelve parts

Comparison of the number sequences of segmentations
into three, six and twelve parts

If the circle circumference is divided up into twelve equal parts, the inscribed rectangle has the following proportions:

a : A = 1 : ctg 15° = 1 : 3.73

The resulting number sequence is:

. . . 0.26 : 1 : 3.73 : 13.9 : 51.84 : 193.38 . . .

Now, we divide the hexagon up into twenty-four identical equilateral triangles. This configuration beautifully illustrates the mathematical relationship we are already familiar with:

$1 : 3 = 1/2 : \sqrt{3}/2 = 1 : 1.732$

———— ✳ ————

Segmentation of a Circle into Four and Eight Parts

In a square, the relationship between base line and diagonal is:

$1 : \sqrt{2} = 1 : 1.414$

This gives rise to the following number sequence:

$0.25 : 0.35 : 0.50 : 0.707 : 1 : 1.414 : 2.00 : 2.82 : 4.00 : 5.65 : 8 : 11.3 : 16.00 \ldots$

The superimposition of two identical squares within the eight times segmented circle leads to the following proportional relationships:

$p : p\sqrt{2}/2 = 0.293 : 0.293\sqrt{2}/2 = 0.293 : 0.207 = \sqrt{2} : 1$

$2p : 1-2p = q\sqrt{2} : q = 0.58 : 0.41 = \sqrt{2} : 1$

The penetration and interpenetration of the star-like configuration with its eight projections gives rise to the following relationships:

$1-p/2 : p = 0.353 : 0.293 = 1.20 : 1$

The number sequence is:

$\ldots 0.48 : 0.57 : 0.69 : 0.83 : 1 : 1.20 : 1.44 : 1.73 : 2.07 : 2.49 : 2.99 \ldots$

and

$p\sqrt{2} : 1-2p\sqrt{2} = 0.415 : 0.168 = 2.468 : 1$

and

$1 : p\sqrt{2} = 1 : 0.414 = 2.414 : 1$

with the number sequence:

$\ldots 0.17 : 0.414 : 1 : 2.414 : 5.827 : 14.067 : 33.95 \ldots$

and

$q = 1-2p = 1-2 \times 0.293 = 0.414$

$q\sqrt{2} : q = 2p : (1-2p) = \sqrt{2} : 1$

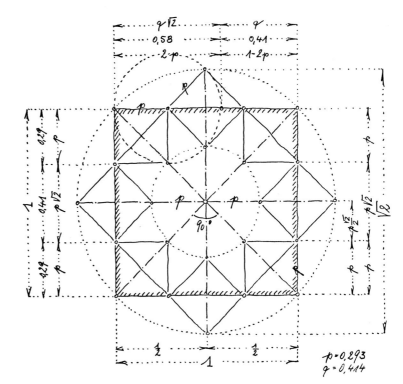

Segmentation of a circle into four and eight parts

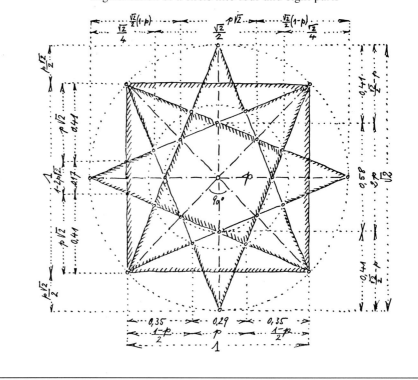

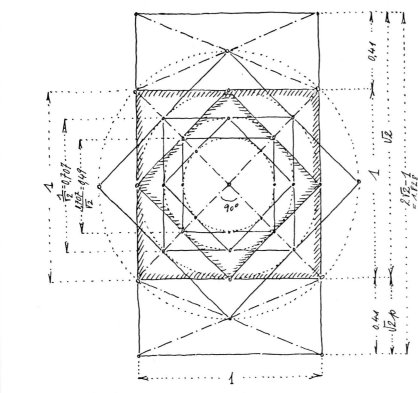

Segmentation of a circle into four and eight parts

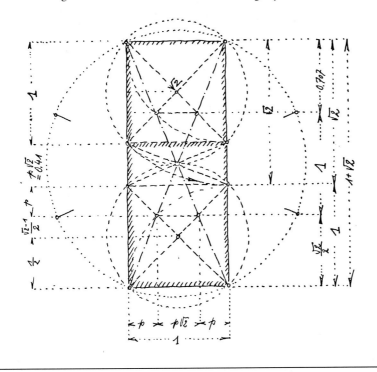

If we halve the sides of the superimposed squares, we automatically inscribe smaller diagonal squares whose sides gradually decrease by a factor of:

$1 : 1/\sqrt{2} = 1 : 0.707$

If we enlarge the initial square by a factor of $\sqrt{2}-1 = p\sqrt{2} = 0.414$, the following relationship is set up:

$1 : p\sqrt{2} = 1 : 0.414 = 2.414 : 1$

and

$\sqrt{2} : 2\sqrt{2}-1 = 1.414 : 1.828 = 0.707 : 1 = 1 : \sqrt{2}$

and

$1 : 2\sqrt{2}-1 = 1 : 1.828$

with a number sequence of:

$\ldots 2.9 : 0.54 : 1 : 1.828 : 3.341 : 6.10 : 11.16 : 20.41 : 37.31 \ldots$

If we divide the circumference of a circle into eight equal parts and join up four points directly opposite each other, we will have constructed a rectangle whose length to width relationship is:

$1 : 1 + \sqrt{2} = 1 : 2.414$

The other mathematical relationships that can be derived are:

$1 : \sqrt{2}/2 = 1 : 0.707 = \sqrt{2} : 1$

and

$\sqrt{2} : 1 + \sqrt{2} = \sqrt{2} : 2.414 = 1.414 : 2.414 = 1 : 1.707$

with a number sequence of:

$\ldots 0.2 : 0.34 : 0.58 : 1 : 1.707 : 2.91 : 4.97 : 8.49 : 14.49 : 24.74 \ldots$

and

$p : \sqrt{2}-1/2 = 0.293 : 0.207 = \sqrt{2} : 1$

and

$0.5 : p = 0.5 : 0.293 = 1.707 : 1$

———— ✳ ————

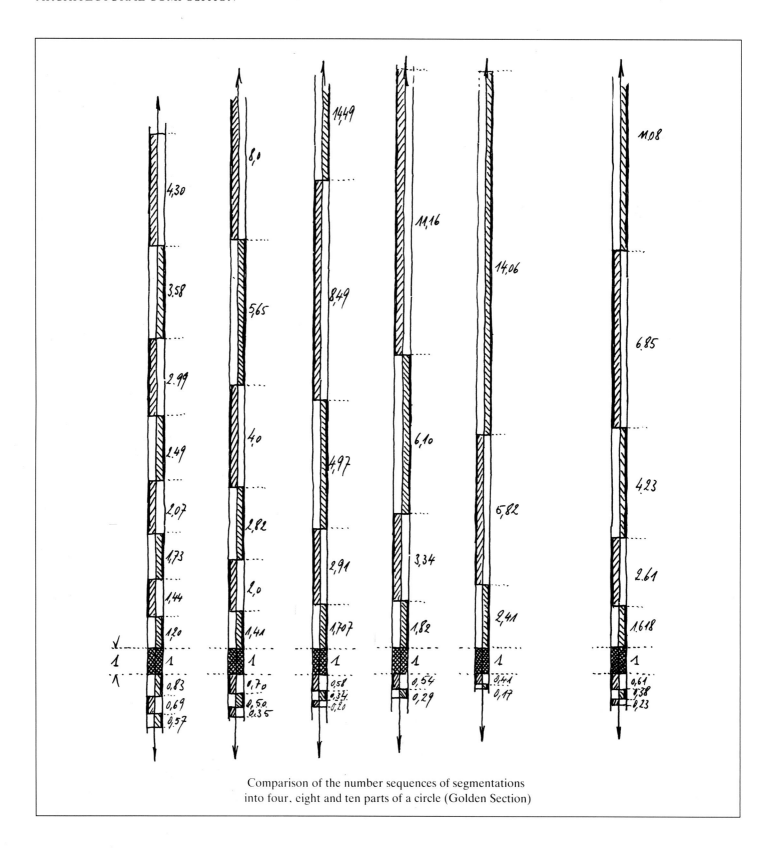

Comparison of the number sequences of segmentations
into four, eight and ten parts of a circle (Golden Section)

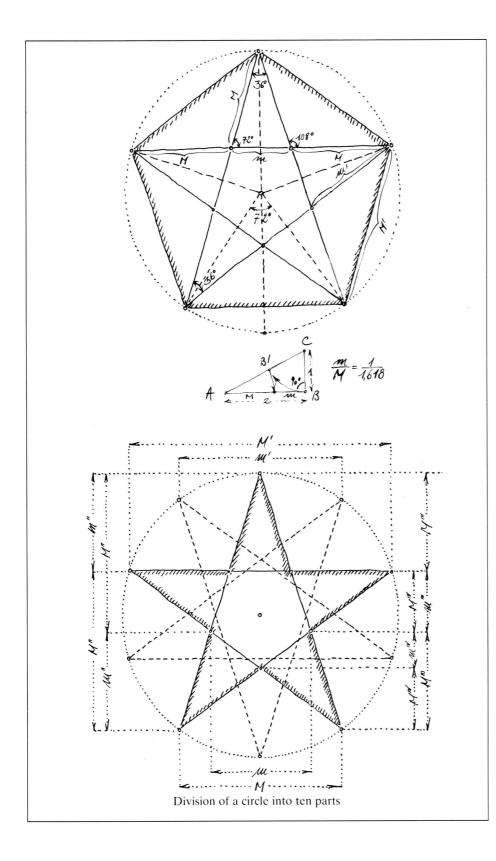

Division of a circle into ten parts

If we join the five points that mark the divisions on the circumference of the circle to construct a five-sided polygon, and then draw a line between every alternate point on the circumference, we get the figure of a star that has five projections. The heart of the star does, of course, give rise to another five-sided polygon configuration.

All the triangles that inscribe an angle of 36° within each point of a star projection have a base to side ratio of m : M = 1 : 1.1618. These are, once again, the proportions of the Golden Section. The resulting number sequence is:

. . . 0.23 : 0.38 : 0.61 : 1 : 1.618 : 2.61 : 4.23 : 6.85 : 11.08 . . .

The relationship between the length M (m^1) and the sides of the polygon ($=M^1$) is also that of the Golden Section:

$m^1 : M^1 = 1 : 1.618$

The simplest method of constructing a Golden Section is to draw a right-angled triangle in which the sides forming the right angle are proportioned 2 : 1. With a compass, using point C as the centre, distance 1 is projected onto the hypotenuse, and the point of intersection marked as point B. Then, using point A as the centre, the compass is used to project point B onto the base line, marked 2.

$AB^1 : AB = 1 : 1.618$

The main characteristic of a division according to the Golden Section is that the smaller distance relates to the larger distance in the same way as the larger distance relates to the overall distance.

Thus: m/M = M/AB

Divide a circle into ten equal parts to form two concentric five-pointed star figures inscribing a small five-sided polygon at their centre. The larger outer five-sided polygon inscribing the star formations has a side dimension (M), which relates to the side dimension (m) of the smaller polygon according to the Golden Section. The distances between the points of 4/10 division (M), and 2/10 division (m^1), also relate to each other according to the Golden Section. Further vertical projections of the points of intersection share the same relationship:

$m : M = m^{II} : M^I = m^{II} : M^{II} = m^{III} : M^{III} = m^{IV} : M^{IV} = 1 : 1.618$

189

The circle is divided as in the previous figure, and the base line of the five-sided polygon is extended outwards. A vertical tangent is then erected on this line. A line is drawn parallel to the base line that intersects the upper two segment points on the circumference of the circle that circumscribes a ten-sided polygon. Two rectangles with the following width to length relationship result from this operation:

m : M

m = radius = 5 units

The verticals are at right angles to the base line and projected from the centre of the circle = 4 units

Half the base line of our five-sided polygon = 3 units

The circle is divided into ten equal segments, with two of the corresponding sides horizontal and parallel to each other. Every side dimension relates to the radius according to:

m : M = 1 : 1.618

Projecting the sides of the ten-sided polygon onto a vertical results in the same relationships:

$m^3 : M^3 = m^4 : M^4$

Equally, projecting the sides of the inner and smaller ten-sided polygon shows the same results:

e.g., $M^1 : M^1$

A star with ten projections can be constructed by starting at any one of the ten segment points on the circumference, and joining it with a straight line to the third nearest point along the circumference, and so on. The intersections of this network define an inner ten-sided polygon with the same star formation.

If the points of intersection of all these lines are projected onto a vertical, the already familiar Golden Section relationships become apparent:

$m^5 : M^5 = m^6 : M^6 = m^2 : M^2$ etc.,

(this figure is taken from Moessel page 12).

———— * ————

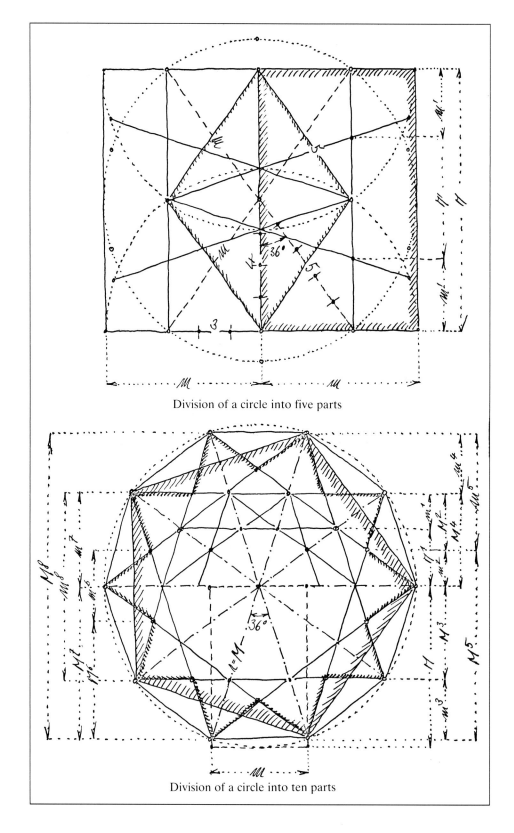

Division of a circle into five parts

Division of a circle into ten parts

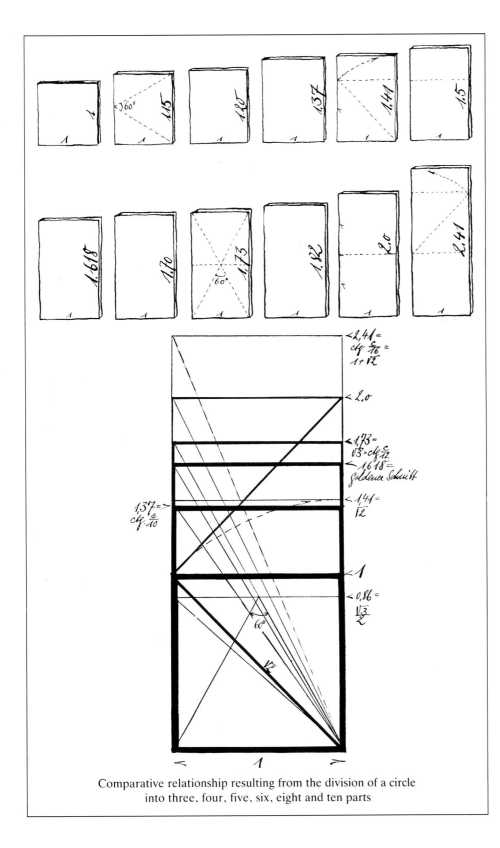

Comparative relationship resulting from the division of a circle
into three, four, five, six, eight and ten parts

In conclusion, the most important relationships that result from the preceding investigations into the three- four- five- six- eight- and ten-fold division of a circle can be illustrated as shown in the adjacent diagram.

Or they can be superimposed onto one figure, as seen below.

Using plexiglass, we can devise an additional control instrument with the following principle:

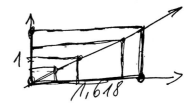

The diagonal fixes the length to width ratios of the rectangle.

Once the most important proportions have been projected, the instrument will look something like this:

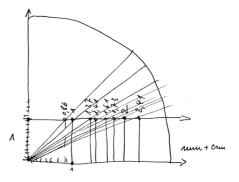

By unravelling the dimensional relationships, this instrument aids greatly the study of proportions used throughout building history.

However before launching into an analysis of a few historic building examples, I would like to draw attention to some observations on the human body and nature – observations we cannot be indifferent about.

I am looking at these things merely through the eyes of an architect, without scientific knowledge, but with pleasure at being able to recognise familiar building plans in the laws of nature.

The Proportions of the Human Body

After the preceding abstract manipulation of numbers, it is a joy to finally prove these relationships through outstanding examples. After all, it was the latter that kindled in me the spirit of curiosity to uncover the secrets of harmonic proportions, not the other way round.

I have been born into an age that for half a century has denounced the tradition of the classical Orders without formulating an adequate theoretical substitute: the structural innovations it has come up with have soon grown old.

I believe that the hope for progress, to which this entire book is dedicated, lies in the clarification of our architectural language. Or perhaps I should say in its 'purification'; in other words its logical use and the integration of its parts must be warranted.

Architecture can no longer fall back onto the classical attributes, even though they have long given good service. Based on the lessons of building history, it is our responsibility to formulate a theoretical basis able to accommodate far-reaching developments.

We can mourn the loss of a rich classical repertoire, but the basics of its typology and

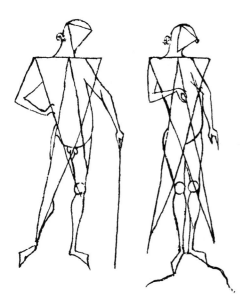

From the thirteenth-century sketchbook of Villard de Honnecourt

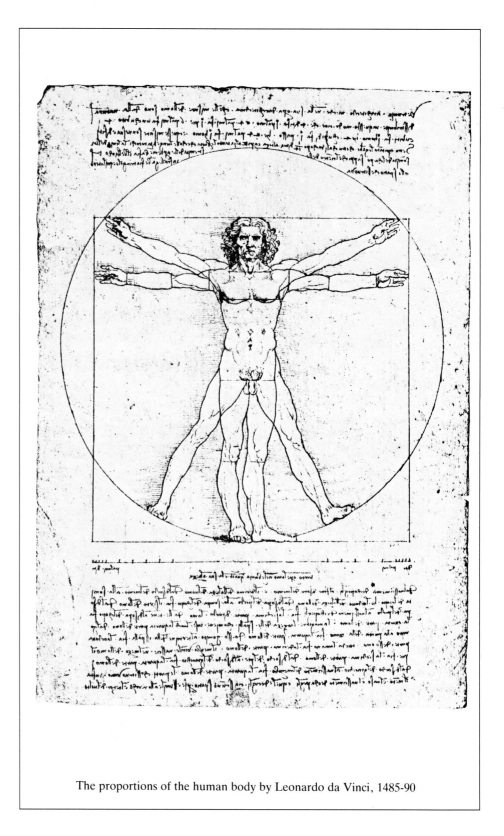

The proportions of the human body by Leonardo da Vinci, 1485-90

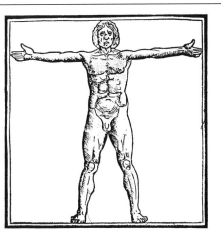

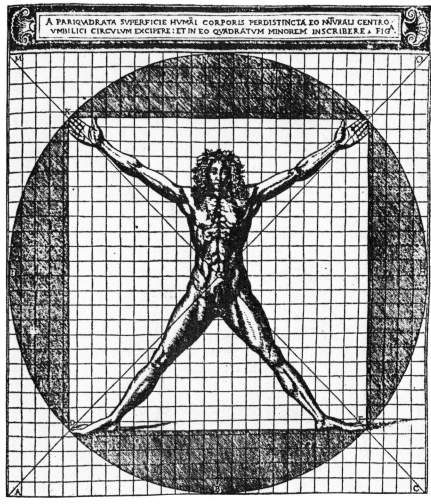

A PARIQVADRATA SVPERFICIE HVMÃI CORPORIS PERDISTINCTÃ EO NÃTVRÃLI CENTRO VMBILICI CIRCVLVM EXCIPERE: ET IN EO QVADRÃTVM MINOREM INSCRIBERE A FIGA.

Caesare Cesariano, Vitruvian figure

elements, to which I devote an entire chapter, are still available to us. Also, we still have its geometry and proportions which guarantee the order of the whole and of the parts to one other.

When we threw the classical Orders overboard, our entire understanding of composition went with them. Therefore today we need to start afresh.

Robert Venturi's essay on complexity in architecture seems like an 'April Fool' to me, in which not even the simplest issues have been understood. So many cosmetics have been used that we've forgotten the colour of the underlying skin. And this skin – this human dimension – gives me the confidence to assert that perhaps all is not lost unless, of course, furious scientific development ruins our planet first.

The dream of beauty cannot be crushed by the ugliness and brutality of our time even if we sometimes despair of its worth.

Before we broach the task of clarifying the rhythmic relationships of buildings and spaces, we should examine the harmonic proportions of the human body and some of the products of nature.

The human body has always been a revered example for architectonic composition. The master builder finds in it the ideal harmonic form. Its functional and structural requirements have been answered to perfection and expressed in a fantastic structure of order and hierarchy. Bones, organs, muscles and tissue are structured not only for optimum function but also for aesthetic fulfilment. Being a bit overweight, I can't say this without smiling, but Dürer's proportional studies illustrate that the proportions of every human body, except the physically malformed, enjoy similarly perfect relationships.

I shall not get involved in a discussion of those instances in which the human body ceases to conform to the norms of 'beauty', since I am primarily concerned with the dimensional relationships that exist between the individual parts of the body and their rhythmic arrangements.

I shall begin my analysis of the human body by considering illustrations taken from a number of proportional studies from Villard de Honnecourt right through to Le Corbusier.

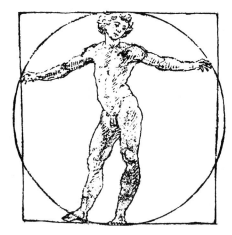

Francesco di Giorgio

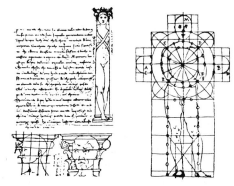

Francesco di Giorgio: a) column and capitals with inscribed figures (Turin); b) plan of basilica with inscribed figure (Cod. Magliab., Bibl. Naz., Florence)

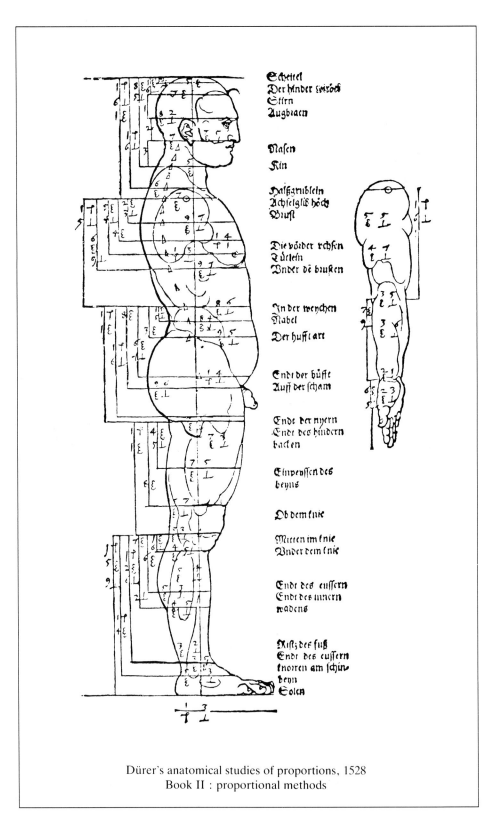

Dürer's anatomical studies of proportions, 1528
Book II : proportional methods

—— ✳ ——

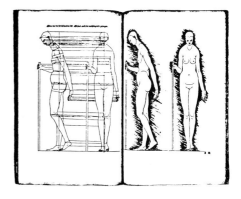

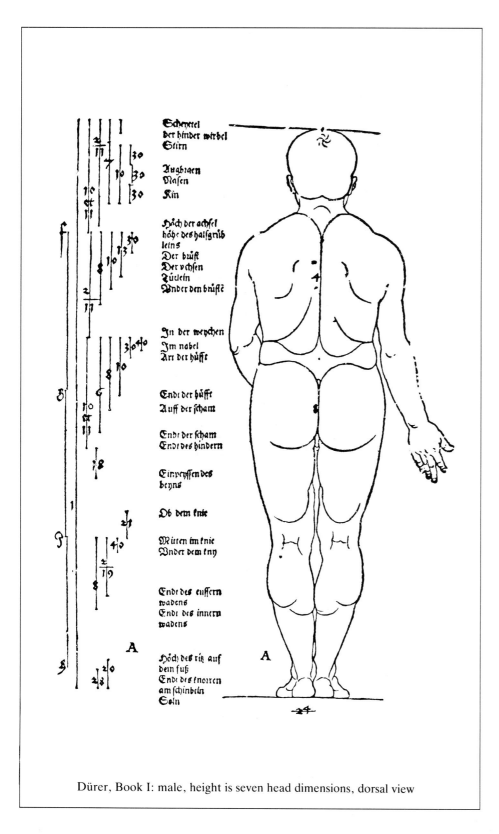

Dürer, Book I: male, height is seven head dimensions, dorsal view

'Human proportions, discovered and described by Albrecht Dürer of Nuremberg, for the benefit of all with a passion for his art. Printed by Hieronymus Andrae Roesch, Nuremberg 1528.

Dürer died on the 6th of April 1528. On the 31st of October the same year his "Study of Proportions" was published. For thirty years Dürer had been studying the proportions of the human body, but did not live to see the publication of the work that established him as a great theoretician. The plan goes right back to the painter's early diaries of 1507-08. In 1523 an edited copy was almost completed, but it was not until 1527-28 that it finally went to the printer after Pirckheimer had proof-read it. The first book described the construction of the figure and some of its limbs with the aid of a special type of rule which had the height of the investigated figure ($= 1$) with fractions marked on its face. The measurements were all in aliquot fractions and taken off fixed points of the body. Constant proportions were determined to enable averages to be established. In the case of head constructions, Dürer offers us three views; by superimposing an equilateral triangle onto the view from underneath, it can be turned 45° and seen as frontal.

The second book deals with the proportions of the human body based on Alberti's Exempeda system. Using a "measuring rod" Dürer measures eight men and ten women, working from fixed points and charting the results in tables. What we end up with is a copy book of certain body types with their relative proportions.

In the third book the eighteen figures are transfigured, but the proportions kept constant. Dürer starts with the reconstruction of the faces, part of his physiognomic studies. He uses a "Trafficker" (reducer) to reduce and enlarge the height, width or depth of his figures. A "Faelscher" (falsifier) is employed to alter the height dimensions. At the end of the third book, Dürer wrote his famous aesthetic excursus as a justification of his proportional studies. With its introduction to the methods of proportional investigations, this forms the core of his art theory.

The last book illustrates "how and where one is to fold the represented figures". Dürer deals with six methods of folding, constructed in frontal and profile view. The second part explains the cube method, whereby the human body is locked into cubes, a plan drawing is produced and the cubes are finally remodelled into spherical bodies.'

(*Extract from the catalogue for the Dürer exhibition, Nuremburg, 1978*)

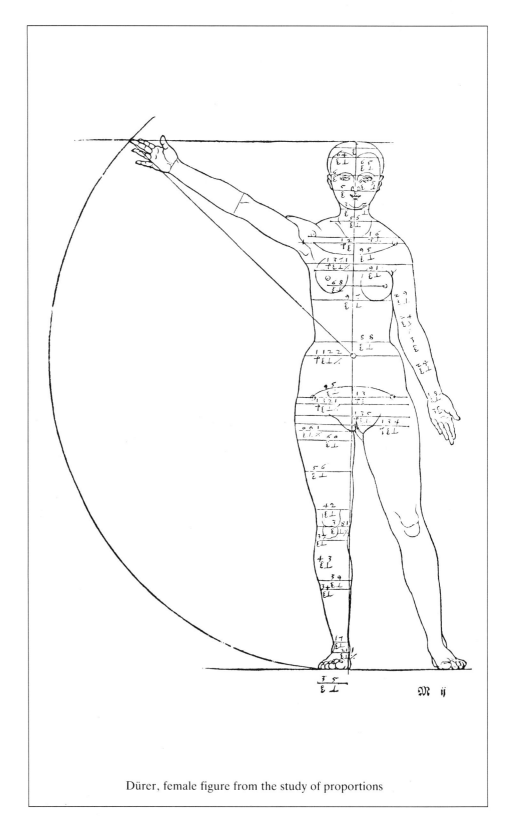

Dürer, female figure from the study of proportions

———— ✳ ————

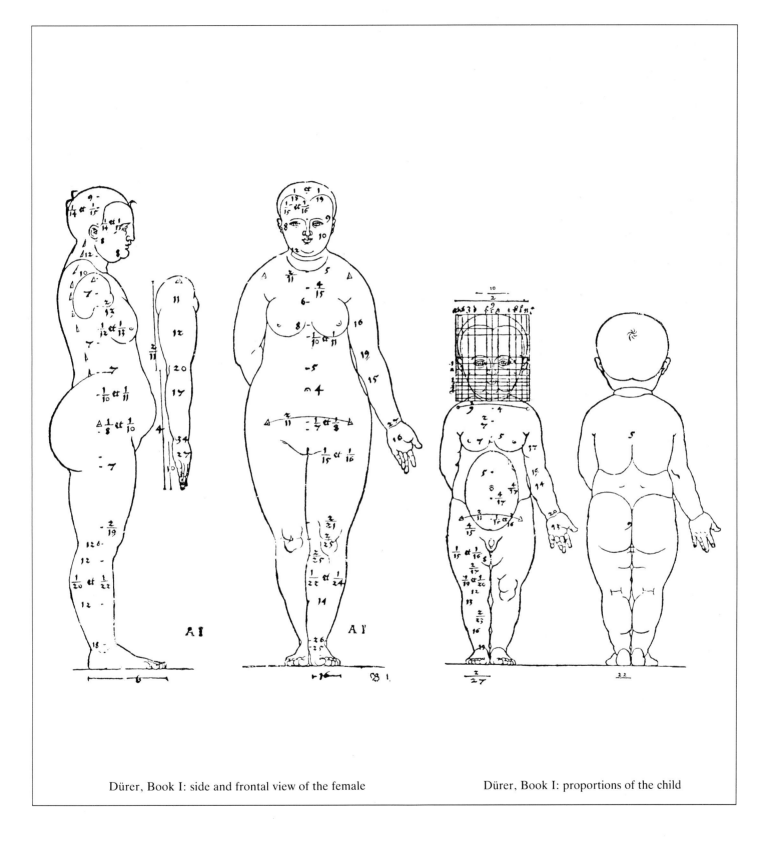

Dürer, Book I: side and frontal view of the female   Dürer, Book I: proportions of the child

Dürer discovers the following dimensional units:

H = overall height from crown to sole

H2 = sole to upper pubic line

H3 = centre knee to navel, upper pubic line to jugular notch

H4 = sole to knee, knee to upper pubic line, from there to armpit and from there to crown

H5 = hip to axis of arm joint, from there to crown

3H5 = leg length, sole to hip

H6 = foot length, three foot lengths to onset of pubic line (my foot is 1/7 of my body height)

H7 = head height, crown to underside of chin

H8 = hand to elbow

H9 = lower breast line to shoulder or to jugular notch

H10 = forehead hair line to underside of chin

The same subdivisions if applied to the dimensional units of Le Corbusier's Modulor (1.83m), give the following dimensions:

H = 183cm

H2 = 91.5cm

H3 = 61cm

H4 = 45.75cm

H5 = 36.6cm

H6 = 30.5cm

H7 = 26.14cm

H8 = 22.87cm

H9 = 20.33cm

H10 = 18.3cm

Superimposition of the figure by Dürer with the Modulor by Le Corbusier. The two harmonic sequences by Le Corbusier are identical with the reference points on Dürer's figure. Using a scale of 1:10 this has been proved graphically:

. . . 27, 43, 70, 113, 183cm . . .

. . . 33, 53, 86, 140, 226cm . . .

———— ✳ ————

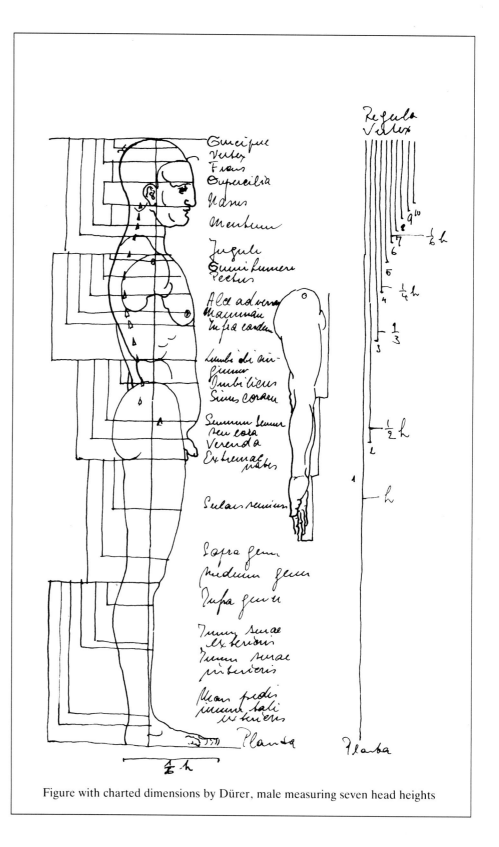

Figure with charted dimensions by Dürer, male measuring seven head heights

198

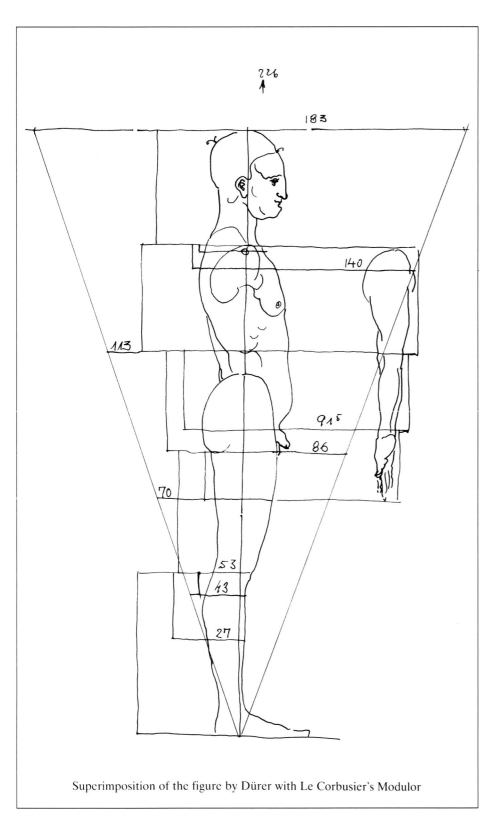

Superimposition of the figure by Dürer with Le Corbusier's Modulor

First sequence:
27cm = sole to end of outer calf (description taken from Dürer)
43cm = sole to lower knee line
70cm = sole to finger-tip of suspended arm, or breast to finger-tip
113cm = navel height
183cm = sole to crown

Second sequence:
53cm = sole to centre knee
86cm = sole to lower buttock line, or sole to crotch
140cm = breast height
226cm = man with extended arm

Proportions of the Golden Section:
The dimensions on the drawing have nothing to do with natural measurements. They are in millimetres and taken from my printed copy.

$m/M = 127.3/206.0 = 113cm/183cm = 1/1.618$

The added centimetre dimensions are measured from my own body and roughly correspond to the dimensions of the Modulor (rounded off measurements).

$m = 113cm = $ navel height
$M = 183cm = $ body height

Thus, the navel divides the human body according to the Golden Section.

$m^{I}/M^{I} = 787/1273 = 70cm/113cm = $ relationship between the distances, navel to skull, and navel height.

$m^{I} + M^{I} = M$

m^{I} is identical to the arm length.

$m^{II}/M^{II} = 486/787 = 43cm/70cm$

Navel height m ($m = m^{II} + M^{II}$) is divided by the lower knee line according to the Golden Section.

$m^{III}/M^{III} = 300/486 = 26.6cm/43cm$

The distance between navel and crown m^{I} ($= M^{II} = m^{III} + M^{III}$) is divided by the neck line according to the Golden Section. The armpit divides this distance equally.

In the lower limb, the division $m^{III} : M^{III}$ is repeated. The distance between sole and end of inner calf and from there to centre thigh or finger-tip of suspended arm shares the same relationship.

$m^{IV} = $ distance between navel and pubic line, 'on the genital organ' (*Auf der Scham*) as Dürer called this position.

$M^{IV} = $ distance between navel and armpit height

$m^{IV}/M^{IV} = 185.6/300 = 16.4cm/26.6cm$

$M^{IV} = 27cm$. This is the length of my foot. My body height is seven times the length of my foot. This dimensional unit is repeated in several other body parts.

$m^{III} = M^{IV} = m^{V} + M^{V}$

The most important of these is the head and neck dimensional unit m^{III}. It is divided according to the Golden Section by the upper edge of the ear lobe.

$m^{V}/M^{V} = 10.1cm/16.6cm$

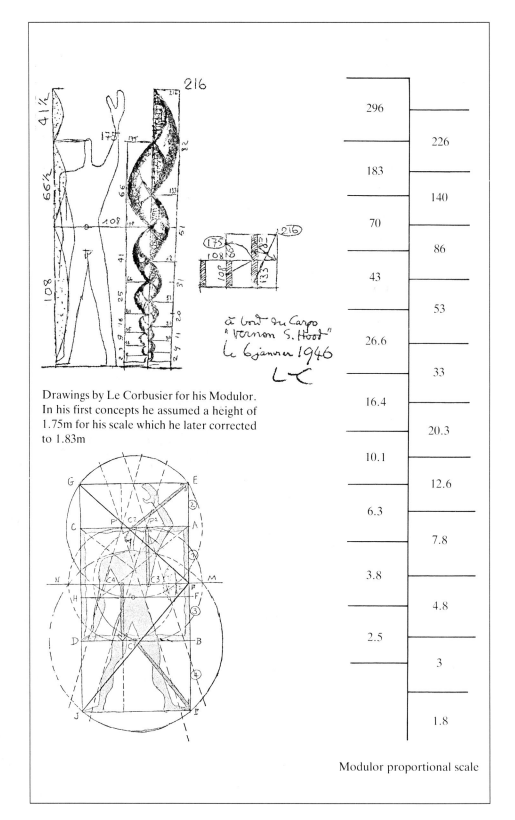

Drawings by Le Corbusier for his Modulor. In his first concepts he assumed a height of 1.75m for his scale which he later corrected to 1.83m

Modulor proportional scale

———— ✳ ————

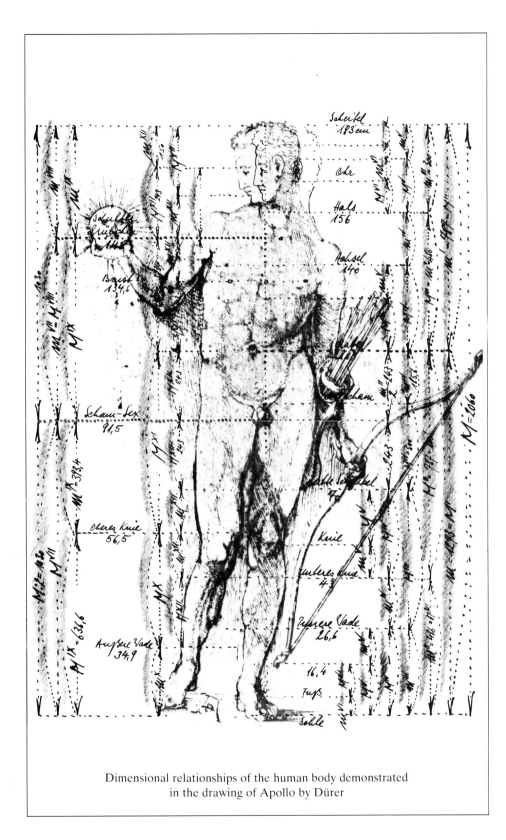

Dimensional relationships of the human body demonstrated
in the drawing of Apollo by Dürer

The size of the ear is $m^{IV} = 6.3$cm. It has m^{III} as its centre, that is $m^V = M^{VI} = 10.10$cm. The genitals divide the body into half.

$M/2 = 2060/2 = 91.5$cm

The trunk divided according to the Golden Section meets the jugular notch or the shoulder height.

$m^{VII}/M^{VII} = 636.6/1030 = 56.55/91.5 = 1/1.618$

$m^{VIII}/M^{VIII} = 393.4/636.6 = 34.95\text{cm}/56.55\text{cm} = 1/1.618$

The area below the waist divided by the proportions of the Golden Section meet the upper knee line, 'above the knee', (*Ob dem Knie*) as Dürer called this position.

$m^{VIII}/M^{VIII} = m^{IX}/M^{IX}$

$m^X/M^X = 243/393.4 = 21.6\text{cm}/34.95\text{cm} = 1/1.618$

$m^{IX}/M^{IX} = m^{XI}/m^{XI}$

m^{XI} = distance between navel and jugular notch

M^{XI} = distance between upper knee line and navel

m^X, M^X and M^{XI} increase according to the same relationship as do m^{XI}, M^{XII} and m^{VII}, developing onwards from the navel height. M^{XII} and m^{XII} is the distance between jugular notch and crown (m^{IV}). The onset of the forehead divides it according to the Golden Section.

$m^{XII}/M^{XII} = 150/243 = 13.34\text{cm}/21.60\text{cm} = 1/1.618$

M^{XII} = distance between chin and crown (21.60cm).

This dimension repeats itself between other points on the body: M^{XII} = distance between navel and nipple, between navel and genitals, between onset of forehead and chin, between centre thigh and genitals, between onset of outer calf muscle and lower knee line. The latter is identical to the size of the sole of the foot (m^X). We may assume this distance (21.60cm) to be the height of the head, which is contained approximately 8.5 times in the overall body height.

Two proportional sequences emerge from these investigations. The first can be found in the Modulor:

. . . 6.3cm : 10.1 : 16.4 : 26.6 : 43 : 70 : 113 : 183 . . .

The second relies on the bisection of the body:

. . . 8.22cm : 13.3 : 21.6 : 34.9 : 56.5 : 91.5 : 148 : 239.5 . . .

1. *The navel divides the overall height according to the Golden Section.*
2. The genitals halve the former.
3. The distances of navel to neckline and crown to neck relate according to the Golden Section.
4. The jugular notch, that shares the same height as the onset of the armpit, halves the distance between navel and crown. The upper knee line does the same with the height of the navel.
5. The lower knee line divides the navel height according to the Golden Section.
6. The crotch height is halved by the lower knee line.
7. The armpit height (m + M^{IV} = 113 + 27 = 140cm) is divided by the knee joint (m^{II} + m^{V} = 43 + 10 = 53cm) according to the Golden Section.
8. Armpit and jugular notch height (M^{VII} + m^{VII} = 148cm) is divided by the genitals according to the Golden Section. The former divide the distance between genitals and crown similarly.
The sole to crown diminishing proportional sequence is, besides the first mentioned, the most important of the entire body structure.

The following ratios emerge:
1. The progressively increasing sequence.
2. The regressive sequence.
3. Symmetrical proportional sequences.
4. Asymmetrical, irregular proportional sequences.
5. Superimposition of dimensional relationships.

These investigations on the human body should remind us of the necessity of controlling the rhythmic divisions of a building.

The human body has been designed to be used with optimum efficiency and ease to serve man. Therefore, it makes good sense that the human body should be the prototype for the composition of buildings.

——— ✳ ———

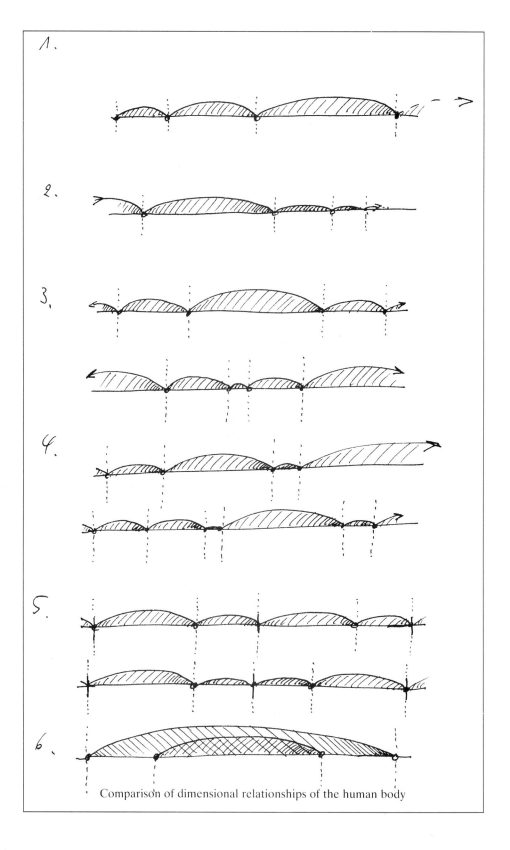

Comparison of dimensional relationships of the human body

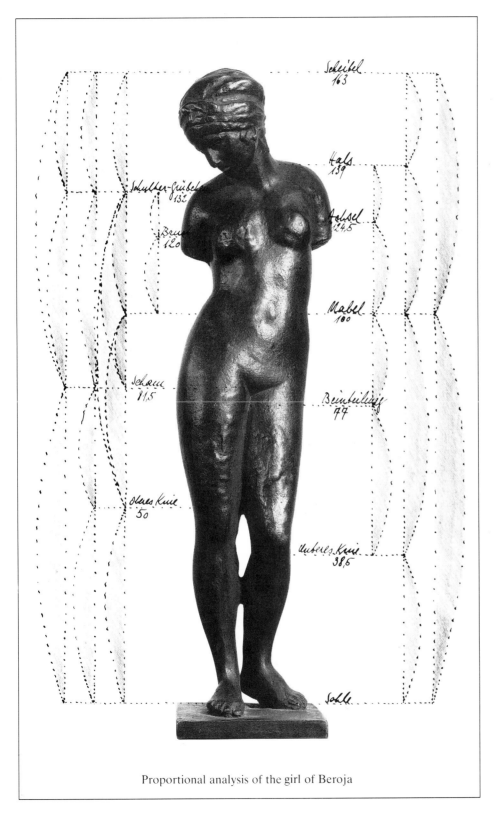

Proportional analysis of the girl of Beroja

The girl of Beroja, Greek statuette,
c.400 BC, bronze cast by Füssel, Berlin, 24cm.
The most important proportional structures of the male body are also, of course, found in the female body. I have left the drawing free of dimensional units, so the rhythm of its proportions may be appreciated more readily.

———— ✳ ————

The following tables contain measurements I have taken of myself (aged 43), my wife Gudrun (aged 40) and my eldest daughter Caren (aged 15). They list natural measurements and ideal dimensions based on the relative body, navel and crotch heights. They also include the ideal dimensions pertaining to the proportions of the Golden Section and calculated only from the overall body height. The middle scale attempts to take the age and growth related proportions into account.

The arm length (70cm) relates to the shoulder width (43cm) according to the Golden Section (Modulor dimensions).

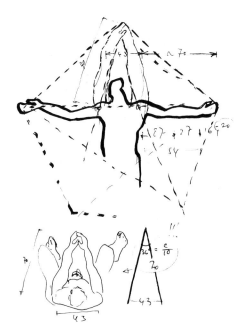

If we join the extended arms in front of our face or above our head so that the fingertips touch each other, they form an angle of 36°. In other words, we can inscribe the human body within the points of a five-sided polygon.

Body Part		Natural Measurements	Ideal Dimensions Related to the Body Structure	Absolute Ideal Dimensions (Modulator)
CROWN	M	182.5cm	182.5cm	183cm
	F	163cm	163cm	163cm
	C	166cm	166cm	166cm
NECK	M	155cm	155.87cm	156cm
	F	136cm	133.5cm	139.22cm
	C	139.5cm	142cm	141.78cm
SHOULDER	M	149.5cm	147.65cm	148cm
	F	131.5cm	131.87cm	131.87cm
	C	134cm	136cm	135.9cm
ARMPIT	M	137cm	139.41cm	140cm
	F	126cm	121cm	124.52cm
	C	129cm	126.5cm	126.81cm
NIPPLE	M	134.5cm	134.33cm	134.6cm
	F	114cm	118.5cm	119.98cm
	C	122cm	124cm	123.19cm
NAVEL	M	112cm	112.79cm	113cm
	F	96.5cm	96.5cm	100.74cm
	C	102cm	102cm	102.59cm
PUBIC LINE	M	91cm	91.25cm	91.5cm
	F	81.5cm	81.5cm	81.5cm
	C	84cm	84cm	84cm
CROTCH	M	84.5cm	86.16cm	86cm
	F	72cm	73.72cm	76.96cm
	C	80.5cm	80cm	78.38cm
ARM LENGTH	M	70cm	69.71cm	70cm
	F	61cm	59.64cm	62.26cm
	C	62cm	62cm	63.4cm
UPPER KNEE LINE	M	57.5cm	56.4cm	56.5cm
	F	50cm	50.37cm	50.37cm
	C	52cm	52cm	51.9cm
LOWER KNEE LINE	M	44cm	43.08cm	43cm
	F	37cm	36.86cm	38.48cm
	C	40cm	38.3cm	39.18cm
FOOT	M	26.5cm	26.62cm	26.6cm
	F	24.5cm	24.5cm	23.78cm
	C	24.5cm	24.5cm	24.22cm

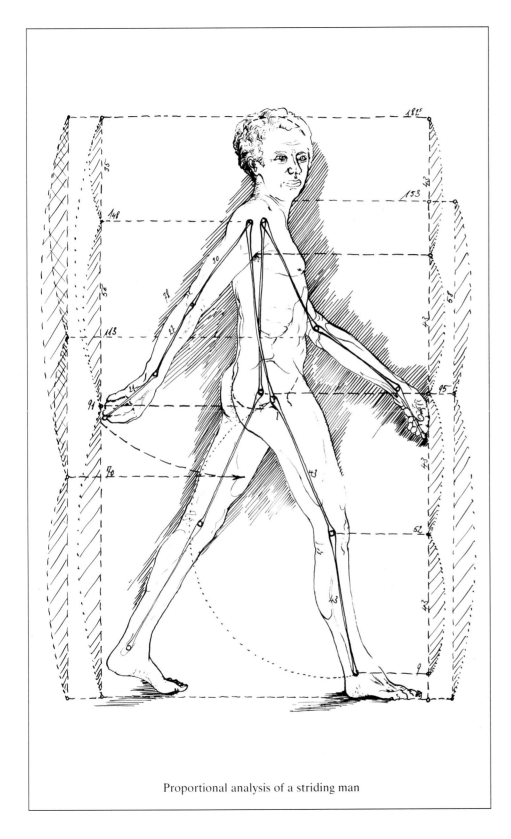

Proportional analysis of a striding man

Striding man
(Traced from a photograph to remain as naturalistic as possible, and annotated with the natural measurements of my own body.)

If we subtract the foot (9cm) from the body height (182cm) and divide the rest by four, 182–9/4 = 43cm, we meet the points on the body related to movement: knee joint, hip joint and armpit. The hip joint divides the distance between the sole of the foot and chin according to the Golden Section. A regressive sequence of the same proportions, that plays a key role in walking, consists of the distances from crotch (91cm), to shoulder joint (56cm), to crown (35cm).

An increasing proportion of the Golden Section is the distance between sole and finger-tip (70cm) of suspended arm and from there to crown (112cm).

The latter is also the navel height. My arm length, measured from shoulder joint to finger tip, is 78cm. This distance is subdivided by the hand (21cm), the lower arm (27cm) and the upper arm (30cm).

Their interrelationships are:
21 : 27 = 1 : 1.28
27 : 30 = 1 : 1.11
30 : 24.27 = 1 : 1.6 = Golden Section
48 : 78 = 1 : 1.62 = Golden Section
One can assume that the most important parts of the body also relate to each other according to the Golden Section when in their dynamic state of movement.
– leg to waist and head
– hand and lower arm to upper arm
During running, bending, squatting, jumping etc. these relationships are enormously important.

——— ✳ ———

The female body in movement

The following movement studies have been traced off photographs. It is only through bending of the joints and movement that the true proportional properties of the human body come to the fore. The stable proportional skeleton of the upright figure begins to waver as some of its parts move forward whilst others go back.

As expected, the Golden Section now takes second place. The centre of the knee divides the distance between sole and crotch.

$m^I/M^I = 74{-}46/46 = 1/1.168$

The leg length M, from hip joint to sole, is 86cm. Its relationship to the back m, is the same.

The arm: upper arm = 28cm
lower arm = 23cm
hand = 19cm

arm length = 70cm

$23 : 28 = 1 : 1.2$
$19 : 28 = 1 : 1.2$

The leg: upper leg = 46cm
lower leg = 38cm
foot = 19cm
(heel to toe tip)

leg length = 103cm

$38 : 46 = 1 : 1.2$
$19 : 38 = 1 : 2$
$38 : 57 = 1 : 1.5$
$46 : 74 = 1 : 1.6 = m^{II} : M^{II}$

M relates to the leg length with extended foot as: $86 : 103 = 1 : 1.2$.

The arm relates to the lower leg with extended foot as: $57 : 70 = 1 : 1.2$.

$1 : 1.2$ is a relationship derived from the quadri- and octa-section of the circle.

——— ✳ ———

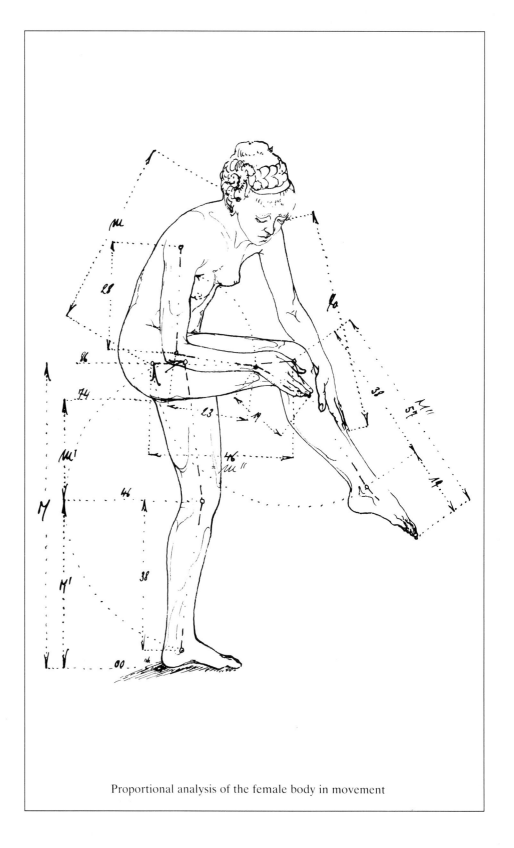

Proportional analysis of the female body in movement

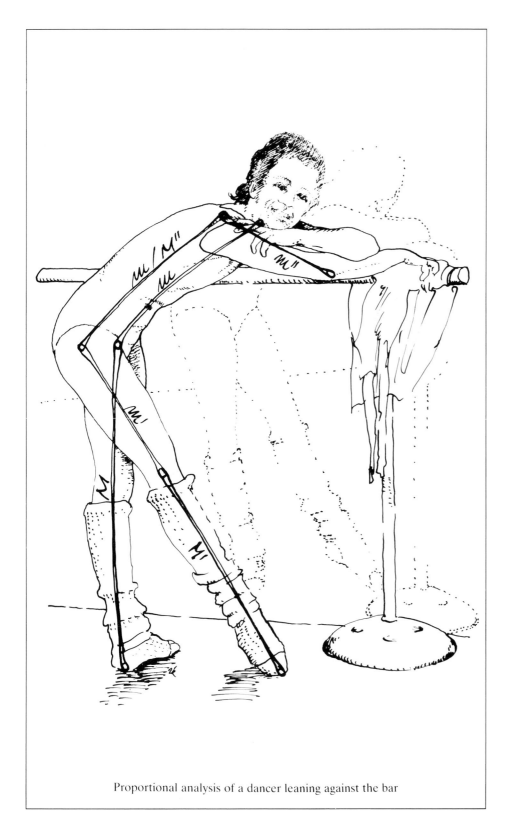

Dancer leaning against the bar
(traced photograph)
Proportions of the Golden Section:
m : M   = body to foot length
$m^I : M^I$ = thigh to calf to toe tip
m   = M^{II}
$m^{II} : M^{II}$ = upper arm to head

Girl with dancing step
(traced photograph)
m : M   = back to leg relationship
$m^I : M^I$ = thigh to calf to toe tip
m   = M^{II}
$m^{II} : M^{II}$ = upper arm to back
$m^{III} : M^{III}$ = calf to foot length
All relationships are of the Golden Section.

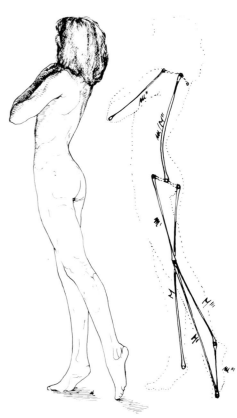

Proportional analysis of a dancer leaning against the bar

Proportional analysis of a girl with dancing step

Proportional observations
on the human skeleton

(illustration from Meyer's *Lexicon*, 1906)
As with the previous investigations on the human body, the skeleton also reflects the major proportions of the body structure.

m : M = m^{I} : M^{I} = 1 : 1.618

m = M^{I}

The distance between pubic bone and shoulder (m = M^{I}) relates to the leg length (M), as the distance between shoulder and cranium (m^{I}) relates to the first mentioned part of the body (m^{I} = M^{I}). This length is equal to that of the humerus. The distance between shoulder height and lower jaw (m^{II}) relates to height of the head according to the Golden Section. The hand length (m^{IV}) relates to ulna and radius (M^{II}) according to the same relationship.

Equally, the shoulder width (m^{V}) relates to the distance between the seventh cervical vertebra and sacrum (M^{V}), as does the width of the femur (m^{VI}) to the length of tibia and fibula (M^{VI}).

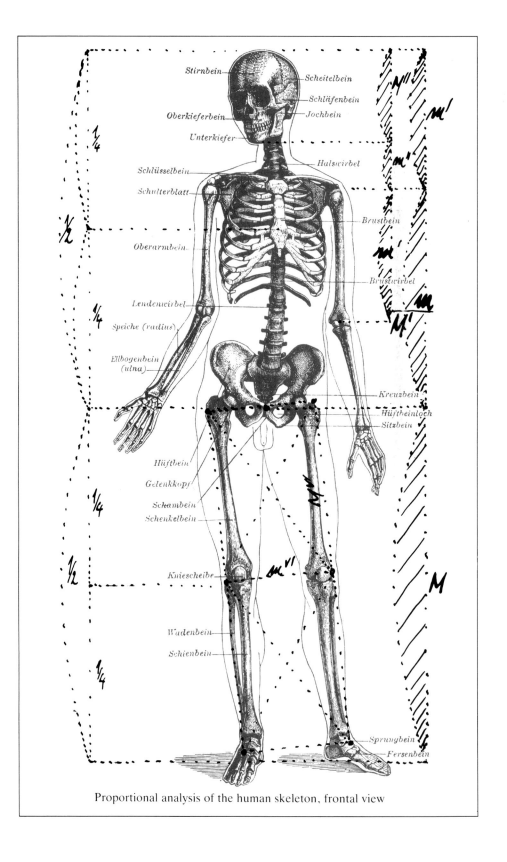

Proportional analysis of the human skeleton, frontal view

———— ✳ ————

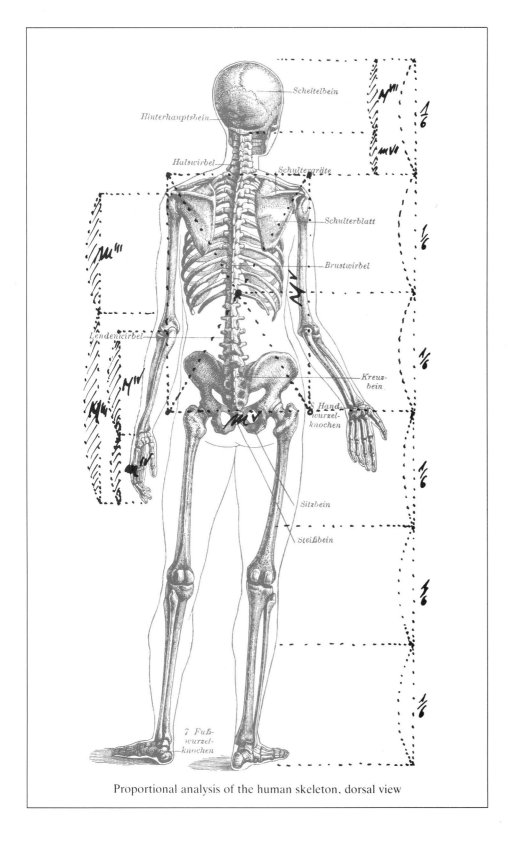

Proportional analysis of the human skeleton, dorsal view

Other divisions of the skeleton:
The pubic bone halves the body height. The two halves are bisected in turn by the widest point of the sternum and the knee-cap.

The cervical vertebrae and the skull represent 1/6 of the overall body height in the illustrated example; equally, the rib cage and the distance between first lumbar vertebra and pubic bone.

——— ✳ ———

The human skull

If we look at the skull sideways and imagine the nose completed, the skull can be inscribed in a square. The auditory canal divides the skull according to the Golden Section (m : M), and so does the orbital roof.

Here we find an important difference to my measurements of the human body. I have always found the division to be in the frontal suture. The anterior nasal spine is on the same level as the auditory canal and divides the total height dimension of the skull in the same way. In the frontal view relationship of skull width to skull height is 1 : 1.26.

Still looking at the frontal view, a horizontal line can be drawn between the upper and lower denture. Measured from the parietal eminence, a horizontal line through the upper and lower incisors completes a square, whose centre point is determined by the nasion. The skull, seen from below, can be inscribed into a rectangle so that the proportions of its sides are true to the Golden Section.

——— ✳ ———

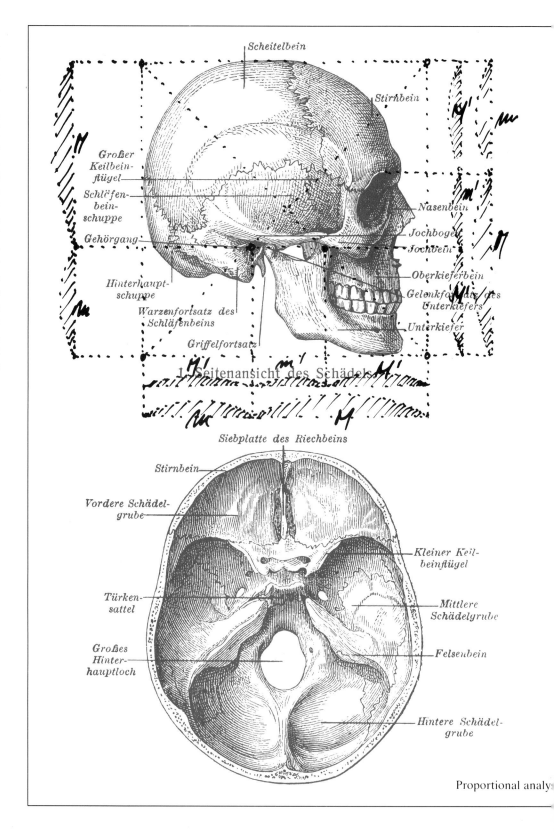

Scheitelbein

Stirnbein

Großer Keilbein-flügel

Schläfen-bein-schuppe

Gehörgang

Nasenbein

Jochbogen

Jochbein

Oberkieferbein

Gelenkfortsatz des Unterkiefers

Hinterhaupt-schuppe

Warzenfortsatz des Schläfenbeins

Unterkiefer

Griffelfortsatz

1. Seitenansicht des Schädels

Siebplatte des Riechbeins

Stirnbein

Vordere Schädel-grube

Kleiner Keil-beinflügel

Türken-sattel

Mittlere Schädelgrube

Großes Hinter-hauptloch

Felsenbein

Hintere Schädel-grube

Proportional analys

210

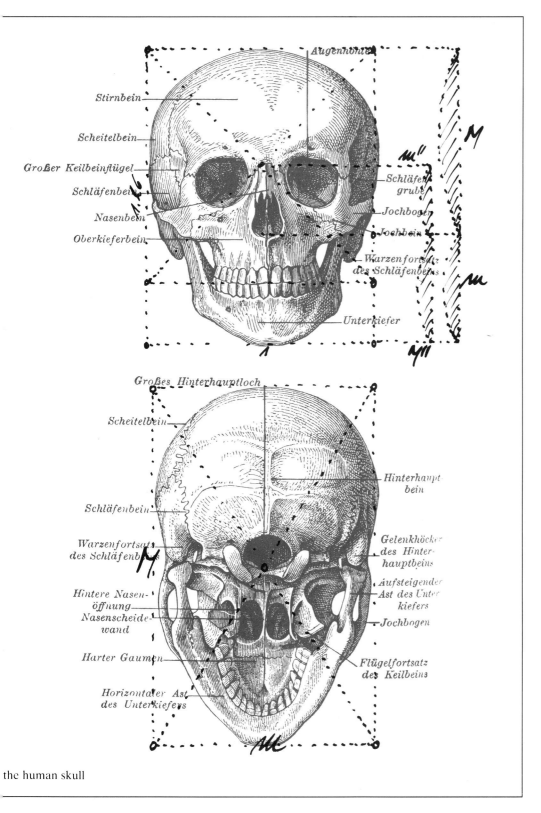

the human skull

Bones of the foot
(illustration from Meyer's *Lexicon*)
From the lateral side:

The dimensions of the distal phalanx, proximal phalanx and first metatarsus of the big toe form a growing sequence equal to that of the Golden Section: $m^I : M^I = m : M$.

The relationship between navicular and the smaller cuneiform follows the same relationship: $m^{II} : M^{II}$.

The joint between the first metatarsus and the first cuneiform halves the length of the foot.

From the medial side:

The base of the fifth metatarsus divides the entire foot length according to the Golden Section: $M^{III} : M^{III}$.

The relationship of the Golden Section is repeated in the metatarsi and the proximal, middle and the distal phalanx:
$m^{IV} : M^{IV} = m^V : M^V = m^{VI} : M^{VI} = 1 : 1.618$

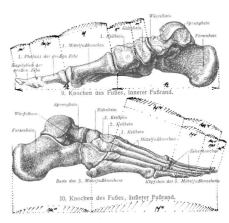

Proportional analysis of bones of the foot

Proportions of the human face

The busts illustrated are portraits of my grandparents on my mother's side, Catherine and Nicolas Lauser. I modelled my grandfather's bust whilst at the Gymnasium in Echternach, 1957, and my grandmother's during Easter 1981, a few years after her death, using photographs to help me.

The measurements on which the proportions are based are true dimensions, taken from the face of my wife and my own. I have since been able to substantiate them on a number of other people.

I always like to compare the dimensions of male and female simultaneously.

Seen from the front, the head can be inscribed in a rectangle whose sides have the proportions of the Golden Section:
m/M = Woman 14.5cm/23.5cm,
m/M = Man 15.5cm/25cm

M^I denotes the facial height dimension between chin underside and frontal hairline (assuming normal hair growth). m^I is the distance between nasion and chin underside and also the facial width dimension between both jaw bones.

m^I/M^I = Woman 11.1cm/18cm,
m^I/M^I = Man 12.6cm/20.5cm

If the facial height M^I is divided, as above, by the nose tip, we get:
m^{II}/M^{II} = Woman 6.8cm/11.1cm,
m^{II}/M^{II} = Man 7.8cm/12.6cm

This enables us to build up two squares, one from the chin, the other from the hairline. The squares overlap at the centre of the face, along the nasal ridge. The side dimensions of the remaining rectangles above and below correspond to the Golden Section. The tip of the nose divides the distance between nasion and chin (M^{II}):
m^{III} = nose
M^{III} = m^{II}
m^{III}/M^{III} = Woman 4.2cm/6.8cm,
m^{III}/M^{III} = Man 4.8cm/7.8cm

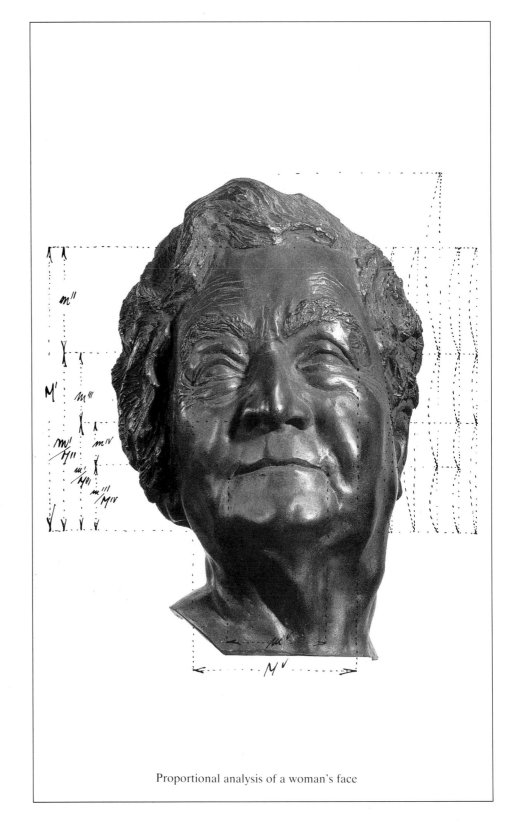

Proportional analysis of a woman's face

———— ✳ ————

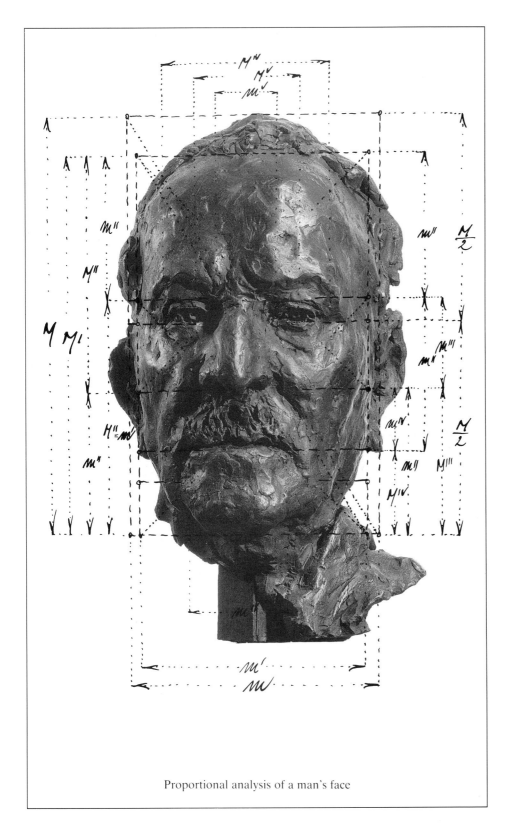

Proportional analysis of a man's face

Equally, the mouth divides the distance between nose tip and chin (m^{III}) according to the same ratio:

m^{IV}: upper lip M^{IV}: chin area

m^{IV}/M^{IV} = Woman 2.6/4.2cm,

m^{IV}/M^{IV} = Man 3cm/4.8cm

The distance m^{II} is repeated three times within the total height dimension. It defines the intervals between chin and nose tip (i.e. mouth), and nasion and forehead height.

m^{V}: mouth measurement

M^{V} width of the eyes (exterior points)

m^{V}/M^{V} = Woman 5.6cm/9.1cm,

m^{V}/M^{V} = Man 5.9cm/9.5cm

m^{VI}: distance between pupils

M^{VI}: distance between the eyes

In this case the eyes halve the total height M. The first figure graphically highlights the rhythmic relationships, the second figure the planar relationships.

$$m^{II}/M^{II} = m^{III}/M^{III} = m^{IV}/M^{IV} = 1/1.618$$

$$\text{where } M^{II} = m^{III} + M^{III}$$
$$M^{III} = m^{IV} + M^{IV}$$
$$m^{II} = m^{IV} + M^{IV}$$
$$m^{III} = M^{IV}$$

Female chin	= 4.2cm
Male chin	= 4.8cm
Female upper lip	= 2.6cm
Male upper lip	= 3.0cm
Female nose	= 4.2cm
Male nose	= 4.8cm
Female forehead	= 6.8cm
Male forehead	= 7.8cm

From the mouth upwards the ratios build up progressively towards the hairline.

———— ✳ ————

The human head in profile

This rather masculine looking bust is the result of my wife's head dimensions (I apologise for this *faux pas!*).

Imagined without the hair-do, it can be inscribed in a square. The face, without the ear, is circumscribed by a rectangle whose sides follow the Golden Section ratio m/M. The profile's rhythmic divisions have already been described exhaustively in the examinations of the face (m^{I-V} : M^{I-V}). The measurements of the Golden Section are superimposed by a simple grid, the side of each square measuring a quarter of the overall square. This confirms that the intervals between chin underside, nose underside, eyebrows, hairline and finally top of the skull, are of equal ratio to each other.

m^{VI} : M^{VI}, the auditory canal divides the head's height measurement in accordance with proportions of the Golden Section.

The horizontal band defining the outer ear hole occurs midway along the vertical head height dimension. The vertical ear dimension is equal to that of the nose and shares the same plane. Both make up a fourth of the overall head height.

Another constant $r = M^{II}$ repeats itself three times in the profile and twice in the side elevation.

r = chin to nose tip
r = mouth to nasion
r = nasion to hairline
r = eyebrow to nose tip
r = ear lobe to corner of mouth and eye.

If one examines the face with a Golden Section divider, the different proportional relationships are not taken from the fixed orthogonal projections, only possible in drawings, but have to follow the accentuations of forehead, nose and mouth. Both types of measurements do, however, lead to similar results. As ascertained already, forehead, nose and upper lip follow a diminishing Golden Section sequence, upper lip to chin an increasing one.

nose m^I/forehead M^I = M^{III} = chin M^{III}/ upper lip m^{III} = 1/1.618

Dimensional proportionality of the ear

The relationship between width (m) and height (M) is that of the Golden Section.

The other proportions are difficult to explain. I suggest you study them for yourself

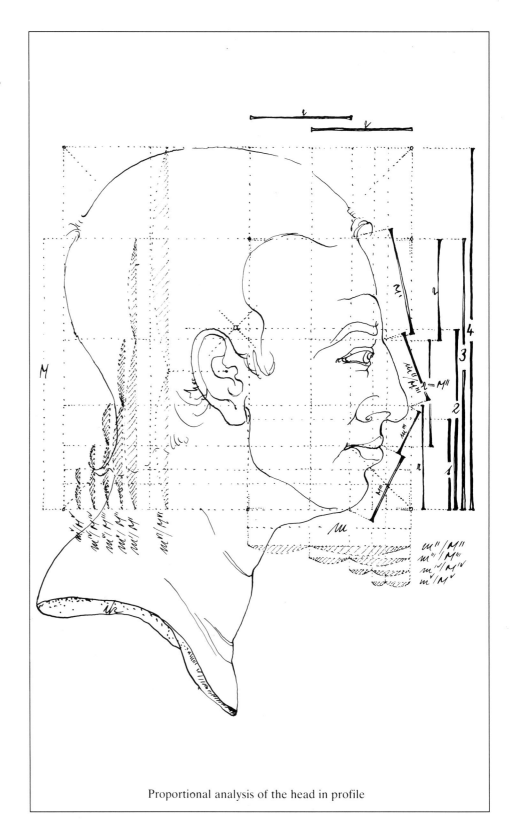

Proportional analysis of the head in profile

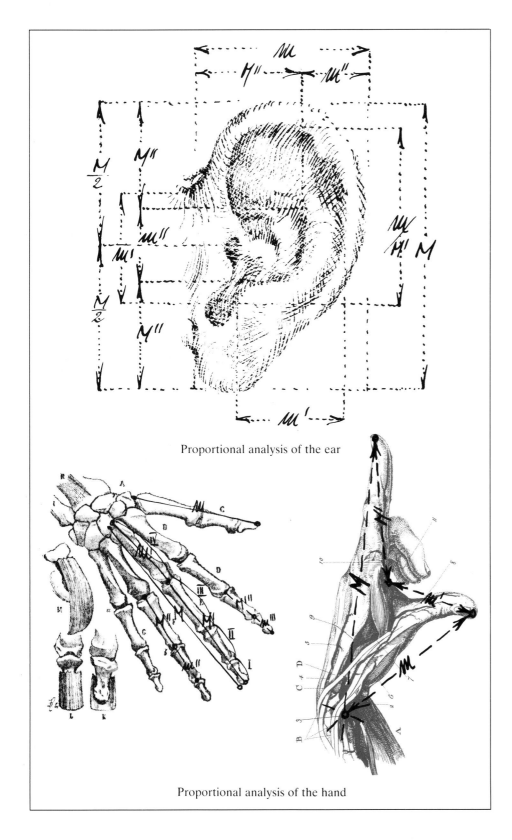

Proportional analysis of the ear

Proportional analysis of the hand

from the drawing or, using a Golden Section divider, project them from a friend's ear. There are some surprising results to be found. It is particularly interesting that the ear hole marks the central position of the overall ear height.

Is the skeleton of the hand ruled by the Golden Section?

I have found this illustration in *Histoire d'un dessinateur* by Viollet-le-Duc. Using the Golden Section divider, I have been able to verify the drawing's proportional relationships using my own hand. Since it is impossible to determine the length of a bone exactly, I am taking my measurements from the approximate joint centres. Except for the thumb, all fingers follow a similar harmonic sequence, which I would like to demonstrate on the middle finger. 1-3 are the distal, middle and proximal phalanx of the middle finger, 4 is the third metacarpus. The following measurements are taken from the anatomical drawing.

1 distal phalanx	= 9.2mm
2 middle phalanx	= 14.9mm
3 proximal phalanx	= 24.1mm
4 third metatarsus	= 29.7mm
sum total	= 77.9mm

$I/II = 9.2mm/14.9mm = 1/1.618 = m^{III}/M^{III}$
$II/III = 14.9mm/24.1mm = 1/1.618 = m^{II}/M^{II}$
$I + II + III = 48.2m = M^{I}$
$m^{I}/M^{I} = 29.7mm/48.2mm = 1/1.618$
All middle finger bones 1-4, are related to the sum of the thumb bones (distal and proximal phalanx, first metacarpus) according to the Golden Section
$m/M = 48.1mm/77.9mm = 1/1.618$

Relationship between splayed index finger and thumb

The measurements are taken from my own hand and transcribed onto a drawing taken from an anatomy book.
$m/M = 12.3mm/19.9mm = 1/1.618$
$m^{I}/M^{I} = 7.8mm/12.6mm = 1/1.618$

———— ✳ ————

Statuette by Michelangelo

wax sketch for a study of a slave, height 18cm, cast by the Staatliche Gipsformerei, Berlin

Since I own authentic copies of both 'The Girl of Beroja' and this statuette, I have been able to take detailed measurements from all sides at my own leisure and without fear of damaging a precious original. It is to be expected that such a perfect masterpiece would not disappoint us in its proportional harmony.

This slumped figure distorts all normal body dimensions. The proportional analysis concentrates primarily on the artistic composition of the piece.

The position of the navel is at the centre of the figure. The chin and genital organs apportion the figure such that its middle part relates to the upper and lower parts according to the Golden Section. The same is true for breast and hip joint, and the distance between them corresponds to the previously mentioned grid patterns of head height dimension.

Viewing the sculpture from the side we are most interested in its points of incurvature. Their three-fold proportional relationship is, once again, based on the Golden Section.

Span 1: the relationship between the vertical measurement of the chest cavity and the distance between hip joint and knee follows the Golden Section.

Span 2: it bisects the body half way. Leg and chest cavity are identical and relate to the hip joint as already mentioned under span 1.

Span 3: this proportion is particularly apparent from behind. The back and buttock ratios are, similarly, based on the Golden Section.

——— * ———

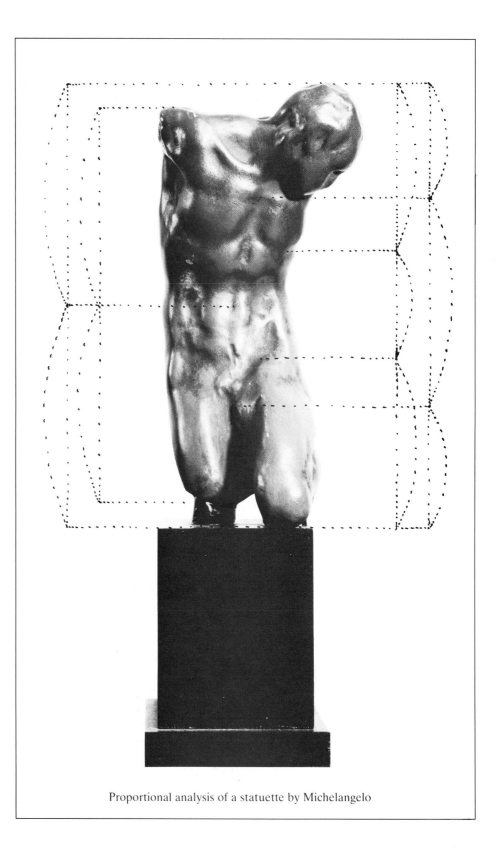

Proportional analysis of a statuette by Michelangelo

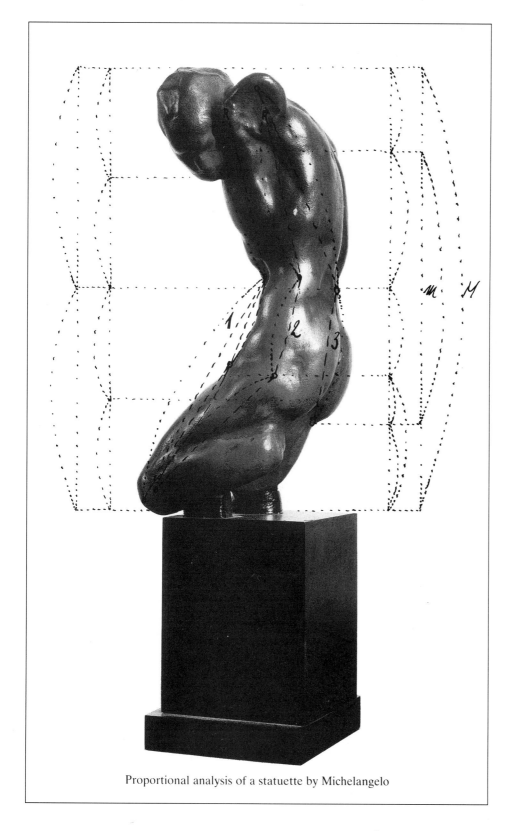

Proportional analysis of a statuette by Michelangelo

Proportional analyses of my own sculpture

Using some of my own works as examples, I would like to illustrate how my sculpture is informed by my observations and understanding of proportions. My predominant application of the Golden Section is never planned or calculated, but is the result of years of tenacious training and of my aesthetic judgement of proportional relationships. None of these figures have been modelled with the aid of a Golden Section divider or any other proportional controlling device.

These little art objects originate from sketches of sculptures for some of my houses; they were never intended as study models to illustrate proportional harmonies. If their involuntary rhythm had not been conspicuous, I would never have thought of mentioning them. I wanted to illustrate, not without vanity, how a rationally worked out and intellectually assimilated compositional system can become second nature and be applied without pedantry or contrivance. This is to encourage the budding architect and artist to uninhibitedly exercise their feelings for proportion through practical application. I would like to anticipate another question that may well arise: 'How do I, as an architect, take it upon myself to meddle in the discipline of sculpture?'

I decorated my house on the Ritterstrasse in Berlin with a large sculpture. With the help and initiative of students, friends and builders I managed to produce and install this monstrosity. The fact that this attempt does not look too professional might perhaps be excused. Not only was it my first enterprise of this kind, but also the client did not cough up a penny – my teaching paid for it!

The project has brought bitter charges from sculptors, accusing me of dabbling in and interfering with their profession. I am, however, convinced that apart from his practical training in one of the building crafts, an architect should have practical experience in the disciplines of sculpture and painting. I am attracted to these art forms, so closely related to architecture, out of an overwhelming zeal for self-realisation that has driven me since my early youth. The fine and applied arts are an intrinsic and indistinguishable part of architecture.

———— ✳ ————

Clay figure of a girl

width 12.5cm, height 23.7cm, 1981
This beautiful piece could not possibly live
with average proportions. So let's examine
it more closely. As an artist I may take the
liberty of completing the drawing and thereby discover that the figure's width, 12.5cm,
is exactly half its constructed height, 25cm.

Navel, nipple and chin subdivide the entire figure into four equal parts of 6.25cm.
The diagonal $12.5 \sqrt{2} = 17.6$cm of the
lower square, if folded up, coincides with
the height of the right shoulder.

The most important proportions in the
Golden Section:
Right Side:
Waist m = 7.7cm to maximum width
12.5cm
m/M = 7.7cm/12.5cm = 1/1.618
Overall height 23.7cm is divided by lower
right armpit line, 14.4cm.
14.4cm/23.7cm = 1/1.618
The shoulder height, 17.6cm, is divided by
lower breast line, 11cm.
17.6cm/11cm = 1/1.618
The distance between navel and chin is divided by the armpit.
18.75cm – 14cm/14cm – 6.25cm = 1/1.618
Left Side:
Working downwards from the imaginary
height of 25cm, we discover a beautifully
diminishing sequence; to nipple height,
12.5cm, to half way mark, to hip height,
4.8cm.
12.5cm – 4.8cm/12.5cm = 1/1.618

———— ✳ ————

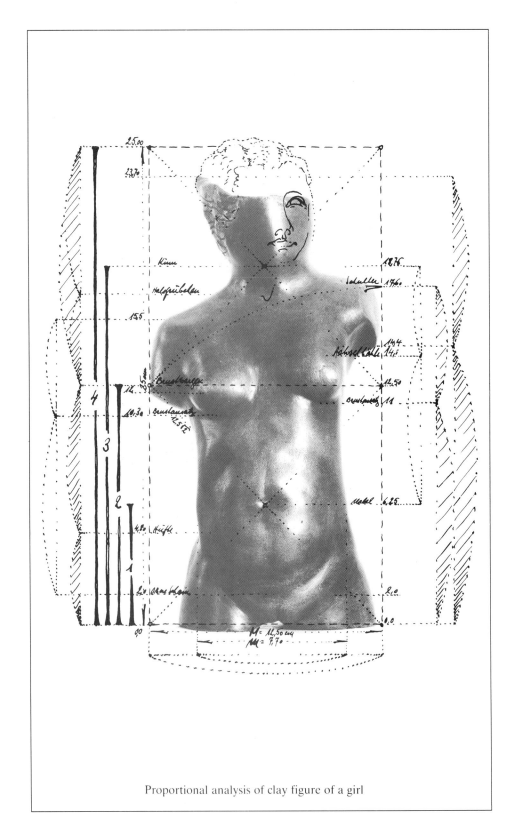

Proportional analysis of clay figure of a girl

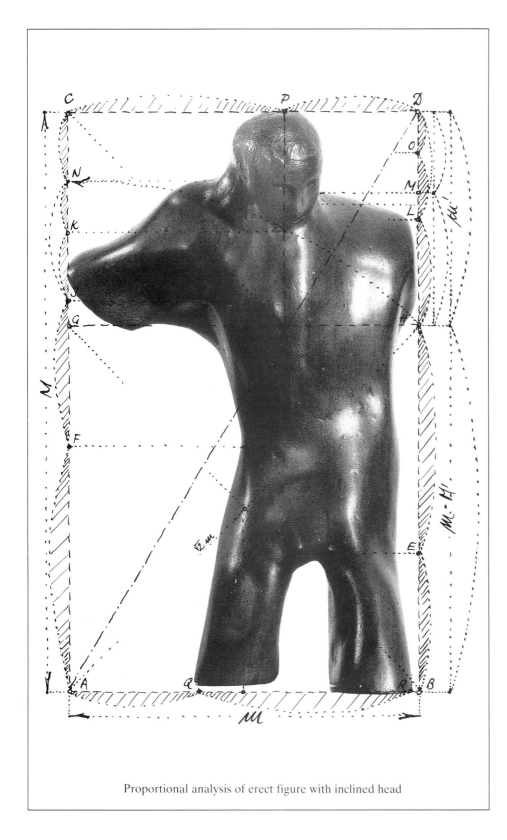

Proportional analysis of erect figure with inclined head

Erect figure with inclined head
clay figure, height 34.5cm, 1981
Seen from the front, the figure can be inscribed in a rectangle, whose sides M : m = AC : AB are in the Golden Section in relation to each other. If one draws a square AGHB, with AB = m, the side AG touches the underside of the severed arm stump. If the diagonal of this square $m\sqrt{2}$ = AH is folded up, it coincides with the left shoulder AH = AN.

On the right side of the figure, the following divisions according to the proportions of the Golden Section, become apparent:
m^1 = distance between breast, right armpit height and crown of the head = HD.
M^1 = right armpit height to arm stump projections = HB.
m^1/M^1 = HD/HB = 1/1.618
M^1 = m
The genital organ E divides m.
EB/EH = 1/1.618
m^1 is equally divided by the seventh cervical vertebra M.
MD/MH = 1/1.618
The right shoulder height bisects m^1.
LH = LD = m^1/2
O = upper hair line, divides LD in the Golden Section.
OD/OL = 1/1.618
A regressive sequence maps the distance between genital organ and crown of head:
EH/HM = HM/MD = HL/LO = LO/OD = 1.618/1
On the left side the following divisions in line with the Golden Section, can be ascertained:
Point J meets the left armpit height AJ in the Golden Section, the hip divided is F.
FJ/FA = 1/1.618
The left shoulder N divides JC equally:
NC/NJ = 1/1.618
Point K demarcates the chin and also divides the same distance according to the same relationship.
KJ/KC = 1/1.618
CN = KJ

Sculpture for Dickes Residence, Luxemburg
fired clay, height 20cm, 1977
Torso with wing that disappears into the house wall.

The superimposed dimensions on the photograph have been projected from the original and follow the Golden Section.

m = figure width, seen from the side

M = height

$m/M = 1/1.618$ = figure's width to height relationship.

The relationship between head m^{II} and wing joint $m^{I} = M^{II}$ obeys the same proportion, as do the following:

$m^{III}/M^{III} = 1/1.618$ = the part of the torso which pierces the base to the section between the upper edge of the base and the upper edge of the wing.

m^{IV}/M^{IV} = base height to distance between base and crown of head.

$(m^{IV}/M^{IV} = 7.64/12.36 = 1/1.618)$

m^{V}/M^{V} = torso base line to wing base line.

$M^{V} = m^{VI}$

$m^{VI}/M^{VI} = M^{V}$ is related to wing height by the same proportion.

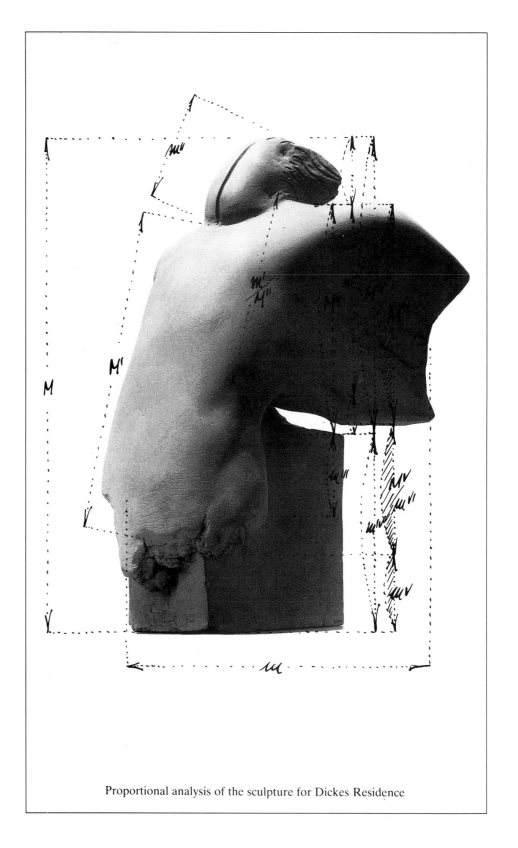

Proportional analysis of the sculpture for Dickes Residence

———— ✳ ————

Double bronze figure on base
Berlin, height 38cm
The visual presence of the base in this com-
pacted figure is minor: m : M.

The armpit divides M in m^I : M^I.

The hip divides M^I in m^{II} : M^{II}, the nose
divides m^I in m^{III} : M^{III}.

The division of the upper base section
follows the same relationship m^{IV} : M^{IV}.

Proportional analysis of double bronze figure on base

Seated figure for the exterior staircase of the gatehouse in the Ravensbererstrasse in Berlin.
clay model, 35.5cm x 29cm, August 1981
One leg of the squatting figure grows into the ascending balustrade. I believe that a sculpture composed for a specific building should be united with it. Without this union, the sculpture is no more than a fragment. The figure is inclined towards the visitor. The proportions, m^{I-III} and M^{I-III} are identical in both sculptures.

The simultaneous, side-by-side comparison of both figures defines their spatial rotation. As with all the other pieces, the dimensions have been taken from the original, not a photograph. m = distance between knee and toe tip, and from buttock to knee (13.5cm). It relates to the shoulder height M (22cm) according to the Golden Section.
$m/M = 13.5cm/22cm = 1/1.618$
m^{I} = distance between knee and hip joint (8.3cm) and relates to m = 13.5 = M^{I} according to:
$m^{I}/M^{I} = 8.3cm/13.5cm = 1/1.618$
M^{I} = also the distance between hip joint and shoulder bone.
m^{II} = distance between knee and ankle joint (11.5cm). Its relationship to M^{II} (18.5cm) is of the Golden Section. The distance between knee and shoulder is:
$m^{II}/M^{II} = 11.5cm/18.5cm = 1/1.618$
M^{III} = distance between buttocks, knee

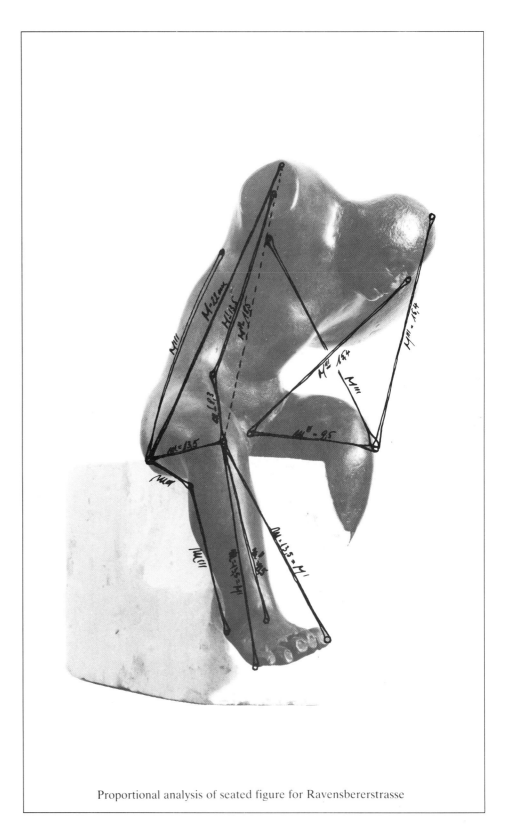

Proportional analysis of seated figure for Ravensbererstrasse

———— ✳ ————

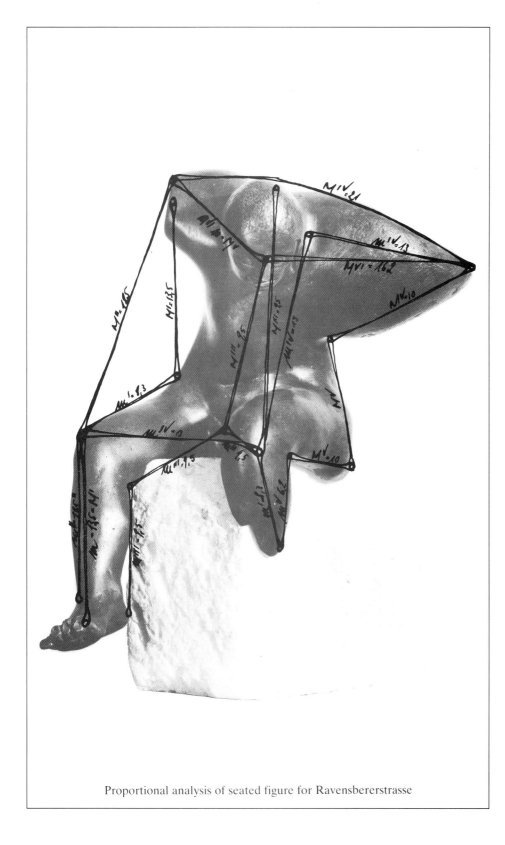

Proportional analysis of seated figure for Ravensbererstrasse

groove and heel. It is identical to the distance between genital organ and knee (9.5cm). Its relationship to distance M^{III} = 15.4cm, genital organ to nose, or knee to cranium, or armpit height is of the Golden Section.

$$m^{III}/M^{III} = 9.5cm/15.4cm = 1/1.618$$

In this oblique view further proportional relationships can be examined:

m^{IV} = distance between wing tip and neck (13cm), and from there to the right knee-cap. m^{IV} is also the distance between both knee-caps.

$$m^{IV}/M^{IV} = 13cm/21cm = 1/1.618$$

Their relationship to the maximum width M^{IV} = 21cm is of the Golden Section.

Of particular importance to the spatial unfolding of the figure is the proportion between the knee distance and the fully extended shoulder and wing span.

m^{V} = right tibia (calf of the leg 6.2cm), which disappears into the base. Its relationship to the distance between knee groove to buttock to wing joint to wing tip (M^{V} = 10cm) is of the Golden Section.

$$m^{V}/M^{V} = 6.80cm/10cm = 1/1.618$$

A last and very important division originates from the nose. It proportions the distance from nose to wing tip M^{VI} = 16.2cm, on to shoulder m^{VI} = 10cm. The latter is identical to the recurring length M^{V}.

$$m^{VI}/M^{VI} = 10cm/16.2cm$$

———— ✳ ————

Proportional Studies on the Horse
(Drawn from a photograph)

Side view:
The following Golden Section relationships have been observed:
M : m = distance between hindquarters and muzzle at loin height.
m = distance between muzzle and ground, in rest position, and between hind heel and front hoof. Legs and loin are inscribed in a rectangle.

The relationship between the length of the animal, and its head height, is: $\sqrt{3/2} : 1$. The whole body is inscribed in a rectangle, with the base/height relationship of an equilateral triangle.
Further Golden Section relationships:
$m^{I} : M^{I}$ = chest diameter : length of foreleg
$m^{II} : M^{II}$ = hip region : length of hindleg
$m^{III} : M^{III}$ = length of head and neck : length of trunk

Frontal view:
m : M = the elbow divides the total height according to the Golden section
$m^{I} : M^{I}$ = head height : maximum trunk height
$m^{II} : M^{II}$ = distance between knee and crupper : hindleg
$m^{III} : M^{III}$ = distance between hock and heel : loin height
$m^{IV} : M^{IV}$ = crupper to head height : maximum trunk diameter
$m^{V} : M^{V}$ = the crupper height is divided by the hock according to the Golden Section

Leonardo da Vinci, *The Trotting Horse*
Drawing
Type and pose are very different from the preceding 'naturalistic' example. The trot movement and the artist's genial line ennoble the figure in a gracious manner. The rampant head and muscular body defy direct comparison with the other figure. (I suspect the drawing was a sketch for a heraldic statue.) The overall figure, including tail, is inscribed in a rectangle, its height to base relationship is that of an equilateral triangle. Trunk and legs are, as in the previous figure, inscribed in a square. The square can be enlarged to encompass the entire figure, with neck and head erect.

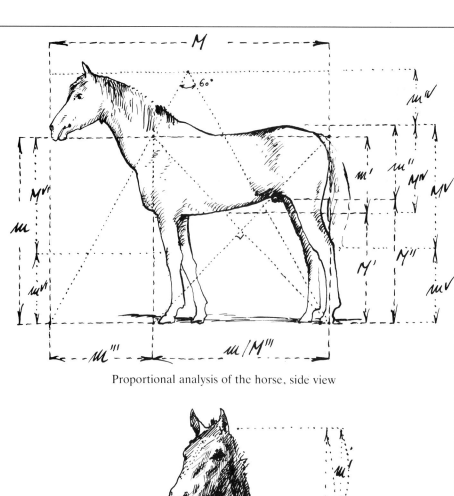

Proportional analysis of the horse, side view

Proportional analysis of the horse, frontal view

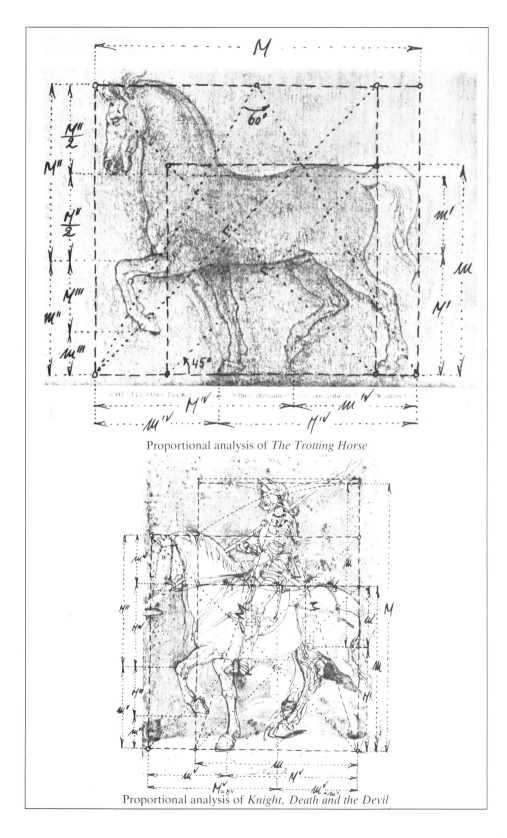

Proportional analysis of *The Trotting Horse*

Proportional analysis of *Knight, Death and the Devil*

$m^{\circ\text{-IV}}/M^{\circ\text{-IV}} = 1/1.618$

m $\quad$ = crupper height

M $\quad$ = distance between crupper and head

m^{I} $\quad$ = vertical distance between saddle height and hindleg onset

M^{I} $\quad$ = hindleg length

m^{II} $\quad$ = floor to knee height of leg drawn up

M^{II} $\quad$ = distance between knee and crest

$M^{II}/2$ = the lips bisect M^{II} at midpoint

m^{III} $\quad$ = distance betwen hoof and floor, leg drawn up

M^{III} $\quad$ = distance betwen knee and floor, leg drawn up

m^{IV}, M^{IV} fix the leg positions.

Albrecht Dürer, *Knight, Death and the Devil*
Drawing
This was a preliminary sketch for the famous copper plate etching of the same title. I have selected this drawing because of its conspicuous geometric grid which corroborates my erstwhile investigations; the square (m x m) transcribes the horse's trunk and legs. Dürer sub-divides the upper side into three equal parts (m/3) and thus proportions the trunk into proximal, medial and distal sections.

$M^{\circ\text{-V}}$ and $M^{\circ\text{-V}}$ are identical to the proportions of Leonardo da Vinci's drawing with only the exception of the head which Dürer under-proportioned a little.

M^{IV}/M^{IV} = distance between throat and chest and the raised knee.

Also of interest are the proportions of the rider saddled on his horse. The height of the horse's hind quarter (m), relates to the maximum height of the rider (M) according to the Golden Section. The rider's visor line runs parallel to the diagonal of the rectangle with base line m, and height $m^{II} + M^{II}$. If we construct a triangle from the base line upwards, with an apex angle of 36°, the relationship between side M and base m is of the Golden Section. The triangle's axis overlaps that of the rider, and its apex occurs on the same horizontal height as the eyes.

———— ✳ ————

225

Albrecht Dürer, *The Greyhound*

Drawing

An analysis reveals proportional relationships similar to that of the horse. The
dimensional relationship of the figure's
length and height is the same as the base/
height relationship of an equilateral triangle,
$1 : \sqrt{3}/2$.

Trunk and legs are inscribed in a square.
The following relationships are true to the
Golden Section:

m : M = distance between shoulder and
buttocks : overall length, or distance between foreleg and hindleg : overall length

$m^I : M^I$ = the inner onset of the hindleg
divides the overall height according to the
Golden Section

$m^{II} : M^{II}$ = chest diameter : chest to floor
height

$2M^{II} = m^I + M^I$ = maximum overall height

$m^{III} : M^{III}$ = length of front leg : distance
between chest and head

$M^{III} = M^I$ = height of hindlegs is equal to
distance between chest and head

$m^{III} : M^{III}$ = the relationship between
length of frontlegs : length of hindlegs is of
the Golden Section.

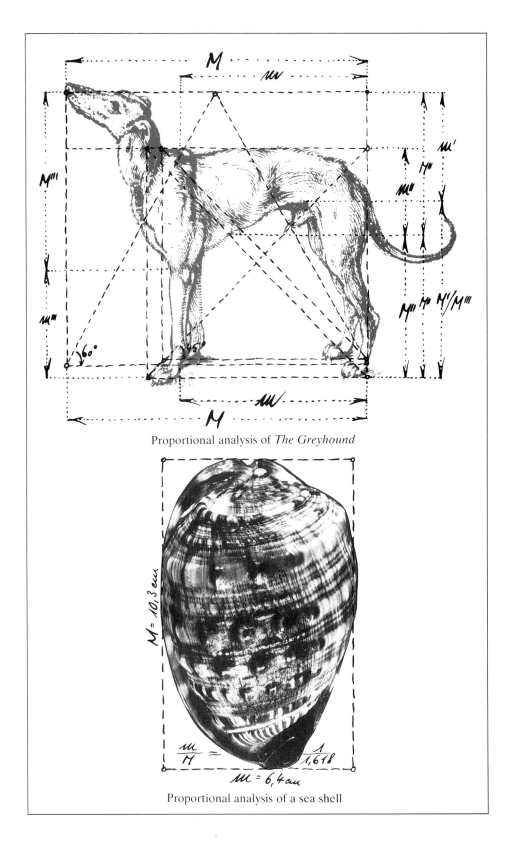

Proportional analysis of *The Greyhound*

Proportional analysis of a sea shell

— ✳ —

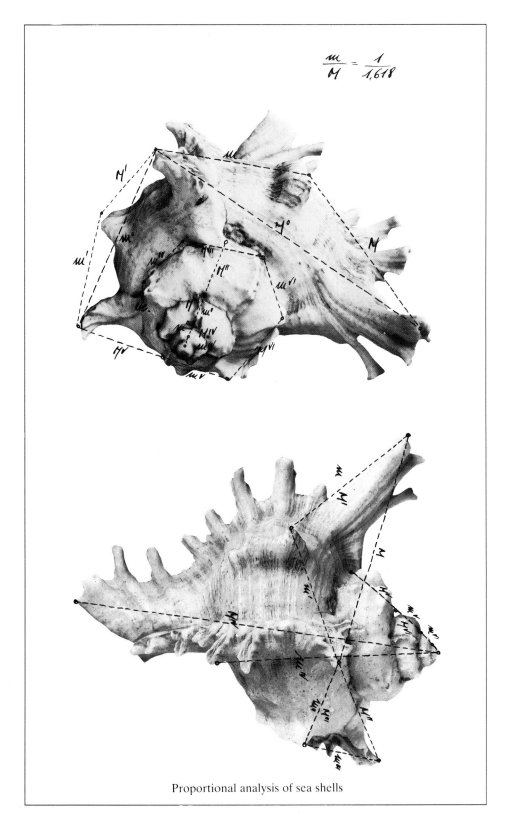

$$\frac{m}{M} = \frac{1}{1.618}$$

Proportional analysis of sea shells

Proportional investigation of sea shells
The large growth rings of these shells approximately follow the proportions of the Golden Section. These dimensional relationships can be mapped and projected with the help of the Golden Section divider. They have to be measured in three dimensions and are therefore not verifiable on a two-dimensional illustration.

This conch is inscribed in a rectangle with sides of Golden Section proportions.
m/M = 6.4cm/10.3cm = 1/1.618

✳

Proportional analysis of five-leaved structures

The leaf structure, chosen at random, forms an irregular pentagon.

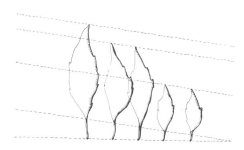

The two leaves on either side of the middle and largest leaf can be seen as two similar pairs. The largest leaf is approximately twice the size of the smallest.

If we inscribe the leaf in a pentagon, and rotate the leaves around the central node, a surprisingly regular configuration becomes apparent.

Five-leaved structures: Ivy and Cinquefoil

Despite all the irregularities, it is interesting to discover that in both species, at least two of the five blades inscribe an angle of 36°. The discernible proportions of the Golden Section are inexact, but represent a beautiful approximation.

Proportions of Ivy

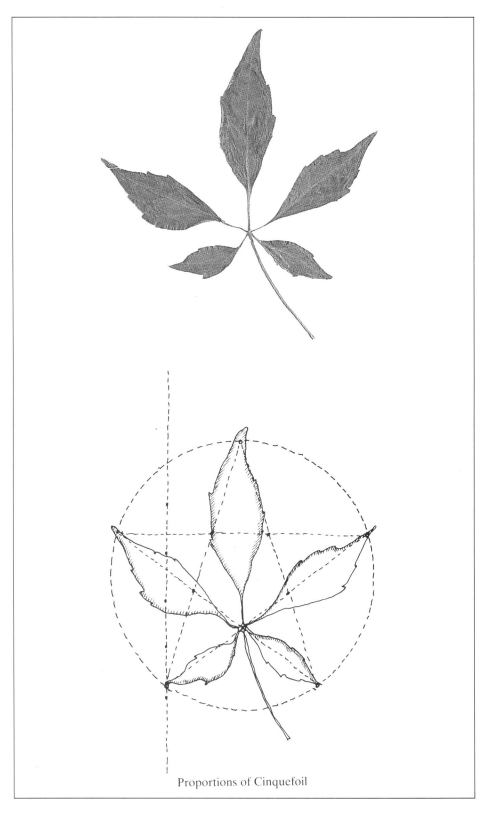

Proportions of Cinquefoil

Leaf proportions: Beech, Walnut, Oak
The proportions of the measured width to height ratios correspond to the segmentation of a circle into three and six equal parts:
1 : 1.15
1 : 1.7
1 : 3

$$\frac{49}{83} \approx \frac{1}{1.5} \approx \frac{1}{1.7}$$

$$\frac{56}{176} = \frac{1}{\pi} \approx \frac{1}{3}\ldots$$

Proportions of Beech and Walnut

Proportions of Oak

229

Page from *Histoire d'un Dessinateur* by Viollet-le-Duc

Viollet-le-Duc, in his book, *Histoire d'un Dessinateur*, expounds the fundamental importance of a study of nature by every drafting apprentice... 'So that the geometric precedence set by nature may guide him towards the abstract geometry of building...'

Measurements on the leaf configurations of worm-ferns

The arrangement of the fronds along the main axis has the following rhythm :

10.7 : 7.6 = 1.4 : 1
7.6 : 4.9 = 1.55 : 1
4.9 : 3.3 = 1.48 : 1
3.3 : 2.6 = 1.26 : 1

On average the distances between the individual fronds along the main axis diminish according to the following relationship:

$1 : 1.42 = 1 : \sqrt{2}$

The ratios between fronds are:

31 : 18 = 1.72 : 1
27.5 : 18 = 1.52 : 1
18 : 13 = 1.38 : 1
13 : 10 = 1.3 : 1
10 : 7 = 1.42 : 1

On average the fronds diminish according to the following relationship: 1 : 1.46.

Measurements of a reed

The leaves point in opposite directions, alternatively opposing each other by 180°. I have numbered the upper leaves as seen on the drawing 1 to 5. Their inter-axial relationships are expressed in the following diminishing sequence :

1. 17 : 15 = 1.13 : 1
2. 15 : 14.8 = 1.01 : 1
3. 14.8 : 12.8 = 1.15 : 1
4. 13.4 : 12.8 = 0.95 : 1

The inter-axial ratios of the lower leaves on the drawing show the following progression :

1. 9 : 8 = 1 : 1.088
2. 7.5 : 7.5 = 1 : 1
3. 6.5 : 6.3 = 1 : 0.92
4. 6.7 : 6.7 = 1 : 1

———— ❋ ————

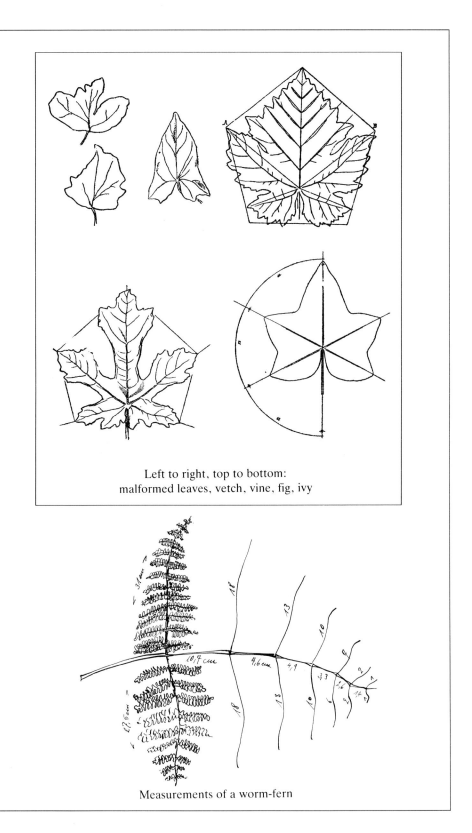

Left to right, top to bottom:
malformed leaves, vetch, vine, fig, ivy

Measurements of a worm-fern

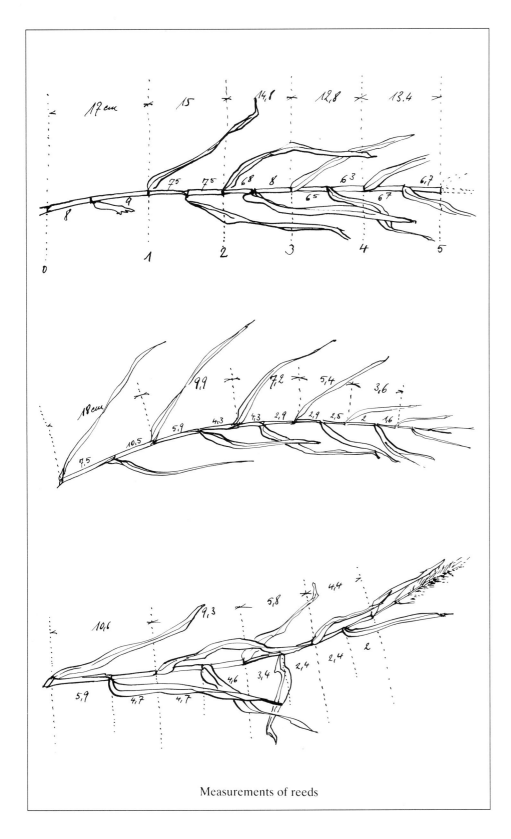

Measurements of reeds

Measurements of a second reed

The upper leaves segment the stalk in the following diminishing sequence :
1. 18 : 9.9 = 1.81 : 1
2. 9.9 : 7.2 = 1.37 : 1
3. 7.2 : 5.4 = 1.33 : 1
4. 5.4 : 3.6 = 1.47 : 1

The lower leaves divide the upper segments thus :
7.5 : 10.5 = 1 : 1.4
5.9 : 4.3 = 1 : 37
4.3 : 2.9 = 1 : 1.48
2.9 : 2.5 = 1 : 1.16
2 : 1.6 = 1 : 1.25

Measurements of a third reed

The upper leaves divide the stalk as follows:
1. 10.6 : 9.3 = 1.13 : 1
2. 9.3 : 5.8 = 1.6 : 1
3. 5.8 : 4.4 = 1.31 : 1

The lower leaves divide the upper segments as follows:
5.9 : 4.7 = 1.25 : 1
4.7 : 4.6 = 1.02 : 1
3.4 : 2.4 = 1.41 : 1
2.4 : 2 = 1.2 : 1

If we monitor the measured reeds it becomes obvious that on average the diminishing relationship is 1.1 : 1. and 1.4 : 1. The odd case might fluctuate between 1.8 : 1. and 1.6 : 1. What apposite lesson can we draw from these observations?

They do not inform our design directly, and except for the pleasure of studying nature, are of little immediate value. Personally, my nature studies have taught me the following : that the magnitude of classes, orders and families in the plant and animal world is vast, and that the infinite varieties of a particular genus are, in turn, uncountable and never exactly the same. There are almost undiscernible differences of part to part, of similar type, grown according to the same building plan, or from the same family, and yet they are not exactly the same.

We human beings all know how dreadful sameness and standardisation is, and how necessary the little nuances and differences amongst us are. Without them we have no identity. Without this surprising and unpremeditated variance even nature would not be as unimaginably rich; in all its parts, in the passing of time, it is always new and always different. This is the lesson.

PROPORTIONAL ANALYSES OF BUILDINGS

The Cathedral of Auxerre

Before examining the proportions of this building, I would like to explain an analytical technique that allows one to encompass the key geometrical properties of a building without even a tape measure.

Let's assume that you are always armed with a sketch-book to jot down the necessary notes. I always carry an A6 (10.5 x 15cm) notebook in my breast pocket. No camera can replace these informed sketches. This 'free-hand analysis' of a building is the best training towards an acute power of observation.

First, I pace the building and estimate the dimensions with the gait of my steps. To be clear about the length of each stride, I have run a series of 'pace tests' over a fixed distance of 20 metres, and determined an average value for fast, medium and slow steps. Taking my height as 1.83m, and my outer foot measurement as 0.96m, I have been able to determine the following average values :

1.05m – fast pace
0.91m – medium pace
0.80m – slow pace

If one doesn't trust such an estimated measurement, the distance can be re-traced several times, at different paces, and a more accurate average value can then be determined by multiplying the number of strides with the corresponding gait measurement. Once the reference values have been determined, the 'proportion detector' can be employed to obtain the best possible estimated values, always taking the distortion coefficient into consideration. The estimates never vary more than 5% to 10% from the real values. An aspiring architect has to train with perseverance in estimating dimensions, so that he can later visualise the built volume on an empty site. He can, of course, use photographic montage to help him out.

It is far more satisfying for him when his preliminary sketches can be worked into drawings that relate the actuality of the building.

The thrill of pacing a cathedral space lies in the gradual unfolding of the rhythmic

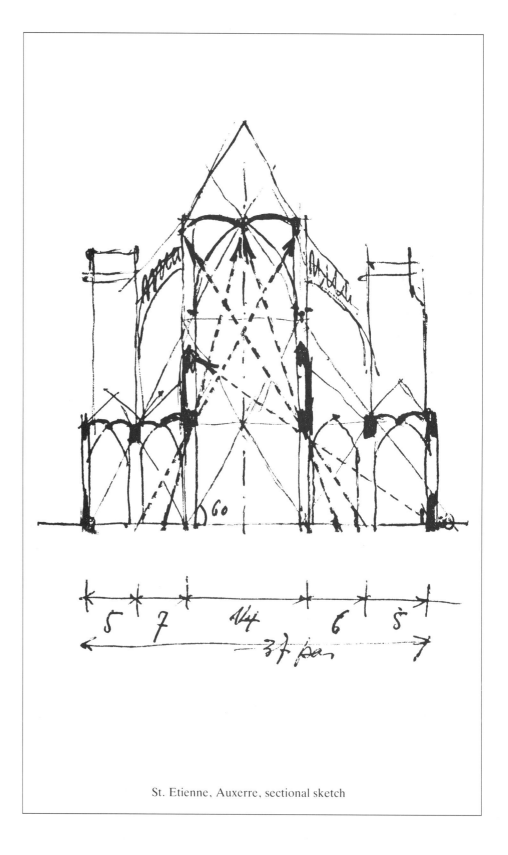

St. Etienne, Auxerre, sectional sketch

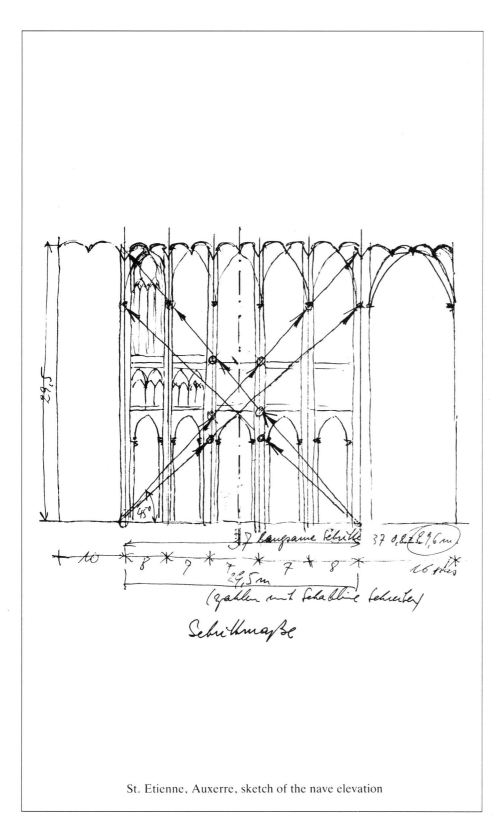

St. Etienne, Auxerre, sketch of the nave elevation

orders that control the arrangement of columns and shafts, along both the longitudinal and transverse axes.

In Auxerre Cathedral the rhythm along the transverse axis has been measured as: side chapel : aisle : nave, is 5 : 7 : 14 paces. In other words, the ratio between chapel and aisle is 1 : 1.4 (1 : $\sqrt{2}$), and between aisle and nave, 1 : 2.

A measured verification of all dimensions determined the ratios as 1 : 1.36 and 1 : 2.11. Due to the built irregularities of the church, these ratios are never constant.

Starting from the west portal, the number of paces along the longitudinal section were found to be 10, 8, 7, 7, 7, 8, 16, the last being the side dimension of the crossing.

$$7 : 10 = 1 : \sqrt{2}$$
$$8 : 16 = 1 : 2$$

The bigger shaft measurement (8 feet) in the transition to the tower and the intersection of the nave is the result of the required structural enforcement of the corner shafts in these areas and with a constant architectonic infill between the shafts.

Structural and aesthetic requirements coexist in perfect symbiosis here. Also, the wall composition, between the axis of the marginal shafts and the height of the vault's central spine, (the structural centre of the stone spine has been measured) can be inscribed in a perfect square, height to base, 29.50m x 29.50m.

At this point, it is worth checking the slowly paced step dimension; 37 x 0.8 = 19.6m. This compares with the accurately measured value of 29.5m. Together with the geometrical properties of the shaft composition according to the Golden Section, which I have verified in the plans, this is a fascinating reconstruction of the design process. Unintentionality and chance are clearly out of the question.

A further important insight that I have gained through the immediate study of buildings is the experiencing of building elements and the observation of central geometrical focal points by means of 'sight lines'. I shall select a few such examples from my sketch-books. The most beautiful proof I would like to document is the following observation on Romanesque and Gothic cathedral interiors.

Imagine yourself standing in the centre of

the side aisle under the apex of the pointed arch. Looking across to the nave wall, you can make out the exact centre of the vault above the nave. In other words, by walking through the side aisle you can experience all the architectonic details of the enclosing nave wall in its unfolding splendour. This experience can be enjoyed in the following Gothic cathedrals : Auxerre, Reims, Laon, Chartres, Beauvais, Bayeux, Cologne, Strasbourg, St. Ouen in Rouen, Veitsdom in Prague, etc.

If one walks past the pillars of the side aisle one can see the vault onset above the uppermost windows. In the case of five-tier plans the field of view diminishes until shortly above the triforium. From every one of these strategic points the harmonic architectural field of the nave can be experienced.

I would like to mention another example from one of my cathedral sketch-books of using 'sight lines': if you stand at the foot of a geometric field and glance across the wall, you will notice that important details overlap (see sketches of the cathedrals of St. Etienne, Auxerre, right, and Paris and Reims).

———— ✳ ————

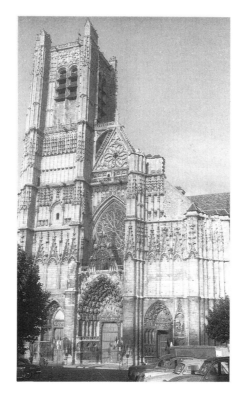

West elevation

West elevation detail

Statues of the main portal

Detail of statue reliefs, main portal pedestal

Aisles leading to chapels

View from the aisle

Triforium of the choir

Nave seen from the triforium

Nave with view of the choir

South portico

Geometric properties of the plan of Auxerre Cathedral

If we project a circle around the centre of the crossing that forms a tangent at the inner west nave wall, we discover that the circle coincides with the inner choir curvature quite accurately. The concentric circle that forms a tangent on the exterior wall of the west portal marks off the outermost projections of the choir chapel. Thus, the crossing emerges as the geometrical centre of the overall plan. What then determined the width of nave and side aisles?

The irregularities of the building make it difficult to reconstruct the planning process. The surveyed dimensions are, however, reasonable approximations. The width of the three-tier sacral space west of the tower is 24.55m, and east of the tower it is 24.70m.

The angle projected from the centre of the crossing point and inscribing the width of the interior church space, is 30°, that is 360°/12. The ctg of 360°/24 = 3.73. The calculated interior space is therefore 24.55m x 3.73 = 91.57m.

The surveyed length of the interior space, to the onset of the inner choir chapel, is 90.25m and 91m to the exterior joint.

We can assert with a clear conscience that the interior space can be inscribed in a circle with twelve segments.

The axial width of the nave varies from west to east, from 12.40m to 13.25m. The minimum width between the wall faces of the nave is 11.40m.

ctg 360°/48 = 7.59

12m x 7.59m = 91m

The width of the central nave approximately inscribes a circle with twenty-four segments. The width of the transept corresponds to the side of a decagon, whose radius/width relationship (19.25/12m) is that of the Golden Section.

$m^1/M^1 = 12m/19.25m = 1/1.6$

The angle projected from the centre of the crossing inscribes the width of the transept and measures 36°. The centre of the crossing divides the distance between the inner west elevation and the beginning of the round end of the choir approximately according to the Golden Section.

$m/M = 28.45m/44.65m = 1/1.57$

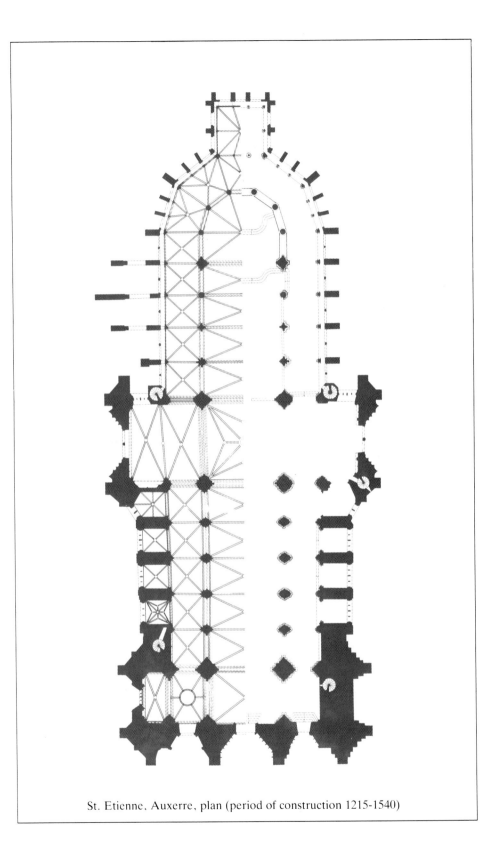

St. Etienne, Auxerre, plan (period of construction 1215-1540)

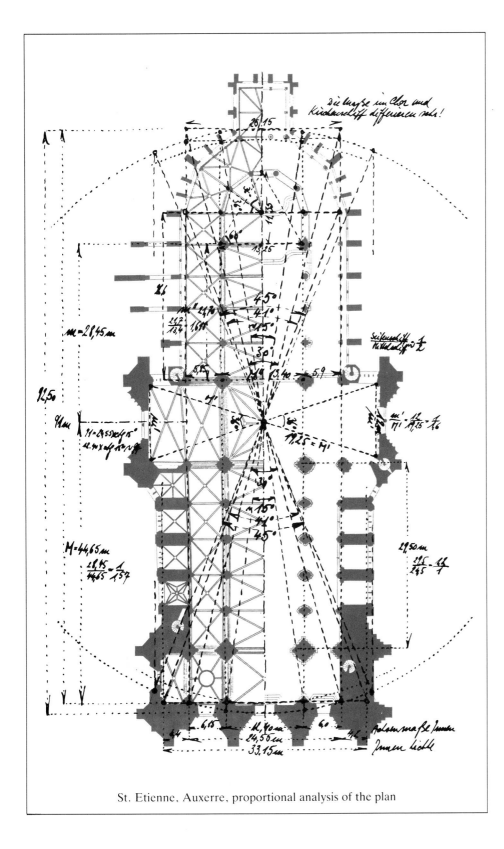

St. Etienne, Auxerre, proportional analysis of the plan

The same relationship exists in Chartres and Amiens.

The relationship between choir width (13.40m) and choir depth (21.70m), up to the already mentioned choir end projection, is exactly that of the Golden Section:
$m^{II}/M^{II} = 13.4m/21.7m = 1/1.618$
The aisles, nave relationship in the choir is:
$5.85m/13.4m = 1/2.29$
In the nave it is:
$6.15m/12.40m = 1/2$
The relationship between choir width (25.15m) and distance between onset of choir line and crossing (21.70m) is:
$21.70m/25.15m = 1/1.15$
a dimension relating to the six-fold segmentation of a circle.

The width dimension of nave and side aisles (24.55m), relates to the distance between the tower composition and crossing (29.50m) as:
$24.55m/29.50m = 1/1.2$
a relation deduced from the division of a circle by eight.

The width of the illuminated interior space including chapels is 33.25m, the exterior width varies between 35m and 36m.

Projected from the centre of the crossing, the interior space (33.15m) inscribes an angle of 41°. The exterior wall inscribes an angle of 45°.

A strong pillar arrangement marks the onset of the choir termination. The axial inter-columnation of the nave is 13.25m. An equilateral triangle can be constructed around this base which determines the axis of the curved choir end wall.
$13.25 \times 0.866 = 11.48m = 11.35m$
The height of this equilateral triangle is 11.35m.

The square of the crossing can be used to reconstruct the key dimensions of the cathedral through simple addition.
(13.3 x 13.4 x 13.3 x 13. calculated mean = 13.25).

The nave, from outside wall of the west portal to the furthermost onset of choir chapel, measures 92.5m. The seven areas in this figure add up to a length of 92.75m. The surveyed length of the transept from north to south portal (exterior wall measurements) is 39.6m, in other words almost three times the mean side dimension of the crossing (13.25m).

Using triangulation around the crossing, the internal transept dimensions can be determined:

13.3 x 0.866 = 11.5m

The true dimension oscillates between 11.5m and 12m. In the central nave of the croning equilateral triangles in the direction of the choir and the west portico each define a pair of vault systems. The equilateral triangle in the choir, projected from its 13.40m base, measures a height of 11.50m, instead of the calculated height of 11.60m, in the nave the height measures 11.75m, instead of the calculated value of 11.26m. This technique of determining dimensions is further substantiated by the fact that the original choir construction consisted of two vaults with six segments each. This can be deduced from the clearly differentiated supports. In Early Gothic this vault technique was very popular, as for example in Notre-Dame in Paris. Vault collapse resulted in a change of construction technique. The unusual reinforcement of the vault supports on the north side are living proof of the disaster. The site of this cathedral was in any case doomed with bad luck. The Gothic building was intended to replace a Romanesque church of the same scale; a typical act of contemporary vanity. Whilst the massive dome was being demolished, its towers stood for a time without the lateral support of the earlier structure, which resulted in their collapse during a fully attended service.

Equally, the construction of the south tower was beset with difficulties. Despite continued strengthening of the foundations and reinforcement of the tower construction, structural defects occurred that jeopardised completion.

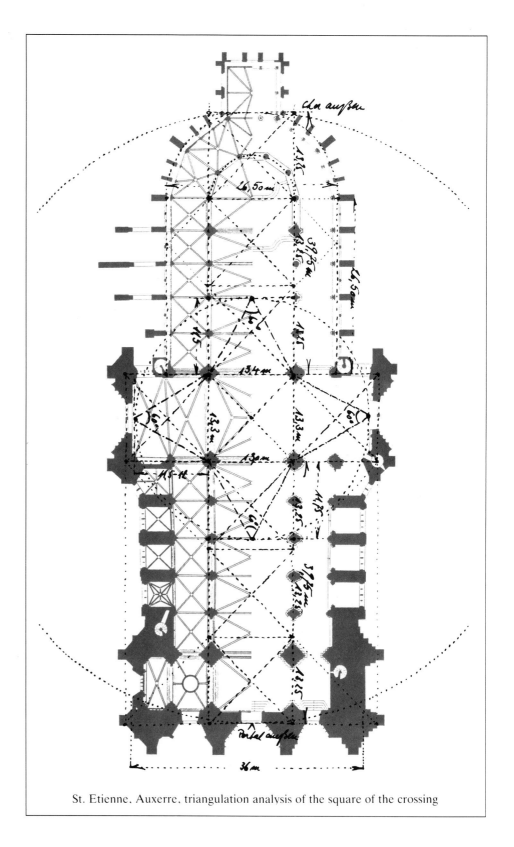

St. Etienne, Auxerre, triangulation analysis of the square of the crossing

St. Etienne, Auxerre, analysis of the plan showing Golden Section proportions

Proof of proportional relationships true to the Golden Section

The centre of the crossing divides east and west nave up to the choir curvature approximately according to the Golden Section.
$m/M = 28.45m/44.65m = 1/1.57$ instead of $1/1.618$

The transept divides the plan in two equal parts with width m^I, and length M^I, following the same relationship:
$m^I/M^I = 24.55m/38.15m = 1/1.55$
east and west nave, inside measurement
$m^I/M^I = 24.55m/39.75m = 1/1.619$
M^I measured to inner portal division
$m^I/M^I = 25.15m/38.8m = 1/1.54$
choir, inside measurement
$m^I/M^I = 25.15m/40m = 1/1.59$
choir M^I measured to outer perimeter
$m^{II}/M^{II} = m^{III}/M^{III} = 22.95m/38.15m = 22.6m/38.15m = 1/1.6$ to 1.7
$m^{IV}/M^{IV} = 13.4m/21.7m = 1/1.618$
This is a key element of the first construction stage started in 1215.
$m^V/M^V = 12/19.3 = 1/1.6$
one half of the transept, interior measurement.

The relationships m^{IV}/M^{IV} and m^V/M^V are convincing, for compositional reasons m/M seems as plausible, especially because other cathedrals, like Notre-Dame in Paris, exhibit the same proportional relationships. This is only the case when the transept halves the floor plan. m^I/M^I in both choir and east and west nave, is too inaccurate to show a mathematical relationship true to the Golden Section. If one considers, however, that the full length of the nave (38.15m) is only 1.60m short, and the choir (38.80m) only 1.20m short of resolving the equation perfectly, I am convinced that my suspected interpretation is justified!

———— ✳ ————

West elevation of the Cathedral of Auxerre

The centre of the third cornice coincides with the central vaulting rib of the nave. We construct an equilateral triangle with this point as the apex. The base line of this triangle (34.80m), corresponds to the width of east and west wing, measured on the exterior wall. We construct a circle around the same centre with a radius of 34.80m. The base line of the already constructed equilateral triangle corresponds to the side dimension of a hexagon contained in this circle. The side of the hexagon directly opposite the base line corresponds to the upper face of the tower parapet.

West elevation, scale 1:50
Proportions of the triangulation
ctg 360/12 = ctg30° = 1.732
1:1.732 is the base to height relationship of the rectangle inscribed in the hexagon.

The calculated tower height is 34.80 x 1.732 = 60.27m as compared to the surveyed dimension of 59.70m.

The height of the third cornice corresponds to the height of the equilateral triangle with its base line 34.80m = 34.80 x 0.866 = 30.13m, compared to the surveyed dimension of 29.80m.

The roof truss is projected on the west facade in the form of a richly decorated equilateral triangle. If its sides are extended to the ground one finds the width of the transept to be 44.75m measured outside the south and north portals.

The flying buttresses supporting the tower and at right angles to the west facade divide it into three almost identical parts. The two outermost parts are 10.37m wide, with the centre part measuring 10.46m. A similar tripartite division is evident in Notre-Dame, Paris.

In Auxerre, the flying buttresses are brutally pushed into the foreground of the facade, squashing the side portals and repressing the main portal. The quality of the portals' sculptural articulation does not come to the fore in the overall composition of the portals. The architect has been overwhelmed by the structural demands. In Reims, Amiens and Laon, the portal figuration is dominant, its genial loftiness balancing the heavy structural support system of the towers. As in all these classic Gothic examples, the centre is carefully set apart

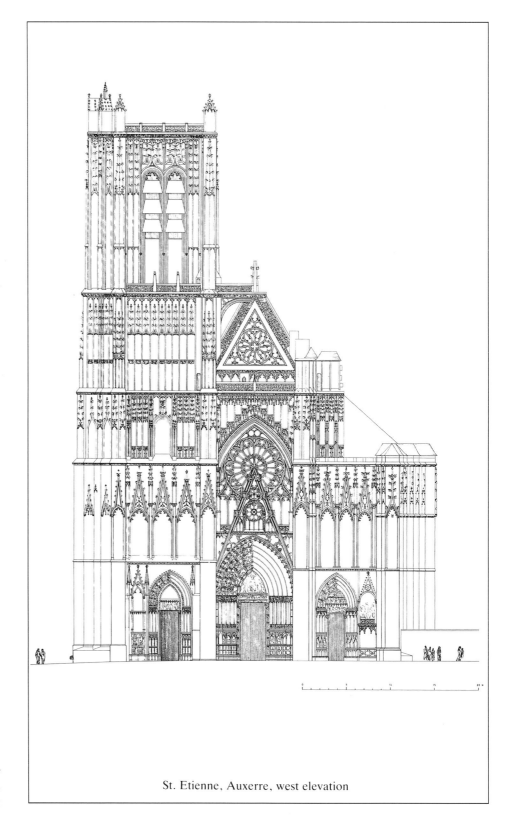

St. Etienne, Auxerre, west elevation

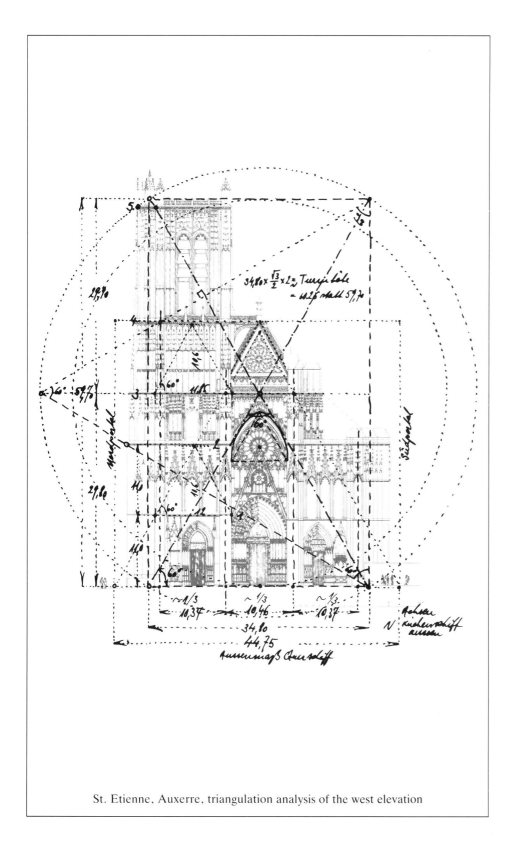

St. Etienne, Auxerre, triangulation analysis of the west elevation

visually from the rest of the composition. Again, proportional relationships close to the Golden Section are to be found. The articulation of the portals in Reims is geometrically independent from its elevations.

Further properties of the west portals, based on the principle of triangulation:

If we draw an equilateral triangle (its sides corresponding to the tower height) into the outer concentric circle of our proportional analysis, its inclined sides intersect the second cornice at the outermost corner of the tower, and the fourth cornice at the axis of the front buttresses.

The two areas on the tower elevation between cornices 1 to 2, and 3 to 4 respectively, inscribe equilateral triangles. The dimensions of both fields are almost identical:
12 (width) x 0.866 = 10.40m (height) compared with a surveyed value of 10.60m.
11.85 (width) x 0.866 = 10.26m (height) compared with a surveyed value of 10.60m.
11.85 (width) x 0.866 = 10.26m (height) compared with a surveyed value of 10.60m.
The mean between upper and lower cornice line is 10.60m.

Proportional relationships resulting from the quadripartite division of the circle

The width of the west facade, taken at the gable line, measures 40.70m. The measured height of the cornice moulding at this point is 40.80m. The centre of this square lies 1.05m below the centre of the rose window.

The datum width of the tower buttresses is 41.65m, which corresponds to the parapet height above the roof cornice.

The diagonals of both squares share approximately the same dimension as the above mentioned cornice and parapet heights of the tower, 57.56m and 58.90m.

The base/height relationship is 1 : 2. The distance between cornices 1 and 2 and 3 and 4 respectively, is 11m. The distance between 2 and 3 is 7.8m.

The relationship between the middle section 2-3, and the outer sections 1-2 and 3-4 is $7.8/11 = 1/\sqrt{2}$

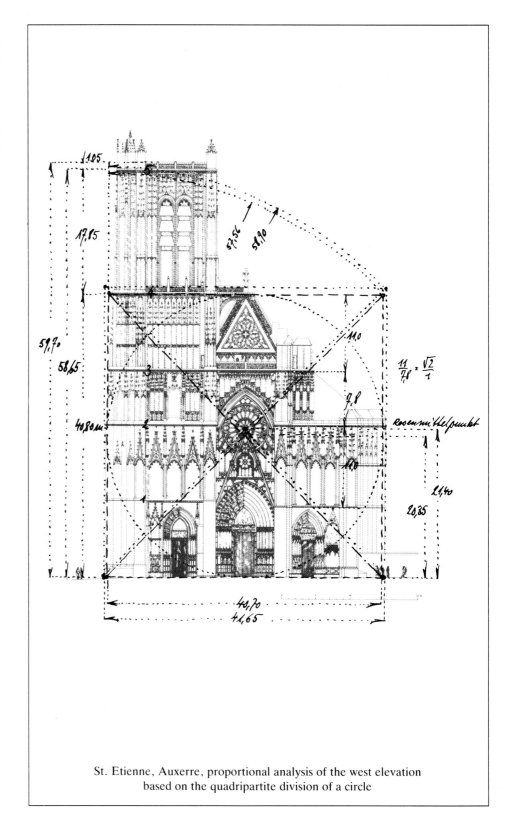

St. Etienne, Auxerre, proportional analysis of the west elevation based on the quadripartite division of a circle

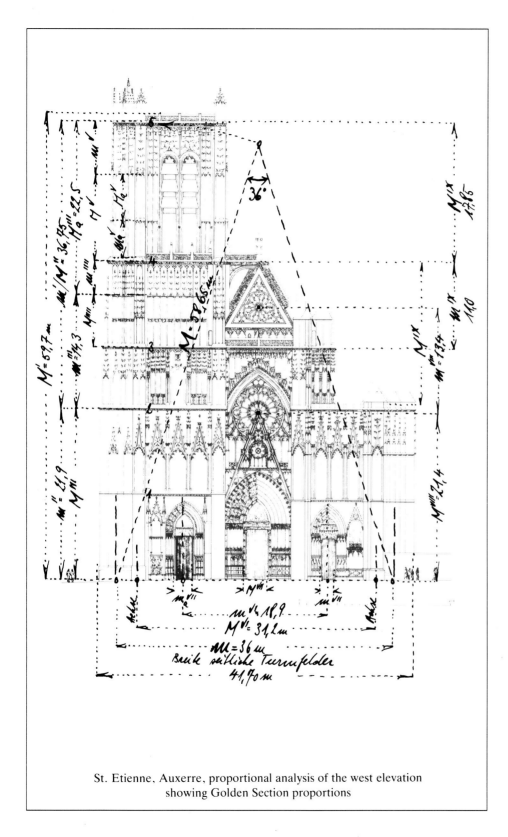

St. Etienne, Auxerre, proportional analysis of the west elevation
showing Golden Section proportions

Proportions of the Golden Section

M = Tower height without parapet (58.65m).
m = Width of building without buttresses, measured between the lateral towers (36m).
$m/M = 36m/58.65m = 1/1.62$
M^{I} = Tower height with parapet = 59.70m.
m^{I} = Area between cornices 2 and 5 = 36.75m.
$M^{I}/m^{I} = 59.7m/36.75m = 1.62/1$
$M^{II} = m = 36.75m$.
m^{II} = string course 2, height measurement = 21.9m.
$M^{II}/m^{II} = 36.75m/21.9m = 1.67/1$
$M^{III} = m^{III} = 21.9m$
$m^{III} = m^{II} = 21.9m$
m^{III} = distance between cornice 2 and wall decoration (between 3 and 4) = 14.3m.
$M^{III}a$ = wall decoration to cornice 5 = 22.5m.
$M^{III}/m^{III} = 36.75m/21.9m = 1.53/1$
$M^{III}a/m^{III} = 22.5m/14.3m = 1.53/1$
For the area between cornices 3 and 4 (11m), a tightly packed row of large statues had been intended, but were never executed. The upper line of the recesses intended for the statues divides the field according to the Golden Section.
$M^{IV}/m^{IV} = 6.80/4.2 = 1.61/1$
The area between cornices 4 and 5 (17.85m) is subdivided according to the Golden Section by the position of its wall decoration.
$M^{V}/m^{V} = 11.03/6.82 = 1.61/1$
Axial distance between lateral tower buttresses = $M^{IV} = 31.2m$.
Axial distance between side portals = $m^{VI} = 18.9m$
$M^{VI}/m^{VI} = 31.2m/18.9m = 1.65/1$
M^{VII} = width of main portal = 3m.
m^{VII} = width of right side portals = 1.85m.
$m^{VII}a$ = width of left side portals = 2.20m.
$M^{VII}/m^{VII} = 3m/1.85 = 1.618/1$
$M^{VII}/m^{VII} = 3m/1.20 = 1.36/1$
$M^{VIII}/m^{VIII} = 21.4/13.4 = 1.6/1$
M^{VIII} = height of rose window centre point = 21.4m.
m^{VIII} = distance between centre of large rose window above main portal and small gable rose = 13.40m.
$M^{VIII}/m^{VIII} = 21.40m/13.40m = 1.6/1$
M^{IX} = tower section between cornices 4 and 5 = 17.85
m^{IX} = distance between cornices 3 and 4 = 11.00m.
$M^{IX}/m^{IX} = 17.85m/11.0m = 1.62/1$

South portal

Blind arcade to the side of the south portal

Sculptures on the south portal

St. Etienne, Auxerre, south portal

St. Etienne, Auxerre, south portal triangulation analysis
and quarter circle proportions

Proportions of the portals

Left side portal = 2.20m width and 5.6m height.

5.6m/2.2m = 2.54/1

Main portal = 3.00m width and 6.40m height.

6.4m/3m = 2.13/1

Right side portal = 1.85m width and 5.25m height.

5.25m/1.85m = 2.83/1

Proportions based on triangulation

We use the width of the main portal, i.e. the distance between exterior face of wall buttresses, 15.65m, as the base line to construct an equilateral triangle whose apex approximately coincides with the apex of the tympanum (13.55m, compared to *de facto* measured dimension, 13.20m).

15.65m x 0.866 = 13.55m

This triangle can be vertically mirror projected three times. The apex of the third triangle is found to coincide with the gable triangle. The measured height between base line of first triangle and the apex of the third is 40.20m, comparable to a calculated height of 3 x 13.55 = 40.65m.

We now determine a second base line (14.00m) between the axis of the exterior wall buttresses – rather than their exterior face, as before – to construct another equilateral triangle. If we project this triangle vertically upwards, we find that four of these triangles near enough determine the height of the two west towers.

14.00 x 0.866 x 4 = 48.50m, instead of a measured 46.50m.

This structural hypothesis hardly requires further proof.

Proportional relationships resulting from the quadripartite division of the circle

The portal width of 15.65m is contained approximately three times in the total height, 46.50m, of the west towers.

15.65 x 3 = 46.95m.

The portal width of 9.3m, without the decorative lateral porch towers, is contained five times in the total height of the west towers.

9.30 x 5 = 46.50m

———— ✳ ————

245

Proof of Golden Section proportions

Since the rose window of the west portal has ten foils, the geometry of the facade is likely to be based on the decagonal division of the circle. If we extend the apexes of the divisions of the rose window from the centre outwards, we find the two lower projections cut the portal base line at the exterior face of the wall buttresses. The angle subtended by the two rose window projections is 36°. Also, m and M near enough relate to the Golden Section:

$M/m = 15.65/25.65 = 1/1.63$

The relationship between the distance of portal base line to the springing of portal gable, and from the latter to the rose window centre point, is of the Golden Section:

$m^I/M^I = 9.3m/15.1m = 1/1.62$

The springing of the portal gable to the portal gallery line is close to the Golden Section relationship:

$m^{II}/M^{II} = 5.7m/9.3m = 1/1.63$

The gallery line of the portal to the centre of the rose window:

$m^{III}/M^{III} = 9.4m/15m = 1/1.596$

The area between the portal gallery line and the parapet of the gable gallery is divided by the centre of the rose window according to the Golden Section:

$m^{IV}/M^{IV} = 5.8m/9.5m = 1/1.618$

$M^{III} + M^{IV} + m^{IV} = 30.3m = M^V + m^V$

The portal gable is crowned by a floral figure whose centre divides the above mentioned 30.30m dimension according to the Golden Section:

$m^V/M^V = 11.58m/18.72m = 1/1.618$

The rose window centre height is:

$m^I + M^I = 15.1 + 9.3 = 24.4m = M^{VI}$

m^{VI} is the distance between the rose window centre point and the base of the lateral upper spires. This geometric reference line is inexact. The same distance m^{VI} is repeated between base line of the gable parapet and the tip of the gable ridge decoration.

$m^{VI}/M^{VI} = 15.08m/24.4m = 1/1.618$

The height to the base line of the gable parapet (30.30m), relates to the distance between the parapet of the portal gallery and the base of the decorated gable triangle, approximately according to the Golden Section:

$m^{VII}/M^{VII} = 18.5m/30.3m = 1/1.63$

$m^{VIII}/M^{VIII} = 30.3 - 18.72/18.5 = 11.58m/18.5m = 1/1.59$

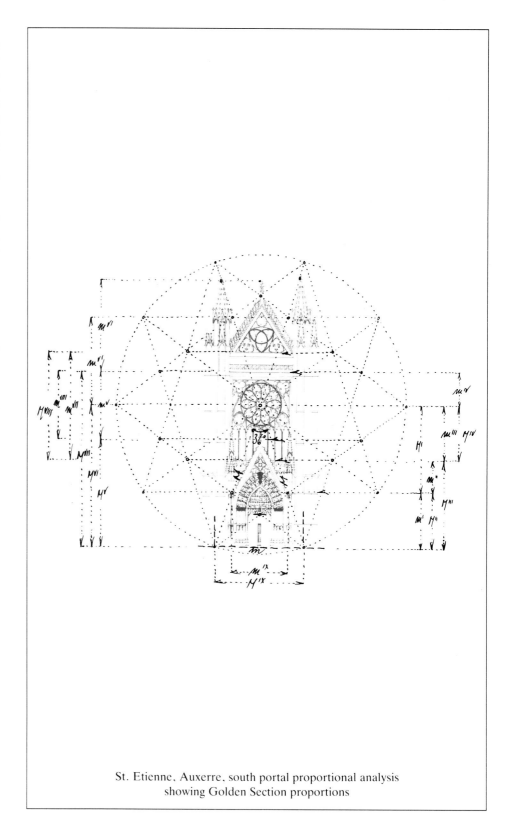

St. Etienne, Auxerre, south portal proportional analysis showing Golden Section proportions

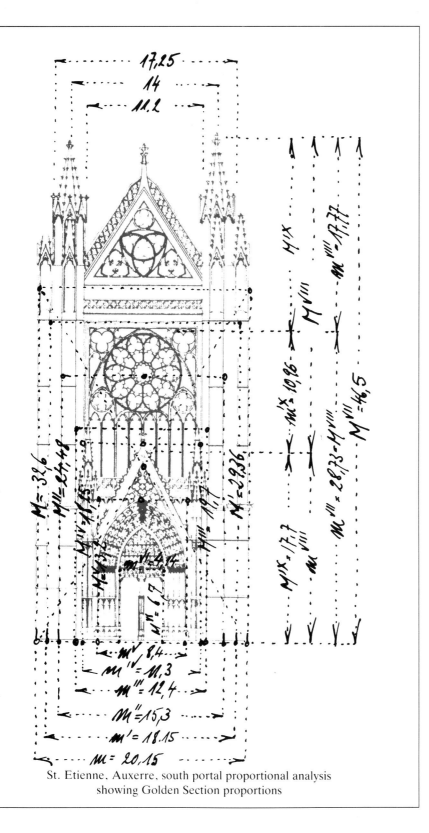

St. Etienne, Auxerre, south portal proportional analysis
showing Golden Section proportions

$m^{IV}/M^{IV} = 9.45m/15.3m = 1/1.619$

The portal niches are hemmed in by lateral piers, extending as turrets beyond the portal gallery. The distance between the inner edge of these supports (9.45m), and the width of the portals measured from the exterior faces of the wall buttresses (15.3m), relate to the Golden Section: m^{IV}/M^{IX}

The following repeated dimensions are strikingly similar:

$m = 15.65m$

$M^I = 15.10m$

$M^{III} = 15.0m$

$m^{IV} + M^{IV} = 15.3m$

$m^{VI} = 15m$

$M^{IX} = 15.3m$

Further analysis of
Golden Section relationships

$m/M = 20.15m/32.6m = 1/1.618$

m = width between external buttresses.

M = height to base of roof triangle.

$m^I/M^I = 18.15m/29.36m = 1/1.618$

m^I = distance between onset of exterior buttresses.

M^I = horizontal string course above the rose window.

$m^{II}/M^{II} = 15.3m/24.48m = 1/1.6$

m^{II} = width between outer faces of the external wall buttresses.

M^{II} = the rose window centre point.

$m^{III}/M^{III} = 12.4m/19.7m = 1/1.59$

m^{III} = inner width between lateral exterior buttresses.

M^{III} = height of the portal gable and lateral turrets.

M^{III} = also the onset of the petal configuration in the rose window.

$m^{IV}/M^{IV} = 11.30m/18.25 = 1/1.615$

m^{IV} = width of exterior face between flanking portal turrets.

M^{IV} = height of the portal gable without the terminal rose.

$m^V/M^V = 8.4m/13.20m = 1/1.57$

--- ✳ ---

247

m^V = maximum width of portal niche.

M^V = height of terminal portal arch.

m^{VI}/M^{VI} = 4.14m/6.7m = 1/1.618

m^{VI} = width of portal opening.

M^{VI} = height to springing of portal vault.

m^{VII}/M^{VII} = 28.73m/46.5m = 1/1.618

m^{VII} = height to onset of rose window.

M^{VII} = pinnacle of right portal turret.

m^{VIII}/M^{VIII} = 17.77m/28.73m = 1/1.617

m^{VIII} = onset or rose window to pinnacle of portal turret.

M^{VIII} = m^{VII}

m^{IX}/M^{IV} = 10.96m/17.77m = 1/1.62

M^{IX} = apex of portal gable and transition into the decorative crown = m^{VIII}.

m^{IX} = distance between height M^{IX} and lower edge of rose window.

South portal blind arcade, cusp detail

The exact and carefully cut stone tracery in Gothic cusped arcades suggest subtle geometric relationships similar to the composition of the south portal itself. The decorative tracery resting on the capitals completes a perfect square, 0.73 x 0.73m.

The horizontal distance between the mid point of the pointed arch radii is 32cm, the horizontal distance between radii mid point and figure frame being 20cm. The two distances relate in the Golden Section:

m/M = 20cm/32cm = 1/1.6

Pointed arch radius = M + m = 32 + 20 = 52cm = M^I

m^I/M^I = 32cm/52cm = 1/1.62

The triangle projected from the crown of the inner arch inscribes an angle of 36°. The two springing points of the arches are connected with the crown of the arch to give an angle of 72°.

The diameters of the foils are, from top to bottom: 18.50cm, 21.50cm and 30cm. The upper and lower ones share the proportions of the Golden Section.

m^{II}/M^{II} = 18.5/30 x 1/1.62

Despite the different diameters of the upper trefoil, the intersections of the circles still form an equilateral triangle with the subtended foil base line, 17cm.

———— ✳ ————

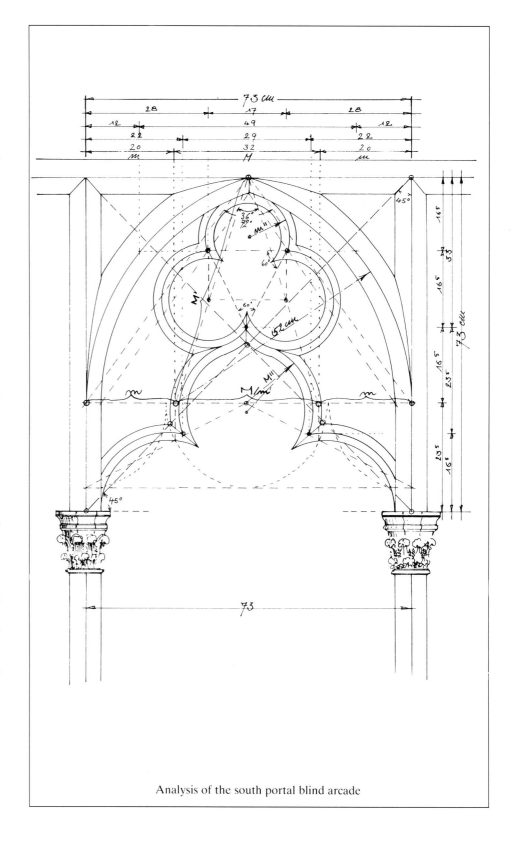

Analysis of the south portal blind arcade

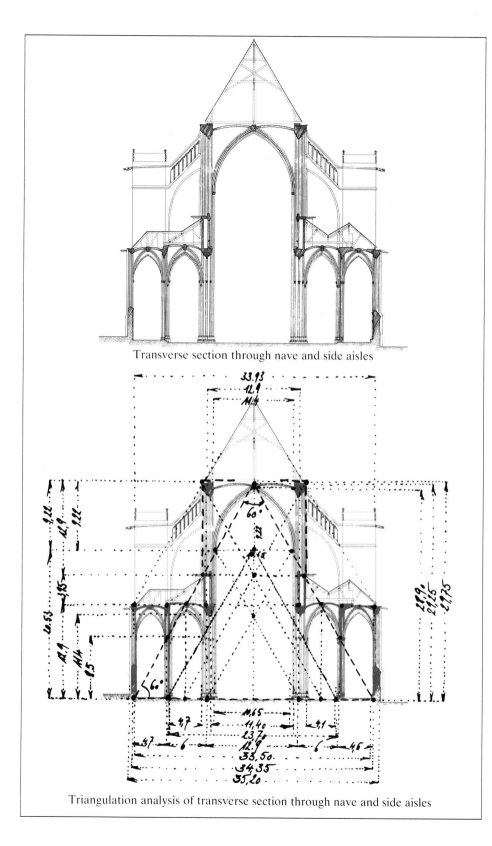

Transverse section through nave and side aisles

Triangulation analysis of transverse section through nave and side aisles

Transverse section through nave and side aisles, an examination of geometric properties with regards to triangulation

The maximum interior width from chapel to chapel measures 33.50m. The height of the equilateral triangle constructed about this base line is 29m, its apex touching the underside of the vaulting boss.

The base of the vaulting boss coincides with the onset of the roof truss, i.e. the upper face of the stone work that supports the enclosing nave walls. This height is 29.75m.

The two corresponding sides of this equilateral triangle meet the cathedral floor on the inside of the external wall.

Working from the apex of the equilateral triangle downwards, the two corresponding sides intersect a number of important structural points with the following height dimensions:

1. Capitals and springing of chapel and side aisle vaulting = 8.50m.

2. Side aisle vaulting boss = 12.90m = height of triforium.

3. Underside of triforium = 16.85m.

4. Capital and springing of nave vaulting = 20.53m. The construction of the vaulting is clearly based on the principle of triangulation, width 10.65m, height 9.22m. The pointed arch configurations give presence to the sacral space, but their arrangement departs from the overriding geometry. I shall return to this point later.

Height to width relationship of the nave:
1. The relationship between nave width and nave height to underside of vaulting boss is:

$11.40 : 28.90m = 1 : 2.53$, i.e. approximately $1 : 2.5$

2. Nave width between horizontally opposed composite piers relates to height of springing shaft line as follows:

$10.65m : 20.53m = 1 : 1.92 = c. 1 : 2$
Neither one of these relationships is based on the sexpartite division of the circle.

To accurately reconstruct the height of 20.50m is surprisingly easy; one simply uses the axial distance between two horizontally opposed piers as the base line for an equilateral triangle. The extensions of the corresponding sides of this equilateral triangle pass through the onsets of the springing vaults and the shaft capitals respectively.

12.9 x 0.866 + 10.65 x 0.866 = 11.17 + 9.22 = 20.39m instead of the measured value of 20.53m.

The height of the triangle determines the onset of the vault springing exactly, and its base line defines the width between the outer aisle walls, 23.70m.

The height can therefore be calculated as: 23.70 x 0.866 = 20.52m. The same extrapolations can be applied in the choir to determine the springing of the vaults in the nave.

Spatial relationships similar to those of the nave are to be found in the side aisles: Vault height to aisle width = 12.9m/4.7m = 2.74/1 thus, a little higher than in the nave (2.5 : 1). Springing of the vault height related to circulatory width: 8.5m/4.1m = 2.07/1. The side aisles are 1.07 times narrower than the nave.

It is interesting to note that the height of the triforium floor, 12.90m, has the same dimension as the axial distance of the nave shafts. The distance between triforium underside and nave vaulting boss is also 12.90m.

If we extend the near enough equilateral triangle of the gable roof we intersect the cornice, and at the same time meet the vault height of the side chapels.

Geometric properties of transverse choir section, triangulation analysis

We construct an equilateral triangle about the base line of the nave. The choir has many different levels and is to be disregarded here. The apex of our triangle extends to the centre of the vaulting boss. The triangle has a height of 29.50m.

The corresponding sides of the triangle intersect important structural points of given height dimension:
1. The parapet of the side aisle windows, 6.00m.
2. The capitals of the cross groins in the side aisles, 7.85m. The same height is shared by the upper face of the capitals of the round nave columns.
3. Height of vaulting bosses in the side aisles 12.70m.
4. Upper triforia ledge, i.e. second choir gallery, 18.10m.
In contrast to the nave, the springing of the choir vault is not intersected by any of the triangle's sides.

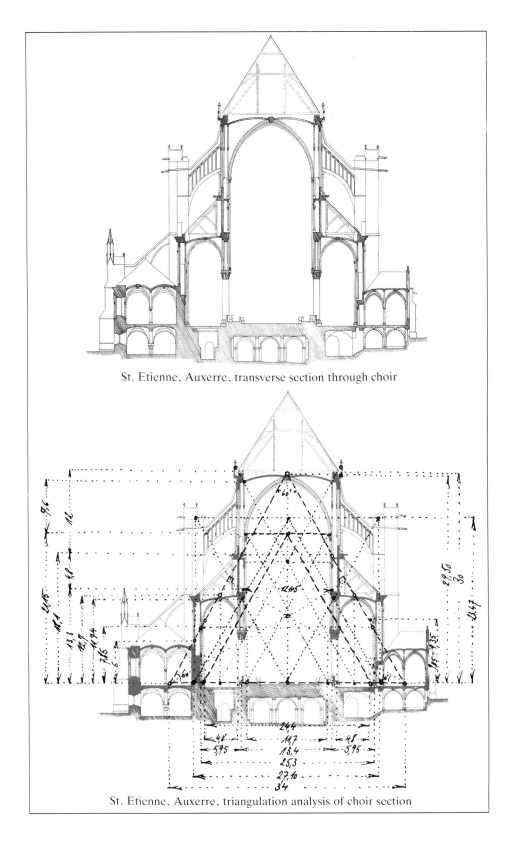

St. Etienne, Auxerre, transverse section through choir

St. Etienne, Auxerre, triangulation analysis of choir section

St. Etienne, Auxerre, choir triforium

Two verticals, one erected at either end of the triangle's base line, intersect the triforium facing at a height of 13.30m. This dimension, give or take 10cm, corresponds to the axial shaft distance in the choir, 13.40m. The same relationship is found in the west nave.

If we project the geometric axis of the side aisles, clearly defined by the central vaulting boss, onto the base line, and use this dimension to build up an equilateral triangle, we find that its apex is identical with the capitals of the triforium arcade (gallery). The triangle's corresponding sides are extended upwards, bisecting the cornice and terminating exactly at the balustrade. If we project the cross-section with 11.7m between composite piers and 12.45m between the walls of the choir onto the base and draw 60° lines from these points to the inside of the choir, the pair of composite piers exactly bisect the front and back edge of the top of the capital on which the rib system of the main vault rests.

The springing of the vault in the west nave could by means of this construction be reached from the column axes. The height of the springing of the vault in the nave can also be determined by means of a second, more accurate method: the height of the triangle, whose base line is the width between the outer passages of the side aisles (24.41m), is exactly the same as the height of the springing vault line of the shaft.
24.41 x 0.866 = 21.15m.

The distance between the axis of the aisle windows, measured across the west nave, is 27.10m. If we bisect this distance and erect an equilateral triangle on each half (13.55m) we find that the apexes of the triangles meet the underside of the pointed arches under the triforium.
13.55 x 0.866 = 11.74m

Because of the choir parapet and the different heights of choir and side aisles, the measurements are taken from the nave level. If we extend the pair of triangles upwards we meet the underside of the buttress termination:
13.55 x 0.866 x 2 = 23.47m.

———— ✳ ————

Geometrical analysis of nave bays based on the principles of triangulation

The axial distance between two adjacent shafts becomes the base line on which we erect an equilateral triangle whose corresponding sides are extended upwards to form a secondary triangle of equal dimensions. In each bay the resulting figure can be repeated 3 times.

5.67 x 0.866 x 6 = 29.46m

Because of irregularities in the plan, the height of the vault varies throughout the nave between 29.25 and 29.75m. The triforium has a height of 4.10m measured to the ledge of its parapet. It occurs exactly at mid height (12.70m) between floor and ceiling vault. The negligible dimensional differences that transpire from the different plans result from measurements being taken at slightly different horizontal levels. For instance, in the transverse section through west nave and side aisles the triforium height is given as 12.90m. Our measurements reveal a height of 12.70m to the ledge face of the lower triforium cornice.

To double check all my listed dimensions would require all plans to be enlarged to a scale far beyond the limitations of this book. As stated already, all of my measurements are based on 1:50 (1m = 2cm) plans.

All analytical evaluations in a structure of such infinite complexity are always flawed by the inevitable shortcoming that the significance of a geometric survey is subject to the interpretation of an individual. Since I am no art historian, but someone who is creatively active, my decisions are guided by a quest for the re-discovery of arhitectural techniques of composition, still relevant in present day practice In other words, I am not interested in establishing art historical data, rather the purpose of this analysis is to inform and enrich my own design repertoire.

Axial distance of the pillars in the choir

The axial distance between pillars is 5.15m. The gallery height above the triforium is 17.80m. To an approximation of 3cm this is exactly four times the height of an equilateral triangle whose base is the axial distance between adjacent pillars:

5.15 x 0.866 x 4 = 17.83m.

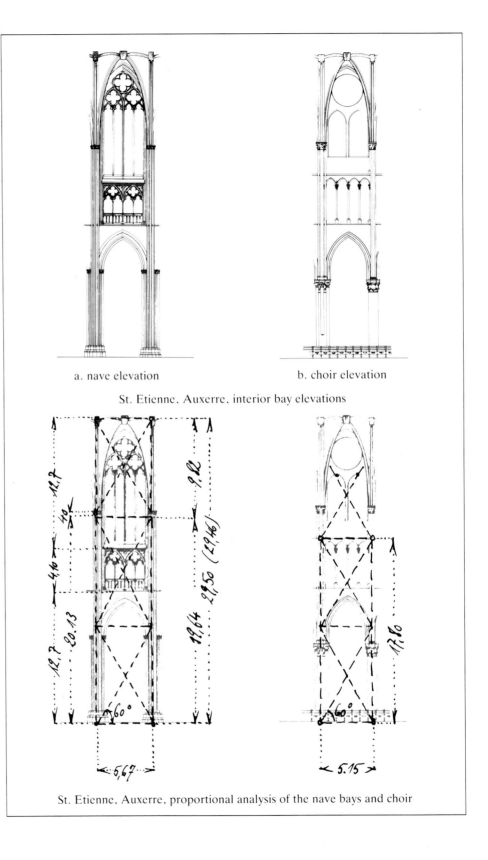

a. nave elevation   b. choir elevation

St. Etienne, Auxerre, interior bay elevations

St. Etienne, Auxerre, proportional analysis of the nave bays and choir

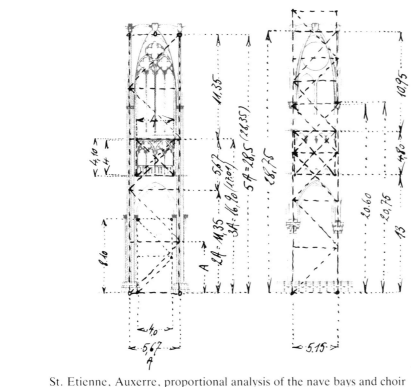

St. Etienne, Auxerre, proportional analysis of the nave bays and choir
based on the quadripartite division of a circle

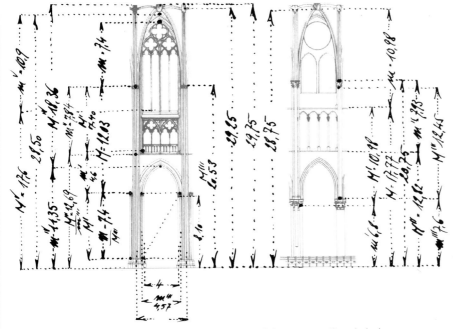

St. Etienne, Auxerre, construction of the nave wall and choir
according to the proportions of the Golden Section

The nave wall

Axial distance between pillars is 5.67m. Height of vaulting boss is 28.50m, approximately 5 times the above dimension (5 x 5.67 = 28.35m).

The apex height of the side aisle arcades, as well as the height of the clerestorey window, are twice as high as the axial shaft distances are wide = 11.35m.

The height of the arcade opening is 4.00m and the height to capital underside 8.10m, a relationship of approximately 1:2. The triforium figuration forms an exact square with sides 4.00m x 4.00m. The dimension 4.10m pertains to the front edge of the triforium.

The choir elevation

The axial distance between supports measures 5.15m. This dimension multiplied by four, 20.60m, is almost identical to the height of the upper face of the capitals in the nave vaulting (20.75m). The height of the pointed nave arches, 28.75m, is roughly 5.5 times the axial distance between supports, 28.32m. The location of the triforium with its height of 4.80m is near enough 2.5 times the axial support distance, (surveyed dimension 13m, compared with calculated value of 12.87m), and exactly twice the axial pillar distance if taken from the crown of the vaulting arch, 10.95m. The latter corresponds precisely to the relationship of the large upper windows.

The triforium arcade marks out exact squares from column to column, 4.80 x 4.80m. The width is of course not identical to the axial distance of the lower supports. The rising composite piers taper the triforium figuration by 35cm.

In the nave

m = compound piers of the arcade configuration, without base = 7.43m.

m = distance betwen vault springing line and intrados.

M = distance between capital of arcade and vault springing line = 12.03m.

m/M = 7.43m/12.03m =1/1.618

M^1 = upper edge of the base to capital of arcade floor.

m^1 = Upper edge of this capital to upper edge of base of the composite piers between the triforium and window above = 4.6m.

$m^I = m^I/M^I = 4.6m/7.4m = 1/1.608$

M^{III} = height to springing line of main vault = 20.53m. The ledge profile of the triforium cornice (string course line) is 12.69m high. This point divides M^{III} according to the Golden Section.

$m^{II}/M^{II} = 7.84m/12.69m = 1/1.618$

$m^{III}/M^{III} = 12.69m/20.53m = 1/1.618$

The relationship between overall vaulting crown height, 29.25m, and vault springing line is approximately $1 : \sqrt{2}$.

$20.53m/29.25m = 1/1.42$.

In the arcade opening of the side aisle an area of Golden Section proportions can be read. It is defined by the distance between capital and base of column (7·4m), and the width between the two opposite responds.

$m^{III}/M^{III} = 7.4m/4.57m = 1/1.618$

m^{IV} = crown height of pointed side aisles arch, 11.35m.

M^{IV} = height between crown of pointed side aisle arch and vaulting boss, 18.36 to 18.41m.

$m^{IV}/M^{IV} = 11.35m/18.36m = 1/1.618$

Vertical distance between cathedral floor and apex of upper gallery window is 28.50m. The ledge of the gallery window divides the height dimension according to the Golden Section.

$m^V/M^V = 10.90m/17.63m = 1/1.618$

Reconstruction of the choir wall according to the proportional relationships of the Golden Section

The base line for the recorded dimensions is not the floor of the nave, as was the case in the transverse choir section, but is taken from the true height of the choir floor.

The maximum vaulting height is 28.75m. The triforium parapet (second gallery) divides this dimension according to the Golden Section:

$m/M = 10.98m/17.77m = 1/1.618$

The triforium height, 17.77m, is equally divided in the Golden Section by the underside of the composite pier capital.

$m^I/M^I = 6.8m/10.98m = 1/1.614$

The height to the upper capital face of the principal vault measures 20.75m, and its Golden Section division is made by the floor line of the triforium.

$m^{II}/M^{II} = 7.93m/12.82m = 1/1.617$

The height to the lower capital face of the principal vault is divided according to the

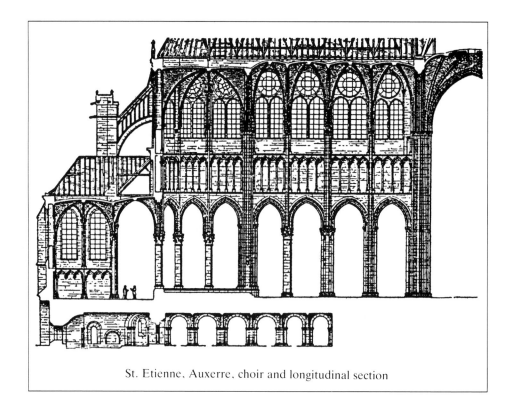

St. Etienne, Auxerre, choir and longitudinal section

Golden Section by the upper face line of the lower arcade capitals:

$m^{III}/M^{III} = 7.6m/12.45m = 1/1.62$

Summary of dimensional analysis of the pointed arch configurations in Auxerre Cathedral

1. Choir vaulting. The centres of the vault radii divide the base in the Golden Section. The proportion between height and base line is also of the Golden Section.

2. The choir vaulting is irregular. The radii have their centres at intervals of one third along the horizontal base line. The height to base ratio is $1 : 0.63$.

3. North portal, blind arcade element. In this case the radii centres occur at intervals of one fourth along the horizontal base line. The height to base ratio is $1 : 0.7$.

4. A classic pointed arch construction is to be found in the west portal, in the large south portal window and in the vaulting of the side aisles. The two radii have their centres on the springing lines, inscribing an equilateral triangle into the arch configuration. The base to height relationship is $1 : 0.866$.

5. Nave vaulting. If we divide the base line by sixteen, the position of the centres of the two radii on the base line can be defined as ten units apart and three units off the onset of the springing line. The height is three quarters of the base line.

6. Pointed arches in the choir aisles. The intersections of the radii move closer towards the centre of the base line. The distance between them is reduced to 1.6 units, their respective distances to the onset of the springing line measures 4 units. The radius to base line ratio is $\sqrt{2} : 1$. The height to base line ratio is roughly the same.

Summary of studies at Auxerre Cathedral

With this dazzling glimpse into the compositional techniques and relationships of Gothic architecture I draw to a close my observations on St. Etienne in Auxerre.

Buried under piles of papers, this study had been shelved for a good twenty years. Its accompanying photographic material has been locked away in a timber coffer that I had embellished with reliefs and dressed in leather. I treasured this study as the key to my architectural education. Now I am glad

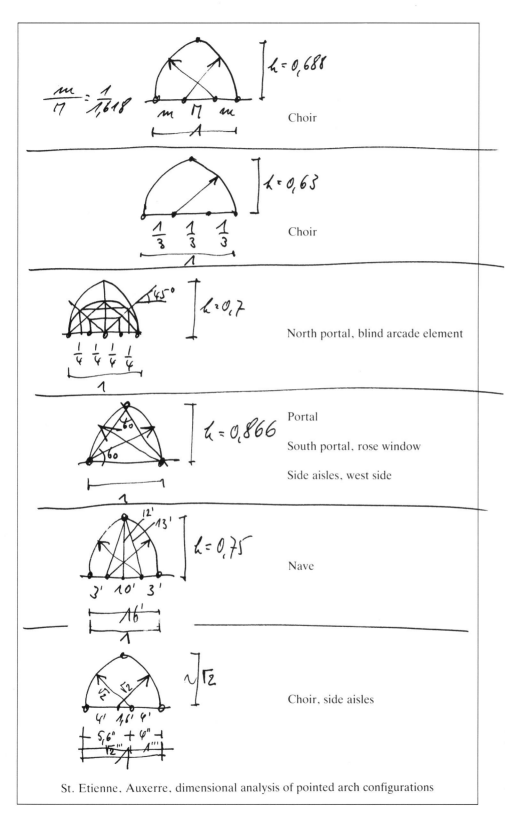

$$\frac{m}{M} = \frac{1}{1,618}$$

$h = 0,688$

Choir

$h = 0,65$

Choir

$h = 0,7$

North portal, blind arcade element

$h = 0,866$

Portal

South portal, rose window

Side aisles, west side

$h = 0,75$

Nave

$\sqrt{\sqrt{2}}$

Choir, side aisles

St. Etienne, Auxerre, dimensional analysis of pointed arch configurations

to have consumed these experiences for the betterment of my architectural activities. I have come closer to understanding the physical unity of a building, its corporeal quality. Plan, section and elevation are magnificently inter-related. All the accidents that have disrupted the building process and lead to innumerable irregularities could not, after all, diminish the impact of the overall artistic expression. The idea of the cathedral remains one of the most magnificent products of architectonic thought. The tenacity with which basilicas were enriched and varied, without sacrificing the unity of the overall form to individual artistic ambitions, is extraordinary. That this uncompromising loyalty to a style was pursued with equal vigour by all participating artists and perpetuated over centuries, is even more remarkable. The craftsmen who gave form to the ideas flourished as much as the creative artists.

Without this healthy inter-relationship, no architectural idea sees the light of day. How sad many of our best modern, twentieth-century buildings look today! They need to be completely overhauled every few years (e.g. Villa Savoye at Poissy by Le Corbusier, the Tugendhat Residence in Brno by Mies van der Rohe, the Weissenhofsiedlung in Stuttgart, the Werkbundsiedlung in Vienna, the Pessac development by Le Corbusier etc...).

If the details of a building are tampered with, its quality suffers significantly. This can go so far that nothing of the original idea remains (e.g. the street facade of the Steiner house in Vienna by Adolf Loos). The way I interpret the proportions of Auxerre Cathedral has a great deal to do with my direct, physical experience of this building, in which we clambered about for a month. The reason for capitalising on one or the other geometric aspect in my explorations, has to do with the fact that the true significance an architectonic theme has on a building and its spatial order can only be analysed in a real-life study and measured drawing exercise on site. No plan analysis will lead to the same results.

As mentioned previously, for me the most significant experience lies in the realisation that in interesting buildings plan, section and elevation always reveal an overlay of several geometric systems. The dimensions of important elements were tested against various proportional sequences and designed to superimpose wherever possible. The cornice and parapet elements of classical architecture facilitated the matching and approximation of analogous parts far more easily than the naked geometric bodies we have at our disposal today. The constructive system of the west facade at Auxerre, for instance, could be convincingly interpreted as the division of a circle into three, four and five parts.

Another aspect of my building studies is worth mentioning: the prolonged and intimate contact with an architectural masterpiece is the best acid test for the vocation of becoming an architect. Those not set on fire by the experience should stay clear of the profession. My fascination for compositional problematics has been compounded by Auxerre. Driven by an all-consuming curiosity, I wanted to read the building in a way it had never been read before. I was, however, always conscious of the risk of misinterpretation. Historically, I was never fixated on Gothic architecture, but rather, since my early youth, I had felt a far more intensive emotional affinity with the Italian Renaissance. However, the extraordinary quality of the old town of Auxerre, with its

damaged but still very tangible medieval character held such a compelling attraction that as a place of study it was as rich a ground as any of the more well-known towns. The Dean of Auxerre offered us hospitality in an ancient timber frame house immediately adjacent to the cathedral, where we could draw up all our plans. Our 'café au lait' in the morning, the Camembert after lunch, the white Jura chalk of the cathedral, the local photographer's participation in our work, the loving interest of the Dean and his chaplain in our work, and the surly moods of the sexton, forever reluctant to part with his keys for the spiral staircase; time has merged all these incidents into one memorable experience. I shall never forget the few remaining stained glass windows in the choir gallery, which often captivated me for hours. They are amongst the most beautiful to be found in France. I have taken close-up photographs of all the ones within reach of the choir gallery. The magnificent ensemble effect that these windows create from afar is, in close-up, heightened beyond belief by the vivid colours and the quality of the drawings. One has to have stood within reach of such a volcano of colour to seize this experience, an experience quite beyond articulation. This broken glass mosaic, held together by its ingenious

skeletal frame, beholds a sensual dimension, not expressed by the artistically layered and sculpted masonry walls of the dome. The message of this building can only be transcended by music which, during mass, fills this space with heavenly vibrations.

Ninety-six clock towers articulated the city's silhouette in the Middle Ages. A few have survived. Even today two imposing churches flank the cathedral not far away. Sadly today, the significance of all these buildings has been reduced to being listed as tourist attractions. Even if the spirit that conceived these monuments seems dispelled, as historic edifices to an artistic idea they remain timeless and of infinite value.

Signatures by stone masons, discovered in hidden places in the church, are shown below; under spiral staircases, in window recesses, galleries, triforia, in tower sections etc. Using charcoal we transferred them onto tracing paper. We amassed a fairly comprehensive collection but, unfortunately, had neither the time nor patience to trace the leads back to the masonry schools that were associated with this building. The example of these fascinating drawings is not intended as a decorative end piece to my study, but as a noble testimony to some of the building's artists – a kind of anonymous signature.

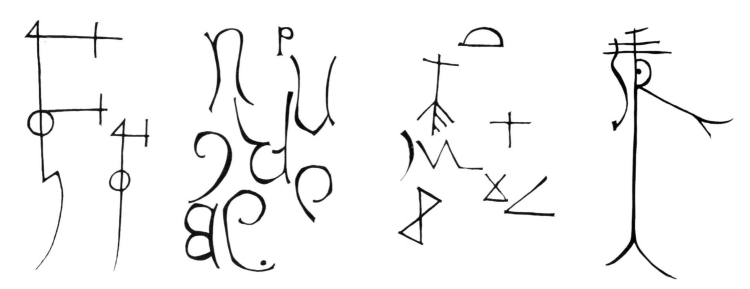

Signatures of stone masons, (*left to right*): North tower exterior, 32m above crossing, 1350-1400; Flying Buttress and columns in central nave, fourteenth century: North tower exterior, 1350-1400; North portico, fifteenth century

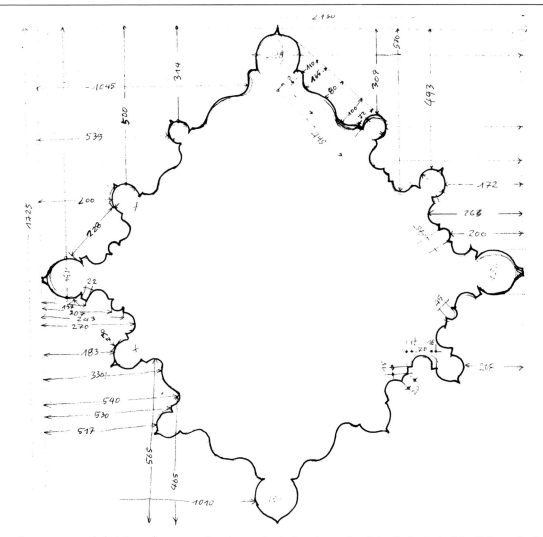

One of our measured sketches of a composite pier made during the study of the Cathedral of St. Etienne in Auxerre

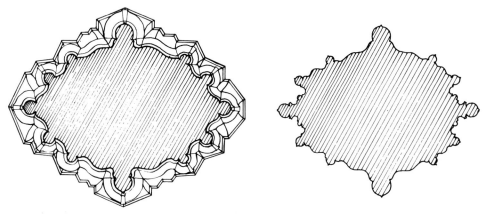

Two different composite piers on the southside of the nave. Here with its plinth, the true configuration of the pillar emerges

Extracts from my sketch-books recording the measuring of Auxerre Cathedral, and trips to Paris and Reims

From left to right and top to bottom:

1 cross-section of nave and side aisles of the cathedral in Sens.

2 cross-section of St. Chapelle in Paris.

3 cross-section of Notre-Dame in Paris. Study of sight lines looking from side aisle across to nave wall. Paced dimensions.

4 proportions of nave wall.

5 triforium window.

6 plan, paced dimensions.

– column bases in the side aisle, amusing transition from circular to square base.

7 column, cross-sections.

8 choir gallery window.

9 capital.

10 transition from nave to transept with interior view of the north portal.

11 column, cross-section.

12 rose window segments from north, south and west portals.

– nave columns, visually superimposed. The view point is the column axis of the two side aisles.

– the view point is the mid point of the chapel portal.

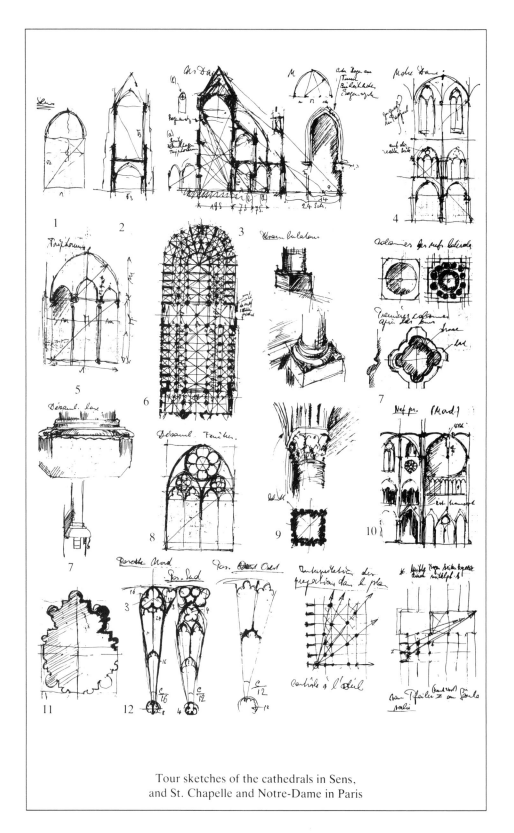

Tour sketches of the cathedrals in Sens, and St. Chapelle and Notre-Dame in Paris

Paced measurements of the west facade of Notre-Dame, Paris

1 exterior wall dimensions.

2 if one glances across the main facade from different view points one observes that important geometric points on the facade overlap.

3 plan of Reims Cathedral, choir detail. Seen from the crossing (16 paces), the inter-columnar distances diminish from 12 to 9 to 7 paces.

4 choir, detail of column base and plinth.

5 section through nave.

6 west portal, interior view.

7 proportions of the nave wall, cross-section through lower shaft.

8 superimpositions on the exterior wall.

9 plan of St. Rémy in Reims.

10 west view of St. Rémy.

11 sketch of transept elevation.

12 cross-section through nave and aisles.

13 choir chapel detail, paced measurements.

14 choir wall.

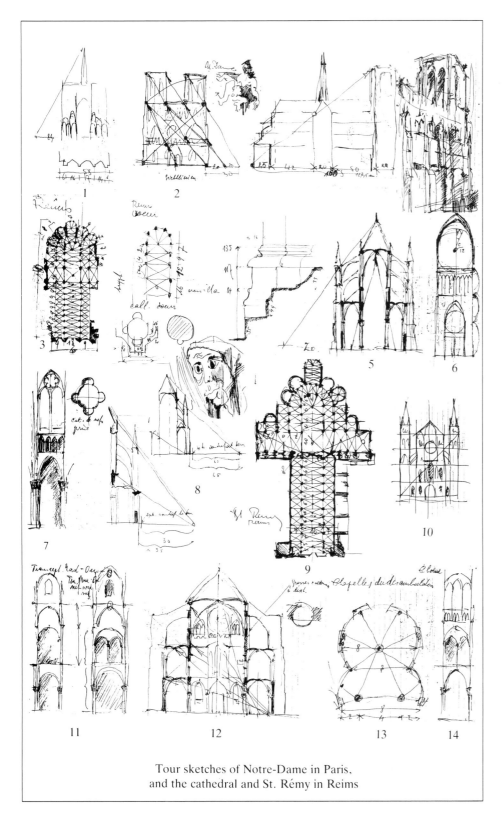

Tour sketches of Notre-Dame in Paris, and the cathedral and St. Rémy in Reims

Notre-Dame in Paris (paced measurements) Similar to Auxerre, the axial distance between the vertical supports is 7 paces in the normal squares. In the crossing transition the distances increase to 8 paces. The mid point of the crossing is also the centre of a circle that inscribes the interior space of the church. The radii of the ten-fold division of the circle define the width of the church, which spans the transept, five naves and aisles.

In cross-section the most important structural points are determined by means of triangulation. The vaulting spine above the nave is the estimated apex of an equilateral triangle, its base line defining the interior width of the church space. If we move this triangle along in either direction, say up to the springing of the vault above the large nave windows, we hit the exterior wall of the side chapels and, once again, the corresponding sides of the triangle cross structurally important points of the vault. Observe the enormous flying buttresses that transfer the load of the vault, above the second storey of the side aisles, down into the chapel walls. The height of the vault springing line in the nave is twice the height of the equilateral triangle whose base line is the width of the nave.

Striding through the first side aisles, alongside the outer supports we experience the unfolding of the nave wall in its full glory. Walking through the outer side aisles we see the whole architecture of the first double height side aisle composition (see section).

For a sketch survey of the entire building in its full height, it was necessary to determine sight lines along which prominent building details would overlap. By marking off the distances from these observation points, the building could be sketched out in its true proportions. In the study of a building pedantic exactitude is not required. The intelligence of the method and how the proportions are recorded is important.

This self-acquired experience is retained in one's memory. One does not easily forget it, being quite different from the abstract knowledge gained through theoretical studies.

As would be expected, a great deal happens on the west facade of Notre-Dame.

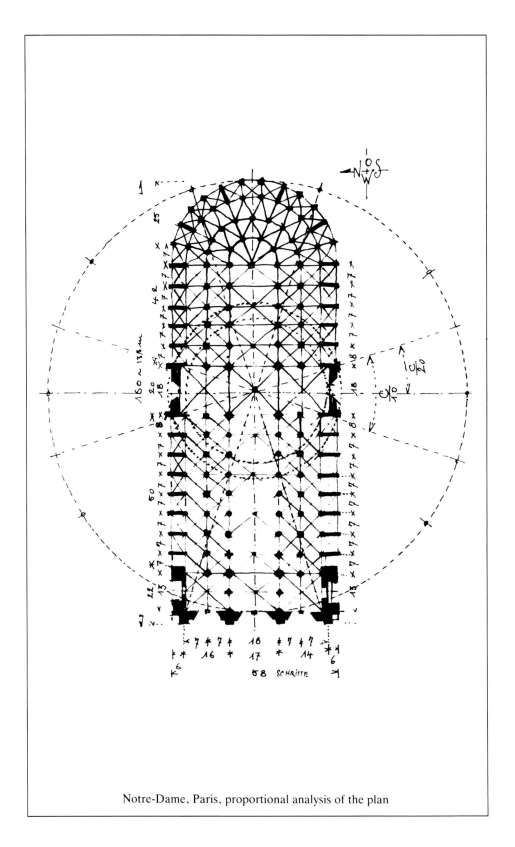

Notre-Dame, Paris, proportional analysis of the plan

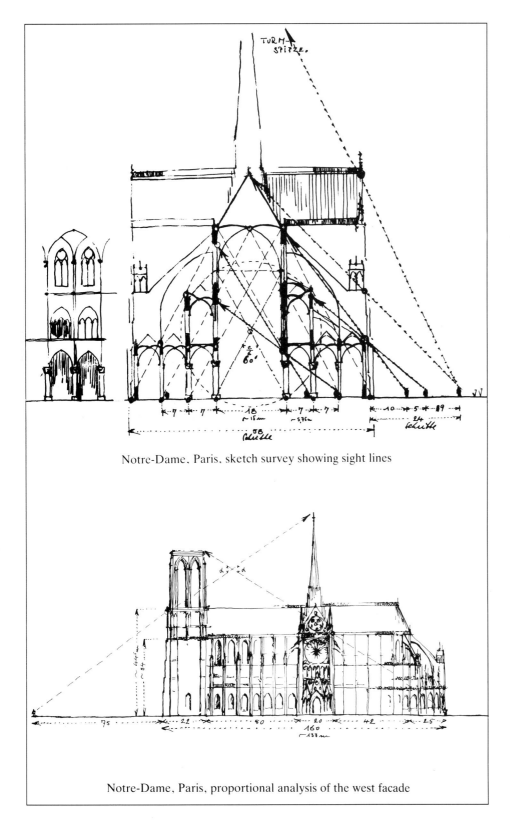

Notre-Dame, Paris, sketch survey showing sight lines

Notre-Dame, Paris, proportional analysis of the west facade

First, with the help of sight lines I try to control my sketch of the building mass (see illustration). The first eye-catching property of this imposing facade is the clear architectonic field that carries the tower projections. Its depth is not as modulated as Reims, Laon and others. The spirit of Romanesque architecture can still be strongly felt. The gable of the roof truss that should logically be visible on the facade is cunningly disguised by a high filigree arcade (compare with Reims, Amiens, Auxerre etc.) The arcade travels across both tower projections and if projected vertically downwards it completes, in a magnificent manner, a perfect square. The diagonal folded up defines the relationship between base line and height of towers as: $1 : \sqrt{2} = 1 : 1.41$.

As we know already, this relationship is the result of the quartering of a circle.

The equilateral triangle constructed around the outer face of the flying buttresses of the west facade touches the cornice above the rose window at mid point. The cornice coincides with the base line of the above mentioned arcade, and if projected into the building it coincides with the central spine of the nave vault. Thus, the height to base relationship is $1 : \sqrt{3}/2 = 1 : 0.866$. So far, using two quite different geometric operations, we have found two important horizontal sub-divisions of the initial square, whose centre is found on the balcony parapet beneath the rose window. The first horizontal above the portals is highly accentuated by a monumental figure group, consisting of 28 statues. In its height it relates to the upper decorative arcade as $m : M = 1 : 1.618$. This relationship is true to the Golden Section.

The most important vertical divisions appear on the facade as a result of the positions of the flying tower buttresses. And here, for whatever reason, we discover an interesting irregularity, the origin of which I cannot trace. I have paced the interaxial distances of the flying buttresses from left to right, and found the distances to be 16, 17 and 14 paces.

16 : 17 = 1 : 1.06
14 : 17 = 1 : 1.21

The portal heights according to measurements taken from the plan, are:

left portal to middle portal: 1 : 1.18
right portal to middle portal: 1 : 1.10

The row of statues above the middle portal consists of nine figures, eight to the left, seven to the right. The irregularity of the left portal against the right portal is balanced by a gable-like relief above the pointed arch configuration.

Now we come to the proportions of the Golden Section. We subtend a circle from the centre of the rose window that has the base line as its tangent. Along a vertical middle axis we divide the circle into 10 parts. We then draw a second concentric circle that has the outer face of the flying buttresses as its tangent, and then connect all points of intersection with the centre. A number of geometric points become apparent that come surprisingly close to the already determined divisions. From a purely mathematical viewpoint they cannot superimpose exactly.

I intend to show that architecture of this complexity is not developed on just the one geometric level, but all available tonalities are employed. I experienced this an infinite number of times in my surveys of St. Etienne in Auxerre.

The irregularities of these overlays are compensated for by the highly modulated and layered profiles. The most important accentuation should always have the most prominent profile that remains clearly visible in the perspective view.

The most beautiful harmonic sequence is defined by the string courses above the figure group over the rose window and the cornice above the uppermost arcade. They are related to each other according to the Golden Section, in a diminishing sequence identical to the composition of the towers:

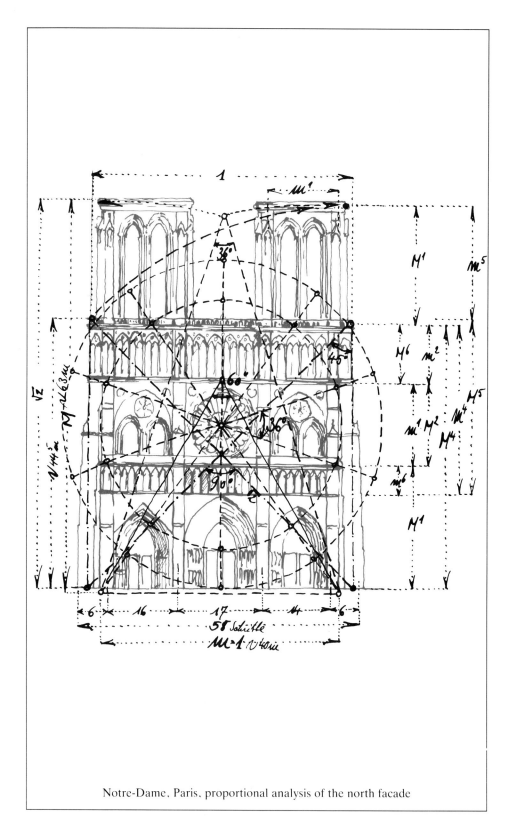

Notre-Dame, Paris, proportional analysis of the north facade

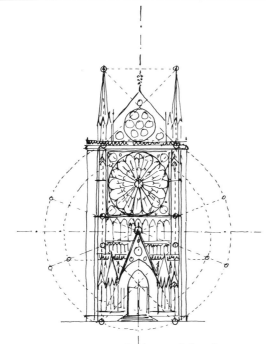

Notre-Dame, Paris, south facade,
drawing based on paced measurements and sight lines

$$ctg \frac{c}{16} = 2,414$$

$$p = \frac{1}{2}(2 - \sqrt{2}) = 0,293$$

$$p\sqrt{2} = \sqrt{2} - 1 = 0,414$$

$$p(1 + \sqrt{2}) = 0,707$$

$$1 - p = 0,707$$

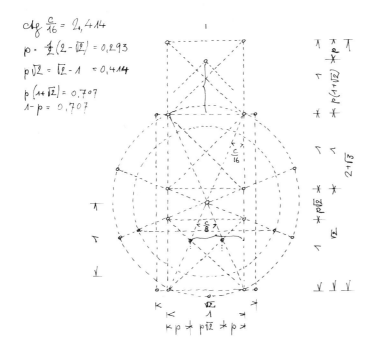

Notre-Dame, Paris, interpretation of the west facade using triangulation

M^I/m^I, M^{II}/m^{II}, M^I

$M^I + m^I + m^{II} = M^{IV}$

m^{IV} plotted from top to bottom defines the lower edge of the figural group

$m^{VI} : M^{VI}$ = figural group of arcade

$m^V : M^V$ = lower edge of the cornice on the tower to m^{IV} + parapet etc.

Moessel tried to establish a Golden Section relationship between the width of the facade and its height.

Properties resulting from the division of a circle into 8 segments are to be found on the north portal.

North Portal of Notre-Dame in Paris

We subtend a circle from the apex of the portal gable that intersects the axis of the flying buttresses along the base line. This distance 1, forms one of the sides of the octagon inscribed in the circle. The cornice forms the octagon side opposite the base line. The base to height relationship of gable gallery is:

1 : ctg c/16 = 1 : 2.414

The two squares contained in this field, horizontally flank a rectangle with sides 1 : 0.414, a ratio identical to that of the monumental blind arcade. The upper square inscribes the 16-segment rose window. Here too, a direct relationship exists between the geometry of the rose window and the overall portal composition.

The same square folded upwards defines the height of the pinnacles that crown the flying buttresses. We can interpret the portal composition also as follows: a rectangle with a base at 1 and top at the square framing the rose window, $\sqrt{2}$, can be inscribed twice, with an overlap, in this portal. The overlapping area with a side ratio of 1 : 0.414 is identical to that of the already mentioned blind arcade. The proportional relationship of $1 : \sqrt{2}$ also determines the compositional framework of our next example, the north crossing house of the Cathedral at Meaux. It too is based on the Golden Section.

---- ✳ ----

263

St. Etienne Cathedral at Meaux

I would like to conclude my observations on the Gothic art of building with the analysis of a magnificent portal composition on the north crossing house of the Cathedral at Meaux. The composition consists of the superimposition of two rectangles with a side ratio of m : M. The area defined by the overlap has sides that relate to the Golden section m^I : M^I, where M^I is identical to m. If one subtracts the newly defined area $m^I M^I$ from the original area mM, one is left with two perfect squares (mm or $M^I M^I$), that flank $m^I M^I$.

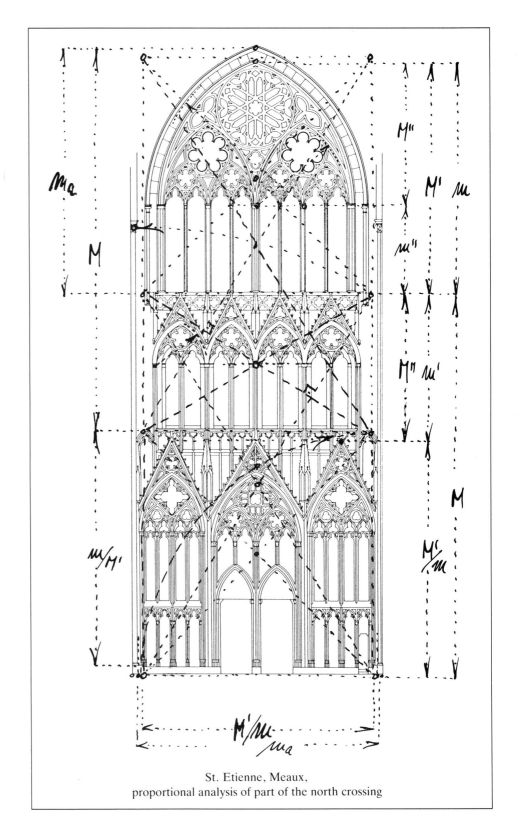

St. Etienne, Meaux,
proportional analysis of part of the north crossing

——— ✳ ———

We find an analogous proportional structure in the human body:
body height is 183cm, width including dangling arms is approximately 70cm, navel height is 113cm, distance between dangling fingertips and floor is 70cm. The key proportions coincide in both figures.

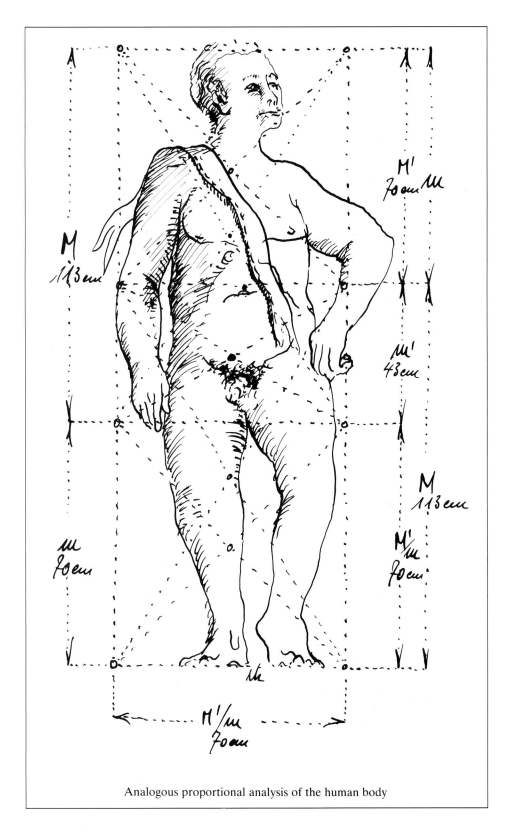

Analogous proportional analysis of the human body

————— ✳ —————

St. Michael in Munich (1582-97),
architects W. Miller and Fr. Sustris
This Jesuit Church which has one of the most beautiful Renaissance interiors in Munich, tempted me to a proportional verification with paced steps.

First, I noticed that if one stands in one of the entrance doors one sees exactly into the corner of the transept. That creates, on entering the building, an illusion of spatial depth that can never be generated on the narrow site. A street on the right-hand side contains this development. I discovered the same 'trick' in the Peterskirche and the Karlskirche in Vienna. Otto Wagner in his Kirche am Steinhof, of the same type as the above mentioned buildings, did not incorporate aspects of successive spatial unfolding. Standing under the choir the geometric space is seen in all its clarity. There are no hidden secrets. It is this philosophical stance that distinguishes Otto Wagner's work. (See illustrations on page 270.) Pacing the Michaelskirche, further important points become apparent with the help of sight lines, as can be seen in my sketches.

———— ✳ ————

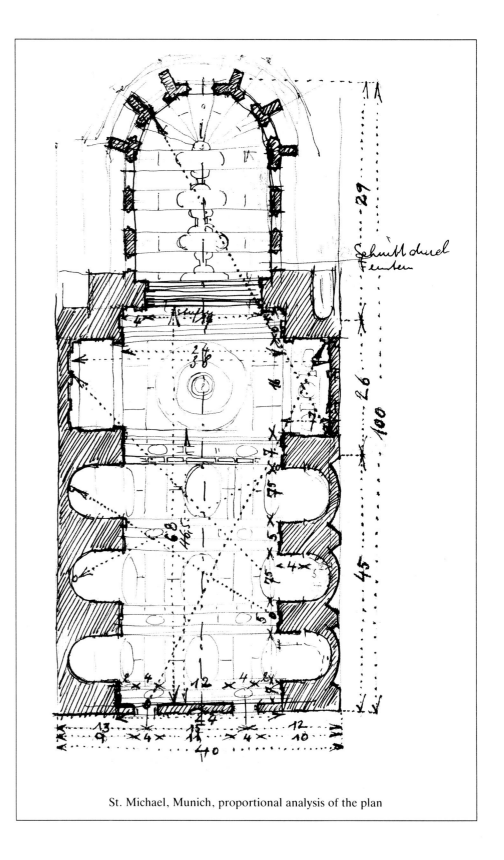

St. Michael, Munich, proportional analysis of the plan

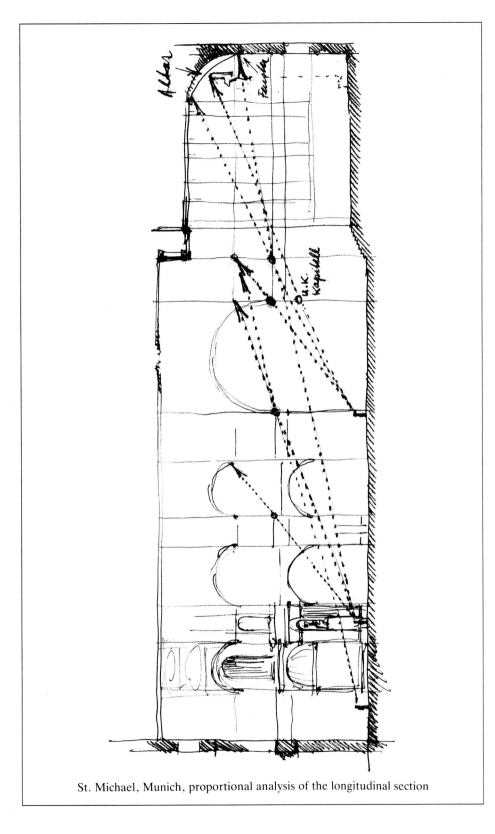

St. Michael, Munich, proportional analysis of the longitudinal section

Checking the relationship between central transept axis and overall exterior length:

$100/45 + 26/2 = 100/58 = 1.724/1 = \sqrt{3}/1$

a relationship pertaining to the tripartite division of a circle.

If we subtract the estimated values for the wall thicknesses, we can prove the already familiar interior space relationship of Gothic churches, i.e. 1 : 1.618.

that is $92.25/57 = 1.618/1$.

(I request architectural historians to check this relationship.)

As I have repeatedly illustrated, the structural demands of a building were always determined by the method of triangulation (Dehio). This also applies of course to exterior dimensions. Looking at the sketches of transept, nave and aisles, consideration should be given to the sight lines.

The most important approximate dimensional relationships of the plan are:

$40 : 100 = 1 : 2.5$ exterior measurements

$24 : 46.5 = 1 : 2$ nave and aisles

$24 : 68 = 1 : 3$ nave, aisles and section of transept

$16 : 38 = 1 : 2.37$

———— ✳ ————

Proportions of the section

Also in this Renaissance building the lateral loads from the main vault are revealed by a system of triangulation. We are talking about the widest spanning Renaissance barrel vault north of the Alps. Between the side chapels massive abutments are concealed from the observer. The central spine of the barrel vault also forms the apex of an equilateral triangle that has the cross-section as its base line. Measured from the outside, the cross-section is roughly 40 paces wide, the height of the vault is therefore approximately:

40 x 0.866 = 34.64 paces x 0.91 = $\bar{3}$1.50m

The width of the church interior is 24 paces, that is approximately 24 x 0.91 = $\bar{2}$2m

I estmate the springing vault line of choir and nave to be: 22 x $\sqrt{3/2}$ = 19m high, which is the height of the equilateral triangle whose base line is the width of the church interior. The height of the vault can also be approximated by interpreting the spatial proportions:

19 + 22/2 = 30m

If we take the interior width as a basis, we can calculate:

38 x 0.866 x 0.91 = 29.95m

The choir width is 17 paces. The outermost aisles are 3.5 paces wide. The height of the choir vault must be approximately 3m lower, i.e. 27m high or

19 + 17 x 0.91/2 = 26.7m or

17 x 0.91 x 0.866 x 2 = 26.79m

that is twice the height of the equilateral triangle whose base line is twice the width of the choir.

Similar to our observations on Gothic buildings, the corresponding sides of the outer triangle meet important structural points of the space. For instance the parapet of the gallery above the chapels and the springing barrel line above the choir.

——— ✳ ———

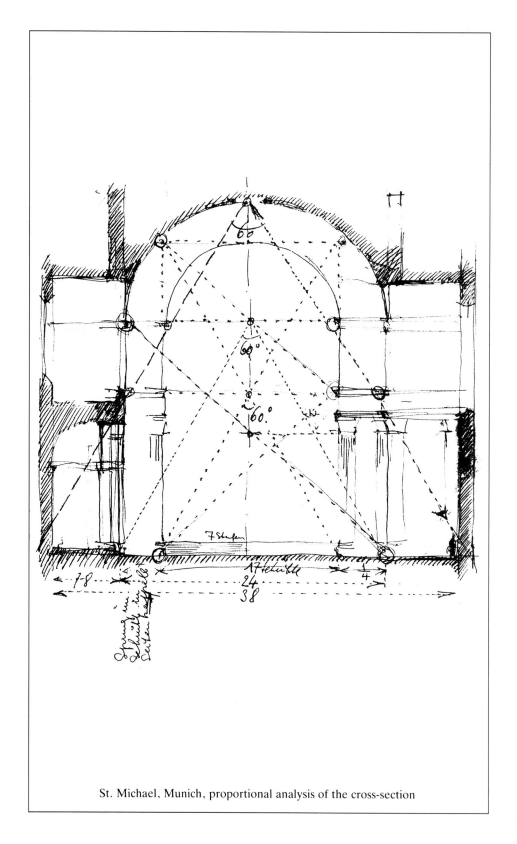

St. Michael, Munich, proportional analysis of the cross-section

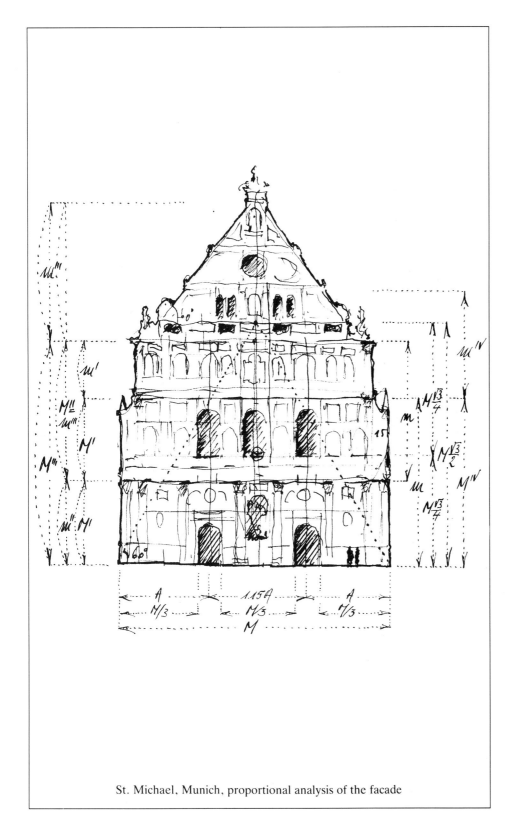

St. Michael, Munich, proportional analysis of the facade

Interpretation of the facade

M = width of the facade (40 paces), and base line of the constructed equilateral triangle.

As expected its apex defines the springing line of the gable ($M\sqrt{3}/2$).

$M\sqrt{3}/4$ = half of building height, which is also the seat of the roof triangle and balustrade of the window in the gallery.

m = the width according to the Golden Section and is identical to the cornice above the gallery windows. At this height the width of the facade begins to taper slightly. This is seen as an architectonic introduction to the imposing gable configuration.

m^I = height of the next storey to the springing of the gable. It is decorated with blind windows and relates to half of m = M^I according to the Golden Section.

m^{II} = height from base line to first string course. It relates to the addition of the next two storeys according to the Golden Section:

$m^{II}/M^{II} = M^I/M^I + m^I = 1/1.618$

The sum total of all three storeys approximately relates to the gable height according to the same proportions:

$m^I + M^I + m^{II} = M^{III}$

$m^{III}/M^{III} = 1/1.618$

$2 \times M^I = m = M^{IV}$

The distance M^{IV} relates to the first gable string course according to:

$m^{IV}/M^{IV} = 1/1.618$

All relationships in plan, section and elevation have been studied carefully and all dimensions I considered to be important (except for the choir) were paced and recorded. The relationships of section and elevation had to be estimated. I am pretty certain that I am not far off the real values. I have not cross-checked my dimensions on the plans. One should, however, normally do this to learn from one's own estimations. I wanted to give an example of how a student can learn to decipher an 'architectonic score' in a few hours and put it to the best possible use of his craft. I carried out these observations in 1961, during my study at the Technical University in Munich.

———— ✳ ————

Sketches of Peterskirche, Karlskirche and Kirche am Steinhof in Vienna

I should like to extend my observations to the spatial composition of the above mentioned churches with notes from my own sketch-books. They have nothing to do with proportions, but a great deal with the complexity of the overall composition which is our concern in this book. With all these examples, I intend to exercise a technique of observation and analysis.

Sketch explanations, from left to right:
1. St. Peter's Church in Vienna.
From the entrance it is not possible to estimate the depth of the side chapel. Even the space of the dome cannot yet be judged. On entering the church interior the impression of spatial depth is very powerful.
2. A similar composition may be found in the Karlskirche by Fischer von Erlach in Vienna. Standing under the gallery on the axis of the entrance passage, the depth of the side chapels cannot be judged, since their back walls are not part of one's field of view. However, the position yields a view right into the lantern of the dome. The oval shape of the room extends the space to an amazing depth. The top light above the altar extends the spatial perimeters even further.
Figs. 3 and 13. In the Kirche am Steinhof, Otto Wagner designed an extremely rational interior space. Standing in the middle of the entrance, the whole interior space can be embraced. Wagner designed the entrance area as preparation for this clear geometric space. Four massive granite columns decorated with figures adorn the entrance. These stele-like portal guardians are penetrated by a filigree canopy made of finely punched copper sheeting. It is supported by delicate bronze columns whose bases line up with the onset of the staircase, (figs. 10 and 11). A row of columns flanking a portal was a favourite theme of Otto Wagner's teacher at the Academy of Applied Arts in Vienna, Theophil von Hansen.

Past the round columns, one enters through glazed bronze grill gates into a sober porch which in turn leads through a pair of glazed oak doors into a space below the gallery. Only here the full spatial experience unfolds. The floor is slightly inclined

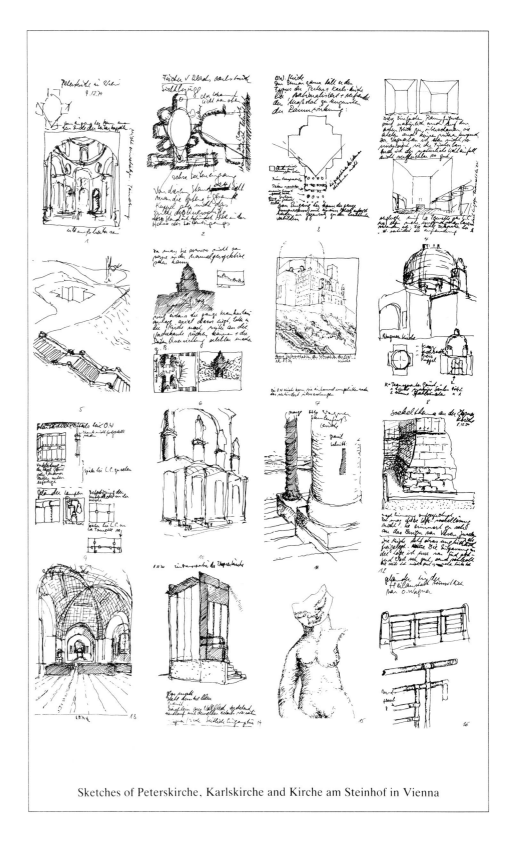

Sketches of Peterskirche, Karlskirche and Kirche am Steinhof in Vienna

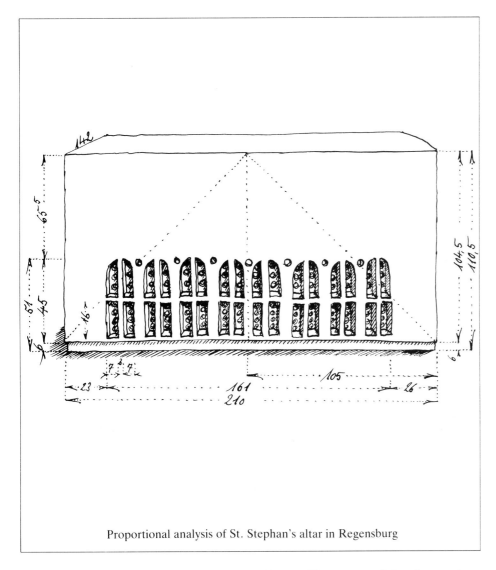

Proportional analysis of St. Stephan's altar in Regensburg

Early Romanesque altar in St. Stephan in Regensburg

The wonderful dimensions of this altar drew it to my attention. Its proportions did not prove to be governed by the Golden Section, as I had initially suspected. They are more closely related to the dimensional relationships of a circle divided into eight parts. Le Corbusier would have enjoyed this stone, since its dimensions are a close approximation to his red and blue Modulor sequence. He had mixed the sequences in a very unorthodox manner, and I suspect that no one other than him could handle them.

The altar dimensions reveal the following relationships: Length/Breadth = 2.10m/ $1.42 = 1.47/1 \cong \sqrt{2}/1$
Length/Base height = 210/104.5 = 2/1
The front of the altar, minus the base, consists of two squares, its diagonals approximating to the altar width.

How does the window band relief sit in the stone?
Altar width/Window band length = 2.10/ 1.16 = 1.3/1
Upper section/Window height = 65.5/45 = $1.45/1 \cong \sqrt{2}/1$
Upper part/Window + base = 65.5/51 = 1.31/1
Window side panels: $51/26 = 1.96/1 \cong 2/1$
$51/23 = 2·21/1$
Side panels without base: $45/26 = 1.73/1 \cong \sqrt{3}/1$
$51/26 = 1.95/1 \cong 2/1$
Halved upper section: 105/65.5 = 1.6/1
I have used this example to show that even without exact geometry, a perfect masterpiece can be created with artistic sensitivity and feeling.

On the other hand, it is quite possible that I have been unable to unravel the secret of the altar's underlying system of proportion.

This precious monolith has probably been left by the stonemason more or less as it was mined from the quarry.

towards the altar.
4. The purely geometric space has been abstracted to the last degree in the church by Rudolph Schwarz in Aachen and by Le Corbusier at La Tourette near Arbresle. With these pure forms, the quality of lighting takes on an even more important role than before.
5 and 6. Location of Kirche am Steinhof. Initial sketches by Wagner suggest a symmetrical staircase along the central axis. Regrettably, the hospital layout fails to acknowledge the church, turning its back on it.
8. The building unit.
9. The tile cladding. Each of the raised tiles is secured from underneath with two bronze bosses. The pattern of the tiles was later repeatedly taken up by Le Corbusier.

I find the rustic base of the church unsympathetic. It reminds me too much of flower vase designs and bedside lamps. What is interesting, however, is the change of material from embossed to smooth granite, to a facade material (marble) hanging on the wall.
14. The side doors. A surprisingly sober and modern design. Even in this unassuming detail, the side walls of the portal clasp the little roof between them, just as in his underground stations in Vienna.
16. Balustrade detail from the sanatorium complex.

———— ✳ ————

Proportional studies of projects
by Claude Nicolas Ledoux

I always advise my students at the beginning of their architectural studies to visit
Ledoux's Saltworks in the forests of Chaux.
There, a true architectural shock awaits
them!

Here is a brief introduction, so that none
of the important nuances are missed.

The Main Entrance to the Saltworks

The imposing portico at the end of an
unswerving street several kilometres long
enjoys a solid, not too complicated proportional framework. It is the centrepiece of
the semi-circular composition, scooped like
the buildings that make up the semi-circle.
m = central engaged portico and side wing
related to the total length M, according to
the Golden Section (congruent relationship).

$m/M = 1/1.618$

This basic proportion is repeated in all the
buildings along the semi-circle.

m^I = height of the massive pediment. Its
relationship to the portico width M^I is of the
Golden Section.

The area m^I x M^I inscribes two squares
with sides m^I. The area where the two
squares overlap denotes the axis of the two
central columns. The ratio between this
dimension and the intercolumnar distance
of the outer columns is 3 : 2.

The theme of overlapping squares extends to other units of the complex. The
height of columns and architrave can be
found by subtending a semi-circle from base
line M^I. Where the arc intersects the axis of
the columns coincides with the termination
of the column capitals and the base of the
architrave.

The architrave and cornice are not part of
the proportional system based on the division of circles. Their inscription reads:
'Royal Saltworks, built under the Regency
of King Ludwig XVI, in the year 1776'.

$m^I + a/M^I = 63/84 = 1/1.33 = 0.75/1 = 3/4$

————— ✳ —————

Proportional analysis of the mai

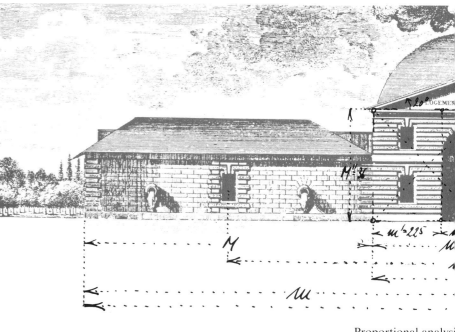

Proportional analysi

ntrance portal, Saltworks at Chaux

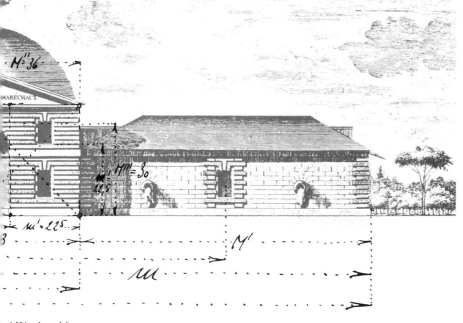

of Workers' houses

Workers' houses with workshops

As with the main entrance portal, central unit and side wings relate in the Golden Section. The height to width relationship of the central unit is also of the Golden Section:

$36 : 63 = 1 : 1.75 = 4 : 7$

The relationship between entrance gate and side parts is:

$18 : 22.5 = 4 : 5 = 2 : 2.5 = 1 : 1.25$

The proportions of the side areas are:

$m^{II} : M^{II} = 22.5 : 36 = 1 : 1.6$

The gate proportions, height measured to the vertex of semi-circle:

$m^{III} : M^{III} = 18 : 30 = 1 : 1.62$

Both proportions are roughly related as in the Golden Section.

———— ※ ————

The Director's Residence

Initially, this house was designed as the centrepiece of circular complex. Since the scheme had never been completed, only half of it was realised, and to this day the house sits in the centre of the semi-circle.

Its magnificent monumental presence is heightened by the clearest of proportions.

The base line of the portal colonnade M, relates to the height of the pediment onset m, according to the Golden Section. The column height is half the base line, M/2

The gable has a gradient of 20°. The diagonal of the rectangle M/2 x m, if folded, meets the inner face of the gable apex.

The height of the gable ridge is m¹, which relates to the total width of the building M¹, according to the Golden Section.

The Stables of the Director

The plan is based on a square with smaller peripheral additions. The gable height of the front facade is identical to the height of an equilateral triangle erected about base m or M¹ (the sides of the square).

The rectangle on which the gable rests is defined in two ways:

1. To cornice head line
2. To cornice base line

In the first case the rectangle has a base to height relationship of 1.53 : 1. The rectangle encloses two overlapping squares whose respective centres denote the axis of the columns. In other words, their distance from the side is half the height, the central overlapping area being identical to the portal opening. The height of the portal arch is the same as half the central engaged portico dimension, including the plinth. This can be demonstrated with a semi-circle subtended around the centre of the engaged portico at plinth height.

We subtend a semi-circle about the same upper plinth line, its diameter defines the total length of the building. The arc intersects the gable springing points and the gable ridge.

The newly fixed geometric points on the semi-circle are joined with the outermost points on the base line and are found to inscribe a 90° angle. Parallel to these projections the same angles can be constructed in the above mentioned semi-circle. If the geometric points on the semi-circle are pro-

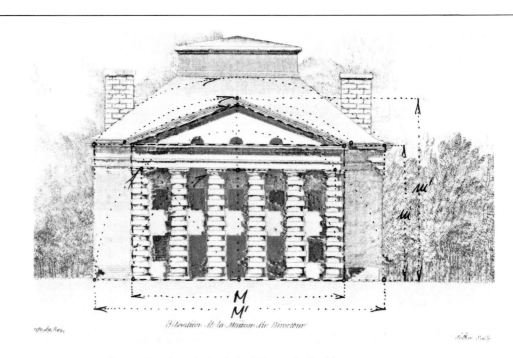

Proportional analysis of the Director's Residence

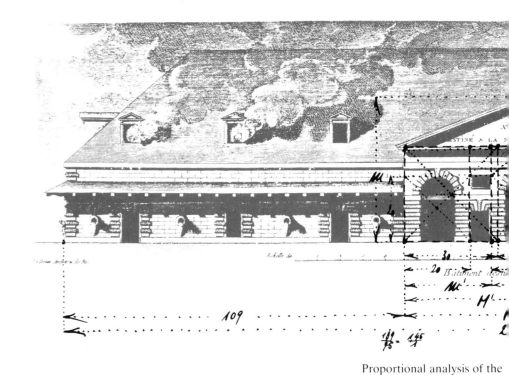

Proportional analysis of the

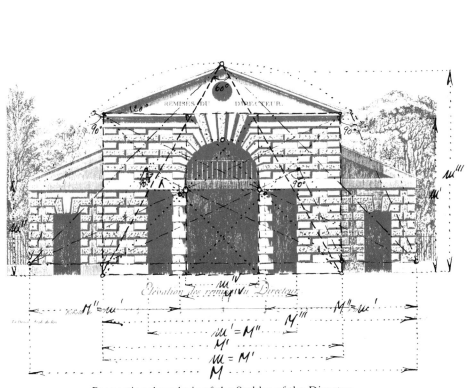

Proportional analysis of the Stables of the Director

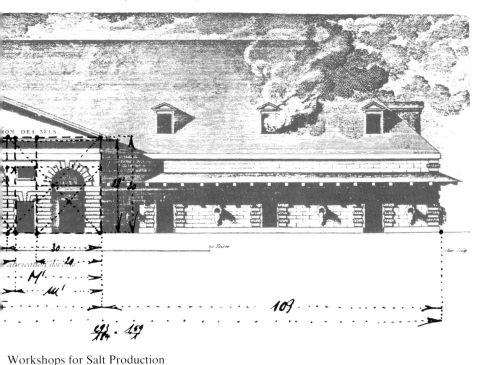

Workshops for Salt Production

jected on to the base, they define the outermost points of the side portals.

The second method of defining the central section of the engaged portico elevation is to determine the height of the lower cornice ridge = m^I. Its relationship to base line M^I is of the Golden Section.

Height m^I is identical to the width of the overall portal configuration and it in turn relates to the central width according to the Golden Section: $m^I = M^{II}$

Height of the portal opening up to onset of the semi-circle = m^{II}

$m^{II}/M^{II} = 1/1.618$

$m^I = M^{II}$ = axial distance between supports, taken to either end of the building.

$m^{III}/M^{III} = 1/1.618$

m^{III} = height to lower gable cornice ridge

M^{III} = central engaged portico plus one side wing

m^{IV} = width of main portal

M^{IV} = respond distance of central portal column and side door

$m^{IV}/M^{IV} = 1/1.618$

The Workshops for Salt Production

Once again the built unit is dominated by a central engaged portico. Its relationship to the side buildings is 75 : 109 = 1 : 1.45.

The overall length relates to the central part plus side wing as 184 : 293 = 1 : 1.59.

The gable height m, of the central part relates to its base line M, according to the Golden Section. This building element consists of three large archways that frame two smaller ones. The width of each archway, 20, relates to the height of the lower cornice ridge, 28.2, as $1 : \sqrt{2}$.

The axis of the pilasters flanking the central archway divide the total width of the engaged portico as follows:

The distance between the axis is 15, the distance between the axis and the lateral side walls of the engaged portico is 30. Thus, the relationship is 1 : 2. The cornice height is 30. The overall dimension of the engaged portico is 30 height and 75 width, that is a ratio of 2 : 5.

———— ✳ ————

The Manager's Residence

Two of these houses mark the corners of the semi-circular plan. The Saltworks facade exhibits a Palladian portal motif similar to the horse stables of the Director's Residence. The inner facing wall of this portal with its entrance door consists of lightly burnished exposed brickwork, a delightful contrast to the white Jura chalk exteriors.

The overall proportions of the facade, with cornice upper ledge 76 and base line 140 is: 1 : 1.84. The distance between lower cornice ledge and upper face of the plinth is the same as half the base. The height to base (width) relationship is 1 : 2. Half the height of this plane meets the upper face of the column capitals. If we take the overall height of the facade to the top of the cornice, and project this line back onto the base line, it meets the inner frame of the entrance door. This type of construction can be found in different designs for these houses. The stone structure clearly emphasises the three sections in the facade; namely, the central portal and the two flanking side parts. The base of the side parts m, is contained twice in height 76. If we construct a semi-circle at plinth height with the entire house width as its base line, i.e. the diameter touching the underside of the main roof truss to form a tangent with it, the points where the semi-circle intersects the vertical demarcation lines between central and side section, coincide with the height of the portal and mark the corners of a square erected about the plinth. The outer faces of the columns, the upper ledge of the architrave and the base line complete another square. The same is true for the inner faces of the columns, the underside of the capitals and the base line.

The gable has a pitch of 20°. From the centre of the base line, at plinth height, the gable height can be determined with the help of a divider.

According to the Golden Section the following sub-divisions can be discovered:
m/M = 1/1.618
m = width of the side section, while M is the remaining central portal section.
M is also identical to the inner portal opening. Thus the inner opening relates to the overall opening according to the Golden Section.

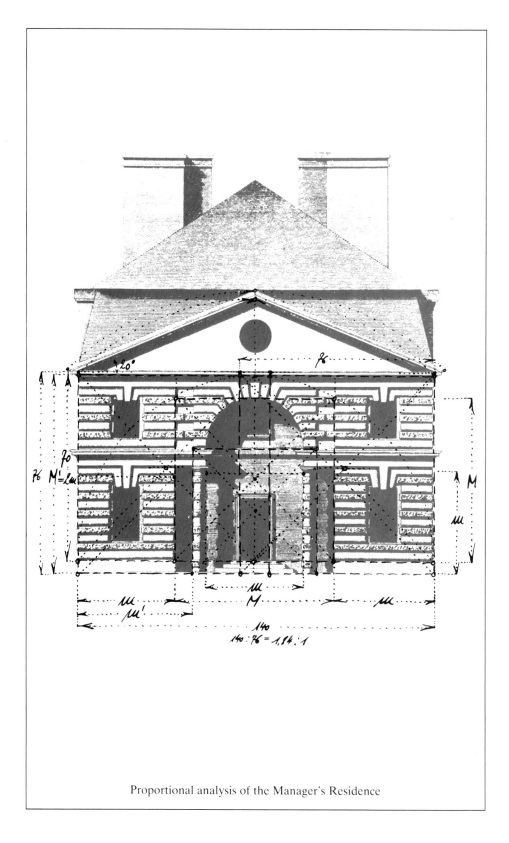

Proportional analysis of the Manager's Residence

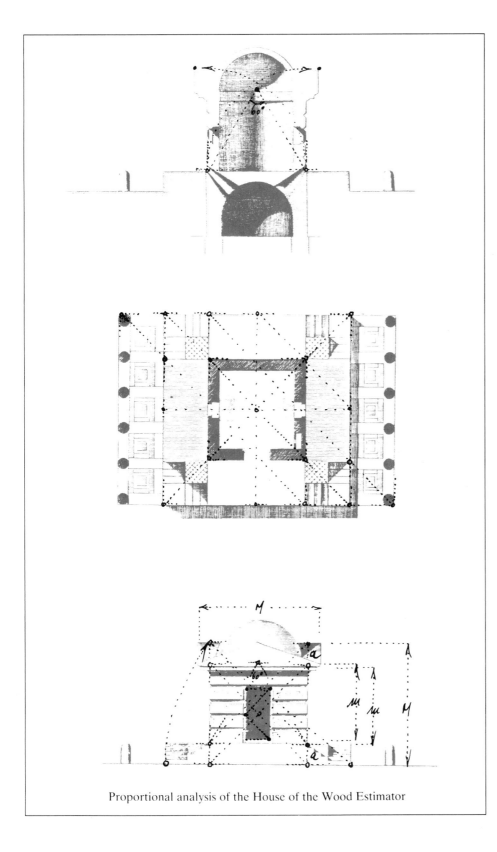

Proportional analysis of the House of the Wood Estimator

House of the Wood Estimator

The layout of the Saltworks holds some wonderful surprises; namely, miniscule buildings, miniature architecture of unbelievable quality. They are to be found near the administrative buildings and in the garden behind the workers' houses. They are not quite executed as the drawings suggest. Plinth and dome are missing. The roof is executed in one piece of stone. Concerning the plan: the square of the plan generates the square of the base, which is four times greater than the plan. Stairs are cut into the corners.

The two flanking stone bollards visually increase the building's presence by a factor of two. The sides of the rectangular plan share a relationship of 3 : 2 determined by the dimensions of the house plan.

The section: the dome springing line is determined by an equilateral triangle erected about the base. The gable heights are identical to the base.

Frontal view: the same relationship is clearly visible in the facade. Gable height a, corresponds to plinth height a, and is half the width of the terrace that runs right round the house.

If one projects the house width onto the ground, the main gable and gable onset complete a perfect square, which in turn is identical to the ground floor plan. The entrance door reveals a relationship of 1 : 2.

Traces of the structural equilateral triangle are still visible in the facade. The relationship between cornice upper face and base line is $\sqrt{3}/2 : 1$

A single Golden Section proportion can be discovered:

M = distance between gable ridge and ground, and approximately the distance between individual gables.

m= distance betwen upper cornice line and door threshold, or cornice centre to upper plinth face.

$20.08/32.50 = m/M = 1/1.618$

The care with which Ledoux designed the gatehouse is extraordinary, as if it were a temple.

———— ✳ ————

A Parisian Gatehouse

If we construct a square on the base line, the architrave with its tympanum rests on its upper side. The diagonals of the square meet the uppermost cornice line, the relationship between base and height being $1:\sqrt{2}$.

A colonnade rests in front of the tower-like building. The height of the architrave above the columns is $\sqrt{2}M - M$. The building has a niche-like recess whose vault sits at the centre of the first square.

A Golden Section relationship can be discovered: the area above the colonnade cornice and the main cornice line of the building, m, relates to base M, as $m/M = 1/1.618$.

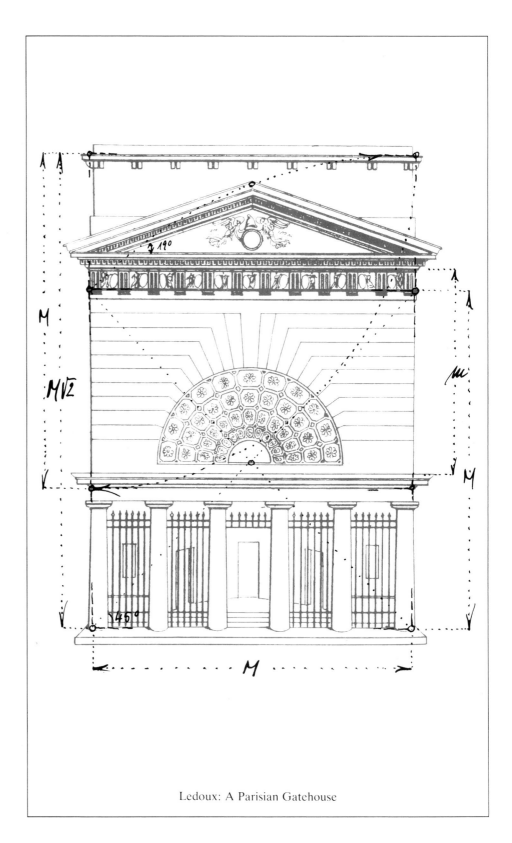

Ledoux: A Parisian Gatehouse

───── ✳ ─────

House with minarets

With its minaret-like towers, this project is reminiscent of the Karlskirche by Fischer von Erlach. The column height and the base form a square, A x A. A is the axial distance between columns. The building between the columns has the width 1. The height of the building measured from the lowest terrace equals its width. The diagonal $\sqrt{2}$ extends from this the lowest terrace to the underside of the column capitals.

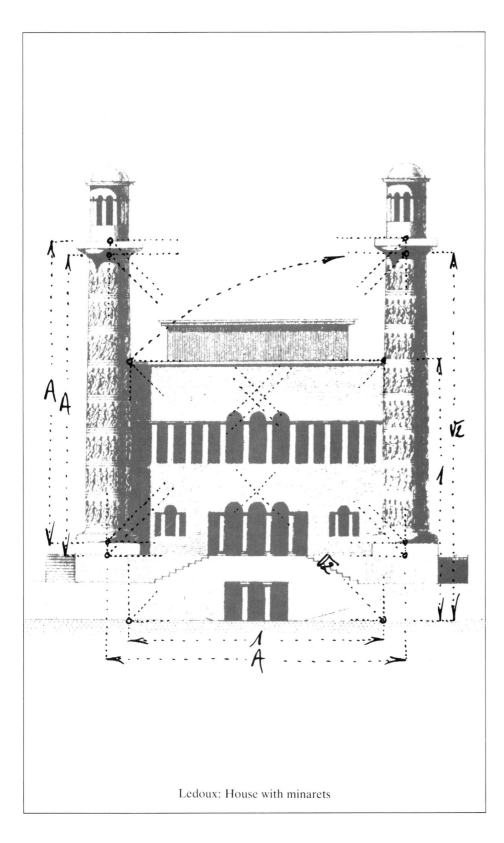

Ledoux: House with minarets

———— ✳ ————

Ledoux's ideal projects have a wonderful typological clarity, and the proportions abound with surprises. The ones illustrated here are the most extraordinary I have ever come across. The base consists of two squares, its height is half of base 1. The diagonal of one of the squares is $\sqrt{2}/2$.

If the diagonal is erected vertically, it denotes the column height in the gallery. The diagonal of this new rectangle, $\sqrt{3}/2$, erected vertically, meets the building's cornice line. It marks the height of an equilateral triangle erected about the base line.

If one of the corresponding sides of the triangle is folded upwards, it meets the gutter of the recessed roof addition, forming an exact square. The superimposition of these different geometries leads to the following geometric progression between base line and eaves:

$0.50 - 0.705 - 0.866 - 1$, or

$0.50 + 0.205 = 0.705$

$0.705 + 0.161 = 0.866$

$0.866 + 0.134 = 1.00$

Guidelines for proportional checks on buildings and their elements

This resumé is a sketchy summary of the design operations that must be controlled by a well-defined system of proportionality, and explains the simplest and most basic steps involved. The selected proportions only serve as examples. It should become clear that when composing a building, analogies between key parts need to exist. There is no need, however, to compulsively restrict oneself to a particular proportional system. The analysis of Auxerre has substantiated my hypothesis, that with increased complexity the superimpositions of different proportional sequences are also intensified. Before looking at proportioning of the built unit, I would like to mention some planar operations. We can imagine the plane to be one of the building's facades:

————— ✳ —————

Ledoux: Project for a house

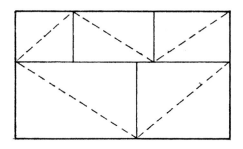

Fig.1 Simple planar relationships, adding up areas to give a sum total.

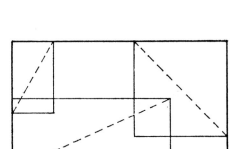

Fig.2 or overlapping of different planes.

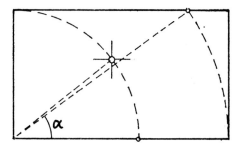

Fig.3 Using a divider, geometric locations are found: angle alpha is connected with the chosen geometric division.

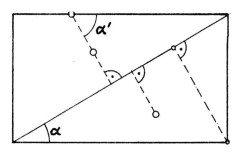

Fig.4 Geometric locations can be projected at right angles onto the diagonal of the configuration. Angle alpha' and alpha correspond to the selected geometric division.

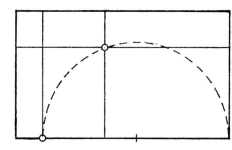

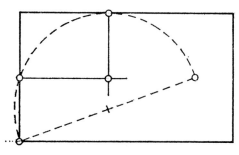

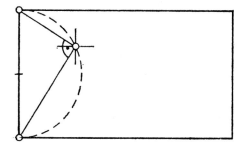

Figs. 5,6 and 7. A geometric location is inscribed in a semi-circle whose base line is identical to the height or width of the overall configuration. In other words, if we connect the point on the semi-circle with the base line we inscribe a rectangle.

Before looking at proportioning of the built unit, I would like to mention some planar operations. We can imagine the plane to be one of the building's facades:

Definition of the entire building unit

Fig. 1. Width to height to depth:
e.g. $b/a = 1/1.618 = c/b$
or $b/a = 1/\sqrt{2} = c/b$
$a/b = 1/\sqrt{3}/2 = b/c \ldots$

The overall proportions of the built unit play an especially important role. They determine its overall impression.

In my experience it is extraordinarily difficult, having taken into consideration all peripheral conditions, like the confines of function, economy etc., to harmonise the external dimensions of the building. In most instances the restricting factors are all too complex. In this case the sub-division and structuring of the building unit should contribute to its ultimate refinement.

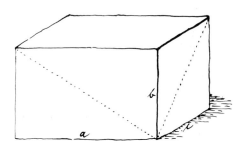

The building block is to be furnished with windows:

Fig. 2. $a/b = a/b^{I} = b^{II}/c^{I}$

The perforation of the building unit is an immensely delicate operation. The impairment of the wall has to be well proportioned and carefully located. In my experience it makes sense to relate the window proportions to the more dominant proportions of the built unit. Between themselves the perforations must display meaningful compositional inter-relationships.

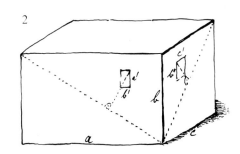

The arrangement of windows in rhythmic configurations

Fig 3. The axis of the window configurations have been determined by a given proportional module.

e.g. M/m = 1.618/1 etc.

These window configurations do, of course, relate to the interior spaces. Purely additive window formations can only relate to an identical repetition of interior spaces.

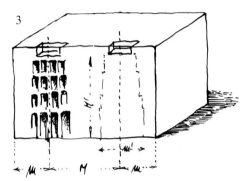

The positioning of the entrance gate

Figs. 4, 5 and 6. The first decision relates to the relative dimension of the gate. A further consideration is the symmetrical or asymmetrical ordering of elements and the composition of the resultant wall areas on either side of the gate. The height of the gate relative to the overall height of the building, and all the other elements of the facade not listed here, must be taken into account.

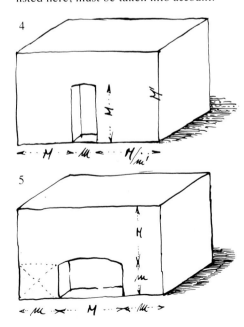

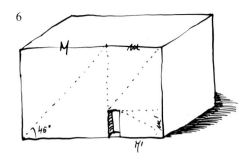

Determination of the base line

Fig. 7. m/M = 1/1.618

If the base line creeps up too high, one gets the unpleasant feeling of the building being truncated in half (for example, as in the Burgareal by G. Semper and K. von Hasenauer in Vienna).

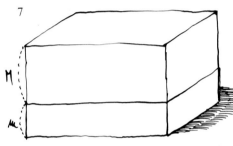

Determining the attic

Figs. 8, 9 and 10. The attic, similar to the base line must be harmonised with the other horizontal divisions of the building unit.

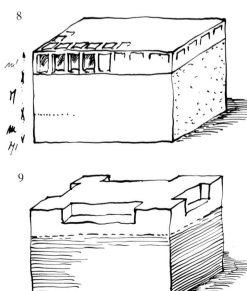

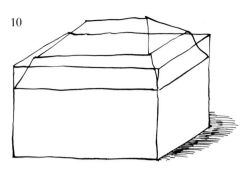

Determining the central engaged portico

Figs. 11, 12 and 13. The significance of a building's key element is judged by its relation to the remaining parts. The central engaged portico may push itself forward to become an independent building element, or rest in front of the building as a tower-like construction.

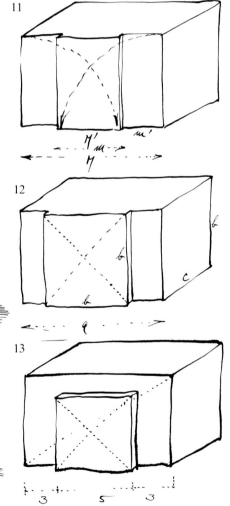

Determining engaged corners

Fig. 14. The centre of the building can also be emphasised by recessing it in relation to its respective corners.

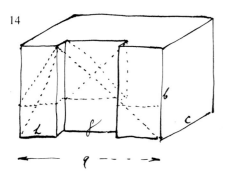

Fig. 15. The corners become independent and form tower-like projections, inscribing a U-shaped courtyard. Our compositional attention must be focused on the proportioning of the projecting elements and the enclosing courtyard walls.

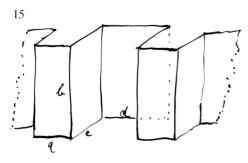

Proportioning free-standing building units relative to one another

Figs. 16, 17 and 18. The distance between building units, like the units themselves, has to be proportioned carefully. The relationship of the building units to each other should be supported by incorporating elements with a similar or regular proportional sequence into the overall design composition.

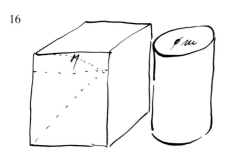

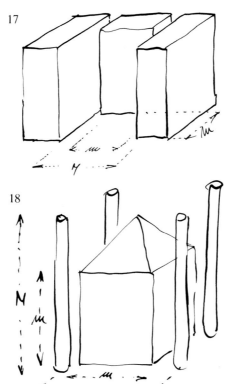

Figs. 19 and 20. In the planning of entire city quarters with streets and squares, the dimension of the blocks as well as the urban space contours must be brought into an harmonious relationship. In the case of the Schinkelplatz in Berlin, the relationship between the height of the two-storey arcade and the width of the square is 1 : 4, the overall three-storey height of the wall enclosing the urban square, including the set back attic, relates to the slightly larger width as 1 : 3.

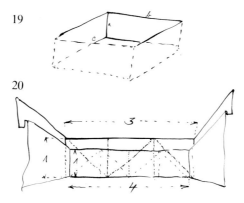

Thus, as in the human body the dimensional systems and their inter-relationships will go on to develop into the smallest detail of the built work.

It is pointless to describe all conceivable geometrical operations here. All figurations must be analysed with the aid of a scale and set square. Only then can one begin to understand the underlying thought processes. Einstein described Le Corbusier's understanding of geometry as 'sensual, irrational and poetic'. I add no other claim to this.

In many design considerations the position of a window or door, for instance, is considerably influenced by its function. There is little room for manoeuvre on the facade. Someone might suggest that given a little practice it should be possible to iron out all geometric irregularities on a facade. This is indeed true. However, the logic of these geometric regulators must go hand-in-hand with functional and structural logic. The *exterior* cannot be designed without an understanding of the *interior* and visa versa.

Le Corbusier has always proved his 'Tracées Régulateurs' with very simple examples, easily recognised by everyone. He shows what is most important and what is the end result of a long sequence of experiments. I have quite deliberately tried to present more detailed geometric proof for my proportional studies, even at the risk of becoming unclear. The drawings illustrated are far more significant for those who themselves carry out proportional studies and may use this material to work with.

This chapter is not intended to cultivate a geometry or number mystique, just as this was not the intention with the Modulor. Proportions are neither a gift of God nor simply rules governed by unmotivated fads. No proportional rule, however refined, can chart an unswerving road towards the composition of dimensional inter-relationships: the *compositional framework*!

Whether or not this exercise has been worthwhile, only the results will tell. The use of rules of proportions and corrective geometrical operations is no guarantee of success.

The same is true for the use of a proportional divider. It is not only an instrument for architects, but for everyone engaged in form-giving problems. Experience in the use of this instrument has taught us that it is deceptive to regard all dimensional derivations as logically correct. It is one of the weaknesses of the Modulor that it relies exclusively on the relationships of the Golden Section and has no additional scale. The missing dimensional units are improvised by the wilful addition of partial measurements that lack geometric logic in their resultant overall composition.

The derivations of the ten-fold division of the circle are, without doubt, the most balanced. They do, however, need to be supported by relationships with other geometric properties. The proportional divider allows us to build up a proportional framework on the basis of a quasi-random dimensional unit, without the dimensional regulatory systems it is important to recognise when the system's limit has been reached and one has to take the liberty of breaking the system's constraints. NOT ALL LIVING PROCESSES CAN BE REGULATED BY MATHEMATICAL RELATIONSHIPS!

Let me list a few number ratios that, except for the first one, could not be ascertained from our circle divisions:

2 : 3 or 3 : 2
1 : 1.5 or 1 : 0.66

3 : 4 or 4 : 3
1 : 1.33 or 1 : 0.75

3 : 5 or 5 : 3
1 : 1.66 or 1 : 0.6

4 : 7 or 7 : 4
1 : 1.75 or 1 : 0.57

5 : 7 or 7 : 5
1 : 1.4 or 1 : 0.71

Additional note

My assistant, Dr. Gaugusch, has dealt with proportions scientifically in his habilitation paper. He advised me to conclude the text with the following historic overview :

The Greek mathematician Euclid, who lived in Alexandria around 300 B.C., posed the following question in his book, *The Elements* (Book 2, paragraph 3) : 'If one divides a length arbitrarily, then the rectangle made up of the full length and one segment is equal to the sum of the rectangle constructed of the segments, plus the square constructed of the former segment'.

If one solves this problem, the resultant proportional relationship turns out to be that of the Golden Section : Major to minor = whole to Major, $M : m = (M+m) : M$

Thus, with three consecutive numbers the product of the smallest number with the largest is equal to the square of the middle numbers. This divisional relationship yields an irrational number that can only be defined geometrically.

In the *Ten Books of Architecture* by Vitruvius, 84 B.C., we can read the following: 'The greatest concern of the master builder must be, when building private houses, that all calculations are ruled by the proportions of a previously determined unit or modulus' (Book 6, chapter 2).

Vitruvius worked with three different proportions for atria:
1) 5 : 3
2) 3 : 2
3) $\sqrt{2} : 1$

(this compares with Alberti: $7 : 5 = 1.4 : 1$)

Colonnaded courtyard: 3 : 4
Triclinium (dining hall): 1 : 2
Ante-room (side room): 1 : 1 (Alae)

The Italian mathematician Leonardo Pisano, called Fibonacci (1180-1240), developed the following irrational number sequence named after him:

2 : 3 : 5 : 8 : 13 : 21 : 34 : 55 : 89 : 144 : 233 : 377 . . .

The second number is added to the first to make up the third and so on. The larger the numbers get, the closer they come to the irrational fractions.

Leon Battista Alberti (1404-72), wrote in Book 9, chapter 6 of *De Re Aedificatoria* (First Edition Florence, 1485).

Proportions of areas (planes) :
1) 1 : 1
2) $1 : 1\frac{1}{2} = 2 : 3$ ⎫
3) $1 : 1\frac{1}{3} = 3 : 4$ ⎬ short areas
4) 1 : 2 ⎫
5) $1 : 2 \times 1\frac{1}{2} = 4 : 9$ ⎬ medium large
6) $1 : 2 \times 1\frac{1}{3} = 9 : 16$ ⎭ areas
7) 1 : 3 the value doubled and $1\frac{1}{2}$ times its fraction ⎫
8) 3 : 8 the value doubled and $1\frac{1}{3}$ times its fraction ⎬ extensive areas
9) 1 : 4

A. Palladio (1508-80), wrote in *Quattro Libri dell'architettura*, Book 1, Chapter 21 (First Edition Venice, 1570) about loggias, entrances, halls, rooms and their forms.

The most beautiful proportions are:
1) round
2) square 1 : 1
3) side of square to diagonal of square $1 : \sqrt{2}$
4) square + $\frac{1}{3}$ = 3 : 4
5) square + $\frac{1}{2}$ = 2 : 3
6) square + $\frac{2}{3}$ = 3 : 5
7) 2 squares, 1 : 2

*   *   *

CHAPTER V

ESSAYS
ON
ARCHITECTURE

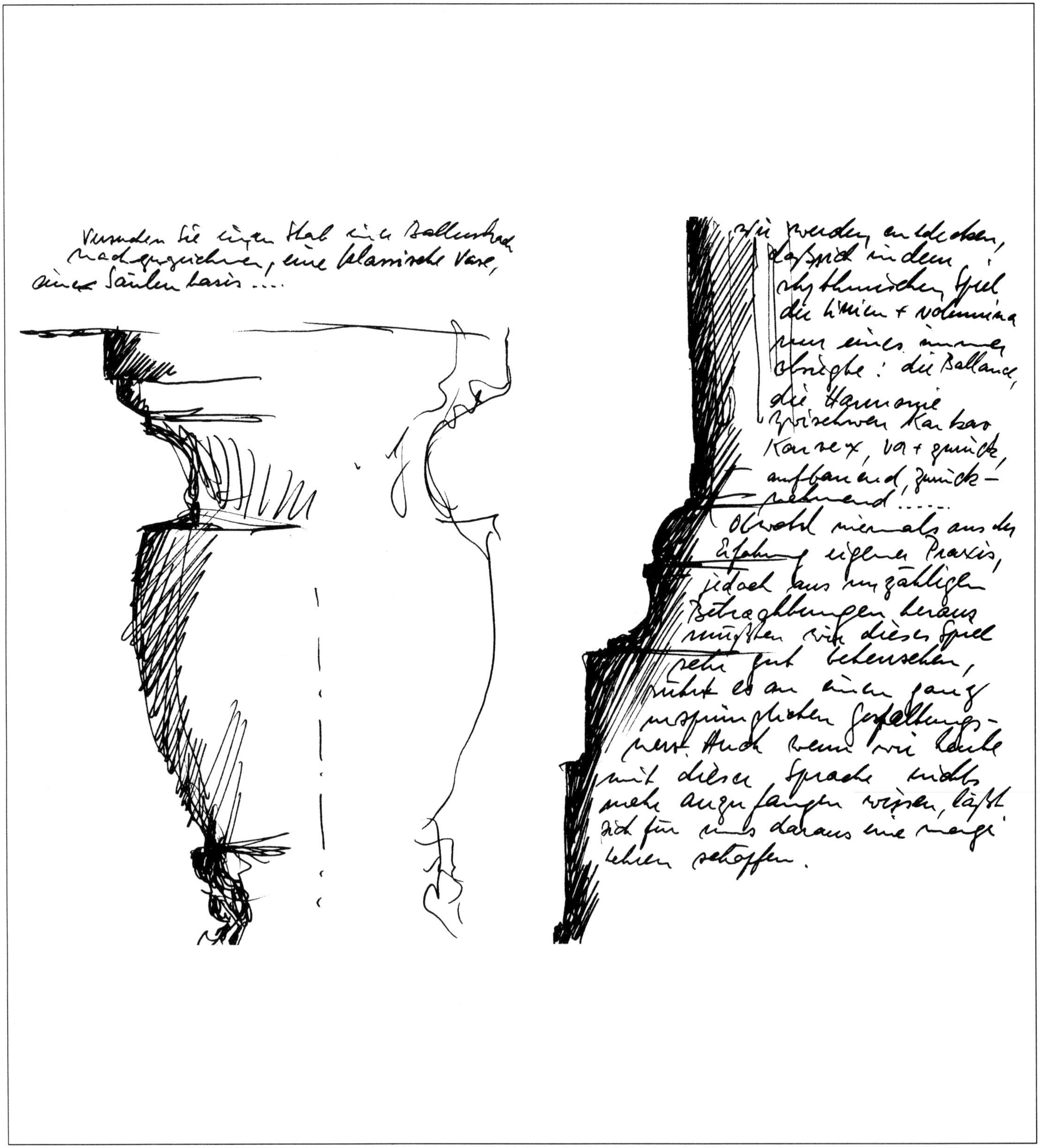
Versuchen Sie einen Stab einer Ballustrade
nachzuzeichnen, eine klassische Vase,
einer Säulen basis ....
Wir werden entdecken,
daß sich in dem
rhythmischen Spiel
der Linien + Volumina
nur eines immer
obsiegte: die Ballance,
die Harmonie
zwischen konkav
konvex, vor + zurück,
aufbauend, zurück-
nehmend .....
Obwohl niemals aus der
Erfahrung eigener Praxis,
jedoch aus unzähligen
Betrachtungen heraus
mußten wir dieses Spiel
sehr gut beherrschen,
rührt es an einen ganz
ursprünglichen Gestaltungs-
nerv. Auch wenn wir heute
mit dieser Sprache nichts
mehr anzufangen wissen, läßt
sich für uns daraus eine Menge
Lehren schöpfen.

ESSAYS ON ARCHITECTURE

SYMMETRY

In classical architecture symmetry was the basis of all architectural thinking. Until the turn of this century it remained undisputed. In the early twenties the Modern Movement began to formulate its intentions programmatically and made no secret of its aversion to symmetry. Only the best artists refrained from this one-sided dogmatism. Yet they could not prevent this discrimination from becoming consolidated and even popular. Asymmetry was celebrated as the redemption from classical architecture, with all its 'false' pretentions. Anyone prepared to poke his nose into our cultural undergrowth will be able to confirm this. Uneducated specialists and laymen generally remain highly suspicious of an architecture that is well ordered and symmetrical. They allude to 'underlying patrician, elitist, even totalitarian and fascistic pretentions'. During a recent competition jury in Moedling, near Vienna, I was subjected to this kind of nonsense directed, as usual, against the best entries. Charges of historicism and eclecticism are also always in the air. These confusions give rise to the misconception that wild, chaotic, asymmetrical and so-called liberalistic humane or 'organic' buildings are a superior kind of architecture. My essay on 'Regular and Irregular Building Types' deals with this controversial issue in far more detail.

My conclusion in this matter is as follows: symmetry is as valid today as it has ever been! For objective and functional reasons it is in many instances the only means of organising a building, and thus geometrical architecture is merely the result of a necessity. On its own, however, it is too cheap a justification.

The study of proportions has taught us that rhythmic succession and the overlaying of dimensional systems call for careful balancing of plan, section and elevation. It should be clear that I am not necessarily referring to an exact axial symmetry, but it is not excluded. To judge the scope of this interpretation we can compare the cathedral with the Greek temple. The conception of the built unit as a physical entity is common to both, whilst interpretation and formal conditions are extremely different. It is the specific conditions that dictate the architectural vocabulary and its formal expression and render it significant! A form whose significance cannot be recognized is no more than 'empty talk'. A meaningful form, expressive of a building's true contents can be enjoyed over generations. This must be our aim if as builders we take our craft seriously and distance ourselves from the short-lived success of capricious fashion makers.

Let us take a look at the figure of the human body: seen from the front and back our body is perfectly symmetrical, but a side view suggests no symmetry. And yet an overall impression of symmetry remains dominant. Most animals, for example the horse, have the same overall body structure, and yet the impression of asymmetry is more dominant. Nonetheless, no one will think of a horse as not being beautiful. Human being and animal alike, only truly reveal the beauty and elegance of their body structure when animated in movement. Just visualize the gracefulness of a soaring bird! We enjoy so readily the harmony of nature – the balance and tension in its opposite forms – but any attempt to copy it leads to sorrow and despair. For all architectonic

creations – the house by the street, the house on the square, a free-standing object – I recommend a compositional recipe: the built unit is to be geometrically taut and of regular overall appearance. All intended or necessary irregularities must be subordinated to the dominant form.

In order to establish a compositional balance, the symmetrical should outweigh the asymmetrical. The facades should have 'faces' that mirror the different programmatic solutions but remain symmetrical within themselves (analogous to the human figure). The side elevation, as such, may play the minor role of balancing front and back elevations.

REGULAR AND IRREGULAR BUILDING TYPES

There are still architects who believe in the reincarnation of Antonio Gaudí, convinced that so called 'organic' architectural forms come closer to human sensibilities. I challenge their contention:

1) All architectural planning, whether of regular or irregular type is an intellectual, i.e. rational, ordering of live sequences. Any ideological parallel with nature's laws of organic growth is far fetched and a poor substitute for an inadequate understanding of geometry.

2) Regular as well as irregular building forms are subject to the same formal considerations. If we are honest we must concede that good irregular building forms are more often to be found in anonymous rather than planned architecture.

3) Man's rhythms of movement are geometrically indefinable, they cannot be delineated by axes or circles. Our overall living habits, however, are more easily

mapped. This has been substantiated by centuries of cultural history. *In no epoch has cultural excellence manifested itself in amorphous building forms.*

4) We are living in a time of total enlightenment which demands equality amongst all human beings and equal opportunity for people with different world views and different ideologies. I need to establish an equal and fair basis for both architectonic conceptions, be it the regular or irregular type. Both expressions must be given their regular or irregular type. Both expressions must be given their intellectual freedom of expression, so as not to discriminate against one another. Only the intellectual discourse between the two is of value. It is always possible for one type to excel in a specific aspect.

The irregular buildings of Le Corbusier, for instance, are highly complex geometric forms, their underlying governing laws never being apparent at first glance.

The building forms of anonymous architecture are relatively easy to grasp, where craftsmanship is developed according to climatic conditions. No special value is placed on over-elaborate artistic expression. Our interest in this kind of architecture springs from a nostalgic yearning for pure an elementary forms.

We have been over-fed with highly developed technology; it bores us, and yet we can no longer do without it unless, that is, a natural catastrophy of apocalyptic proportions reverses the prevailing trend to point zero. On the other hand, the aping of primitive building forms can be particularly embarrassing.

Note on the classical profile sketches

We discover that in the rhythmic interplay between volume and line, one dimension always has to have the upper hand: the balance and harmony between concave and convex, foreground and background, recess and prominence . . . We should have learned to play this game well as a result of numerous observations rather than our own praxis, since it extends infinitely to many creative activities. Even if it seems that we no longer have anything to do with the formal classical language, we can still learn a great deal from its vocabulary. For example, how a base step is expressed as a step-ping stone to a staircase, how its generous tread introduces the first steps, how the stairs are flanked by wall and balustrade, how the steps themselves are profiled, how risers relate to treads, how the transition on to the landing is expressed and how the railing partakes in this sequence of movement . . . All this is rhythmic composition put to practical use and remains no less complex than the profile of a classical vase.

THE SENSE OF SCALE IN ARCHITECTURE

In present-day architecture, the significance of scale is technical and economic, unlike the Renaissance, for example, where scale in architecture grew out of a humanist commitment.

Those who build small today do so because they cannot afford to build any bigger. And those who build big have the potential to manipulate our society.

This difference, this division of class, has basically always existed. Today, however, it is exacerbated by seemingly unlimited technological resources which have been used largely to surpass the natural limits of height in building construction. A new dimension of scale has entered today's building industry; an unstemmable flow of ominous monsters that stalk across the looming landscape.

Since the 1920s and until recently, these achievements of modern technology gained praise as high and abundant as the constructions themselves. Latterly, this euphoria has been dampened, not because our technocrats have come to their senses, but rather because the public outcry and condemnation is now so loud that it is easier to quietly submit before such a sensitive issue and avoid kicking up any dust.

The question of scale in architecture pierces the socio-cultural nerve of our time. I shall limit my observations to purely visual and aesthetic considerations of architecture and refrain from discussing the more complex socio-political aspects – I am an architect, not a politician.

All architectural types, in their conception and composition of parts, are ruled by considerations of scale and proportion.

Let us begin with the smallest unit – the private house. It epitomizes the most popular and seemingly innocuous expression of architecture, and its *scale* is healthy and beyond reproach. However ugly and vile its architecture might be, as a last resort it is always possible to hide its shame behind a lucious growth of trees and vines. The winter months will just have to be endured, although even snow and ice can contribute to the integration of architecture into the landscape. Provided the occupants can overcome their fear of spiders, insects and other creepy-crawlies, ivy and wild vines remain the best means to disguise the exterior walls of a building. The 'green facade' has been, since ancient times, the most effective architectonic correction. It is not coincidence that Le Corbusier was fond of quoting the ancient Turkish proverb: 'Where you build you must plant trees'.

This perfect building unit, the one-family home, only becomes a problem of scale if it is subjected to a process of infinite addition.

I would love to enjoy my legitimate claim to live on this planet – if only I could afford it! I am fond of remembering my parents' and grandparents' house, and how vitally important it was for us, as children, to have our own garden to play in and enjoy the infinitely rich perceptions and discoveries brought about by this close contact with nature.

In a tightly knit village the same effect can be achieved by lining the streets with trees, planting public spaces with flowers and shrubs and treating parks more like natural landscapes.

I am convinced that a house should only be as high as I can comfortably climb without gasping for air; this amounts in my case, being an average sort of chap, to four floors. From this height a mother can still maintain contact with her child playing in the courtyard below. If a sensible block dimension of 65m x 65m, and a courtyard dimension of 40m x 40m is established, a very high ratio of habitation can be achieved: the block's usuable floor area would be twice the total site area. This density facilitates good urban living conditions. In the heart of the city – the centre point – one can build up to six floors and, where necessary, to a maximum of eight floors. This is assuming, of course, that the normal mixture of living and working accommodation takes place in these buildings.

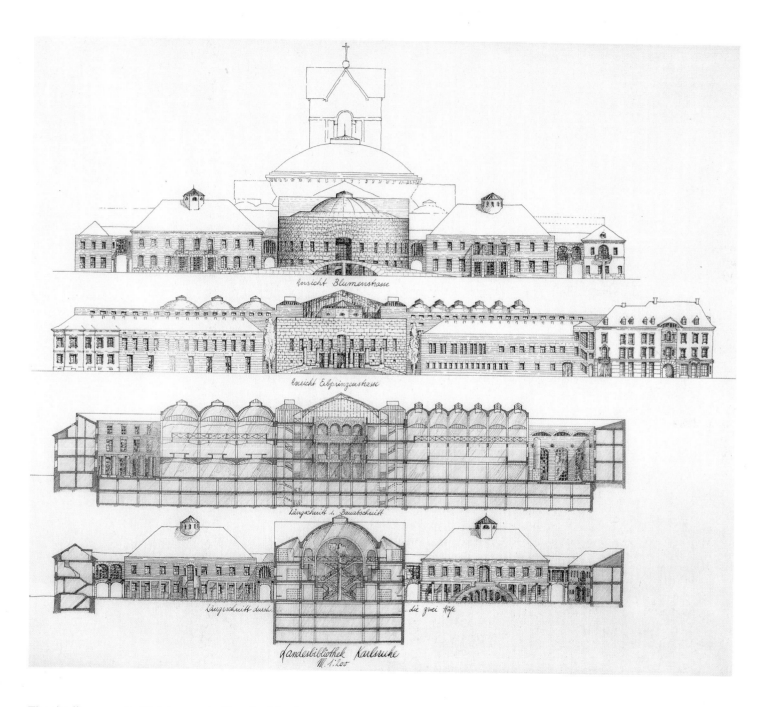

The site lies opposite Weinbrenner's Church of St. Stephan, which has had a major influence on the design. The large reading rooms are conceived as three different types of construction. The main room has a vaulted ceiling without supports, the left-hand room has two aisles, the right three, all with study areas along their sides. The visual appearance has been varied as much as possible throughout to facilitate orientation.

On the left in the background is Weinbrenner's Kurfürsten Palace. I would suggest improving the bad facades of the post-war years without impairing the function of the houses or affecting their construction.

Weinbrenner, who built the market place at the beginning of the nineteenth century, wanted to have two U-shaped market halls in the front part of the square. The city council has taken this idea up again and asked me to present a design.

1

2

3

4

5

6

7

8

9

The rear facades on Kaiserstrasse (in yellow) are corrections to facades dating from the 1950s. The ghastly advertisements which disfigure these houses from top to bottom should be confined to the ground floor.

I am fundamentally opposed to high-rise buildings. Nothing coud be more deadly to human interactions and a spirit of community than this form of building. I would like to encourage philosophers to re-open the public debate.

I can do no more than express my fears of the overscaled and colossal. Our natural defence mechanism might react to these fears with bouts of dizziness and vomiting. Man has broken his ties with nature and driven our cities to heights of absurdity. It is this irresistible drive to challenge the laws of nature that has led to the distortion of scale in architecture. The resulting high density conditions do have some advantages as well as disadvantages; on the one hand their unbelievable cultural intensity, and on the other their insurmountable social crisis.

Some of these high-rise ghettoes have long overstepped the threshold of physical possibility. They are only held together by an inappropriate application of technical resources and a shameful waste of energy, without which they would simply fall apart.

Man has lost the instincts which regulated his behaviour towards the natural world, and unbounded by this he has overstepped the boundaries of nature.

Our building sites are no longer bustling with the activity of skilled craftsmen. Buildings are no longer embellished with artful decorations, and finely crafted with an attention to detail which increases their durability. The quality and life-expectancy of today's houses are on a steady decline. Wherein lies the profit of all this?

I don't wish to dismiss or ridicule the technical advances of our age, but they have to become more widespread, more readily available and we have to succeed in turning them into profit-spinning investments. To believe in the advances of the future, as Le Corbusier did with characteristic intensity and vigour, sounds today like a naïve illusion!

Industrialization has *not* become the 'cultural coat-hanger' for a better architecture; on the contrary, it has forced building culture to the point of ruin and despoiled our cities and countryside with disgraceful banalities.

It is the architect's prime responsibility and a question of professional ethics to safeguard the human condition by maintaining an architectural scale appropriate to our physical requirements.

The high-rise block is the lowliest of building types – a derelict result of shrewd and profit-making commercial manipulation. It cannot command any legitimate value, other than its being a form of speculative optimisation, which fails to take the social and hygienic condition of the city into consideration. The capacity of our public amenities is absurdly overstretched and our built environment offers no benefits to compensate the citizen.

Another generating force not to be underestimated in the development of high-rise buildings is man's quest for power, his compulsion to be in charge. This thirst to influence and manipulate has never gone hand-in-hand with a genuine concern for the needs of human beings.

I don't dispute the fact that some skyscrapers are fantastic architectural achievements. It is an age-old dream of mankind to build clocktowers that would rise into the clouds – a mere delusion that never enjoyed more than a symbolic significance. Recent technological advances, however, have brought this dream into the realms of reality.

Skyscrapers have long lost their novelty value. Their abundance internationally has robbed them of any significance or attraction they may once have had. In any case, the 'right of light' regulations in Germany are such that over a given area four-storey housing blocks have the same density ratio as a battery of high-rise buildings.

The consideration of scale is not only limited to the exterior dimensions of houses, but is equally relevant to the details of construction.

Compared to human dimensions, the gigantic and overscaled portal of a Gothic Cathedral is legitimized by its cultural significance. Moreover, crowds of people and entire processions have to pass through it. Priests and doormen of civic buildings often share the same apprehension of large doors. It is for this reason that these doors often remain shut and even side entrances are seldom fully opened. The solution, to cut smaller openings of a more human scale into huge solid gates, is one I find particularly amusing. This curious double function is found in skyscrapers and barn doors, as well as in churches. These cat-flap versions all share the same principle of the door within the door.

The dimensions of windows in relation to a room is, equally, a question of scale. The toilet window will have a different dimension to the kitchen window, which in turn will vary in scale to the lounge window.

The problem of room heights should also be mentioned. Physical human dimensions as well as perceptions of space and comfort must be taken into consideration. Unless the architect knows the prospective occupants, it is difficult for him to anticipate what are totally subjective spatial perceptions. This personal feeling of well-being is often governed by irrational socio-economic conditions. Bodily dimensions, since only slightly variable, are of secondary significance. It is well known that very low and flat ceilings tend to oppress a room and create an unpleasant living environment. We feel much more comfortable in a room of consistent height, where the ceiling expresses itself by the sense of its structural system. Apart from minor and personal considerations, which should be left to the individual's sensitivity, the optimum ceiling height lies, in my opinion, betwen 3.20m and 4m. Proof of this can be found in buildings of bye-gone ages, which we tend to treasure more than our modern houses. Not only the generous room heights, but also the general spaciousness of these old houses contribute to their amiable living comfort. Sadly, in social housing we cannot even dream of reaching those old standards of spatial composition.

To respect scale and the harmony of proportions in all architectural composition, in order to better living conditions and improve the state of mankind, is every architect's moral and professional responsibility.

Green in the City
'Where one builds, one plants trees.'

(Turkish proverb)

I am almost inclined to let this wonderful proverb stand by itself. It encapsulates everything I have to say.

Johann Kraefter, whose support has been

invaluable in compiling this book, has produced a beautiful work about the 'architectural tree'. I would like to draw attention to his rich pictorial material which serves to illustrate many of the aspects of this problem.

Nature takes an essential part in the experience of architecture. Without its contrast, that softens the harshness of built geometry, a building seems cold and abstract. In many examples of good architecture, the concept springs from an understanding of the prevalent topography or the existing tree planting. Even during the design process nature is the generating force. If forgotten, she will invariably claim her rights sooner or later. She possesses the magical power to dress even the most defacing building mistakes. Mediocre designers should take this to heart, but they especially insist on exposing their unmitigated stupidity, not ashamed of destroying our landscape in the most brutalistic way. This happens particularly in the case of service buildings, industrial developments or Ministry of Transport buildings. In the case of housing one normally contends oneself with a minimum of 'good manners green'.

One cannot help noticing that the way man disregards nature bares close resemblence to his behaviour towards his fellow man. Again and again I see how trees are felled with a positive lust for destruction.

I would speculate that this flagrant decline of quality, from nature to modern city development, is the protagonist for so much social destruction. Nature's beauty and harmony exposes all built ugliness, the latter seeking assimilation to cover its shame!

I know that nature is resilient and hope that man's wilful destruction will, in time, effect a turn-around in his ultimate respect for nature. Even nature itself has a habit of turning its harmony on it head and whirling about confusedly.

I don't intend to give instructions on nature's compositional inclusion in the drama of architecture. This would be a book in itself. For this I would recommend old text books. Until the First World War there was still a certain understanding of this art. Stuebben, in his book on urban planning, describes how trees are to be planted in the city and how parks should be planned.

In long avenues I recommend strictly disciplined tree planting as dense as the necessary light penetration into the houses permits. In the case of park planting, the gardeners should respect nature's laws of growth and restrain their husbandry. We can rest assured that nature knows exactly why it grows and develops the way it does. There is no need for us to intervene constantly with our laughable and pedantic allures.

'Where one builds, one plants trees . . . '

ARCHITECTURE IN THE CITY
All new planning in the city has to subordinate itself to the existing overall framework, and offer in its physical manifestation a formal answer to the given spatial conditions.

THE URBAN SPACE
has been forgotten in twentieth-century city planning. Our new cities consist of a conglomeration of free-standing and isolated buildings. Five thousand years of city planning history are living proof that the complex structures of streets and squares have been successful as zones of communication and points of orientation. Our traditional urban concepts are still valid in today's modern city.

The house is the basic building block for village or city structure. It is important to define this unit before dealing with structures of a higher order – like housing developments – and forgetting about the basic unit. A city structure is the summation of various permutations on the theme of the house, from the free-standing house in the open suburb, via the housing unit as part of a development, to housing on an urban scale.

Since the twenties two factors call into question the housing unit as part of a multi-storey city structure:
1. The patrician landlord who was in a position to build merchant banks and rented accommodation in the city became an increasingly rare species. Correspondingly, collective and private property development consortiums able to amass larger sums of capital came to take charge of the building sector. The traditional site allotment, as regulated by the city hall, was taken over by urban planning on block sites.
2. The growing industrialization of the building sector demanded the mass production of identical parts, from wall panels to doors, windows, staircases, etc . . . I shall discuss the sense and nonsense of this trend in a separate essay.

Through the repetition of identical parts, houses lost their individuality. In our more recent larger housing developments we see the helpless attempts by architects to compensate for the loss of orientation by designing over-size house numbers and using coloured concrete for the stair wells. The brightly coloured circulation systems in large building complexes reflect smilar errors of scale. Despite ambitious planning methods by the big planning offices, large scale planning programmes still fail due to a singular disregard for human scale.

All new planning in the city should fit into the existing structure. This vague assertion can only be clarified with the help of examples. In the documentation of my own planning programmes, I refer to the following projects that clarify my theory: Leinfelden, Stuttgart; Royal Mint, London; Rennweg, Vienna; Via triumphalis and Bibliothèque, Karlsruhe; Community hall, Brunn am Gebirge; Ballhausplatz, Vienna; and the Berlin projects.

Even amongst my learned colleages the subject of urban planning is lately becoming noticably more fashionable. I hope they will also learn to deal with this problem in their own designs. Amongst the young ones some have already understood it much better and are even winning competitions with the concepts we have preached so passionately. And even their drawings are almost indistinguishable. As for myself, I am happy that all our efforts are bearing fruit. In the seventies I would not have dreamt that five years later I would be given the opportunity to work on a proposal for a large enclosed courtyard on an urban scale. I thought then that I could not possibly strike this unbelievable professional luck before the age of eighty.

This premonition could still be true since in the mean time unforseen difficulties have jeopardised the realization of the Schinkelplatz scheme in Berlin. During a first building phase only one enclosing courtyard wall is to be erected. As an incurable optimist I am still convinced that the next building phases will follow suit without interruption or delay. I was wonderfully surprised to see the Schinkelplatz development included in the Kleihues plan for South Friedrichstadt of 1981, and this fills me with hope. To gain a better understanding at this stage, I would recommend that you study my plans for South Friedrichstadt development in Berlin.

There is no need to elaborate on the theme of urban space much further. My book on the subject has, against all expectations, enjoyed a surprisingly large circulation. In some official places 'urban space' has now become a household term, but this does not stop critics from condemning my ideas as reactionary planning ideologies devoid of any aesthetic component and an understanding of social needs. The best criticism came from the Karlsruhe regional library competition jury. They accused me of planning 'alongside the *Zeitgeist*, to which I replied that the *Zeitgeist* is formulated by creative activities, not by critics. We are blessed with an entire army of people involved in creative pursuits, all driven by the anarchic desire for innovation, all intent on formulating our *Zeitgeist*.' I am suspicious of those who proclaim their stake too readily. Let us reserve judgement until our ideas have withstood the test of time!

To sling mud at colleagues is insolent, especially when one has no taken time to study their work. I remember the hostility James Stirling was subjected to after winning the competition for the Staatsgalerie in Stuttgart. That was no starlight hour for the German critics scene.

In the chapter on 'The Decline of the Building Arts' in this century, I am not exactly restrained in my observations on the work of some of my respected colleagues. I do however hope to be objective!

It is important to stress that space in the city – in the form of streets and squares – does not only get its quality from the general disposition of the buildings and their geometric contour but equally from well-resolved facades that shape and contain the space. City plan and architectural detail must always be equal in status and depen-

dent on each other. Some urban plans have a highly promising aerial view, but on closer inspection the architecture turns out to be of inferior quality, with the experience value of the urban space remaining zero. An example would be the 'anger villages' in the Burgenland in Austria, which have to a large degree been spoilt in the last few years. There are, however, many inconspicuous city spaces that have been wonderfully enriched by the quality of their architecture.

If the composition of the urban space does not have a scale appropriate to its functions, then even the best architects cannot compensate for this basic mistake. The dissonance will remain blatantly obvious. In this case only nature can heal the broken harmony. But, tragically, mistakes are infectious and one never wants to admit them. The villages we perceive as awful have hardly any trees in their streets or squares. If they were to be green our impression would be very different. Ugly houses radiate a fearful aggression. They kill the spirit for generations.

On a recent journey through Czechoslovakia, I passed through the village of Telč with its beautiful and spacious square. Here stands not a single tree. Architecture alone, in its often naive and burlesque strength, supporting the haughty staging of a proud bourgeoisie of times past. In the social levelling process of today's CSSR this beautiful urban space has not forfeited its attractiveness. Yet it seems incomprehensible how such quality could not have been an inspiration to the new housing developments in the area. The outskirts of Telč is depressingly ugly. If only beauty could be as infectious as ugliness!

The worst shock came on a journey to Brunn. Coming from Prague, the approach to the city is framed by a modern housing development of no less than 70,000 people. All the houses, on average eight storeys high, are constructed of the same prefabricated concrete system and are strung alongside the motorway in an endlessly monotonous chain. They stand as a devastating monument to systematic human degeneration. This way of building houses cannot even be justified by the most acute housing shortage. The Berlin kitchen sink poet Zille was right: 'buildings CAN kill . . .'

THE RUIN OF THE BUILDING CRAFTS, OR THE SENSE AND NONSENSE OF THE INDUSTRIALISATION OF BUILDING

Everyone who has learned a building trade knows the physical hardship involved. It is heavy work and often leads to painful physical condition in old age, advanced by voluntary overtime to supplement income. Many builders have to leave the job for medical reasons and look for less physically demanding work. Recently, a taxi driver told me how twenty years of rendering buildings had done his back in.

A multitude of new machines are making jobs less physically demanding than they used to be. The prefabrication of building components in factories is doubtlessly contributing to this trend.

The architects' hope in the early twenties that industrialization would improve the quality of building components, has sadly not been fulfilled. On the contrary! As a result of mass production details had to be simplified to respond to mechanical processes that would turn out crude and rough forms. The creative contribution by the skilled craftsman to the shaping of building details has sadly been lost for ever, together with all the invaluable experience evolved and handed down by generations.

Try to order a curvilinear patio window with tracery from a window firm. You will have a lot of fun! First they will try to talk you out of the curvature and then the tracery. If you supply them with a 1:1 detail drawing, they will tell you that this detail is not available, or can only be produced at an exorbitant price. My personal reaction to these experiences, at least in social housing, is to limit those critical details to an absolute minimum. Under the circumstances it is best to realize most ideas during building construction. The result is an architecture enlivened by its corporeality rather than complicated details. In today's critical financial situation it has become a personal challenge to arrive at a simple and powerful architectural solution, despite limited means and the near extinction of skilled labour. This demand might even be a chance for the salvation of architecture.

In a sarcastic address to the 'Elfenbeinturm' (Ivory Tower) Foundation in Kassel, I proposed to close all schools of architecture and instead train students to become specialized craftsmen in the building industry. Unfortunately, this idea is not enforceable. One could, however, insist that all architectural students serve an apprenticeship in one of the building-related crafts.

During the student riots in the late sixties many schools in Austria and Germany became complacent and slack, and lifted the previous requirement of a practical apprenticeship. It was thought that theory would solve everything and that in the 'golden age of industrialization' the machine would solve problems far more efficiently.

This euphoria has long since evaporated and the one-time revolutionaries, in despairing of their own limited competence, have barricaded themselves behind different pseudo ideologies. On the other hand, I do know colleagues from the same generation who are seeking a return to craftsmanship. They spare no painstaking effort to relearn forgotten building skills, and using cheap materials turn theory into practice.

I know a carpenter who for many years used to work in a small three-man workshop as an apprentice. Since there was no chance of promotion in the small family firm and as he could not raise enough capital to set up his own business, he agreed to work for a large firm in the city which offered him a higher salary and a tempting promise of promotion. After a short time the brutal consequences of his decision became clear, the wonderfully intimate working atmosphere he was accustomed to no longer existed, his personal involvement and decision-making on a piece of furniture, door or window from start to finish was no longer required. All the decisions were made in the planning office and components were pre-cut using templates with great precision. My friend no longer had the faintest idea who had commissioned the piece or how and where it was going to be used. He was part of a production line shuffling components identified by numbers and passed on to another specialized team responsible for on-site assembly. His promised promotion was never again mentioned and his extra earnings were swallowed up by his longer daily journey. Above all, he could not even return to his old firm since a younger member of the family had taken his place.

During a seminar in Sopron, I had an extraordinarily serious discussion with a Hungarian student. I felt that my call for the revival of craftsmanship would fall on receptive ears in a communist country. And indeed the young people did come down on my side, but the facial expressions of the older generation revealed shocked disapproval; 'we have so arduously fought for industrialization, why should we now go back and question it . . . ?' I went on to point out some of the built examples which happen to look more decrepid in the East than their Western counterparts. Did they honestly believe a better society could grow from these miserable constructions? Did not their social structure, especially, aim to raise work ethics, quality of the working environment and quality of the product? In a society where no one can make a personal killing in the construction industry where does the motivation for this wretched architecture stem from? Poverty does not necessarily produce ugliness. The latter is a product of stupidity, incompetence and a singular lack of vision. How free and vivacious, skilful and intelligent must the self-sufficient farmers have been, many of whom could not even read or write, to produce such wonderful buildings. Barn and stable were treated just as lovingly as the house. Their wealth was their power of invention.

Excessive organization and mass production only alienate the working environment, depersonify the workman, disparage him by schematising the work processes and dishonour him with the loss of personal responsibility. His reaction is the quiet suppressed boycott. He becomes inattentive and sloppy wherever possible. His lowliest satisfaction is to seek retribution against the system he hates. On this level capitalist and communist social systems sadly share a common ground.

'In times past, a builder's board would evoke images of joyful expectation, today, it evokes only fear . . .'
Julius Posener, building historian.

What are the gifts industrialization bestowed upon us? Have we earned higher profits, have we built faster, have we built more, have we built cheaper, have we built

more rational, more intelligent, more modest, more functional, more beautiful and better houses . . . ?

Yes, we have gained higher profits, but that is all! Construction workers are earning more than they used to and they deserve it far more than developers and speculators. But unfortunately, without the latter little more than family houses would get built. What a dilemma!

My call for smaller building trades and specialized workshops is lost in the fierce competition of large, high-capital construction firms, whose services reach even the most isolated and secluded villages. Imagine my shock when one day, enjoying a fine afternoon with friends in a rented farmhouse at Loretto in Austria, a deafening announcement from a car-top public address system came blasting across the valley. As I leapt to my feet I was horrified to find a van, doubling as a showroom, parked in front of the door to our house, unashamedly brandishing prefabricated doors and windows in all their ugliness. They even distributed leaflets illustrating one's old and their new windows; the old ones were depicted in thick, heavy lines, crossed out in red and captioned: 'Old out, New in'. In stunned amazement I watched the driver who mistook me for a prospective customer and promptly reduced the volume of his deafening hailer. After an exchange of glances, however, he knew better and in fear of having his mobile showroom vandalized swiftly took flight towards a curious looking group in the distance.

Not long after, I was subjected to a similar shock. I had to replace one of my floorboards and visited the local joiner. He no longer stocked timber floorboards only large sheets of chipboard and was determined to sell me the excellence of this 'modern' material. He even suggested I covered my floor with PVC to protect the timber, and assured me this had now become the accepted practice. It would conceal the patched up floorboards and, above all, would give the room a 'modern' appeal. When he finally realized that I remained unconvinced, he directed me to another joinery in the neighbouring village, where I finally obtained the desired floorboards.

Today, neither of the two joineries still

produce their own windows and doors. They buy in prefabricated frames and their 'joiners' merely install them.

Grown timber is demanding to treat and work with, it stretches and shrinks and at worse it warps. This has been the carpenter's headache since the beginning of time. Still, he knew how to store and dry timber, and select the best boards for a particular job. Today, carpenters and joiners are no longer prepared to worry about storing timber since it is too space consuming and cost intensive. Thus, we cut down fully grown trees, reduce them to pulp, add glue and press them into standard size boards.

The sandstone in the votive church in Vienna came from the stone quarry in the village of Loretto. Today, the broken sandstones are ground to sharp sand for the manufacture of artificial tiles and stones. Sandstone has gone out of fashion.

I am sure we can all recount similar experiences. They have become so commonplace that they no longer surprise us. Our children probably think it has always been like this. A great deal more could be said about the infamous conduct of the cement and plastics industry, but I do not have the energy for it.

THE HISTORY
Proper evaluation of our historic inheritance allows us to use the experiences of the past to plan for a better future.

Around the turn of the century, inspired minds in pure and applied arts denounced their historic inheritance and with revolutionary gestures threw overboard all handed down commitments and affiliations.

In the early nineteenth century, the calm of an ensuing classicism was a welcome antidote to the tempestuous eruptions of the baroque and rococo periods, and as a result the time of advancing Enlightenment almost suffocated under the clutter of its calm. This reaction was without historic precedence, unless one dares compare it with the social upheavals of the French or Russian revolutions. The latter initially identified itself with the endeavours of its young artists until their quest for freedom of expression became too dangerous for the reigning dynasty.

The final split between 'plush and trash'

came with the collapse of Imperial Europe. The Church followed the lead of the aristocracy and withdrew its cultural patronage.

Artists were prepared to exchange financial support for freedom of artistic expression. This unrestrained expression degenerated into true eruptions which found their most extreme forms in Expressionism. For the first time in history, the artist could without inhibition comment on social problems and express them critically. Despite desperate efforts by ensuing dictatorships to undermine these developments, the flow of the once initiated movement could no longer be stemmed.

While architecture had been hobbling along, paces behind the fine arts, it finally managed to find its definitive concept in the twenties. In the chapter on 'The Decline of the Building Arts' I shall deal with its evaluation. The pure engineering structures of the mid nineteenth century prepared architecture for its looming upheaval, an upheaval without revolutionary pretentions.

New socio-political conditions demanded rethinking. We had to learn to walk all over again and throw overboard traditional and historic truth. Sadly, in the field of architecture and city planning too much has been surrendered without first weighing up the consequences. It remains incomprehensible to me how the great artist Le Corbusier could have conceived and formulated such catastrophic city planning blunders as the 'ville radieuse'. Members of his own generation and the next unreservedly applauded this form of Modernism. It is high time to clear up the half truth, to throw overboard the revolutionary fetish and to fill the gaps we so wilfully cut in our quest for a sensible architecture. It is for this purpose that I have collected the material for this book.

Allow me to repeat here a few sentences from the closing paragraph of my book *Urban Space*.

OUR DEFECTIVE SENSE OF HISTORY . . .
is to blame for much false interpretation of the past and also characterises our relationship with the future. The wish to cut oneself off from the heritage of the past is extremely shortsighted. By doing so, one deprives oneself of thousands of years' worth of ex-

perience. At the beginning of the century, the pioneers of the Modern Movement frivolously flaunted this attitude. And yet all of them had enjoyed a sound education and were very knowledgeable about history. Their attitude can easily be dismissed as a defiant reaction, intended above all as a harangue against their position in society, and against their fellow students at the Academy who remained stuck in their old ways. It was a different matter with the pupils of these pioneers, and with their students in turn. They felt able to do without the grounding which had fitted the pioneers for their transformations into 'moderns'. And we today, armed with our pitifully inadequate know-how, must make up for a great deal that has been neglected. I have a faint suspicion that a new pioneering situation will grow out of this.

We have learned how little is achieved by technological advance and how rapidly the glow of new inventions fades when they are backed by nothing more than technological novelty. This does not denigrate the usefulness of experimental technology: it simply puts it into perspective. Care must be taken that it does not attempt on its own to initiate new development while making unjustifiable claims for universality.

I would go so far as to maintain that nowadays it is more useful to imitate something 'old' but proven, rather than to turn out something new which risks causing people suffering. The logical and attractive building types and spatial structures left to us by anonymous architects have been improved upon by countless succeeding generations. They have matured into masterpieces even in the absence of a single creator of genius, because they were based on a perfectly refined awareness of building requirements using simple means; the result of an accurate understanding of tradition as the vehicle for passing on technical and artistic knowledge.

All my dire warnings inspire considerable gloom, and one fears it will prove impossible to do justice to the demands I have outlined.

However, not all the blame should rest on architects, whether they are involved in building or administration. To be fair, some of the rubbish should be dumped back in the universities, for it was there that the whole avalanche started rolling.

THE RESPONSIBILITY
OF THE ARCHITECT

The architect alone is responsible for the final product, it springs from his drawing board and carries his signature. No politician or financier will share the architect's blame for an ill-planned environment. Our schools of architecture must prepare the new generation of young architects for this devastating ethical and moral task.

The Zille quotation, 'Architecture can kill', is a strong expression of the architect's responsibility.

I am well aware that architects have always been better off than other artists. Mozart complained that his patron, the Bishop of Salzburg, made him eat with the riff-raff in the kitchen and paid him as miserably as a cheap entertainment artist. Michelangelo almost pushed his patron, Pope Julius II, down the scaffolding of the Sistine Chapel in a wild fit of bad temper. The following amusing anecdote of artistic revenge has been passed down from Babylonian times: a stone mason, asked to chisel a granite bust of his sovereign, carved his own name into the base where his emperor's should have appeared. He then covered the whole bust with a layer of plaster. After the emperor's death, it was the artist's name that survived for posterity.

How often do the rich and powerful try to lay personal claim on their acquired portraits? Man can own, protect or destroy an acquired painting, but the idea will never be his. It belongs to the artist and is the only pride left to him.

'Built by Emperor Franz . . .' these pretentious words were carved with pride and clarity into many buildings of the Hapsburg Empire, the emperor boasting his excellent choice of fine artists. But fortunately, their enforced modesty – only archives reveal their identity – is outshone by the quality of their artistic creations. If a building has true quality its message will duly spread, even without exhibitionist publicity.

This is the quiet invigorating satisfaction of the artist. He may work for a client who in the long run might well become richer as a result of his commissioned acquisition. Still, a house built in the city or countryside belongs not only to its owner, but in a wider sense is also part of the cultural heritage of the city or landscape. Thus, the client, whether he likes it or not, becomes a patron of culture, sometimes in a positive, more often in a negative sense.

Houses cannot be hidden like furniture, they stand in the public's eye and they offer enjoyment or despair, as the case may be.

All too often the architect makes excuses for his botched-up work by pointing the finger at the client, political circumstances, lack of funds or the sloppy workmanship of the builder. He is tempted to dress his crime in banners proclaiming everyone else's guilt except his own. Of course, he cannot be held responsible for everything, but as the executor he carries the largest part of the blame. He has given birth to his creation on his drawing-board and its features are the result of the architect's personal whim. My brother Leon had the idea of introducing a form of 'Russell tribunal' to try all rotten architects. In *Archives d'architecture moderne* under the heading 'Public Vice, Private Virtue', Leon Krier and Maurice Culot used to publish regularly the buildings of successful architects together with the houses they themselves lived in. The contrast was devastating.

The cultural temper of our time is reflected in our buildings, not inside our opera houses nor in the libraries we keep to decorate our living rooms.

THE PLIGHT OF OUR
ARCHITECTURAL SCHOOLS

I must come clean and admit that I hated the educational system at the Technische Hochschule in Munich where I studied architecture, from the bottom up. It had a lot to do with the form of mass education and the totally anonymous academic set-up. This was compounded by my then-devastating realisation that I could not admire a single one of my tutors' buildings. I hope they no longer hold this confession against me! Real buildings, far more than any theoretical teaching, are the bedrock of an architectural education. It follows that the student can only learn on site.

Anonymous buildings and monumental architecture flourished as long as we did not have schools of architecture, as long as the student could learn his skill in a workshop in direct contact with master and site, just as painters, sculptors and musicians have always been taught.

To have been a pupil of Palladio was a ticket that needed no endorsement by the state. Our anonymous diplomas are worthless in comparison, and at best good enough for a career in the Civil Service.

Today, a genuine talent for architecture only unfolds itself after about ten years of practical experience. I am taking the liberty of regarding my own experience as the norm. This should offer some consolation to those architects who despair at the age of thirty.

There is no need to discuss exceptions, since they normally dispense with the formal school education themselves.

The insurmountable problem, in almost all the schools I know, is the sheer number of students. Ideally, I would like to enjoy the same working relationship with my students as I have with members of my office, where I can only properly supervise and instruct between four and seven people, rather than 200.

I hardly get to know my students, and feel unable to follow their educational development let alone their professional careers. Of the 1,500 or so students who have registered with me in the past five years, there are no more than a dozen I can clearly recollect. A hopeless situation!

Only a fraction of students eventually manage to have their own office. I appeal strongly to all ministers of education and culture to re-evaluate this student intake problem. The excessive number of students in the master classes at the Vienna Academy should serve as a typical example.

The overflowing architecture faculties of our universities render the disproportionately small body of staff ineffectual and helpless. My own desperate fight for commissions only underlines the unbalanced architect/client ratio.

In the present situation, the few talented students end up suffocating in throngs of second-rate competition. I gladly admit that my becoming a professor spared me from the sordid battlefield of fierce competition. I could not have supported my family from my building commissions unless I had invested less in my own office, which would have jeopardised the quality of my design work.

If nothing else, a university does fulfil the

role of an indirect patron. As a gesture of gratitude for this support, I am happy to persevere with this hopeless task.

Maybe one should simply not overrate the significance of a course in architecture. After secondary school it could just be a worthwhile general education! Perhaps in this way a more considered appreciation of architecture might reach a wider audience?

This would be a small consolation. Another comfort is the fact that with the vehement and missionary application of my assistants, we have at times succeeded in teasing out an extraordinarily rich average from the masses and have allowed them to outgrow themselves. The amazing pictorial material in the chapter on 'elements' proves this point beyond doubt.

The problem of the academic proletariat is not of course unique to architecture, but concerns all branches of science and the arts.

This realisation might give rise to a purely social commitment which the universities can only meet from a political standpoint. This would mean coming to terms with the fact that the standard of education would decline rapidly as a result of growing numbers of students. An advanced post-university course designed to iron out mediocrity would be a possible solution.

Reading Le Corbusier's writings as a student, I developed a growing contempt for the architectural teaching profession. In his view all evil stemmed from the academies. He could not have envisaged the enormous influence his genius was to later exert both through his theoretical role as urban planner and through his demagogic manner.

As a student, I never dreamt that I would have to seek refuge in the teaching profession simply to support my existence. My continued and frustrated attempts to win architectural competitions have made me very humble. Also, I never suspected the enormous manoeuvrability a university could offer, and how much the relief from the pressures of naked existence could mean. Also, the persistent scrutinisation of one's theories by diverse critical students is enormously valuable to one's own creative work. The correction of student designs demands terrific patience and unfailing flexibility. I not only have to prove to the student his mistakes, but kindle in him the willingness to accept them and nourish the motivation to correct them.

This is only possible if the student respects me both as human being and artist and somehow accepts the integrity of my theory and plan. It is only much later that he can hope to prove it exactly. The student should be allowed to sense my personal uncertainties, so he may see his own as merely relative. He must feel that he is taking part in my development and that his learning is supportive of mine.

To meet this pedagogic commitment the professor has to step down from his elitist rostrum, dispose of his tie, turn up his sleeves, run the university as a workshop and turn the students into partners.

The incestuous title breeding in Austria and elsewhere makes a natural student/tutor relationship very difficult. This hierarchical order has been indoctrinated since the nursery, so much so that most of my students automatically resist any kind of 'familiarisation'. When asked not to call me Professor, they prefer not to address me at all. After the Second World War, imperial titles were abolished in Austria. There remains the hope that the whole nonsense of awarding titles and medals will reach saturation point and burn itself out.

Tutors should keep alive their ateliers within the universities, so that students have direct contact with the work of their Professor. Physicists and chemists have their laboratories at the university. Such a set up also encourages a healthy reassessment of the design work. It is a Professor's responsibility to design buildings that are in every sense exemplary. He must never exploit the standing and public regard that he enjoys as a result of his position to intensify his commercial building activity.

This is a cautious appeal to my colleagues to tread softly with a prayer. As Dean of the Faculty, I was forever being subjected to my colleagues lamenting the miserable quality of student material. 'Gentlemen, our schools of architecture are only as good or as bad as their tutors . . .'. Every charge against a student is an admission of our own failure. The Ministries of Building and Science should ensure that important research as well as building projects are offered to the various schools of architecture. Tutors must be given the opportunity to design potential key buildings, without outside competition.

At present, this is certainly not the case. On the free market, the architecture Professor's influence is little to none. He is lampooned as an eccentric out of touch with reality. Anyhow, his claim to design cannot be evaluated financially.

Who is to blame for this situation? We can only blame ourselves! We have misused our position and it will take a long time to regain public respect.

The *laissez-faire* atmosphere within an academic institution is, unfortunately, rather tempting and attractive for second-rate and less committed members of staff, and once established they enjoy the protection of a secure government position and barricade themselves behind a packaged set of lectures involuntarily regurgitated *ad infinitum*. Guaranteed job security without continuous reassessment is always problematic. This is where we could learn a lesson from the private American universities. Our highly acclaimed teaching continuity often leads to stagnation, to being out of touch and to bitter boredom.

I consider increasing fluctuation and a higher turn-over of Professors to be very important. I also believe that the rotation of subjects according to a predetermined plan would afford a healthy challenge, impossible in our present rigid system.

The burden of our administrative responsibilities poses a menacing threat to our intellectual mobility and hence, far too often, it becomes a refuge for mediocrity.

Since the introduction of the EDV system in Austria, the administrative staff has increased ten-fold. Tighter control, the object of the exercise, has now been lost under tons of extra paper work.

The drawn-out meetings and setting up of endless commissions are in the same category of activities that only distract from the real issue – the standard of teaching. Decisions concerning the running of an academic institution are regurgitated *ad nauseum* in countless commissions until all parties have reached a tired compromise.

I would plead for the example set by English and American schools, where the

Dean is given far-reaching organisational powers. He has to keep abreast with teaching experience but is never burdened by it. To a large extent, the Dean should be able to organise the teaching staff and mastermind the running of the school with his charisma and personality. He should be elected by teaching staff and students, be appointed from the outside as leader of the faculty, for a fixed term of office. This would be a chance to dispel the stagnant image of our schools and inject fresh impetus.

At this point, it seems appropriate to recall an essay I wrote shortly after my graduation from the Technical University in Munich in May 1964. It was intended as a critique of my then just completed course and at the same time an exploration of my hopes and expectations for my professional career. I still feel the fear of the unknown that these lines radiate. The piece was published in a student magazine and I have decided to reprint it here in full, without further editing. To this day, many of the passages remain valid, while others, perhaps, raise a smile. At that time, my faith in the development of modern building technology was still irreproachable. Out of this spirit I later worked with Frei Otto for a few years, and admittedly this experience taught me a great deal and helped me towards finding my own way.

THE TRAINING OF ARCHITECTS

'And so I shall lay the foundation stone for a generation of true architects, true in the sense of honest men and visionaries of action.'

L. H. Sullivan, 1964

I was presented with a diploma a few days ago. For a few years now I have been engaged in the study of architecture and now feel the urge to reflect what I have gained from this training, both as a human being and as a professional. I would like to examine to what extent this institution, the Technical University in Munich, practised what it preached.

What was our position forty-five years ago?

'Architects, painters and sculptors must once again learn to recognise and understand the multivalent form of architecture in its totality and individual parts, then their works will be filled with the architectonic spirit without further ado. The spirit that has been lost in the art of the saloons . . . the basis of workmanship is indispensible to any artist . . . Bauhaus, the reunion of all craft disciplines . . . '

Gropius, 1919

And what is our position today, in Germany? In every profession there is invariably a hierarchical ordering according to title. This categorisation has lead to the fragmentation of our educational institutions and the formation of engineering schools, academies and technical universities. Every one of these institutions believes it has something to do with so-called architecture, on a building technology or artistic level. Van de Velde, and later Gropius, energetically questioned this situation. A great deal of literature has survived them and is dutifully and passionately being revealed today.

Indeed, our situation is once again the same as it was around 1900. Only a handful of the experiences and lessons of the twenties have survived the Second World War. The sentences by Gropius, above, are as much of a revelation today as they were then.

For the present let us accept the facts in all their unrelatedness and consider them from the 'Technical University' point of view by looking at the education system from its highest vantage point where all weaknesses are most conspicuous.

My first contacts with lectures and projects aroused in me an unhealthy confusion. There was no feeling of what to expect. In school master fashion we were indoctrinated with primary and secondary subjects, apparently in preparation for a profession few of us knew anything about. Young people who have struggled that far, able to think for themselves and be independent, are likely to pack in the course at the outset.

Any thought that cannot be formulated clearly is suspect. In the ensuing chaos, one is bombarded with basic principles of higher mathematics, statistics, building construction, applied geometry, building technology, art history, building history, design, surveying, measured drawing, sketching, perspective . . .

Building Construction

We learned to insulate a house against rain with a given set of materials. We neither knew what went on inside this house that we had been asked to insulate, nor did we understand the logic of the materials used. We completed the exercise for its own sake. A window, for instance, was seen as an isolated object, not in relation to anything, not even its own function. The design process was tackled back to front, only to cloud and obscure the design problem. Even building practice, or as it was the hawking around of bricks on site, did nothing to clarify the issues of architecture.

Statistics

Without a proper scientific grounding a statistical calculation is unthinkable. For the engineer it might be the ultimate goal. For the architect it is a tool, he needs a form of statistical 'imagination' to feed his creative impulse. Mastery of complicated mathematical calculations is unlikely to ignite his powers of invention.

The Basics of Higher Mathematics

We are taught these during secondary education. To repeat them without gaining further insights seems futile and unnecessary, quite apart from their being of limited usefulness to the architect. His calculations are unlikely to extend beyond the limitations of the slide-rule.

Basic Design Principles

Design . . . what? . . . and why? A relic from a Bauhaus course. What has remained? Watercolour painting, Calligraphy, Paper folding, Structural investigations.

A rich and wonderful field has only been touched; spatial geometric forms. This could be the starting point from which to transcend the superficiality of the decorative and to break away from pure design characteristics.

Whether I am able to draw good or bad lettering onto a facade is a question of my inner strength as an artist. The less I know about lettering and script writing, the clearer, the more honest and the more immediate my handwriting is likely to be. Paper folding may stimulate the powers of imagination and encourage a sense of playfulness. As purposeful, abstract play, paper techniques may be useful. As a teaching method, however, it fails since the mental attitude necessary for an act of creation cannot be bred.

In practice these exercises result in curtain-like metal hangings in entrance lobbies, suspended stucco ceilings in origami patterns, facades treated like curtains, sunshade patterns, masonry with shadow effects, colour contrasts between high-rise buildings – one beige/grey/baby blue, the other dark umbra with a delicate touch of green . . . in a word, art in building!

Oh God, the fragrance of so much perfume is nauseating!

Through this subject most students turn rotten at their roots. They learn deceit and trickery . . .

For all this cream we lose sight of the cake. But, oh wonder, the cake can still be found. The subject of architecture holds the unequalled potential to lay the foundations for the development of a spatial vision on a geometrical or free basis, as well as to inspire the discovery of harmonic proportions.

The Study of Building Forms
This subject deals with the history of building forms from antiquity and their structural details.

To realise that by studying architecture one is only supposed to be looking at things presupposes a deep insight into the whole problematic of buildings.

The classical column in Greek Antiquity is the end-product of a long development. What we are looking at today is not the support as structural element, but a pure form, developed and elevated from its most basic functional form to an element of symbolic significance. The Japanese have never robbed the column of its intrinsic function, and yet still raised it to a level of perfection of the highest order. I am mystified as to why the Japanese building aesthetic is still not taught at our universities. It has influenced the thinking of our generation unlike any other architectural expression. Our outstanding engineers, such as Auguste and Georges Perret, probably drew too many classical capitals in their youth! They never got away from them.

Without doubt this subject can be interpreted according to the spirit of its time. In its historic form it only breeds malaise, as for example by encouraging the idea of turning a simple joint to 'form' by overworking it artificially, yes, by deforming it. Yet the ambiguity of a structural detail adds a richness of meaning that cannot be surpassed by those designers who aim for stylistic effects.

History of Architecture, Painting and Sculpture
The study of history imparts the basic knowledge for a meaningful understanding and relates realisations and experiences.

What I do not understand is why contemporary work – the history of the present – does not get sufficient mention when it is this we need to build on.

Building Surveys
Are only done on qualitatively 'proper' buildings, not trams or motor bikes, whose inner functions we as architects are not able to comprehend fully. Only then can this exercise in the technique of surveying relate something of the architectonic spirit which finds its expression only partly in numbers.

The harmony of numbers is a sure control in the design process. It disciplines the spontaneous impulse and tightens the structural framework.

Applied Geometry
This undergraduate subject seems somewhat overrated, for in the undergraduate course it is given more emphasis than building construction. It is a complicated scientific method that defines the construction. It is a complicated scientific method that defines the space accurately, but its visual distortions do not allow us to experience the space as it really is. For the architect this subject is only valuable if taught with perspective drawing.

Except for a few competition entries during the vacation, the student in Munich is not given the opportunity to design during the first two years of his course. If he is waiting for an introduction into this key problem of design, he is only wasting his time. The first independent semesters in the post-graduate course that are more like aca-

demic study, are not only the toughest but doubtless also the most momentous. Those first designs are ripe with the desire for creation.

The conversion to architecture as an intellectual discipline and organising framework of society, does not spring from a young person spontaneously. First, its logical framework has to be discovered and understood. What draws him to its truth is fascination, the spiritual intoxication radiated by the 'perfect play of bodies under the light' (Le Corbusier).

Master and pupil, united by the urge for creation, can only join hands in the quest for personal realisation.

Frequently the first attempts of a young person are richer in their conceptions than the more matured and mellowed works of the experienced master.

This freshness, this forever regenerated originality must, despite experience and age, never wane.

It is a master's task to help his carefree young friend mature and develop!

A tutor, however, can only communicate when he himself confronts every situation with creativity, not with an automatic catalogued reaction.

These observations give rise to the following educational demands:

1. To radically reduce the student intake from 150 to 50 students per semester, or to increase the teaching staff three-fold. The student has the right to individual tuition!

Equally, one would not expect a mother to bear twelve children when her strength is limited to bearing four, just as a mother cannot see the sole purpose of her existence in procreation without taking into account the protection and development of her siblings.

There are ways of making a reasonably fair choice of 50 students from among the 500 or so applicants. Not in one afternoon, of course. We need to get to know the applicants and test them, not for their thirst for knowledge, but for their motivation and sense of direction. We expect confidence and a trusting relationship to help us over our first stumbling steps.

2. Our Professors run their own independent offices, (some of them accommodated

within the university), to keep in touch with architectural practice and supplement their income since their salaries are not exactly brilliant.

These offices could be a significant and meaningful link between practice and research (as the example set by Wachsmann has shown). It is obvious that universities should cultivate contacts with industry, and not only support industry in its research and development programmes, but also to make valuable suggestions (for example, Frei Otto's research centre for lightweight construction). Frei Otto: 'I would like to be surrounded by people who learn and search with me.'

If our tutors saw themselves as students amongst students, the 'podium' would vanish – in the literal and true sense of the word – from our classrooms and would make room for a chair amongst chairs arranged in a circle. The guarantee of success lies in the authority and radiance of the tutor. However, it alone is not enough, a regular '*presence*' is essential, and not once a week for cold comfort.

We demand that we not only get to see or hear our tutors, but are allowed to experience them, since we take it for granted that they have turned to education out of fascination and idealism, not a vain hankering for a highly regarded title, or for prestige, social standing or a career for its own sake.

Well, up to this point we have constructed an ideal relationship between tutor and student. What is missing is the structure, the system that is to support this learning process.

After serving the cards we play the game . . . sitting round a circle. Suggestions are made, evaluated, tried and tested. Yes, this applies as much to statistics as reinforced concrete, urban planning, industrial construction, prefabrication . . . and if there is no space to experiment at the Technical University, then we have to create this space elsewhere.

It calls for courage to recognise the situation. Every department is allocated its laboratory, so why not architecture?

But fear not! A government subsidised institution seldom pays the penalty, especially not an educational institution, since demands on it always far outweigh its allo-

cated investment. In any case, its results are never quantifiable.

'EXPERIMENTING' is as essential a function as 'CHEWING'.

I suggest that students, during their five month vacation, are given the opportunity to come into contact with materials and methods of construction, and under instruction examine the problem of the chair just as much as the problem of the parabolic hyperbole. Thus, the practical experience arranged by the school would not just mean contact with what is commonplace, but a chance to discover the as yet unknown.

Here, one could learn how cautious one has to be in accepting handed down experiences, because tired experiences are as dangerous as rusty tools.

It is incomprehensible why in our schools (especially in Munich) building sanitation is limited to drains, wastepipes and man holes . . . and building physics ends with properties of materials, expansion co-efficients and thermal values.

It simply is not enough to refer the student to building exhibitions and trade literature, essentially only found in advertising catalogues and industry.

It must be said, however, that some German universities have been making remarkable efforts.

It is the task of an architectural faculty to skim off a number of young people from the prevailing average of business minded students, who are prepared to confess to their work, who take it upon themselves to form a solid united front, who create first the legal conditions, then secure craftsmanship and industrial means for healthy professional continuity.

A superior once told me: 'The school is no place to carry out experiments . . .' What he meant was, no place for fooling about! I regard this utterance as a defamation of the Technical University, reducing its status to that of a breeding box for architects.

Here is another remark from a different Professor: 'I don't understand why so many students come to Munich. It must be common knowledge by now that there is nothing much going on here.'

Well, it is an open secret! We no longer need to feel embarrassed about it and can get on with rocking the boat.

3. An introduction to the key architectural problems of PROGRAMME, PLAN and DESIGN is the best preparation for the first semesters.

4. The student has to understand right from the beginning that the house constitutes only one small detail of the urban plan, just as the waste pipe is only a small detail of the house. It is essential from the outset to clarify and define the terms spatial order, urban structure, rural structure . . . The student has to know the object of his investigation by its name before he can hope to classify its characteristics.

Just as a building detail cannot be drawn up before the overall concept has been worked out – since it is derived from it and dependent on its structure – a house cannot be designed without first studying and if necessary revising the existing urban structure.

The interest in our task leads us first to the spatial order, in the widest sense of the word (what Buckminster Fuller called 'universal order'), then to the morphological structure, and eventually to the individual spatial units; the houses and apartments, the factories and workshops, then to the space of intermediate rooms and thresholds and their function as 'breathing spaces'. In this 'BREATH' life itself is contained: exchange, encounter, relaxation . . .

What is the young student being confronted with? A mass of disciplines that only make sense and fall into place once the over-riding concepts have been grasped. What is the use of studying proportions, without understanding terms like 'volume' or 'body'? What is the use of studying structures without knowing their origins?

The great shortcoming of our education is the fact that it does not help the young student to attack the problematic of his profession p r o g r e s s i v e l y.

5. The study of details and construction must run parallel to design and architectural history, systematically extend over the entire course and capitalise on the truly great buildings of our time. Theoretical subjects

must always be taught in relation to design work.

It should always be possible for an architectural student to specialise in the invention of structures (Nervi, B. Fuller, Wachsmann, Frei Otto, Candela, R. Le Richolais, J. Prouvé . . .), as well as urban planning, and be given the opportunity to make it the subject of his diploma dissertation.

The medics are streets ahead of us architects. We are still clinging to a universal, all-encompassing knowledge that today can no longer be carried by one person. We pride ourselves with a false 'vision' to justify our complacency and backwardness.

6. Every university should have a permanent exhibition area for the display of tutors' work and student designs both at home and abroad – this is one of the most important pre-requisites for a true forum. Apart from that it allows visitors to enter the spirit of the school. I would not encourage anyone to visit the corridors of the Technical University in Munich, they would think of the school far worse than it really is. This is not ill-tempered criticism; I am only stating the all too obvious.

7. Also, the stipulated eight semester course is not long enough to digest the set curriculum. The medics have long accepted a minimum study period of six or seven years, and architecture can be seen as equally universal. The same holds for the six weeks we are allocated for our diploma dissertation. Whatever technical or organisational reasons come into play here, they can never justify this measure. We applaud strict and clearly defined deadlines, as will be expected of us in practice, but they must also be realistic.

The observations here drawn up constitute only a rough outline, and in no way do they represent an exhaustive educational reform. Such a reform has long been discussed. One intends to level out the curriculum by redirecting subject emphasis, engage in some insignificant regrouping; perhaps a few more lectures here, a few less exercises there . . .

To implement a reform at a Technical University calls for some fearless young Professors who are prepared to undertake the lengthy task of reorganising this precarious work.

EPILOGUE

Man identifies himself not so much with the objects around him, but rather with their acquired familiarity and habit of use. And so it happens that objects, genuinely and persistently harmful to our society, are with time, that turns contact to habit, quite inconspicuously shrouded in a veil of innocence.

The interchange of opposites is a basic law of life. The single mindedness of their confrontations are an expression of their zest for survival.

Le Corbusier . . . 1929: 'They had not warned me sufficiently of the impossibility of following a career outside the teaching given in schools, or of practising as an architect without the famous diploma that crowned these studies with such pomp, and sometimes virtually stopped the period of creation.'

At my final exam, the chairman of the examination committee came up to me and said: 'You, even though you think we are all cuckoos, we have still accepted your diploma submission!'

The mark was adequate but by a mere hair's breadth it would have been inadequate.

To the Architecture Councils (Governing Bodies)

They should not only organise the professional body, guarantee pensions and liability insurances, regulate competitions and professional status and dish out awards and titles, but their powers should also extend to architectural quality control beyond the bounds of universities!

This is only possible if the best architects are prepared to co-operate with the council of architecture. Since the council is presently, however, occupied by mostly administrative and commerical functionaries, there remains little hope for a changing trend.

This instrument, that guarantees state job protection, could be the generator for a great impetus towards a better architecture.

The Chief Planning Officer and the Planning Authority

The function of the chief planning officer should not be reduced to carrying out administrative responsibilities. During his term of office he should and must have been creatively active as urban developer and architect to set an example to the architectural community of his town, just as Fritz Schumacher had done during the pre-war years in Hamburg.

The planning council, responsible for control and implementation of the building laws in a town, must be trained to recognise and encourage true architectural quality.

It is normally at the discretion of the chief planning officer that building regulations can be relaxed to allow for architectural innovation.

I know from my own jovial encounters with civil servants that the slightest relaxation of a narrow-minded regulation may lead to an insufferable conflict of their conscience. However, where fire regulations are concerned I always concede, even if I don't always quite understand them. But, if the issue is a purely aesthetic one, as for instance the apportioning of placement areas in living spaces or such like, I as the expert assume to have an understanding that extends beyond the limited horizon of the paper-pushing civil servant. With infinite patience and a lot of discussion, I try to get the respective civil servant to identify with my project. Sometimes I stick my head out too far, only to find it chopped off by the guillotine of bureaucratic injustice. Then one has to start all over again.

My fear that the bureaucratic apparatus can break the strongest spirit has often been confirmed. An experienced colleague confessed to me that the most stupefying plans get accepted provided they meet all the regulations. But I cannot bear to go back to any of these houses, let alone show them to anyone.

This is the worst guilt that bureaucracy has loaded upon itself. Unfortunately, no one individual is ever responsible! Everyone takes cover behind the law.

It is, of course, difficult for an architect who, for whatever reasons, has joined the ranks of the civil service and has not drawn a creative line since his last college project, to overcome his own frustration and grant building approval to his colleague in the private sector without some self-gratifying tampering with the proposed design.

A certain degree of correction by the

planning officer is doubtless necessary, since no architect knows all the building regulations by rote. The crucial point is the extent to which the design is 'corrected'!

How often have I had to restrain myself from exploding into a fit of wild temper and ruining everything? How often have I had to redraw plans for no good reason but to spoil them?

In my experience, the quality and presentation of a submitted set of plans is directly proportional to the scrutiny they are likely to be subjected to. A sloppy and badly drawn plan, on the other hand, represents identifiable and therefore acceptable mediocrity. I once had plans rejected because the elevations were too 'fascistic'. In a fit of despair I rendered the drawings unintelligible by randomly covering them with trees, flowers, people and projected shadows, and by defacing the suspect windows at will. As a result the scheme was accepted!

Later, the facades were executed according to the original plan. But somehow I don't think the planning officer would let me get away with the same trick a second time. He was generous enough not to make me accountable. The house has since been published extensively and I would not hold it against him if he boasted to his colleagues about his involvement in the scheme.

All officials I have had dealings with up to now were essentially nice guys. Even if my 'Viennese charm' could not deceive them, in a roundabout way we managed to get along. My stubbornness has always been a great help. I even go down on my knees if necessary, or in extreme cases play a cunning trick. None of this should be necessary! The planning officer could just as much be our partner!

Comparison of the Arts
Music, the most abstract of arts, stimulates our innermost feelings more than any of the other art forms.

No other artistic experience has had a more devastating effect on me than listening to a beautiful musical composition. The contemplation of a perfect painting or a virtuoso drawing are in comparison mere suggestion of this sensuous ecstacy.

Likewise the calm radiated by a painting's formal composition and its tonal quality are dimensions unbeknown to music. Paintings are fixed, permanent things, and being visually stable they can be read at leisure. Like the pages in a book they do not overpower one like the remorseless energy of a musical climax.

I feel less threatened by the static quality of a painting than by the abstract tonality of music. Surely it is as a result of my weakness, my inability to find self-expression in music – the highest art form. Resigned to the role of listener, I suffer torment and anguish.

Architecture, the most sober and rational of the arts, is shaped by functional and structural demands that all too often draw the energy from its spatial and plastic composition.

In this century, architecture has been gratuitously prostituted. Even its most ardent protagonists have contributed to its shameful disgrace.

An efficiently running motor is not, even in the widest sense of the word, a work of art, however beautiful it may look. If it ceases to run, it invariably ends up on the scrap heap. Le Corbusier's comparison between the Parthenon and an automobile in the twenties was epoch-making nonsense. These things cannot be compared, just as one cannot compare Bach's music to a Sachertorte . . .

Building is so constrained by programmatic requirements that it becomes increasingly difficult to isolate the aesthetic component from the torrent of relative trivia.

As an architect, I wish to dissociate myself from those who merely serve the physical and practical needs of society without indulging in a pleasurable personal artistic experience.

As long as consumer art is traded like canned meat, devoured and treated with the same spirit of superficiality as popular music, the artist has but one option, to retreat and await society's saturation point and the inevitable vale of tears that will cultivate a fresh desire for all that is beautiful.

Excruciating transistor music can be turned off at the push of a button. The visual insults that deface our cities and countryside are not so easy to wipe out.

A Call to Boycott Ugliness
Our planet is covered with schools, universities and educational institutions of all kinds, and our knowledge of the make-up of things has increased enormously but sadly our understanding of the beauty of things has diminished in proportion. Beauty can no longer take root in this transient world of throw-away objects where the tranquility it needs to feed off has been suffocated by the fumes of superficiality.

Beauty, however, is the only and ultimate aim, it alone fires my commitment to this profession.

I would like to be spared the insipid boredom of meeting only operational demands and be spared the bitter after-taste of only profit-orientated design devoid of ethical or symbolic significance.

The veil of ugliness that shrouds our world will tie itself like a fatal cord around the necks of our children and rob them of their remaining breath. In the trail of destruction and catastrophy that is befalling our century, my call to boycott is but a strangled whisper.

*   *   *

The Poetry of Building
We can only speak about architecture when
buildings embody a richness far beyond the
purely functional . . .

There is no poetry
in our sterile
day-to-day
functional implements.
Poetry rests in the
multifaceted
beauty of objects,
in the lustre of materials
and the grace and care they demand.

Poetry rests in the
life-giving breath of a building,
the aroma that exudes
from all its nooks and crannies,
saturated by the sweat of generations,
polished and worn by its use,
treasured in memory
and harassed by its multiple use.

Poetry rests in the
unruffled calm of its catalepsy,
hollowness and desertion,
the secrets of all the destinies,
buried in your walls,
they serve as shock absorbers for energies,
we have no powers to tame.

The unspeakable shock
of a corpse horrifies us,
it numbs our senses
as a sharp reminder of our own mortality.
We are all so alike.
Death only comes
to those who are in love.

Stronger than flesh is bone,

the bedrock.
Once divided and split,
despite careful arrangement,
you are affected and weakened,
since only our organic framework
gives you stability and strength.

My windswept bride,
your veil moribund with malice
and spite.
You have choked
on my innocence.

I cannot believe
that natural materials broken up
will gain in significance
through artistic arrangement,
to be more beautiful
than what nature grows from compost.

There was a time,
when man tried with all his intelligence,
to create something better, more beautiful,
without offending nature.

Today we have abandoned
regard and respect for nature,
we are filled with arrogance,
the spirit poisoned,
the earth's surface mutilated
and treated like a giant rubbish dump.

He who can contain
this primaeval urge to conquer this world,
who can meet rain and cold
with cunning aptitude,

who can retain his powers of perception,
he will understand,
that to build one's own dwelling
is a primitive urge
that need not be reinvented

The cloth, that covers your body,
that absorbs the moisture of your skin,
that retains your body heat,
it is an embarrassing substitute
to the natural coat of fur.
Nature has punished us
with nakedness
for our vanity.

Now, man has to protect
his goose-pimpled skin,
decorate it, cover its imperfections
and wrinkles of old age,
and powder away the agony of living.

The second skin, the dress,
the third, the walls, the building,
they hold similar significance and meaning
Who wants to dress to the disadvantage
of one's features.
Who wants to advertise his cack-handedness
by living in a cowshed?

The house is a basic need of both
body and mind.
If when you furnish it
you neglect one part,
the others will take over,
and smother what little is left,
to the disgrace of mankind.

*   *   *

About My Plastic Works

Besides working as an architect, it gives me untold pleasure to immerse myself in the poetic sphere of visual expression.

At last I am freed from the constraints of functional justification.
At last the burden of structural limitations has been lifted.

No client, no owner, no specialist consultant, no clever-clever boy, to scrutinise my every line,
or to rob me of my pen,
only to impose with arrogance his own identification problem on my design.

Tampering with my architectural drawing, he compensates for his own creative impotence.

There exists neither client nor customer in this world of poetic expression.
Here, I am accountable to no-one but myself.
I forgo recognition and waive success.

I need not quarrel with my dreams,
need not convince or astonish,
nor boast or impress.
With the things one can only love,
never hate,

things like book markers or hand warmers,
things that always accompany one . . .

The themes of architectural and urban form shape the cultural expression of our cities,
This thought ignites my innermost passions –
the structures of our time can cause such harm to mankind.

We must fight the stupidity and ugliness of our built environment.

Here I grow flowers that blossom eternally,
play with dolls that breath the sweet air of paradise
and dance to the melodies of singing birds.

Here the colours are filled with aroma,
and the walls breath out and expand into unknown dimensions.
Here geometry stretches like the tissue of our lungs,
here bodies shed their skin and metamorphose like larvae.
Here where love and suffering is as much transfigured as exhausted,

screams of ecstasy and screams of death dissipate into clouds of smoke.

I would like to file the edges of human dilemma,
tame the hatred
that bears such wretched misery.
This world,
that adorns itself with all the wordly glitter,
its surface shudders,
its breath inflames with rage,
that exterminates entire generations.

Every day, we are served up a dish of beauty and ugliness,
life and destruction,
wherein lies the significance?
You watch this theatre,
you sit motionless,
you internalise your despair,
your comatose stammer remains unheard.
Don't be too inquisitive,
the sun can blind you,
the shadow levels the abyss,
the days evaporate and consume your thoughts.

*   *   *

A CRITIQUE OF MODERN ARCHITECTURE

I do not intend to put certain personalities on trial, or to produce a lexical review with the aim of analysing every architectural contribution on the basis of its theoretical stability. What I want to do is to take a good look at architectural tendencies which, widely supported, have influenced whole decades; further, I wish to separate theoretical substance from fashionable trends, and to formulate propositions according to my own personal conviction. These will allow me to make a critical statement, and to give an outlook on an architecture which outlasts the present.

Modern architecture, in a disastrous way, has ruined cities throughout the whole world. The loss of spatiality in the modern city is most especially deplorable. Some years ago, I published a book on this traumatic issue in which I tried to fathom the reason for this destruction. Spatial urban systems have been radically and callously ignored, while the repertoire of architectural composition has been degraded just as brutally, to become the most primitive formulae; and all this with poor economic and technical 'reasons'.

This development took place with the euphoric support of the entire professional world which finally, during the time of the post-Second World War building boom, saw the chance to realise the architectural revolution dreamt of in the twenties. The principles of the CIAM Athens Charter, which concerned the separation of functions in the city (zoning), were incorporated into building law at an international level and carried out with the rigour and scrupulousness of bureaucratic machines. This deplorable state of affairs was primarily helped by the indescribable misery in Europe after the Second World War. But oddly enough, in Warsaw for instance, where the situation was worst, areas in ruins which were important for the city's identity were rebuilt with a heroic certainty. Of course this operation was criticised by some people as producing merely stage-sets. Yet the Polish people had been disgraced without being at fault. They therefore made Warsaw a symbol of their national strength. Our modern cities and their buildings are merely functional objects, without any ethical meaning. They are simply production areas or housing estates which people occupy avidly but leave without sorrow, because ugliness sooner or later creates contempt and disgust in every human being, and sometimes leads to delinquency.

The mass housing shortage was abused by speculators in order for them to become rich in a short period of time. The profit-seeking attitude of these people forced the building industry into the use of prefabricated systems and certain other materials regardless of their durability. The planners, as if struck by madness, agreed to this profiteering: by building extremely densely, they made it even easier for building companies to make fast money – a vicious circle, still rotating, but now conscious of its limits. Some planners even welcome the consumer/disposable ideology as a substitute for non-existent architectural concepts.

The revolution of modern architecture has failed. Even if it is difficult for professionals to admit this fact, for years journalists and lay-people have been heaping reproaches on us and have given us the most appalling reports. Citizens' initiatives, more than before, vehemently take up urban design problems. The press spies out and hunts down, with increasing success, the dubious operations of big building companies.

Industrialisation has not led to the perfection and reduction in price of building components as it was expected by Le Corbusier and his generation. All that has been achieved is that through mechanisation, the architectural detail has been submitted to the laws of production technology. Of course the calculation of the maximum yield simplifies the constructional solution. Also, reducing production time often offends against all practical reasoning. Decadence in architecture and the ruin of building craftsmanship go together, and can only recover together.

Yet I hope that, despite the discredit architects and the building industry have brought upon themselves by their own faults, there might be a chance for 'renewal'.

Mankind in our century continues to demonstrate its apocalyptic destructive power. The brutality of self-slaughter is reflected in all parts of industrialised society. The architectural problem that worries me is no doubt one of the most obvious, but certainly not the most threatening problem the twentieth century has given birth to. The architectural problem will neither explode nor emit fatal radiation. But the illnesses which may be created by chemicals which new buildings are stuffed with, I hardly dare to foresee. We wait with dis-

Piazza Navona, Rome

Gropius-Stadt, Berlin

Computer Centre, Vienna

trust and desperation for the results of all these experiments which have plunged us into a meaningless venture.

Of course the individual case does not matter so much, but a host of bad architecture becomes threatening. A few ugly buildings would not be that serious a threat, but if they spread so that in the end hardly one per cent of real quality is left in building activities, then the time would have come to sit up and take notice.

Bombed street in Warsaw

The same street after reconstruction

Unfortunately this ugliness, this private kitsch, in millions of variations flooding city boundaries and countryside in the form of single family houses, is not viewed that way by their inhabitants, as it is the case with their standard upholstered furniture and

New buildings on the Alexanderplatz in East Berlin. General planning by H. Henselmann

wall decorations. Education, which at one time everyone enjoyed, has suffocated under empty aestheticism. A society, wealthier and better schooled than ever before, is in danger of wasting away because of its selfishness, which is often accompanied by ridiculous gestures. In philosophical terms, this development seems to represent a logical result. In historical terms it is certainly not the only example of this kind of development. But the decadence in culture to which I refer is by no means confined to the private sector; it is even more obvious in these gigantic, hypertrophic building complexes. Aristocratic power was successfully fought against, and when it finally ceased to exist, we were indeed left with an immensely lavish but tasteful heritage. If the modern bureaucratic and technocratic power structures were taken by storm what would then be left? Only a gigantic rubbish heap of useless equipment and, of course, a scorched earth.

Bourgeois dining room in the 'international moderne' style

Can we, with good conscience, enter into a heritage of such dubious value? Who would be willing to take over all this hideousness; who would further enjoy all these shapeless idylls?

I think we will put the 'throw-away' ideology into practice and pull down all the rubbish. This would be necessary anyway for economic reasons.

Such is the sad starting-point of contemporary architecture. He who has not yet realised this should open his eyes and name me the modern buildings in his close vicinity which will go down in building history for having met high architectural demands. I live in the centre of a metropolis called Vienna. If I think about the banalities which for the last thirty years have emerged from a ground that is pregnant with tradition, I am on the verge of tears. The illustrations which accompany this essay have been deliberately picked from anonymous modern architecture to be found in all our cities. I am convinced that many lay-people consider these examples as serious contempor-

Modern alpine hotel architecture, Salzburg, 'accommodating Nature'

ary architecture. After all, similar criteria are applied when, from a holiday catalogue, somebody makes a decision about his 'seaside hotel'. What then should one be guided by? In case of doubt, certainly by the buildings which are close to the heart of the ruling parties; in Vienna these would be the UN-City, the Allgemeines Krankenhaus (hospital), the Franz-Joseph railway station or the Hilton Hotel. What also gives certainty is the taste of big companies and banks which, by way of trendy architects, try to pep up their image and, indirectly, their products and services. So it is that laypeople are spell-bound and terrorized by the taste of magnates, who abuse architecture for their own publicity and to be celebrated publicly as cultural patrons.

Vienna, building by Staber ' . . . following closely Fischer von Erlach, Otto Wagner and Loos . . . ' (quotation by the architect about his building)

As an example of how evident the opportunism of powerful clients and architects can be nowadays, I would like to mention two building programmes in Vienna concerning the Ballhausplatz and Schwarzenbergplatz, which have become political issues. After their first glass-facade designs had been successfully rejected by local initiatives, architects and clients changed their attitude and architectural style, proposing for the two sites buildings with historicist facades. Nobody knows whether these games were an attempt to deceive the citizens, or whether they were meant to be an ironical affront. The architects concerned, being among the busiest in Vienna, are experienced tradesmen and entrepreneurs. They are too clever not to have a precise strategy for these kinds of prestige objects. Anyway, different groups got very concerned about the architectural tradition of Vienna and initiated meetings and panel discussions, certainly to the amusement of their supposed enemies. These 'enemies'

however, veered round to go the 'alternative way': the citizens were invited to discuss proposals, to reject or agree, their choices being manipulated according to the strategy of clients and architects. These 'link' (left) tactics for the fooling of citizens are disgraceful. Architecture has been degraded to a masque, which changes according to a required role in a strategy. It was characteristic of the ensuing discussion that the plans were never dealt with. Only the facades were discussed. Later it became apparent that the former did not exist at all. The 'Mother of the Arts' must have gone astray in a brothel. She has fallen to the market value of a car-body. If this is not capable of being changed abruptly we could end this chapter with some lascivious swearwords, and could better devote our time to a good game of golf.

Rudolf Hospital, Vienna

So much for the 'atmospherical'. Now we can begin our analysis with a relaxed and enlightened mind.

At the beginning of this century, the revolt against traditional architecture took place in several stages and with different shades of opinion.

The garden city movement fought against the overgrowing of the city. Art Nouveau, Vienna Secession or artists and architects like Antoni Gaudí, Tony Garnier, Otto Wagner, Josef Hoffmann, Adolf Loos, Henry van de Velde, and many others, attempted successfully to halt the industrialised historicism of the nineteenth century.

At the moment I live in an apartment block typical of the last century, and enjoy the room heights and the cross-section of the three front rooms. But everything which lies behind this front is not worth mention-

ing, although the flat is 27 metres deep. Twelve metres in front of my window is a facade which could be ours, decorated with this successful industrial ornamentation in neoclassical style, exchangeable, but more bearable than an aluminium-profile facade.

Franz-Joseph Railway Station, Vienna, by Schwanzer and Hlaweniczka

All this of course does not reach the level of architecture. The young artists and architects of the nineteenth century detested this kind of work for which the busy plasterers were in demand, and intended to put an end to such activities. They were seeking forms and themes which would be good enough to take the place of the classical styles such as the Romanesque, the Gothic, the Renaissance, the baroque and neoclassicism, which in the nineteenth century were employed arbitrarily.

Street in Vienna, late nineteenth century

Mackintosh achieved this liberation by taking refuge in geometry. He did without classical symbols and relied on the aesthetic values inherent in well-proportioned forms, surfaces and structures. The traditional way of composing the building body and its interior were not questioned by him. His

Glasgow School of Art by C.R. Mackintosh, 1897-1909

conception became very influential for architectural development in the twentieth century.

With Gaudí the liberation from the classical language happens almost like a sensuous eruption. The sculptural quality of his architecture can be solely attributed to Gaudí the artist. His individual play with interpretations is too irrational to set a precedent.

Casa Milà, Barcelona, by A. Gaudí, 1905-10

Where his architecture was taken as an example, the results were often awkward *faux pas*. Still, straight-forward geometry is also a good protection for mediocre architects. The realm of irregular design can only be mastered by extremely talented artists.

This may be a warning to all those young architects who think that the spontaneous individual line and liberation from geometry are the pre-conditions for becoming an artistic personality.

The Casa Mila, an immensely powerful architectural event, just cannot be repeated at every corner. It is a unique building. The analysis of the Casa Mila, a steel-structured building on a free plan with a sculpted sandstone facing, reveals a very interesting building type which was only possible because of new technology. But this is a specific quality which was certainly not exploited superficially by Gaudí. Even if he had had to use a traditional solid structure, a similar effect would have resulted. The passion for constructional subtleties is deeply rooted in the Catalan building tradition, and Gaudí certainly benefited from this background.

Casa Batlló, Barcelona, by A. Gaudí, 1904-06, facade detail

Whoever builds up and teaches an architectural theory must examine every theorem in terms of its universality. This means that the margin of possible interpretations of principles has to be anticipated, and all tangible experiences in history have to be reviewed for practical application. Thus,

Casa Batlló, view of courtyard

only solid principles remain a matter for instruction in order to guarantee sound high quality of work. The truly great artists have indeed a command of this alphabet, but they are also aware of its limits. With their secure instincts, they only abandon approved rules once, after a long search, they have found a yet unknown variant.

Roof construction of Gaudí's Casa Mila

The Art Nouveau movement was an international revolt against the historical styles being trivialised. The classical decorative elements were replaced by floral and other ornaments borrowed from nature.

But although the results were fresh, powerful and often effusive, as best seen in the works of Victor Horta, Henry van de Velde and Hector Guimard, they were too individual in their interpretation and therefore could not last for long.

Maison du Peuple, Brussels, by V. Horta, 1896-99

The artists of the Vienna secession led by Otto Wagner, Hoffmann, Plećnik etc. had essentially a more classical attitude and abstained from expressionist gestures. Wagner's Post Office Savings Bank in Vienna and Hoffmann's Palais Stoclet in Brussels are wonderful highlights of this movement.

Hôtel at no. 4 Avenue Palmerston, Brussels, by V. Horta, 1895

Where Hoffmann still formally celebrates the detail, Wagner exposes the constructive and technical qualities of the building's parts. Because of the numerous engineering buildings he executed for the 'Stadtbahn' network and the Donaukanal, his attention was drawn on the design qualities of unmasked constructive details. The banking hall of the Post Office Savings Bank is designed with great technical precision as

Métro station, Paris, by H. Guimard, 1899-1900

glass-steel architecture, which until then was only applied to halls and greenhouses.

In retrospect, one is amazed that in the nineteenth century architecture and engineering were kept at a distance from each other and that the latter, where it was found to be necessary, employed the classical orders as if ashamed of its nakedness.

Palais Stoclet, Brussels, by J. Hoffmann, 1905-11

Road bridge over the river Norderelbe by Meyers, Hauers and Pieper, 1884-88

Adolf Loos always played a special role in the scene in Vienna. He did not join any group, and vehemently criticised the romantic air of the Viennese studios under Hoffmann. How his battle against ornament should be understood is evident in his own work. He had a passion for panelling the walls with precious materials. He also used hollow piers and non-supporting beams when, in his terms, this was required by the composition of the room. Some of his interiors were decorated with classical friezes in plaster: the Doric columns which emphasise the main entrance of the Goldman commercial building at Michaelerplatz in Vienna are mere 'decorations' (to be naughty).

Water Tower, Hamburg, by von Lindley and de Chateauneuf, 1854

To accomplish this architecture, long spanning concrete beams were inserted storey by storey which, in the photographs of the skeleton, gave the impression of being suitable for oblong window bands. Far from it! They were filled in with bricks and, after plastering, a simple perforated facade appeared. This Viennese 'naughtiness' is not easy to tolerate. Very often Loos took up contradictory themes which he then pieced together like collages. Different facades in one building are often joined together as if they have nothing to do with each other. The interior composition of spaces, according to his 'Raumplan' (room-

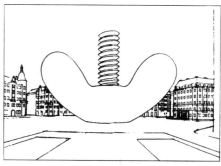

Claes Oldenburg, 'The Big Screw', design for a monument on Karlaplan, Stockholm, 1966

one reflects on its meaning. An office tower among many others in an American city with millions of inhabitants would soon have lost its spirituality.

Building at Michaelerplatz, Vienna, by A. Loos, 1910

plan) concept, is interlocked and diversified, and surprising in terms of their different heights. One of his projects, the administration building of the Herald Tribune in Chicago, is one of the strangest and most misleading statements in recent architectural history, not only because of its gesture, but because of its anticipation of many representations in contemporary art and architecture. Loos was a biting critic of the International Style, and I can only understand his entry for the Herald Tribune competition as a grandiose affront against modernism à la Gropius, Hilberseimer, et al.

I think that if this building had been realised, idea and reality would not have agreed with each other. This building, in among all

Competition design for the Chicago Tribune by A. Loos, 1922

the other kitsch, would have looked monstrous and ridiculous. Steinberg's drawings picture similar American situations. Considering the appearance of the Herald Tribune Building, one might associate this gigantic Doric column with the wonders of the antique world. But this is not possible if

Saul Steinberg (before 1945)

Hans Hollein, Vienna, 1963: 'Transformation', a technical object becomes a cultural statement

Vienna, benefiting from her topographical situation, has always been a place where cultural controversies have been fought out. Here, the south German baroque celebrated its splendid alliance with foreign styles in the masterly collage of the Karlskirche by Fischer von Erlach. Hildebrandt was by no means an orthodox classicist. His Upper Belvedere for Prince Eugen is a marvellous architectural achievement. It is a building which is not deep in plan, yet its clear geometrical facade and carved decoration gives the impression of a gigantic complex when viewed from the city. The enormous solemnity of the buildings on the Ringstrasse is still experienced with pleasure, although as cultural achievements they cannot compete with the unique musical creations of Beethoven, Schubert or Brahms, creations

Karlskirche, Vienna, by J.B. Fischer von Erlach, 1716-23

which have not been surpassed anywhere in the world.

Gottfried Semper, who was commissioned to design the Burgtheater, left Vienna head over heels after only three years. He could not cope with the intrigues and the manoeuvres of the Viennese partner Hasenauer with whom he had to work, and who

First Court Theatre, Dresden, by G. Semper, 1838-41

bestowed Semper's plans with an effusive local hue. So the Burgtheater, with the exception of the stage-set depot, as one of his late works has little in common with the strict discipline of his buildings in Zurich and Dresden.

In the twentieth century the music of Berg, Schönberg and Webern has gained an international reputation. The very few modern buildings in Vienna have not reached the same level. Like neoclassicism at the beginning of the nineteenth century, the clear, rational Modern Movement was only half-heartedly supported in Vienna.

Burgtheater, Vienna, by G. Semper and C. Hasenauer, 1874-88

Former stage-set depot, Vienna, by G. Semper, c.1875

Only in the romantic expressionism of the Viennese 'Gemeinde' (community) buildings of the twenties and thirties has a generation of architects found its identity. This tendency, which was partially rooted in the school of Otto Wagner, gained spontaneous

'Karl Seitz-Hof', Vienna, by F. and H. Gessner, 1926

public acknowledgement because many details employed were known by the population as classical motifs. Architects who adhered to the Bauhaus ideology certainly made fun of the playfulness of their Viennese colleagues. The latter were branded as secret traditionalists, and for that reason they were not appreciated for a long time. These 'Hof-Siedlungen' (courtyard estates) have a particular spatial quality, especially in terms of urban design when compared to the schematic linear housing estates; as for example the Dammer-stock estate in Karlsruhe by Walter Gropius or Onkel-Toms-Hütte and Siemensstadt in Berlin. (This subject has been dealt with at length in my book *Urban Space*, and therefore I can do better than to repeat myself, but concen-

Wittgenstein's House, Vienna, designed by himself down to the last detail

trate my thoughts on the architecture of the buildings themselves.) I hope nobody minds that Vienna, at present my adopted home city, is always the focus of my reflections. In a similar way in which I teach my students to learn exemplarily from this city, my observations of architectural events receive their orientation from this background.

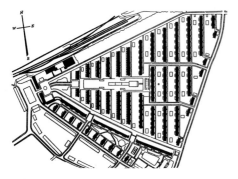

Plan of the Bad Dürrenberg quarter, Berlin, by A. Klein, 1930

Heinrich Tessenow, despite his lectureship at the Akademie für Angewandte Kunst (Academy of Applied Art) which lasted for five years, never became an 'echter Wiener' (real Viennese). But because of his very honest, restrained architectural language, he certainly had some followers among the architects of council estates not only in Vienna. One aspect, however, should be pointed out in Tessenow's work. Shortly after the turn of the century, at a time when many architects were still concerned with heroic design themes of the nineteenth century Tessenow concentrated all his efforts on workers' housing. In Rome, Tony Garnier was designing his

Gymnasium (Dalcroze Institute), Hellerau, 1910

Housing estate near Schwechat by H. Tessenow

'Cité Industrielle' at the same time. The beauty and freshness of these drawings were never reached in Garnier's actual buildings. Both Tessenow's and Garnier's projects can be compared here as being representative for future generations.

In every cultural era there are two camps, the one of the traditionalists and the other of the avant-gardists. The two are mostly standard bearers of the same age and educational background but with different attachments to cultural heritage; the one cautiously weighing tradition, the other boldly questioning tradition. Attitudes can change with the life of an artist. However, at the time of competing for bread and recognition, not the most polite comments are exchanged. These, however, will be knowingly smiled at thirty, forty years later . . . One 'reactionary', the other 'progressive' . . .

Can art be the one or the other? After a short time ideological hostilities disappear and what is left can be put in simple words: he was proficient, but incapable.

Art lives solely on the quality of meaning and the embodiment of it. All *ad hoc* publicity should therefore be handled cautiously, at least until superficial effects have died down. Even in times where culture is imposed by dictators, the so-called reactionary and opportunistic pieces of art will only

reveal their true artistic quality and become recognisable for everybody after the ideological aspects have become meaningless. The artist is at liberty to freely choose his means of expression. He only disqualifies himself through sloppiness and incapability in terms of skill and design. Cézanne has created a fantastic œuvre with his innocuous landscapes and portraits; the Cubists with their violins, bottles and cuttings; Morandi with his arrangements of vessels etc. And none of them asked permission of the public to do this or that. Sometimes the price for the artist's freedom in his choice of theme and way of expression is life-long isolation and a concomitant undervaluation of the artistic quality of his work. The artist's biggest enemy is the arrogance of the 'cultured' public. It only appreciates what is established and familiar. If one asks for personal judgement where no common interpretation exists, then a spiteful criticism breaks out condemning everything that is not understood. This has always been the case, and this touchstone of every new artistic generation is at the same time its challenge.

Drawing from *Une cité industrielle* by T. Garnier, 1904

In this sense my criticism of the contemporary architectural scene should not be understood simply as being bitter about failed successes. They help me to clarify my point, to strengthen my position even at the risk of judging unfairly. Recently I was accused of working beyond the 'Zeitgeist' (spirit of the age). Indeed, for years this is what I have been doing with all my strength and devotion. My congratulations to the critic who has understood this. However, to be precise, I have always thought that I was working beyond contemporary needs, and that this was the reason why my architecture was not in demand. That it was all to do with prescribing a 'Zeitgeist' never came into my mind. The 'Zeitgeist' is solely created by artists and not by the public. It is a very natural thing that the older generation has to cope with their achievements being questioned, and therefore we do not mind their struggling against us. We for our part will not be hypersensitive either, but nevertheless ask for a fair fight. Despite all hindrances, better arguments and achievements always receive the merit they deserve.

To recapitulate the aim of this essay, I would like to mention that my extensive words have only the purpose of putting my criticism on a solid basis. I am not concerned about the normal change of generations, but that the arts worldwide are being made bankrupt. To posit and prove this has required this long prologue. However, the dispute between 'reactionaries' and 'avantgardists' has another aspect; the former, building on a safe repertoire, benefit from immediate success; the latter, seeking new ways, are existentially threatened. Today, as the 'Moderne' in all its banality is enjoying cultural acknowledgement, everybody who tries to avoid this cul-de-sac by way of thorough studies of history is branded as a reactionary. Now it is he who is called to bear the pioneer's standard and to suffer the privations of a renewer. In both camps, only the best talents will survive the hardest test, while struggling for the realisation of their ideas.

Drawing from *Une cité industrielle* by T. Garnier, 1904

Tony Garnier, who won the Prix de Rome in 1899, renounced the traditional Beaux-Arts programme and devoted himself to a theme neglected in the nineteenth century: the industrial city. His architectural concepts are of ingenious clarity and void of any decorative romanticism. If one looks at Garnier's design for the Prix de Rome in the Beaux-Arts publications, one will notice that it is still fully in line with the bourgeois fashion-architecture of the fin de siècle. All the more astonishing is his reversal afterwards, which had very much to do with his sojourn in Rome. His projects are disciplined by an almost antique attitude.

Abattoir de la Mouche, Lyons, by T. Garnier, 1909-13

He was using the qualities of reinforced concrete, still new and revolutionary at the time, and refined this new material by way of an aesthetic design which respected its inherent constructional rules and logical composition. *Une cité industrielle* is a book

Maison Cassandre, Versailles, by A. Perret, 1926

Théatre des Champs Elysées, Paris, by A. Perret, 1911-12

which belongs to the most beautiful theoretical contributions of this century. Garnier had a strong influence on the 'Moderne' which was developing in the twenties. But personally he rejected the idea of becoming a promoter of this scene. His buildings, however, did not fulfil the expectations of his powerful early work. Unfortunately he ended up in a structuralism, à la Perret, which was popular in France. Yet his Olympic Stadium and his abattoir de la Mouche remain outstanding achievements. Thus an avant-gardist became a bourgeois traditionalist. It was similar with Perret. Perret's early work contrasts in the same way with his later buildings in Le Havre. Unlike Garnier, Tessenow developed from being a poetic traditionalist into a classicist of the thirties.

This pre-Second World War scene, so colourful and rich as it was, was abruptly ended in the middle of the thirties when, on the Continent, dictators assumed political power. The official architectural canon for public buildings in German cities prescribed a primitive and inflated neoclassicism which had nothing to do with the delicacy and elegance of the era of Schinkel, Weinbrenner or Klenze. Buildings in rural areas were to represent the 'Heimatstil' (homeland style). Only industrial building was spared regimentation and could realise clear modern construction without problems. The debate on the architectural history of the Third Reich is immensely burdened, despite the fact that it is an issue of the past. The new rulers quickly realised that neither the aesthetics nor the technology of modern architecture were suitable to serve as the pretence of the Party. The same applied to modern art with its critical social aspects. The sober building bodies were anything but popular, their building technologies not fully developed, and therefore not reliable enough. To impress the masses, the Nazis fell back upon the approved monumental orders which, given the pressure of time they were under, could still be mastered in terms of craftsmanship. There was no time for new developments, and they did not

Albert Speer's studio, Upper Salzburg, 1936

want to run any risk. The model for a late neoclassical monumental architecture was found in the USA, and in colonial cities. Here, not only public buildings but also banks, office buildings and business premises were all alike in terms of the style described above. That the Nazis used the best materials and craftsmanship for the few pompous edifices they were able to build, can hardly be criticised. They sought to disguise the brutality of their regime with an appropriate (in their terms) architecture. In the history of urban design, the plans for

Factory in Westphalia by F. Schupp and M. Kremmer

Domed Hall planned for Berlin by A. Speer, 1938

Berlin are of 'excessive grandeur'. The urban geography would, however, have benefited from them. If one examines the different stages of planning, it appears that the initial proposals were much more differentiated and sympathetic to the urban structure in terms of scale. Only later did they become coarse in texture and lost in terms of space. A gigantic domed building of Boullée-like dimension was to establish the high point in this Berlin apotheosis. Sometimes one is tempted to think to oneself: 'They should have built all this stuff instead of making a war.' But this would probably have meant that the fascists would have been in power for an even longer period of time. In the Eastern Block this kind of idiotic despotism is perpetuated. The Stalinallee which could well have sprung from Speer's Bebauungsplan (development plan) by means of an oppressive architecture, became the symbol for the rise of a young, communist state which did not want to be one. Later on, as soon as the images of socialism were fading away, the feeble architectural theory of capitalism came back into favour. If today the Berlin Wall was pulled down, the difference between the two Germanies would only be economic. Otherwise East and West do not contradict each other on the level of general cultural taste. The East simply did not succeed in finding an architectural language for its kind of society. It was not possible because its social order is that of a police state.

I was very shocked to find the Wall being dealt with as an architectural monument in

an architectural journal published in East Berlin. We do not care for this kind of macabre joke.

A schizophrenia drug seems to exist in modern states, the effect of which is very unpleasant and painful. That a majority of the world allows itself to be placed under schizophrenic tyranny can only be explained by an analysis of power mechanisms which have got out of the hands of society. Or are there indeed pleasant sensations about self-destruction?

Or are there any natural automata which, in case of surfeit, order self-destruction?

Literature, music and art anticipated the apocalypse of the forties long before it happened. I fear that the state of architecture, this mute imagery, has to be understood as a warning of an imminent spiritual abyss. The

Karl-Marx-Allee (formerly Stalinallee), East Berlin, by Paulick, Henselmann, Hopp, Leucht, Souradny and Hartmann, 1951-57

last time that this abyss opened up was after mankind had inflicted the biggest self-destruction in its existence. I remember the boom of the bombers very well. But today they would sound like light music in comparison with the vast amount of destructive material available now. How can beauty ever grow on such a brutal background?

Architectural culture is interconnected but divided into two parts: the wide basis of common functional buildings for dwelling and working, and rising from that, the small apex of buildings which accommodate special functions for society. It is legitimate to design the latter in distinct manner, in order that they differ from functional buildings.

During the nineteenth century when the bourgeoisie was getting rich, it embellished

No 6, Sandwirtgasse, Vienna, c 1860

its residential premises with all the attributes which were used by the dethroned aristocracy to stand out from the masses. The architectural language got so confused that it became necessary to find another way of distinguishing public buildings from private ones. The former, therefore, were isolated from adjacent buildings and set into a square, a park or sited on top of a hill. But this step soon found its followers. In the twenties the free-standing object as such became desirable for better living, working and resting in general. Only one aspect was not taken into consideration; given that everybody had the same rights, this demand would have meant the death of the city. Today this no longer needs to be proved. Modern cities are the built evidence. The majority of Americans claim that they do not want to have anything else other than the modern 'anti-city'; that only some 'fanatics' would still prefer New York, Boston or San Francisco. Let us wait and see what happens if, because of a new energy crisis, legs have to be used for walking again. Maybe then Americans will remember the good old European city again!

The confusion in architectural language became even more profound after the Second World War. As historical architectural features had been abused so much, architects thought that they had been left without any good examples and therefore attempted to express the special significance of a building by way of employing novel methods of construction. For the last thirty years the whole range of exotic structures has been tried out, for example, on churches. Flicking through publications dealing with this subject, one shudders at so much kitsch. In terms also of ground-plan design, anything conceivable has been put to the test. The underground church at Lourdes, or the one by Nervi beside Saint Peter's, can at best be called well-structured garages. These buildings have nothing to do with churches. Many modern churches can be mistaken for being industrial halls; some of them are deliberately designed that way to supposedly reduce the distance between the church and the faithful. To undermine the sacred in this way, given the significance of churches in the history of architecture, is for me the worst aspect of our present

No 42, Linke Wienzeile, Vienna, by Kmunke and Kohl, 1896-97

cultural decline.

Temples and churches have been acknowledged and valued at all times, even by unbelievers, as the most noble symbolic buildings. They received the best of artistic and artisan achievement. They exemplified the architectural tradition of an epoch. After the antique, they also became the most magnificent interior public spaces. Are there any other functions available now to compensate for the loss of religious feeling? The reading rooms in public libraries, the resting rooms in swimming pools or sport centres, station halls, concert halls or theatres? None of these functions can ever reach the mystic and symbolic significance of a place of worship. Every human being is touched by the enigma of life and death. The fateful and inscrutable dimensions of existence and non-existence are as overwhelming as they are frightening. Nature, in its monumentality and beauty, being the background for everything that happens, only cautiously reveals her secrets. To soothe his fears and to calm his senses, man has erected symbolic places on earth for the spiritual interpretation of his being. These buildings served as places of mediation between him and the unnameable enigmas; the addressee in this fictitious dialogue: a glorified human being, a God; the building: an idealised accommodation for the supernatural. I do not know whether this subject is definitely lost in architecture. For the time being, I am satisfied with the sacral buildings which history has passed on to us. We can live with these for a while longer. If an idea cannot be celebrated genuinely anymore, what else can one do but stick to things one is good at? In this consumer world people are not very interested in spiritual values.

At the beginning of the fifties, the confusion about forms gave a fresh impetus to the development of new structures. Technology was less loaded a term than form, and immune from ideology. After a short period of time, the attitude spread that once the constructional requirements had been met, one had done justice to architecture. In a similar one-sided way, efforts were also concentrated on the solution of functional problems and cost-effective construction processes.

But despite the miseries of the post-war period, there are of course examples of an 'architectural' attitude towards design, and nowadays some buildings from that time gain sympathy despite their clumsiness.

One phenomenon, however, hit the devastated Middle Europe quite unexpectedly: an exploding economic prosperity and in connection with that, an unrestrained building boom. In order to encourage building activities, governments offered special finance and depreciation schemes which could easily be abused. It is perhaps only too natural that in this competition between 'more money' and 'more architecture', the Muse was the loser.

It is a long time ago that a person who commissioned a building demanded the best skills of architects and craftsmen, because his building was to demonstrate his honourable position in society. Also, the house of the poor and the house of the rich were easily comparable in terms of elegance, despite the difference in expenditure and embellishment.

The idea of making a lot of money in a short period of time has destroyed the quality of a building as such. Even the majority

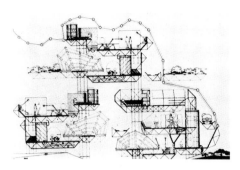

Design by Archigram, London, 1960s

of buildings that do not need to meet high architectural demands have lost the elegance which I have mentioned above. That is also due to the fact that because of quick industrialisation, the building crafts have been ruined.

Responsible for all this are first and foremost the architects and planners who, burdened by growing competition, sell their souls and professional credibility with the empty phrase: 'If I don't do it, another colleague will'. Can this fatal lack of self-respect still be overcome? Who is the first one whose eyes must be opened, the one

who buys or the one who produces? Both are cheated at the moment.

The client who relies on cheap technology will soon have to pay for its defectiveness. He will also be bored quite quickly with superficial architectural cosmetics. The architect has tricked himself out of the most elementary professional fulfilment; and I cannot imagine that the easy money he earns can make up for the shame of blatant opportunism.

There are no less talented architects today than in the past. But now, to a much greater extent, they are condemned to inactivity or their creativity is just not asked for. Very often they take refuge either in the arts scene where it is still possible to get fair acknowledgement, or they lecture at schools of architecture which guarantee artistic freedom and survival.

But without a practical challenge every theory is meaningless. I would very much like to prove my arguments with my own work instead of letting others do this for me. But to build under today's conditions is a damned humiliating business, not very sympathetic to the fulfilment of theoretical and artistic ambitions.

ERRATA

p. 17, centre caption should read 'Good example – IIT, Chicago, architect: Mies van der Rohe'; p. 122, third column, end of first paragraph should read '... all create the rhythm of masses, planes and lines'; p. 238, fourth paragraph, third line, for 'croning' read 'crossing'.

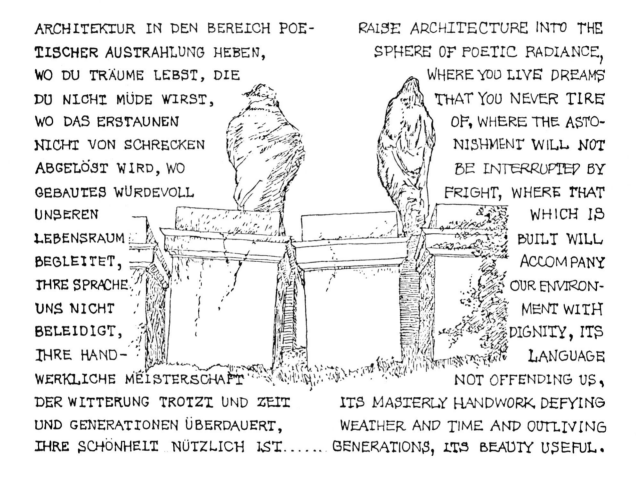

ARCHITEKTUR IN DEN BEREICH POE-
TISCHER AUSTRAHLUNG HEBEN,
WO DU TRÄUME LEBST, DIE
DU NICHT MÜDE WIRST,
WO DAS ERSTAUNEN
NICHT VON SCHRECKEN
ABGELÖST WIRD, WO
GEBAUTES WÜRDEVOLL
UNSEREN
LEBENSRAUM
BEGLEITET,
IHRE SPRACHE
UNS NICHT
BELEIDIGT,
IHRE HAND-
WERKLICHE MEISTERSCHAFT
DER WITTERUNG TROTZT UND ZEIT
UND GENERATIONEN ÜBERDAUERT,
IHRE SCHÖNHEIT NÜTZLICH IST......

RAISE ARCHITECTURE INTO THE
SPHERE OF POETIC RADIANCE,
WHERE YOU LIVE DREAMS
THAT YOU NEVER TIRE
OF, WHERE THE ASTO-
NISHMENT WILL NOT
BE INTERRUPTED BY
FRIGHT, WHERE THAT
WHICH IS
BUILT WILL
ACCOMPANY
OUR ENVIRON-
MENT WITH
DIGNITY, ITS
LANGUAGE
NOT OFFENDING US,
ITS MASTERLY HANDWORK DEFYING
WEATHER AND TIME AND OUTLIVING
GENERATIONS, ITS BEAUTY USEFUL.

315

SELECTED BIBLIOGRAPHY

ALBERTI, LEON BATTISTA
De Re Aedificatoria, 1452, 1485, 1550

———.
Ten Books on Architecture, London, 1965
BERTOTTI SCAMOZZI, O.
Le fabbriche e i disegni di Andrea Palladio raccolti e illustrati, 1776-83
CESARIANO
Di Lucio Vitruvio Pollione de Architettura . . ., Como, 1521
CURTIS, N.C.
Architectural Composition, New York, 1923
DEHIO, G.
Untersuchungen über das gleichseitige Dreieck als Norm gotischer Bauproportionen, Strasbourg, 1894

———.
Ein Proportionsgesetz der antiken Baukunst und sein Nachleben im Mittelalter und der Renaissance, Strasbourg, 1895
DURAND, JEAN-NICOLAS-LOUIS
Recuel et parallèle des édifices en tout genre, 1800

———.
Précis et leçons d'architecture, 1802-5
DURER, A.
Underweyssung der Messung mit Zirkel und Richtscheid in Linien, Ebenen und ganzen Corporen, Nuremberg, 1525

———.
Vier Bücher von menschlicher Proportion, 1528

———.
Befestigungslehre, 1527
GARNIER, TONY
Une cité industrielle, 1904
HARBESON, J.F.
Study of Architectural Design, New York, 1933
LE CLERC
Architecture, 1714
LE CORBUSIER
Le Modulor, Boulogne-sur-Seine, 1950, London, 1954
Modulor 2, Boulogne-sur-Seine, 1955, London, 1958
LEDOUX, CLAUDE-NICOLAS
L'architecture considérée sous le rapport de l'art, des mœurs et de la législation, 1804
LEONI, GIACOMO
The Architecture of Leon Battista Alberti in Ten Books, London, 1726
LOTZ
Römisches Jahrbuch für Kunstgeschichte, 1955
MOESSEL, ERNST
Die Proportion in Antike und Mittelalter, Munich, 1926
PALLADIO, ANDREA
Quattro Libri dell'Architettura, Venice, 1570
PICKERING, E.
Architectural Design, New York, 1933

PFEIFER, HERMANN
Die Formenlehre des Ornaments, Handbuch der Architektur, Stuttgart, (nd)
ROBERTSON, H.
Principles of Architectural Composition, London, 1924
ROBINSON, J.B.
Architectural Composition, New York, 1908
ROWE, COLIN
The Mathematics of the Ideal Villa and Other Essays, Cambridge, Mass., and London, 1976
SCAMOZZI, VICENZO
L'idea dell'architettura universale, Venice 1615
SCHOLFIELD, P.H.
The Theory of Proportion in Architecture, Cambridge, 1958
SEIDER, HANS
Urformen der abendländischen Baukunst, (nd)
SERLIO, SEBASTIANO
L'Architettura, 1537-51, 1575

———.
Libro Extraordinario, 1551

———.
Quinto libro d'architettura, 1600
VAN PELT, J.V.
Discussion of Composition, New York, 1902
VARON, D.
Architectural Composition, New York, 1923
VILLARD DE HONNECOURT
Thirteenth-century Sketch-Book, Bibliothèque Nationale, Paris
VIOLLET-LE-DUC, EUGENE-EMANUEL
Entretiens sur l'architecture, Paris, 1863, 1872

———.
Histoire d'un Dessinateur, (nd)

———.
Histoire de l'habitation, (nd)
VITRUVIUS POLLIO, MARCUS
De Architectura, Rome, c.1486. First illustrated edition by Fra Giocondo, 1511

———.
Ten Books of Architecture, 84 B.C.
WITTKOWER, RUDOLF
Architectural Principles in the Age of Humanism, London, 1949. 4th edition, 1988
WOTTON, SIR HENRY
Elements of Architecture, 1624
WYNEKEN, K.
Leitfaden der Rhythmik, Berlin, 1912
VIGNOLA, GIACOMO BAROZZI DA
Regola delli cinque Ordini d'Architettura, 1562-3

INDEX

Figures in italics refer to pages containing illustrations